# The Economics of the Good, the Bad, and the Ugly

The highly praised Western, *The Good, the Bad, and the Ugly*, has been used in many game-theory courses over the years and has also found its way into leading journals of this field. Using the rich material offered by this movie, alongside other elements from popular culture, literature and history, this book furthers this exploration into a fascinating area of economics.

In his series of Schumpeter lectures, Manfred J. Holler uses his analysis of Sergio Leone's movie as a starting point to argue that combinations of desires, secrets and second-mover advantages trigger conflicts but also allow for conflict resolution. Many people and organizations have a desire for secrecy, and this is often motivated by a desire to create a second-mover advantage, and by undercutting the second-mover advantage of others. This book demonstrates that the interaction of these three ingredients account for a large share of social problems and failures in politics and business but, somewhat paradoxically, can also help to overcome some of the problems that result by applying one or two of them in isolation.

This book has been written for curious readers who want to see the world from a different perspective and who like simple mathematics alongside story telling. Its accessible approach means that it will be of use to students and academics alike, especially all those interested in decision making, game theory, and market entry.

**Manfred J. Holler** is Emeritus Professor of Economics at the University of Hamburg, Germany; research professor at the Public Choice Research Centre at Turku, Finland, and a member of the board of the Center of Conflict Resolution. He is founding editor of the *European Journal of Political Economy* and the journal *Homo Oeconomicus* (now one of its three editors-in-chief), and also serves as assessing editor or board member for a number of other journals.

# The Graz Schumpeter Lectures

*Series Editor: Richard Sturn, University of Graz, Austria*

**Exchange Rates and International Finance Markets**
An Asset-Theoretic Approach with Schumpeterian Perspective
*Erich W. Streissler*

**An Unholy Trinity**
Labor, Capital and Land in the New Economy
*Duncan K. Foley*

**Politics and Economics in the History of the European Union**
*Alan S. Milward*

**The Dynamics of Industrial Capitalism**
Schumpeter, Chandler, and the New Economy
*Richard N. Langlois*

**Growth, Distribution and Innovations**
Understanding Their Interrelations
*Amit Bhaduri*

**Complex Economics**
Individual and Collective Rationality
*Alan Kirman*

**Public Economics in an Age of Austerity**
*A. B. Atkinson*

**The Economics of the Good, the Bad, and the Ugly**
Secrets, Desires, and Second-Mover Advantages
*Manfred J. Holler*

For a full list of titles in this series, please visit: www.routledge.com/The-Graz-Schumpeter-Lectures/book-series/SE0392

For more information, please visit the Graz Schumpeter Society's website: http://www.uni-graz.at/gsg

# The Economics of the Good, the Bad, and the Ugly

Secrets, Desires, and Second-Mover Advantages

**Manfred J. Holler**

Routledge
Taylor & Francis Group

LONDON AND NEW YORK

First published 2019
by Routledge
2 Park Square, Milton Park, Abingdon, Oxon OX14 4RN

and by Routledge
52 Vanderbilt Avenue, New York, NY 10017

First issued in paperback 2020

*Routledge is an imprint of the Taylor & Francis Group, an informa business*

*British Library Cataloguing-in-Publication Data*
A catalogue record for this book is available from the British Library

*Library of Congress Cataloging-in-Publication Data*
A catalog record has been requested for this book

ISBN 13: 978-0-367-58777-2 (pbk)
ISBN 13: 978-1-138-60698-2 (hbk)

Typeset in Bembo
by Swales & Willis Ltd, Exeter, Devon, UK

# Contents

**4    Secrets: how to create and how to deal with them**                    121

**5    Justice in the end?**                                                 230

# Preface and alternative facts

Instead of submitting a lengthy preface, I strictly recommend reading Chapter 1 "The trailer" that follows. But there are two pieces of information that I want to give in advance. First, some chapters contain some mathematics, or more general, formal analysis. This is not meant to put readers off or to impress them, but to shorten the presentation, to make it more precise, and to add lucidity where the verbal presentation might suffer from ambiguity. Knowledge of the four basic arithmetical operations is enough to master the mathematics in this book. Readers who find mathematics boring should just flip the pages. Secondly, this book does not presuppose the knowledge of the movie. However, if you detest movie Westerns, you might not enjoy reading this book. Sergio Leone's *The Good, the Bad, and the Ugly* is not just one of the best movie Westerns – Quentin Tarantino called it "the best-directed film of all time" and "the greatest achievement in the history of cinema"[1] – but it also delivers rich material to analyze and to exemplify the interaction of desires, secrets, and second-mover advantages which is the focus of this book. My thanks for inspiration, motivation, and support are given in the Acknowledgments section at the end of "The trailer," just like in the movies.

Since the formal level of this book is rather modest and the use of mathematics limited to its basics, the question could arise whether the book can be used in a classroom situation. The answer is "Yes," if your students are interested in decision making and market entry, George Orwell and *Lady Chatterley's Lover*, creative destruction and the making of war, or learning how other people make money, or at least in some of these issues.

---

1 Quotations are taken from Wikipedia and cross-checked with the original sources: Rob Turner, "The Good, the Bad, and the Ugly," *Entertainment Weekly* (June 14, 2004).

# 1 The trailer

Combinations of desires, secrets and second-mover advantages trigger conflicts but also allow for conflict resolution. Many people have a desire for secrecy. Often the desire of secrecy is motivated by creating a second-mover advantage and by undercutting the second-mover advantage of others. This book will demonstrate that interaction of these three ingredients accounts for a large share of social problems and failures in politics and business but, somewhat paradoxically, can also help to overcome some of the problems that result from applying one or two of them in isolation. An adequate design of secrets can be a tool to circumvent second-mover advantages and to avoid or solve social conflicts. This observation was the point of departure, yet, also the conclusion of the Schumpeter Lectures which I gave at the University of Graz, November 7–12, 2013. The title of this series of four lectures was "The Good, the Bad, and the Ugly: From Ethics to Economics and Back Again." Two of the four lectures were directly inspired by Sergio Leone's 1966 masterpiece *The Good, the Bad, and the Ugly*. I showed sequences of the three-person duel, an icon of the history of movie making, and of the rather dramatic "sharing" of the treasure between the Good and the Ugly towards the end of the movie, both taken from a DVD version.[1] In the other two lectures, I made some occasional remarks related to the movie in order to emphasize the coherence of the lecture project and the universality of the discussed topics, but also to prepare the audience for more direct references.

What looked like a simple exercise – writing down one's lecture notes – turned out to be a rather complex project. As I cannot expect the reader to look at the film material, when reading the book, I had to rearrange the material of the lectures for this volume. On the other hand, the writing-down of the text allows a much more thorough discussion of the basic concepts analyzed here – i.e., desire, secrets, and second-mover advantage – which were

---

1 I would like to thank Jörg Altekruse and his Zeitfilm Media company (in Hamburg) for their assistance in preparing classroom media materials from the film. This was a rather complicated and time-consuming project. I also would like to thank my son Michael (Mikko) Holler, who gave me a DVD of *The Good, the Bad, and the Ugly* as a Christmas present.

fundamental for the movie, and are of eminent importance to social life, in general. In what follows, the movie serves as a point of reference and source of inspiration, but it is not pivotal for the generalization of the issues and results.[2]

As already noted in the Preface, this book does not presuppose that the reader knows the movie. However, if you detest Westerns, you will not enjoy reading parts of this book. Yet, there are enough pages without reference to Sergio Leone's movie to keep the reader busy. Also, in the Preface I suggested that readers who find mathematics a nuisance should just flip the pages which show formulas or diagrams. They will not lose much. The other half of the readership, however, may profit from the more concise representation offered by using mathematical language. However, the level of mathematics offered here is very low from the technical point of view.

## 1.1 The confession

I have to confess that when I chose the title of my lecture series I was not aware how popular Sergio Leone's film was and still is. Probably this is partly so because of its German title *Zwei glorreiche Halunken*. This is not a very attractive title and a rather unfortunate translation. An English equivalent would be "Two Glorious Scoundrels." Before the shooting began, the working title of the movie was *I due magnifici straccioni* which comes close to "The Two Magnificent Tramps." Obviously, the working title and *Zwei glorreiche Halunken* select Blondie and Tuco, i.e., the Good and the Ugly. However, in the last pictures of the movie, Tuco does not look glorious with a hangman's noose around his neck balancing on the wooden cross of a tomb, not to lose control and get his neck broken or his throat sealed forever. Moreover, calling the two scoundrels is a euphemism, given the number of corpses they produced and the sadistic tortures they occasionally exercised on each other and others. And why "Zwei" (i.e. two)? What happened to the Bad, called Angel Eyes, who played such an important role in bringing the story to its end? It needs three for the three-person duel which is perhaps the most outstanding scene of the movie. Given the misleading and unattractive German title, it is not surprising that when I was young this movie was not as popular in Germany as it was in the Anglo-Saxon world. For quite some time I did not even relate *Zwei glorreiche Halunken* to *The Good, the Bad, and the Ugly*.

Over the years, the three-person duel, also called "truel," became a major device to illustrate the problem of strategic interaction. I was told that this sequence of Sergio Leone's movie was used in many game-theory courses and it also found its way into leading journals of this field (see Kahn and

---

2 This approach concurs with a project that uses movie or theatre material for distilling ideas and concepts of individual decision making in a social context. See Holler and Klose-Ullmann (2008, 2013) and Klose-Ullmann (2015).

Mookherjee's (1992) *"The Good, the Bad, and the Ugly*: Coalition Proof Equilibrium in Infinite Games," published in *Games and Economic Behavior*). However, earlier I read Marc Kilgour's analysis of the truel (Kilgour 1972, 1975, 1978) without relating it to Sergio Leone's *The Good, the Bad, and the Ugly*, "*GBU*" in what follows.

My interest in *GBU* grew after I had watched *A Fistful of Dollars* (1964) – Sergio Leone's first film of the so-called "Dollars Trilogy" – in the guest apartment of the Indira Ghandi Institute of Development Research in Mumbai where I spent two weeks in September 2004 teaching Law & Economics to Ph.D. students and guests. (The second movie of the "Dollars Trilogy" is *For a Few Dollars More* (1965), and *GBU* (1966) completed the trilogy.) When watching *A Fistful of Dollars*, there was the noise of a fan in my living room. I felt very hot watching the movie, although the thermometer indicated that the room temperature wasn't excessive. I remember that the next day I discussed some episodes of the movie during lunch and in class. I do not remember their names, but I would like to thank my sparring partners and send apologies for exploiting them. These thanks go to many people around the globe, not just in India.

Finally, about seven years ago, my son gave me a DVD of *GBU* for Christmas. I watched the movie three or four times in full length before I started to prepare my Schumpeter Lectures at Graz. As I tried to document it in the subtitle of my lectures, I found much more in this movie then the notorious truel. Still, the truel is an outstanding scene and it triggered my interest from a game-theoretical point of view. Its overwhelming theatrical impact derives from the assumption that there is a second-mover advantage – and therefore there is no rational justification for a first action, i.e., for action at all. As a spectator, I was pushed into a choice situation that does not allow me to form helpful expectations and to suggest rational actions. Again and again, when watching this scenario, I get a feeling of forlornness and desperation, and I find this feeling mirrored in the eyes and fingers of the three duellers.

There seems to be no solution to this situation – neither for the duelers nor for the spectators. Obviously, Sergio Leone enjoys the hopelessness embedded in the intractability of the decision problem – every minute the duelers watch each other and the audience watches them – perhaps in order to demonstrate how smart his own resolution is. I have to confess that I found his solution somewhat disappointing. Nevertheless, it offers food for thought. Some of it entered the agenda of this book. I hope that the book demonstrates that the issue captured by Sergio Leone's truel is far more general than *GBU* suggests. The analysis of the truel will be a major item on the agenda of this book.

## 1.2 The agenda

Interestingly, Kilgour and Brams (1997) do not cite *GBU*, even when they give examples of truels referring to movies and competing television networks. Perhaps this is the case as in Sergio Leone's truel, the probability of each player hitting the chosen target does not matter, while it is an important issue in Kilgour (1972, 1975, 1978) and Kilgour and Brams (1997). The immense excitement and tension of the situation in *GBU* is the result of the expectation that if A shoots B, then C has time enough to shoot A. If so, then there is an obvious disadvantage for the one who shoots first, i.e., there is an advantage for the second-mover. However, it is not obvious who will be the second-mover. Will there be a second-mover at all?

If there *is* a second-mover advantage, then a likely outcome is that nothing at all will happen as there will be no first-mover, i.e., the second-mover advantage implies a first-mover dilemma. This is a rather general phenomenon, as the discussion will reveal. We expect an underprovision or underperformance in cases of second-mover advantages. The sequence of moves – i.e., time in its strategic form – matters. Of course, time could also matter if the environment changes and, with it, the decision situation. However, in Chapter 3 of this volume we will focus on the strategic aspect of time or, more generally, time defined by history. It is neither the time measured by the clock on the wall nor the one captured by the calendar. It is defined by events and decisions. The sequence of decisions and events determines the information of the decision makers and reshapes the decision situation and thereby the possible outcome. This is essential to many game situations in which "historical time" boils down to strategic time, and a second-mover advantage can be one of its implications. Another implication is information: "historical time," i.e., the data of past events, defines what decision makers could know and incorporate in their decisions.

As historical time is bound to events and decisions, a look into the future is identical with forecasting events. It is not enough to follow a horizontal time axis to count hours, days, weeks, months, and years when we talk about the future.

Historical time and, more specifically, strategic time seem to be decisive for the *GBU* truel. There are numerous examples also in the world of politics, production and trade that demonstrate its effect. For an illustration of the latter, we will take a look into the history of diapers, video recorders and "lite" beer, and comment on hedge-fund managers who made up to $2.2 billion a year.

When it comes to underprovision or underperformance, then the potential of an exogenous agency, the government, could be a solution. In her study, *The Entrepreneurial State*, Mariana Mazzucato (2014) gives a long list of examples which demonstrate that outstanding success of private businesses often results from government activities (i.e., public investments), overcoming the disadvantages of a first-mover. Apple and Google are just two of them that we will discuss in what follows – perhaps the most popular ones. These cases indicate that information often is an essential spin-off of public investment, ready for private use. On the other hand, government might also try to reduce information if it prefers underprovision or underperformance, or if it does not want to accept responsibility for such failures. In extreme, but not so rare cases, it chooses a policy of obfuscation and authorizes secret agencies for implementing such a policy. Whenever information matters, secrets and the creation of secrets have a strong impact on decision making. This book contains some nice examples that we will discuss in Chapter 4, e.g., the Zimmermann Telegram (a major event of World War I), George Orwell and his notebook, and the CIA's cultural policy. The latter two are byproducts of the Cold War in the aftermath of World War II.

The truel in *GBU* could be a perfect illustration of how a secret could map a second-mover advantage into a first-mover advantage. Blondie knew that Tuco's gun did not have any bullets. He had made a first-move in this truel by unloading Tuco's gun the night before the truel. Therefore, when he is dueling with Angel Eyes, he had the advantage that Angel Eyes did not know about Tuco's incapacity. Perhaps Sergio Leone was not aware of the strategic impact of this modification as he made Angel Eyes draw first, but with no success: Blondie was much faster in drawing and shooting. One might argue that Blondie was faster as he knew that Tuco was no danger to him while Angel Eyes, who did not have this information, was handicapped in his attention and the speed of his operation. This assumption could save the rationale of the outcome, but somehow devaluates the decision problem of the truelists.

Before discussing the strategic implications of time (i.e., second-mover advantages and their consequences) and the implications and creation of secrets, Chapter 2 of this volume will introduce desires as the driving force. If there are no desires, then second-mover advantages and secrets are "vacuous experiences," and individual and social decision making miss their point of reference. Obviously, the heroes of *GBU* – Blondie, Angel Eyes and Tuco – have very strong desires, especially when it comes to money. The greed for money is the dominating motivation for most of what we see on the screen. There is also some lust for killing and torture, but lust seems to be secondary, and the sexual dimension of it is marginal, even missing: their focus is on money and how to get it. There is no alternative that competes with the desire for money. However, the last scene of the movie suggests a second thought.

Of course, a movie is not real life. Kaplan and Rouh (2013: 40) observe that the average pay (in 2010 dollars) for the twenty-five highest-paid hedge fund managers climbed from $134 million in 2002 to an astonishing $537 million in 2012. I presume that these twenty-five people have other desires than just the one for making money, but I think making money is of utmost importance to them. Otherwise, it is even more difficult to understand what they do and what they earn, than it already is.

Given this, it seems amazing that we do not find references to desire in modern economics textbooks. Greed is absent, too. How do people decide and why? Standard economics models individual decision making with the assumption that individuals have preferences over given alternatives and they pick the alternative that they appreciate most, given various constraints like, e.g., the budget. However, Blondie, Angel Eyes, and Tuco did not think about alternatives when they were hunting for the $200,000 treasure – not even the danger of losing one's life or taking the life of a rival mattered. As standard economics does not consider desires, it cannot analyze the behavior of Blondie, Angel Eyes, and Tuco. Of course, this might not be a great loss, because their objectives and environment are rather different of what we find in everyday life. But even in everyday life, desires matter.

I have argued (Holler 2014) that standard economics took refuge in comparing the value of given alternatives in order to submit the subject to the constraints of mathematical analysis. (See Jevons (1888 [1871])) for this research agenda.) I will further elaborate this argument in what follows and demonstrate that puzzles, like Sen's Liberal Paradox, will resolve or become irrelevant, once we accept that decisions are motivated by desires, and not necessarily the result of comparing given alternatives. However, whether desires matter – i.e., whether they determine behavior or at least have a significant impact on it – is an empirical question. This raises the question of how we measure desires. To make a long story short, there is no immediate answer to this, neither in the literature nor in this book. But, in many cases, it seems that individuals try to rank their desires. Introspection shows that we can expect that the individual editing can lead to a partial ordering, giving priority to a particular desire. Alternatively, individuals can be expected to form classes of desires so that hierarchies of set of desires result. We will discuss this approach in detail below.

My conjecture is that there will always be limits to measuring desires and to submitting them to a formal treatment. Perhaps I should warn the reader that Chapter 2, on desire, will be rather abstract despite references to the Marquis de Sade, *Dr. Jekyll and Mr. Hyde*, and *Lady Chatterley's Lover*. Chapter 3, on second-mover advantages, and Chapter 4, on secrets, are likely to be more entertaining – when we meet *The Good, the Bad, and the Ugly* again. Readers who are not interested in desires – lust, wants, needs, dreams – are recommended to skip Chapter 2 and jump right into Chapter 3, which discusses second-mover advantages.

*Figure 1.1* Desires, strategic time, and secrets

Figure 1.1 outlines the program of this volume. It relates desires, secrets, and strategic time. The latter will be specified by the second-mover advantage. The interior of this triangle expresses social situations that combine these three components. However, the equilateral triangle should not be read as a simplex, as the three components do not satisfy a Cartesian measure. Distances cannot be added up or be divided. They only illustrate a monotonic relationship. In some instances, we may conclude that the social situation X implies more of desires and less of secrecy than the social situation Y. If so, we may conclude that situation X is more strongly characterized by second-mover advantages than situation Y. In case of *GBU*, the situation can be characterized by all vertices simultaneously: there is no single point that captures the degree of desire and secrecy, and the relevance of the second-mover advantage in this movie. Perhaps this is the secret of its success.[3]

Dedicated followers of economics are likely to miss a welfare analysis, especially when effects of government interventions on private decision making are on the agenda. There will be some standard references to Pareto optimality, now and then, but, in principle, I have tried to avoid welfare arguments. Whether secrets are good, whether desires are justified, whether second-mover advantages imply inefficiency, depends on specific circumstances and second-order conditions – and how we want to see the world.

## 1.3 The story

The version of *GBU* underlying this text is on a DVD sold by the leading German daily newspaper *Süddeutsche Zeitung* (*SZ*) as part of a collection of the 50 favorite movies of the *SZ* film desk. The playtime of both the English and the German version is exactly 171 minutes. It seems that the German version is the result of the English-language version, and not taken from the Italian original. The much shorter version presented in German cinemas showed differences in the visual presentation. I presume that in the U.S. a much shorter version was on show in the cinemas, too. Details may vary from version to version.

In the course of this text, some prominent scenes of the movie will be described in more detail when they are applied to introduce or to illustrate core issues discussed in this text. For instance, the three-way duel introduces the issue second-mover advantage in Chapter 3. The so-called "bridge scene" is used in the discussion of hierarchies of secrets in Chapter 4. Finally, Chapter 5 discusses the last scene of the movie, which offers some material to elaborate on the question of fairness.

---

3 Figure 1.1 is a close relative of Aristotle's Rhetorical Triangle which has ethos, pathos and logos – the Aristotelian Triad – as vertices. Of course, an argument can simultaneously satisfy all three to a high degree.

The issue of fairness was already raised when Blondie and Tuco were partners in the bounty-hunting game. Blondie delivered Tuco to the authorities and cashed a $2,000 premium. In the twinkling of an eye, Tuco was brought to the hanging tree and a rope placed around his neck as he faced an audience who wanted to see him put to death for the long list of crimes he had committed. The list was read out before his execution, citing a great number of murders, robberies and rapes. As the noose was tightening around Tuco's neck, Blondie cut the rope with a shot from his rifle. They both escaped, ready to share the money and to look for another round of the bounty hunting game. However, the sharing of the money became a problem when Tuco was no longer satisfied to get only half of it. His argument was that his job was much more risky and unpleasant. Blondie's reaction was sphinx-like in its ambivalence:

*Blondie*:   You may run the risks, my friend, but I do the cutting. We cut down my percentage . . . liable to interfere with my aim.

*Tuco*:   But if you miss, you had better miss very well. Whoever double-crosses me and leaves me alive, he understands nothing about Tuco.

Before I close this trailer with thanking the numerous people who contributed with their comments and suggestions to the writing and publishing of this book, I must warn the reader: by their very nature, movie trailers are incomplete and tend to be biased, trying to coax the still undecided client into the role of a committed customer. In movie trailers, we see all kinds of tricks applied in order to accomplish this transformation. However, there is a trailer of *GBU* on the Internet that simply confuses the Bad – i.e., Angel Eyes – and the Ugly, Tuco, labeling Angel Eyes the Ugly and Tuco the Bad. It is easy to see that this obvious mistake is due to the Italian title of the movie: *Il buono, il brutto, il cattivo*. Here Tuco is listed as "il brutto" in the center position and Angel Eyes as "il cattivo." The ranking of "il buono, il brutto, il cattivo" is also reflected in advertising material such as posters that show Tuco in the center position, framed by Blondie to the left and Angel Eyes to the right, with the misleading subscript "The Good, the Bad, and the Ugly."

In the Italian version and in the original script, Angel Eyes is named "Sentenza." Sentenza is also used for Angel Eyes when I click onto the German (language) version of my DVD. Possible translations for "Sentenza" are judgment, decree, sentence, adjudication and ruling. None of these fit my interpretation.

## 1.4 Acknowledgments

First of all I want to thank Heinz Kurz and Richard Sturn for inviting me to give the Graz Schumpeter Lectures at the Schumpeter Centre of the University of Graz in November 2013. The two are not responsible for this book's contents, but for the writing of it. They are responsible that I was thinking three years about the text which is now in front of you. I read many thousand pages on desires, secrets and second-mover advantages seeking answers to open problems and found many new questions. I spent many evenings, nights and early mornings typing my reactions to these questions into the computer. A third of these pages survived the revisions and the focusing of the text – although the focus of the text is less than strict. One early reader of the manuscript said that this is due to its interdisciplinary approach. While Heinz Kurz and Richard Sturn are not responsible for this, I am grateful for them motivating me to go on this reading and writing journey, combined with some thinking. Next I would like to thank my wife Barbara Klose-Ullmann. She read every line of this text and did not agree with everything it still contains. Special thanks go to Heinz Kurz: he read the text in detail and made numerous valuable suggestions. I would also like to thank Marlies Ahlert, Luciano Andreozzi, Timo Airaksinen, Rudolf Avenhaus, Niclas Berggren, Helmuth Blaseio, Friedel Bolle, Daniel Eckert, Hartmut Kliemt, Klaus Kultti, Vikas Kumar, Alain Marciano, Hannu Nurmi, Rigmar Osterkamp, José Reis, Florian Rupp, Raymond Russ, Donald Wittman, who all read shorter or longer parts of the text. My thanks also go to copy-editor Jeanne Brady and Adam Bell of Swales and Willis for their work on the book.

I have borrowed ideas on desires from Timo Airaksinen without asking his permission, but I have quoted from his publications, and I've made use of earlier publications of mine which were not widely read. Most of this material was published in the quarterly journal *Homo Oeconomicus*. As this journal was published by ACCEDO and I have been and still are one of the directors and owners of this company, it was not necessary to ask for permission. However, I have asked Bengt-Arne Wickström for permission to cannibalize our joint paper "The use of scandal in the progress of society" and he agreed (see Section 4.4.4 for a reference to this paper). Ashgate Publishing has permitted me to republish parts of my 2007 article "The artist as a secret agent: Liberalism against populism," in A. Breton, P. Galeotti, P. Salmon and R. Wintrobe (eds.), *The Economics of Transparency in Politics (Villa Colombella Papers)* (Section 4.4 contains a condensed version of this paper). Edward Elgar gave me permission to republish parts of my 2005 article "George Orwell and his cold wars: Truth and politics," in: J.-M. Josselin and A. Marciano (eds.), *Law and the State: A Political Economy Approach* (see Section 4.6). Domenico Da Empoli has granted permission to make use of my 2010 article "The Two-dimensional Model of Jury Decision Making," published in his *Journal of Public Finance and Public Choice* (*Economia delle Scelte Pubbliche*), saying he is "very glad" to give his permission. Traces of this article can be found in Section 3.6.4.

# 2 On desires

Modern economics is considered a decision theory. This presupposes that the objectives (i.e., preferences on the alternatives) are given and well ordered, and finite. Desires do not always satisfy these requirements and therefore cannot be handled in this framework without some "editing." In this chapter, we will discuss the relationship of desires, preferences and choices, and illustrate their relationship with reference to Sen's Liberal Paradox. It will be argued that the mathematization of economics, as proposed by Jevons, and, more specifically, the calculus of pleasure and pain, presupposes a focus on preferences and a neglect of desires. This calculus can neither explain the driving force in Sergio Leone's *The Good, the Bad, and the Ugly* nor help to understand why Columbus crossed the Atlantic Ocean. Obviously there is a demand for a theoretical framework for dealing with desires. What follows is a preliminary discussion and a draft of such a framework.

## 2.1 Why desires?

A focal object of the social sciences, including economics, is to explain human behavior, be it for pure curiosity, or to forecast social outcomes, or to manipulate individual behavior and social outcomes. It seems obvious that desires have a strong impact on human behavior; however, the mechanism that transforms desires into action is less obvious. Desires trigger decisions, but the correspondence is not always straightforward as we shall see below, and the relationship of decisions and outcomes, i.e., the individual and social behavior that we observe, sometimes looks rather "disconnected." For a better understanding, we have to rethink desires. This is not an easy project because desires are not merely a theoretical concept, which can be constructed to fit into the rest of our theory. There is a real-world understanding to them and there are empirical interpretations that produce paradoxical results. For instance, Airaksinen (2013: 375) suggests that "desire is a happiness maker," an intended or "prima facie happiness maker," which mostly disappoints us. Following Schopenhauer, Airaksinen argues that desires can never be satisfied, unless our level of demands is low enough.

Hegesias of Cyrene (about 300 BC) argued that happiness is impossible to achieve, as conventional values such as wealth, poverty, and freedom produce no more pleasure than pain. Here is a dilemma: incomplete satisfaction does not make us happy (Airaksinen 2012: 405), and complete satisfaction is not possible. This view is supported by the argument that desires are unbounded, especially the desires for luxury goods (see Adam Smith (1981 [1776/77]: 181)) and desires of lust and greed (see Marquis de Sade's *Justine*, discussed below).

A second argument is that desires are intransitive, unordered, and very often incompatible. They are allowed to contradict each other as they are not choices. And yet decisions may follow from desires, even when intransitive, unordered, or incompatible. However, in standard economic modeling, desires have to be transformed into preferences in order to derive decisions. If the preferences on the desired alternatives are transitive, complete, and reflexive and therefore form an ordering, they can be represented by a utility function. Then textbook economics applies and decisions can be derived. There is a budget, there are preferences, and there is an optimal choice, but no desires, on the one hand, and no happiness, on the other. The budget represents limited resources, i.e., scarcity, which "lumps together one person's desire to obtain a subsistence diet with another person's desire for precious jewelry" (Northrop 2000: 54).

However, desires cannot always be shaped into a preference ordering that supports a utility function, and still trigger decisions. Section 2.2 discusses the relationship between desires, preferences, and choices. Well-known results from social choice theory and multi-criteria decision making (MCDM) will be applied to illustrate the potential of cycles and incompatibilities in the ordering (and editing) of desires and the shaping of decisions. In view of these issues, we will discuss Sen's Liberal Paradox in Section 2.3. It will be argued that, on the one hand, the aggregation procedure mixes desires and alternatives for the given example and, on the other, the Paradox is due to the fact that the personal spheres of the members of the liberal society are ill-defined. The analysis demonstrates that without an adequate definition of the personal sphere (and the desires assigned to it), the concept of liberalism remains vacuous.

We also give an interpretation of the Paradox as a MCDM issue. Once we give up the claim of a complete ordering of desires, we may waive the condition of ordering entirely and have recourse to comparing sets. In Section 2.6, we propose a set approach that could serve as a prerequisite to testing whether people with larger sets of desires behave differently from people with smaller sets of desires. (For example, are the former more frustrated if their desires are not satisfied?) The theoretical apparatus suggested in this section is identical to what has been developed in the theory of freedom of choice.

Of course, frustration is a form of pain. It can be the price of unsatisfied desires. In Section 2.5.2, the calculus of pleasure and pain, suggested by Jevons, will be confronted with the Marquis de Sade's "calculus of desires." Sade's heroes do not calculate: they act. They want to have more and more, and more of the same, while economists like Jevons and Senior observe a "love for variety." However, economists face a problem with variety, especially if the dimensions of the commodity space have to be extended to describe novelties, i.e., alternatives that do as yet not exist or did not exist when decisions were taken. Economists also face a problem with respect to specifying the wants, beliefs, and desires. In Section 2.7.2, this issue will be discussed making use of Tennessee Williams's play *A Streetcar Named Desire*. Finally, Section 2.8 presents a simple microeconomic model, in line with Fehr and Schmidt (1999). The model illustrates how desires could be integrated into standard theory. Of course, "others" would assign this model to the neoclassical repairshop where we find bundles of similar solutions.

## 2.2 Desires, preferences, and choices

Can we learn from the choices of an individual about his or her desires? Or are we restricted to the verbal communication or an interpretation of emotions (of happiness) to find out about desires and their degree of satisfaction? Perhaps we come closer to an answer to these questions when we consider what we learned from preferences. The theory of revealed preferences, introduced in Samuelson (1938), tells us that we can deduce "relevant parts" of its preferences[1] from the choices of an individual.[2] One might argue that the assumptions on the preferences we have to make in order to accomplish this deduction are rather restrictive. However, there is little "real substance" to the preferences; they are like a black box with well-defined corners and walls. For instance, an essential precondition is that preferences are ordered. Preferences are based on a comparison of at least two alternatives, and preference orderings are derived from comparisons of pairs of *given* alternatives that get connected (and extended to all alternatives) via transitivity: if $A \succ B$ and $B \succ C$ then $A \succ C$. Yet, nothing has been said what these alternatives are; it seems that they could be anything. Preference revelation assumes that individuals have such an ordering and choose the highest-ranking alternative that they can achieve. This, of course, is identical with utility maximization, which is in fact an optimization as there are constraints, in general, introduced as budget or resources.

However, this revelation does not always apply. As, e.g., pointed out by Lehtinen (2011), we cannot reveal preferences from the choices when the choices are not alternatives, but strategies, as is the case in game theory. The decision makers have no preferences with respect to strategies, but with respect to the outcome. But outcomes in strategic decision situations are "only to

---

1  In order to avoid the "his or her," I will address the individual and use "it" and "its" in what follows.
2  One should add, "without reference to particular preferences or utility functions," assuming that the consumer's price reactions are consistent and tastes are stable, and the consumer spends their full budget on consumption. One implication is that the consumer will buy every time the same bundle of goods unless prices or income change. Another implication is that the substitution effect will always have a negative sign.

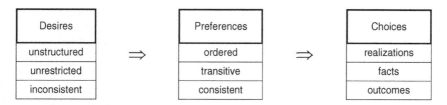

*Figure 2.1* Desires, preferences, and choices

some extent" determined by the selected strategy of an individual decision maker. Of course, strategic decision situations are ubiquitous, but often decision makers are not aware of the complexity of the situation that they are confronted with. Thus, if we ignore strategic decision making, this might seems admissible as a first-order approximation to reality, especially when we relate decision making to desires.

Given this simplification, can we then extend the reasoning behind preference revelation to desire revelation? Is there a way to deduce his/her desires from the choices the individual made – and derive a measure of the intensity of various desires? If so, then we have made a first step to integrate happiness and desire into a standard economic model.[3]

A possible conclusion is that desires are more exciting than preferences, as they have a greater potential for explaining behavior because they can even support inconsistent decisions. However, this does not imply that all decisions derive from desires. Often there are necessities, routines, and social pressures that determine what we decided, and desires may only determine to which degree we like or hate the alternatives that we have chosen. In fact,

> we may well prefer A to B and want neither. You will be executed by a bullet or rope, which one do you prefer? Many of our preferences are coerced, which is to say we do not want them. We do not want this choice; yet, we cannot avoid it. We hope we could.
>
> (Airaksinen 2014a: 459f.)

In Holler (2015), I made use of Figure 2.1 to illustrate the relationship between desires, preferences, and choices that is assumed here, and discussed several

---

3  There is an immense literature in economics about happiness and empirical/experimental research related to it. Frey and Stutzer (2002) tried to answer the question "What Can Economists Learn from Happiness Research?" Up to now, the results of happiness research are strangely disconnected from the main body of economic theory, especially the neighboring microeconomic theory. The fact that desires have no entry in modern textbooks of economics could be a possible reason for this disconnectedness.

paradoxes of multi-criteria decision making (MCDM) which result from an application of well-known paradoxes of collective decision making to the internal aggregation problem of an individual. The language and instruments of (modern) social choice theory, pioneered by Duncan Black (1948, 1958) and Kenneth Arrow (1963 [1951]), were applied to individual decision making, e.g., by May (1954), Holler (1984) and, under the label of MCDM, by Nurmi (1988, 2010), and Nurmi and Meskanen (2000).[4] This material tries to explain the formation of preferences as an aggregation over various characteristics (i.e., dimensions). There is a potential "impossibility" of preference orderings embedded in this aggregation, quite similar to the message of Arrow's impossibility theorem with respect to social preferences. In Holler (2013a, 2015), these results are applied to desires. For instance, a possible illustration of the inconsistency of desires is a cycle $X > Y$ and $Y > Z$ and $Z > X$. Here $>$ represents the binary relation "larger": it reflects the everyday language when an individual states that "my desire for X is larger than my desire for Y," etc. Of course, this "evaluation" is related to a particular individual: the one that has the desires X, Y, and Z.

If we force the individual that shows a cycle $X > Y$ and $Y > Z$ and $Z > X$ to structure its desires in accordance with three dimensions (e.g., feasibility, emergence, and social acceptability) – or the individual forces itself – then a desire profile as shown in Figure 2.2 is a possible point of reference, given that these dimensions are of equal weight and a majority aggregation rule applies. For instance, if we hypothesize "one dimension, one vote," then $X > Y$ is supported by a 2:1 "vote," and so are $Y > Z$ and $Z > X$.

In his Tanner Lecture on Human Values, Schelling (1982) discusses a multiple-self pattern that corresponds to the aggregation problem that the decision maker in Figure 2.2 faces. He concludes that

|        | Dimension 1 | Dimension 2 | Dimension 3 |
|--------|:-----------:|:-----------:|:-----------:|
| Rank 1 |      X      |      Z      |      Y      |
| Rank 2 |      Y      |      X      |      Z      |
| Rank 3 |      Z      |      Y      |      X      |

*Figure 2.2* A Condorcet-like cycle of desires

---

4 This literature reflects the discussion of the multiple self by psychologists which "gives up the idea that there is just one self per head. The idea is that instead, within each brain, different selves are continually popping in and out of existence. They have different desires, and they fight for control – bargaining with, deceiving, and plotting against each other" (Bloom 2008: 4/18). He illustrates the case: "Late at night, when deciding not to bother setting up the coffee machine for the next morning, I sometimes think of the man who will wake up as a different person, and wonder, *What did he ever do for me?* When I get up and there's no coffee ready, I curse the lazy bastard who shirked his duties the night before" (Bloom 2008: 5/18).

we should not expect a person's choices on those matters that give rise to alternating values to display the qualities typically imputed to rational decision, like transitivity, independence of "irrelevant" alternatives, and short-run stability over time. We should expect the kinds of parliamentary strategies that go with small-group voting behavior.

(Schelling 1982: 58f.)

The illustration in Figure 2.2 is well known in social choice theory as the "Condorcet cycle." Of course, we do not expect that the individual votes, but suggest that it decides in accordance with more than one dimension – and considers weighted averages when comparing two items like X > Y. It is assumed that the individual can rank its desires in accordance with each specified dimension. However, we argue that each dimension is defined by a particular property such that the desires can be ranked in accordance to it. If there is no ranking possible, then there is no dimension. While desires are hardly ever measurable, if not expressed in money values, some of their dimensions could be mapped even in a cardinal scale. Think about the dimension "speed" if your desired Porsche is compared to the perhaps less-desired Ferrari. Speed is quantifiable; however, maximum speed seems not decisive for the strength of desire in this case (if it is higher for the Ferrari than for Porsche).

Standard economic theory assumes that decision makers (can) assign preferences to all alternatives irrespective of whether these alternatives are available or not. They might even contradict the laws of nature. There is no room for desires in this conceptual framework. But does it make sense to draw conclusions on the basis of alternatives that are not available or even not feasible? They might have an impact on the alternative chosen. If we relate preferences to desires, then such an impact is rather likely. Even if we do not assume that desires are the root of preferences, we might consider that desires have an impact on decision making and a discussion of desires seems to be "desirable."

## 2.3 Sen's Liberal Paradox and the mixing of preferences and desires

Figure 2.1 assumes that desires and preferences are distinguishable and separable, and preferences reflect desires such that preferences are the images of desires. However, these assumptions do not necessarily hold: desires and preferences can mix in real life and in theorizing. In fact, it seems that the mixing of desires and preferences can explain many of the inconsistencies that people show in decision making, especially in experiments that take place in laboratories where the decision makers have no real-world equivalents that demonstrate the difference between choices and outcomes, on the one hand, and ordering alternatives or editing desires, on the other. To illustrate this issue, we will take a closer look at Sen's Liberal Paradox and argue that it mixes preferences (on alternatives) and desires. It nicely demonstrates the pitfall of assigning preferences to alternatives that are not available to the decision maker (and will never be), a standard procedure in standard economics. First, we will discuss the Paradox in its original social-choice setting and then, addressing *Dr. Jekyll and Mr. Hyde*, give it the interpretation of a MCDM problem.

Let us start with the story of Prude and Lewd, introduced in Sen (1970), referring to D.H. Lawrence's scandalous novel *Lady Chatterley's Lover*, first published in 1928. When, in 1960, the full unexpurgated edition was published by Penguin Books, the publisher faced a trial under the British Obscene Publications Act of 1959. The verdict was "not guilty" because a number of academic critics and experts, called as witnesses, testified that the book was of literary merit. This proposes that social values have changed and words like "fuck" and "cunt" are now deemed acceptable to be read by a wider audience. Sen's Paradox is about a social evaluation of reading Lawrence's book and illustrates some of the problems that are of relevance to the court's decision.

### 2.3.1 The 1970 Paradox

The modeling in Sen (1970) assumes that there is one copy of *Lady Chatterley's Lover*, and three alternatives to be ranked: (x) individual 1 reads the book; (y) individual 2 reads the book; and (z) no one reads the book. Individual 1 has the preference ordering $z \succ x \succ y$ where " $\succ$ " reads, usually, as "prefer to." Individual 1 would prefer that he reads the book himself "rather than exposing gullible Mr. 2 to the influence of Lawrence" (Sen 1970: 155). On the other hand, individual 2 "takes a delight in the thought that prudish Mr. 1 may have to read Lawrence, and his first preference is that person 1 should read it, next best that he himself should read it, and worst neither should read it" (Sen 1970: 155). Therefore, this individual's preference ordering is $x \succ y \succ z$. The two orderings suggest that individuals 1 and 2 will be renamed Prude and Lewd, respectively.

But what is the social ranking of x, y, and z? What does society consider best and what worst? Sen (1970) proposes three conditions that a social ranking should satisfy: Unrestricted domain (U), Pareto optimality (P) and Liberalism (L). Because of U, the relevant individual preferences can be as controversial as the preferences of Prude and Lewd. (Note they could be even more controversial.) Sen's definition of (weak) Pareto optimality (P) is standard: "If every individual prefers any alternative x to another alternative y, then society must prefer x to y" (Sen 1970: 153). However, his definition of Liberalism (L) is disputed. It says. "For each individual *i*, there is at least one pair of alternatives, say (x,y), such that if this individual prefers x to y, then society should prefer x to y, and if this individual prefers y to x, then society should prefer y to x" (Sen 1970: 153).

In a footnote, Sen (1970: 153) comments:

> The term "liberalism" is elusive and is open to alternative interpretations. Some uses of the term may not embrace the condition defined here, while many uses will. I do not wish to engage in a debate on the right use of the term. What is relevant is that Condition L represents a value involving individual liberty that many people would subscribe.
>
> (Sen 1970: 153)

However, in their critical note, Hillinger and Lapham (1971: 1403) argue that Sen's definition of liberalism "does not correspond to any common or acceptable notion of liberalism at all and that the only generally accepted principle of liberalism, far from conflicting with the Pareto principle, is in fact a special case of it," i.e., of the Pareto principle.

Given Sen's definition of liberalism, the Liberal Paradox says that there is such a conflict: "There is no social decision function that can simultaneously satisfy Conditions U, P, and L" (Sen, 1970: 153). In other words, there are individual preferences (i.e., preference profiles) such that there is a conflict between Sen's notion of liberalism and the Pareto principle. The case of Prude and Lewd is an example. The preferences of the two are summarized in Figure 2.3.

If there is a choice between Prude reading the book (i.e., x) and nobody reading it, then, according to Sen, in a liberal society Prude's preferences should matter and his individual ranking $z \succ x$ becomes the social ranking $\mathbf{z} \succ \mathbf{x}$. (Note in what follows symbols printed in bold represent social rankings.) Similarly, if the choice is between y and z, i.e., Lewd reading the book or nobody reading the book, then Lewd's preferences $y \succ z$ should be decisive for the social ranking so that the social preferences are $\mathbf{y} \succ \mathbf{z}$. As Prude and Lewd prefer x to y, however for different reasons, an application of the Pareto principle proposes the social preferences $\mathbf{x} \succ \mathbf{y}$. Now, if we look for transitivity with respect to the social preferences $\mathbf{z} \succ \mathbf{x}$, $\mathbf{x} \succ \mathbf{y}$, and $\mathbf{y} \succ \mathbf{z}$, we get a cycle. This demonstrates that the Pareto principle (P) and Liberalism (L) are in conflict with each other.

Should we restrict the domain, i.e., not allow for the preferences of Prude and Lewd as they are? This definitively questions liberalism.

Restricting the domain by excluding "deviating citizens" from political decision making is a common feature in liberal societies. Minors can be viewed as an instance of such restriction when it comes to voting. Another case is given by felon disenfranchisement. In the State of Iowa, almost 35 percent of its African-American population are barred from voting by felon disenfranchisement laws. Iowa is not an exception and felon disenfranchisement is not restricted to the African-American population, although the latter

| Prude | Lewd | |
|:---:|:---:|:---|
| z | x | x = Prude reads the book |
| x | y | y = Lewd reads the book |
| y | z | z = nobody reads the book |

*Figure 2.3* Preferences of Prude and Lewd, as in Sen (1970)

seems to be hit harder than other ethnical groups in the population. It is a nation-wide phenomenon:

> By Election Day 2004, the number of disenfranchised felons had grown to 5.3 million, with another 600,000 effectively stripped of the vote because they were jailed awaiting trial. Nationally, they made up less than 3 percent of the voting-age population, but 9 percent in Florida, 8 percent in Delaware, and 7 percent in Alabama, Mississippi, and Virginia.
>
> (DeParle 2007: 35)

Is it fair to conjecture that most of these people had preferences that deviate, perhaps substantially, from the preferences of the average US voter?

A first reaction to the Paradox is to point out the externalities implied in the preference orderings of Prude and Lewd. For instance, if Lewd reads the book then Prude cannot achieve his most preferred alternative z, which is "nobody reads the book." In fact, in Sen (1970), all three alternatives are conditional as there is the implicit assumption that the book can be read only by one person, and of course z can only be achieved if both do not read the book. In Sen (1982), there is the possibility that both read the book; however, this alternative cannot be achieved by the decision of one individual only. Standard microeconomics tells us that, in general, we do not achieve Pareto efficiency if there are (positive or negative) externalities. How is this related to the aggregation problem discussed here? Hillinger and Lapham point out that if there are no externalities,

> then liberalism follows as a special case of the Paretian principle. Pareto optimality will be attained when individuals are not at the mercy of the collective and coercive actions of others – when each individual makes choices on the assumption that no other single individual can cause him to take a particular action.
>
> (Hillinger and Lapham 1971: 1403)

However, as Sen made clear in his rejoinder to the comment by Hillinger and Lapham, his notion of liberalism (Condition L) is relevant only when there are externalities. Otherwise, liberalism "would say nothing on minority rights, nothing on the right to privacy, and nothing on the noninterference in personal lives. It would defend a person's freedom of action only so long as nobody else objects to that action" (1971: 1406). But what externalities are acceptable under the umbrella of liberalism? "What kind of externalities are these, and how can they be distinguished from those where the application of the condition would be inappropriate?" (Hillinger and Lapham 1971: 1404).

Sen was not explicit on this issue when he first introduced the Paradox (Sen 1970). However, in Sen (1982), obviously aware of the problem, he defines the concept of personal sphere:

> An individual's personal sphere contains some choices that directly affect the way he or she lives, but does not directly affect others, and if others are affected at all they are affected only because of their attitudes toward the personal lives of those who are directly affected.
>
> (Sen 1982: 208)

As a consequence, individual liberty implies some power of the respective individual to determine social judgments or social decisions over his or her personal sphere: if two social states x and y are different only by the color of agent i's shirt and i prefers x to y then the state x is socially preferred to y. That is, liberalism assigns power to the individual to determine social judgments. However, does this presuppose that the individual has the power to accomplish the underlying choices on the individual level? The choice of a particular shirt does not seem any problem; however, the example of Prude and Lewd indicates that agents could be rather powerless with respect to choices on the individual level. Neither Prude nor Lewd have "the chance . . . to realize their own will in a communal action even against the resistance of others who are participating in the action" (Weber 1948 [1924]: 180).[5]

Liberal people are likely to consider the color of a shirt as an item of the personal sphere, although certain colors are also a challenge to the environment. But if the shirt shows the Swastika, even liberal people may raise some objections – in fact, there are legal systems that rank the public showing of the Swastika as a crime. However, Prude and Lewd do not seem to be "true liberals." They want the other(s) to behave in a particular way and these "desires" have an impact on the issue of social ranking: it fails to produce an ordering. It seems that you cannot have a social welfare function that satisfies Pareto optimality and liberalism, if the agents are not liberal and do not respect the personal sphere of the other(s). For instance, given Lewd's preferences, how can we consider Prude's choice between z and x to be the personal sphere of Prude, if a cycle of social preferences follows from this qualification? On the other hand, Prude is only interested in reading the book, because it implies that Lewd cannot read the book. Does this respect the personal sphere of Lewd? Obviously, the aggregation of the individual preferences into a social ordering fails because Prude wants Lewd not to read the book. If this is the consequence of Prude's preferences, then we can hardly accept that Lewd's personal sphere is given by the choice between his reading of the book and no one reading it. Moreover, how can "no one reading it" be ever an element of a personal sphere?

---

5 This is the translation of Weber's definition of social power given in *Wirtschaft und Gesellschaft* (Weber (2005 [1922]: 678). Sen (1982) discusses "control" which comes close to the power issue. For liberty as control, see Sudgen (1985). Obviously, the relationship of desires, power and control power deserves further elaboration. See Section 2.3.4 below.

The design and acceptance of the personal sphere seems to be decisive in this case – as in almost all cases of liberalism. It seems to be the quintessential problem of liberal society. This issue is, however, not elaborated in the Liberal Paradox. On the other hand, one may wonder whether x, y, and z are alternatives that are subject to choices, although they are elements of the personal sphere of Prude and Lewd, respectively (if there are personal spheres at all). Clearly they are not independent of each other. On the one hand, if x or y is chosen, then z is no more feasible. On the other hand, if Prude chooses x, then y and z are no longer feasible, and Lewd has no choice at all. The latter case presupposes a particular sequential structure which is not specified in Sen (1970).

### 2.3.2 The 1982 Paradox

Perhaps as a reaction to this problem, in Sen (1982), the set of alternatives is enlarged by the possibility that "both read the book." This implies that both can choose between the alternatives either to read the book or not to read the book. However, still there are joint alternatives that are subject to aggregation; those are "both read the book (b)," "nobody reads the book (o)," "only Prude reads the book (p)," and "only Lewd reads the book (l)." Obviously, neither Prude nor Lewd can choose any of the four alternatives independent of the other one: the outcome will be a social choice. The alternatives represent individual *desires* with respect to the two-person society that we have discussed thus far, but not alternatives to choose from. Perhaps this is most obvious from the individual rankings of p and l and how controversially they are motivated (see below). There are either two copies available, or there is an arrangement that allows that both read the same copy. In the case of two books, the enforcement of p and o, respectively, seems very unlikely unless there is a social ordering that is accompanied by an implementation mechanism. But if p is unlikely, then b is unlikely, too.

It seems that Sen takes into consideration that the quality of the preferences underlying the Paradox differs from the quality of the preferences assumed for consumers in standard microeconomics. "An important distinction exits," it seems to him, "between person i *preferring* x to y, and person i wanting his preference for x over y to *count* in determining social choice" (Sen 1976: 236; original emphasis). One may add: particularly if this preference is not exclusively individual i's concern as in the case of Prude and Lewd. But Sen does not stop here. He notes that "extending this reasoning, I may decide, for the sake of consistency, not to insist that my preferences be taken into account ever in choices over some pairs that are not exclusively your concern" (Sen 1976: 236). If individual i does not *want*, for instance, that her preferences for x over y should count at the collective level, she may still *prefer* x to y and y to z. and contribute to the Paradox as the preferences of Lewd do. Obviously, there is a difference between *wanting* and *preferring* in this case if individual i follows her desire for a social preference order. Should we follow our desires, and not our preferences? This problem is well-known from the theory and the reality of strategic (or sophisticated) voting: voters may vote for their second- or third-best candidate, to let their first-best win (as in the case of strong non-monotonicity), or at least achieve a better result than in the case that they vote for their first-best candidate. Nurmi (2002, 2006) offers a rich set of examples of strategic voting and related paradoxes that illustrate that it is not always wise to strictly decide in accordance with one's preferences.[6]

Not to follow one's preferences, but trying to satisfy one's desires, could be beneficial. Sen's above suggestion – not to insist on the realization of one's preferences – clearly involves some sophistication and implies strategic behavior. Proposing (or not proposing) an alternative becomes a means and is no longer an end. As a consequence, it is not always possible to reveal the (social) desires by looking at the choices, i.e., the representation of preferences over alternatives, in the process of aggregation. As already indicated, there are obvious limits to a revealed-desires approach in the tradition of Samuelson's theory of "revealed preferences."

Figure 2.4 summarizes the assumed preferences of Prude and Lewd. The ranking of $o$, $p$, and $l$ corresponds to the preferences in Figure 2.2; however, there is the additional alternative (outcome) "both read the book ($b$)."

If the personal sphere of Prude implies that Prude is decisive for the social ranking of $p$ and $o$, then $o$ should be judged to be socially preferred to $p$. We

| Prude | Lewd |
|-------|------|
| o | b |
| p | p |
| l | l |
| b | o |

$o$ = neither read the book;

$p$ = Prude and only Prude reads the book;

$l$ = Lewd and only Lewd reads the book;

$b$ = both read the book.

*Figure 2.4* Preferences of Prude and Lewd, as in Sen (1982)

6  However, Lewis points out that there is also a *belief* that an alternative is good, that can make us deviate from our desires. His illustration is as follows: "The Department must choose between two candidates for a job, Meane and Neiss. Neiss is your old friend, affable, sensible, fair-minded, co-operative, moderate ... Meane is quite the opposite. But it is clear that Meane is just a little bit better at philosophy. Gritting your teeth and defying all desire, you vote for Meane, because you believe that Meane getting the job instead of Neiss would, all things considered, be good. Your belief about what's good has moved you to go against your desire to have Neiss for a colleague and to have nothing to do with Meane" (Lewis 1988: 323). I will not further discuss the relationship between beliefs and desires here, as Lewis emphasizes the difference mainly to defend David Hume (also see Lewis 1996) – which is not our concern.

express the social ranking by $o \succ p$. If, correspondingly, Lewd should be decisive for the social ranking of $l$ and $o$, then $l$ should be put over $o$: we write $l \succ o$ to express the social ranking of the two alternatives $l$ and $o$. An application of the Pareto criterion tells us that we get the social ranking $p \succ l$. If we sum up the social ranking, we get the preference cycle $o \succ p \succ l \succ o$. This demonstrates that transitivity is violated. Thus, there is no consistent social ranking under the given assumptions: a social preference ordering does not exist.

Again, neither Prude nor Lewd can choose any of the four alternatives $o$, $l$, $p$, and $b$ independent of the other one. The alternatives express desires, referring to the two-person society that we have discussed so far, but they represent neither for Prude nor for Lewd alternatives to choose from. For example, Prude cannot choose that he is the *only* one who will read the book. Perhaps this is most obvious from the individual rankings of $p$ and $l$ and how controversially they are motivated (see above). Or, does Prude have the power to prevent Lewd from reading the book? If so, then Prude is a dictator and we are no longer in a liberal society.

Perhaps it is irritating that the preference cycle $o \succ p \succ l \succ o$ does not refer to alternative $b$, i.e., both read the book. Yet, $b$ is neither subject to a personal sphere nor does its individual rankings allow a relevant Pareto ranking. However, Sen (1982: 211) also offers an alternative cycle $b \succ p \succ l \succ b$. Here $b \succ p$ is a consequence of the ranking of Lewd, given that Prude reads the book anyway – then $b \succ p$ represents Lewd's personal choice. (The assumption on Prude's reading corresponds with Prude's preferences, if $o$ is not feasible, but is it plausible? Does it correspond with Prude's desires?) Further, there is $l \succ b$ as Prude prefers not to read the book while Lewd reads it in either case. Again, an application of the Pareto criterion tells us that we get the social ranking $p \succ l$. This completes the cycle.

### 2.3.3 Dr. Jekyll and Mr. Hyde

The underlying model of the Liberal Paradox and more specifically the story of Prude and Lewd can also be used to discuss the editing problem that an individual $i$ faces in case of an multi-criteria decision making (MCDM) problem (see, e.g., Holler 2013a, 2015). Perhaps we should no longer speak of two individuals Prude and Lewd but of two versions of the same person like Mr. Hyde and Dr. Jekyll. Let us take the story as in Sen (1982), so that both "versions" can read the copy of *Lady Chatterley's Lover*. This makes, however, especially sense if there is just one person. But there are these two versions of this person characterized by two different preference orders as summarized in Figure 2.5.

Obviously, the prudish Dr. Jekyll wishes to read (the book) if Mr. Hyde threatens to read, and the wicked Mr. Hyde prefers that Dr. Jekyll reads if only one of them reads. However, if Dr. Jekyll reads, we can be sure that Mr. Hyde will also read the book. Then Dr. Jekyll prefers not to read the book.

| Dr. Jekyll | Mr. Hyde |
|:----------:|:--------:|
| z | b |
| x | x |
| y | y |
| b | z |

b = both read the book
x = Dr. Jekyll reads the book
y = Mr. Hyde reads the book
z = nobody reads the book

*Figure 2.5* Dr. Jekyll and Mr. Hyde's preferences, based on the example in Sen (1982)

However, if the wicked Mr. Hyde manages that both read, which is his highest-ranking alternative, then Dr. Jekyll will be very unhappy.

Let us try to aggregate the preferences of the two versions (i.e., dimensions or criteria) of the same person in the way suggested for Prude and Lewd in Sen (1982). First, it is assumed that (z, x) is the personal sphere of Dr. Jekyll such that the aggregated preferences are $\mathbf{z} \succ \mathbf{x}$. Next, we assume that that (y,z) is the personal sphere of Mr. Hyde such that the aggregated preferences are $\mathbf{y} \succ \mathbf{z}$. Then we assume that person represented by Dr. Jekyll and Mr. Hyde applies the Pareto principle. As a result, we have the aggregated preferences $\mathbf{x} \succ \mathbf{y}$. This completes the cycle $\mathbf{z} \succ \mathbf{x}$, $\mathbf{x} \succ \mathbf{y}$, and $\mathbf{y} \succ \mathbf{z}$. Obviously, the aggregation of preferences fails, if we ask for transitivity (and completeness). The Dr. Jekyll and Mr. Hyde person cannot rank his preferences. If we interpret the preferences as desires, we have to note that trying to satisfy these desires is likely to lead to inconsistency as there is no guiding ordering – and this is what Robert Stevenson's novel *The Strange Case of Dr. Jekyll and Mr. Hyde* is about: the Good and the Bad cannot be separated into two personalities of the same person without causing inconsistencies.

Throughout the above discussion, it was assumed that the two versions of the Dr. Jekyll and Mr. Hyde are of equal weight. Once Mr. Hyde takes over and Dr. Jekyll transforms more and more often and even in public into Mr. Hyde, the aggregation problem could be solved, but the drama approaches its end: Mr. Hyde is not able to survive without the second version of the person he represents; as a consequence, it seems, he committed suicide in Dr. Jekyll's laboratory.

Note that, contrary to what Emily Northrop (2000: 54) observes, failing to discern a hierarchy of desires does not "put all desires on equal footing." For instance, if there is no hierarchy, then we cannot assume an ordering and execute an optimization calculus as we learned to do it with reference to preferences and budget constraints. In any case, it is up to the decision maker to decide. However, if we cannot distill a hierarchy of desires then we cannot forecast future behavior and explain past behavior. The latter is a grave problem for the historian while the first result is a challenge to a social planner.

### 2.3.4 Power analysis and strategic reasoning

Liberalism, as defined in Sen (1970), assigns power to the individual to determine social judgments. Sen introduces the concept of minimal liberty (ML) which presupposes "at least two persons each having a nonempty personal sphere over which they respectively have such powers" (Sen 1982: 208). Does this imply that the individual has the power to accomplish the underlying choices on the individual level? And what choices? The choice of a particular shirt does not seem any problem; however, the example of Prude and Lewd indicates that agents could be rather powerless with respect to choices on the individual level. More specifically, in case that there is only one copy of the book and this copy is given to Prude, then nobody will read the book, irrespective of Lewd's preferences. We conclude that Lewd has no power in this case and ML is not satisfied. If, on the other hand, Lewd receives the copy he will read it, and not pass it on to Prude despite the fact that he prefers $p$ to $l$, since Prude will not read the book anyway, irrespective of whether Lewd reads it before him or not − if he is not a hypocrite. (However, if he is, then this should be reflected in the preferences.) Note that Lewd's least preferred alternative $o$ prevails if he gives the book to Prude without reading it. But if Lewd does not give the copy to Prude, then ML does not apply to Prude.

Sen must have seen this dilemma and the possibly missing ML. In Sen (1982), he allows for two copies, since otherwise it is not likely that both can read the book. But if we are serious about personal spheres, then Lewd cannot make Prude read the book, which excludes outcome $b$, and Prude cannot block Lewd from reading the book, which results in $l$. The outcome $l$ is rather low ranking in Prude's preference, lower than $p$. However, if Prude also reads the book, then $b$ results, which is lowest ranking for him. If there are two copies, then $p$ cannot prevail and the personal sphere of Prude is empty unless Lewd sacrifices his taste for *Lady Chatterley's Lover* and throws away his copy so that Prude has a choice between $p$ and $o$, and chooses $o$. But if preferences have any meaning, then Lewd is not expected to do so. Neither Prude nor Lewd have "the chance . . . to realize their own will in a communal action . . . against the resistance of others who are participating in the action," to repeat Weber's definition of power (Weber 1948 [1924]: 180).

|        |               | Lewd            |            |
| ------ | ------------- | --------------- | ---------- |
|        |               | Reads the book  | Does not … |
| **Prude** | Reads the book | $b$          | $p$        |
|        | Does not …    | $l$             | $o$        |

*Figure 2.6* The *Lady Chatterley's Lover* game form

We can illustrate the power issue by looking at the game form describing the choices of Prude and Lewd and the possible outcomes in Figure 2.6.[7] In the liberal setting of the problem, the two decision makers can either "read the book" or "not read the book," given there are two copies (or more). In game theoretical terms, this defines the strategies of the two players Prude and Lewd. Obviously, no individual player has full control on a particular outcome. Prude can block his least preferred outcome by choosing strategy "Does not . . ." whereas Lewd can prevent *o*, his least preferred outcome by reading the book. Thus, if the two decision makers use their blocking power, defined by their personal spheres, then *l* will result – which is not a poor result for a liberal society. However, this notion of liberalism does not concur with Sen's definition if people care what other members of the society read and their preferences (or desires?) matter for the evaluation of the social outcome.

Note that the most preferred outcomes *o* and *b* are desires of Prude and Lewd, respectively, and these desires will not be satisfied. They are "*imaginary features* of a possible world, which feature is such (a) that it is, for me, possible to *identify* with it and (b) it is *plausible* to consider the satisfaction of the demand" (Airaksinen 2014b). Note further, that the players do choose strategies, but not outcomes – however, they have no preferences on strategies, but on possible outcomes.

In Figure 2.7, we assigned numbers to the possible outcomes that represent the evaluation of Prude and Lewd in Figure 2.4. Only the ordinal rankings of these numbers matter, so any monotonic transformation of these expresses the same evaluation. In the corresponding game, Prude and Lewd have the dominant strategies "Does not . . ." and "Reads the book," respectively, so *l* will prevail. This confirms the analysis of the game form in Figure 2.6. Note that

**Lewd**

| | | Reads the book | Does not ... |
|---|---|---|---|
| **Prude** | Reads the book | (0,3) | (2,2) |
| | Does not ... | (1,1) | (3,0) |

*Figure 2.7* The *Lady Chatterley's Lover* reading game

7 In fact, what follows can be analyzed by means of effectivity functions. See Moulin and Peleg (1982), Miller (1982), and Vannucci (1986, 2002). An effectivity function describes the set of subsets of the outcome set X within which a coalition of players can force the final outcome by means of some coordinate action. Obviously, if Prude and Lewd coordinate their actions, they can select any outcome in the matrix of Figure 2.6. The coalition {Prude} can assure that the final outcome is either in the set {*b, p*} or in the set {*l, o*}, while {*b, l*} and {*p, o*} are the corresponding sets for coalition {Lewd}.

the outcome violates Pareto optimality. This does not come as a surprise because Figure 2.7 represents a Prisoners' Dilemma game (see page 163). However, in the non-cooperative setting implied, one might wonder whether Prude still prefers $p$ to $l$, if $l$ results anyhow. The preference $p \succ l$ is difficult to derive if Prude chooses "Does not . . ." in the equilibrium of the game. Wasn't Prude's preference $p \succ l$ motivated by the "desire" that Lewd will not read the book, if he reads the book?

In general, outcomes in strategic decision situations are "only to some extent" determined by the selected strategy of an individual decision maker. It has already been argued that as a consequence, in most game situations, we cannot reveal preferences from the choices. Can we conclude that Prude's preference ordering on the outcomes is $o \succ p \succ l \succ b$, if he chooses "Does not . . ."? Prude's preference order could be $o \succ l \succ p \succ b$ and he still chooses "Does not . . ." – in fact, in this case Prude has even stronger arguments to do so. Of course, there is also the possibility that Prude has a preference on the (strategy) choice itself such that she strictly prefers "Does not . . ." to "Reads the book," e.g., for moral reasons. However, by assigning preferences to strategies, we are outside of the game-theoretical framework, although preferences on the actions themselves could be most relevant for the observed behavior. In fact, the observed behavior could be the result of a combination of the evaluation of the expected outcome and the strategic reasoning and the evaluation of the available actions.

## 2.4 Preferences on desires

The game theoretical analysis suggests that we consider *preferences on desires*. To repeat, in Figure 2.7, an individual player, say Prude, cannot determine the outcome. Prude has some control on the outcome as by his choice of strategy he can exclude some alternatives from realization. But the realization of a particular outcome $\xi$ needs the corresponding strategy choice of Lewd, i.e., perhaps $\xi$ is a desire of Prude, but it is not an alternative that he can choose. As a consequence of his desires, Prude may *wish* that Lewd does not read the book – and perhaps even tells Lewd so. Correspondingly, Sen's examples, summarized in Figure 2.3 and 2.4, can be interpreted as preferences on desires. If we accept the notion of preferences on desires, then Figure 2.1 reads like (i) "there are desires and these desires will be ranked according to preferences" and (ii) "the ranked desires trigger decisions that have an 'impact' on the choices (i.e., realization, outcomes, etc.)." However, since we deal with desires, the "impact" does in general not "fully determine" choices. In fact, it could well be that no desire will be realized as they are "imaginary features of a possible world," only.

It "is plausible to consider the satisfaction of the demand" implied by the desire, but that does not mean that satisfaction follows. To be sure, *preferences on alternatives*, which populate textbooks of microeconomics, do not guarantee satisfaction either: there are budget constraints to the consumers and market constraints and technological restrictions to the firms. However, different from the "imaginary features of a possible world" that define desires, the set of alternatives is *given*. It might be very large, but it is assumed to be bounded such that there is scarcity ("rareté" in terms of Walras) which assures "value." This relationship has been proposed by Walras (1954 [1874])[8] and successfully submitted to a rigorous formal analysis by Debreu (1979 [1959]). But Debreu's formal apparatus does not apply, i.e., it does not allow proving the existence of an equilibrium, if the set of alternatives is unbounded, or more specifically, if the set of alternatives is not given.

Blaseio (2016) argues that formal economic analysis fails to deal with novelties, i.e., goods that we do as yet not know but we want to exist in the future and therefore invest in invention and innovation. Such an investment is not covered by standard economic decision calculus, although there are many approximations that try to capture the essence of the underlying decisions. However, the essence is that we do not know the results of the decisions in the case of pure novelties – resembling that, in general, we do not know the outcome of desires. Therefore, preferences on desires are quite different from preferences on (given) alternatives, and we cannot expect a complete and transitive ranking.

Preferences on desires imply a close relationship of the two concepts, but also demonstrate a clear distinction and a fundamental asymmetry: the meaning of assigning desires to preferences is not straightforward; one might even argue that it is nonsensical. If we do not make a distinction between preferences and desires, or completely neglect desires, we could face a major deficiency in understanding human behavior, the functioning of markets and nonmarket social relationships, and in coping with future developments and challenges. In her review of Scroble and Israel's book *Age of Context: Mobile, Sensors, Data and the Future of Privacy*, Sue Halpern (2014: 23) stresses the fact that "cars themselves are becoming computers on wheels, with operating system updates coming wireless over the air, and with increasing capacity to 'understand' their owners." Quoting Scroble and Israel, cars

> not only adjust seat positions and mirrors automatically, but soon they'll also know your preferences in music, service stations, dining spots and hotels . . . They know when you are headed home, and soon they'll be able to remind you to stop at the market to get a dessert for dinner.
>
> (Halpern 2014: 23)

It seems that the driverless future has already begun. In September 2016, taxi service Uber "launched a fleet of driverless Volvos and Fords in the city of Pittsburgh . . . Uber's Pittsburgh venture marks the first time such cars will be available to be hailed by the American public" (Halpern 2016b: 18). As of yet, these cars do not know our preferences, i.e., cars can learn your preferences on given alternatives, but not on desires if they are imaginary features of a possible world. (See Airaksinen (2014b) for this definition.) To satisfy your desires, you

8 See the "Preface" chapter of his *Éléments d'économie pure ou théorie de la richesse sociale.*

have to "operate" the steering wheel yourself. Of course, the "operating" can be strongly supported by a computerized search for the imaginary features of a possible world. However, cars may develop their own preferences on the available alternatives – and their choices could be in conflict with your desires. Your car could bring you home like it did ten days before, while you have the desire to go to town, have a fresh beer and perhaps meet new friends. This conflict seems to be easy to solve by switching off the computer – as long as there is a switch and the car has a steering wheel. It should be noted that autonomous vehicles, however, will not have a steering wheel. If you think this scenario to be exaggerated, please note that there already exist weapons that "pick whom they kill." The *New York Times* of November 11, 2014, reported that

> Britain, Israel and Norway are already deploying missiles and drones that carry out attacks against enemy tanks or ships without direct human control. After launch, so-called autonomous weapons rely on artificial intelligence and sensors to select targets and to initiate an attack.
>
> (Markoff 2014)

If this news does not affect you, then please read André Dhôtel's *L'île aux oiseaux de fer* of 1956. It is about desires in a society literally governed by computer.

## 2.5 The calculus of desires and preferences

The beauty of the formal proof in Sen (1970) somehow glosses over the problems which we discussed above. In fact, in order to keep the formal proof simple and lucid, it is necessary not to differentiate between preferences and desires – and not to discuss what defines the personal sphere of the decision makers. Sen's analysis nicely demonstrates that even under his rigorous assumptions on preferences, the aggregation of preferences may imply serious problems. The story of Dr. Jekyll and Mr. Hyde and the results of studying multi-criteria decision making (MCDM) suggest that even the forming of individual preference orderings is a problem. Experimental research confirmed such problems. The results of Kahneman and Tversky (1979) triggered a plethora of research and publications pointing to framing effects, certainty effects, status quo bias, preference reversal, etc. that explain that individuals violate expected utility theory, on the one hand, and transitivity of preferences, on the other.[9] They are labeled as examples of cognitive biases. Sales managers and advertising specialists knew about these effects long before they entered footnotes and appendices of economics textbooks, where preference orderings still prevail.

---

9  See Allais (1953) for the pioneering paper and Lichtenstein and Slovic (1971) for an early discussion of preference reversals.

### 2.5.1 Pleasure, pain, and mathematics

There is a long tradition of making use of preferences as a black box. The assumption of an ordering and the conditions for revealed preferences add some constraints, but still one might almost always find a preference ordering that supports a particular observed behavior. Experimental economics challenges this state of the art. However, many experiments are in fact analyzing desires, and not preferences, just like we saw in the *Gedankenexperiment* illustrating Sen's Liberal Paradox. On the other hand, much of economic theorizing is still based on a "calculus of pleasure and pain" – which makes even stronger assumptions than implied by a preference ordering, as it assumes a cardinal measure of utility which allows for deriving decisions and actions from an optimization calculus. In the introduction of the first edition of *The Theory of Political Economy* of 1871, Jevons ((1888 [1871]): vii) writes: "The nature of Wealth and Value," which derives from the calculus of pleasure and plain, "is explained by the consideration of indefinitely small amounts of pleasure and pain, just as the Theory of Statics is made to rest upon the equality of indefinitely small amounts of energy." The underlying assumption is that progress in economics can only be achieved by the application of mathematics, thereby mimicking physics. In the *Preface* to the second edition of 1879, Jevons postulates "all economic writers must be mathematical so far as they are scientific at all, because they treat economic quantities, and the relations of such quantities, and all quantities and relations of quantities come within the scope of the mathematics" (Jevons 1888 [1871]: xx).

Jevons emphasized this message by giving a long list of literature that used mathematics as an analytical instrument in economics. In the second edition of *The Theory of Political Economy*, he explicitly substituted political economy with economics, but left the book's title unchanged: "Though employing the new name in the text, it was obviously undesirable to alter the title-page of the book" (Jevons 1888 [1871]: xiv). He asserts that "all reasonable exertion have thus been made to render complete and exhaustive the list of mathematico-economic work and papers, which is now printed in the first Appendix of this book" (Jevons 1888 [1871]: xx), i.e., the second edition of *The Theory of Political Economy*.

Only recently, a quite lively debate, also as a consequence of the economic crisis and its perhaps inadequate treatment in the academic arena, erupted, at least in Germany and in the U.K. The issue was whether there is too much or too little mathematics applied in economic analysis. The dividing line can be illustrated by a letter to Her Majesty The Queen of July 22, 2009, signed by Professors Tim Besley and Peter Hennesey and a response letter to the Queen of August 10, 2009, signed by Professor Geoffrey M. Hodgson.[10] In his letter, Hodgson complained that the

---

10 The two letters – together with comments by Peter Skott, John Hudson, Andreas Freytag, Leif Helland, Gebhard Kirchgässner, Alain Marciano, and Heinz Kurz – have been published in the form of a Symposium in *Homo Oeconomicus* 27(3), 2010: 329–389.

letter by Professors Besley and Hennessy does not consider how the preference for mathematical technique over real-world substance diverted many economists from looking at the vital whole. It fails to reflect upon the drive to specialise in narrow areas of enquiry, to the detriment of any synthetic vision. For example, it does not consider the typical omission of psychology, philosophy or economic history from the current education of economists in prestigious institutions.

(Hodgson 2010: 335)

Further, Hodgson pointed out that

leading economists – including Nobel Laureates Ronald Coase, Milton Friedman and Wassily Leontief – have complained that in recent years economics has turned virtually into a branch of applied mathematics, and has been become detached from real-world institutions and events . . . Far too little has since been done to rectify this problem. Consequently a preoccupation with a narrow range of formal techniques is now prevalent in most leading departments of economics throughout the world, and notably in the United Kingdom.

(Hodgson 2010: 335)

One might argue that this did not happen just in recent years. My estimate is that more than half of all Nobel Laureates in Economics are trained mathematicians. Most of them focused on economic issues and used mathematics as a tool for economic analysis, while some seemed to use economics as a playing field for mathematics. In his *Theory of Value*, Nobel laureate Gerard Debreu (1979 [1959]) starts with a chapter on mathematics. This chapter does not seem to be written to help the reader to understand what follows, but to keep those off the text who are neither competent nor interested in mathematical analysis. It is surprising to learn from his Presidential Address to the American Economic Association (December 29, 1990), "The Mathematization of Economic Theory," the qualification that the dominance of mathematical analysis can be explained only partly by its intellectual successes." Even more surprisingly, he adds:

Essential to an attempt at a fuller explanation are the values imprinted on an economist by his study of mathematics. When a theorist who has been so typed judges his scholarly work, those values do not play a silent role; they may play a decisive role. The very choice of the questions to which he tries to find answers is influenced by his mathematical background. Thus, the danger is ever present that the part of economics will become secondary, if not marginal, in that judgment.

(Debreu 1991: 5)

There is still Keynes's verdict that

> human decisions affecting the future, whether personal or political or eco-
> nomic, cannot depend on strict mathematical expectations, since the basis
> for making such calculations does not exist; and that is our innate urge to
> activity which makes the wheels go round, our rational selves choosing
> between alternatives as best we are able, calculating where we can, but
> often falling back for our motive on whim or sentiment or chance.
>
> (Keynes 1936: 163)

Note that the central hypothesis of this section is that desires have vanished
from the menu of economic research (and consideration) and are completely
substituted by preferences and utilities because the latter concepts are closer to
mathematization – at least, as seen from the contemporary state of the art. And
there is some evolutionary dynamics involved that supports further mathematization. What Debreu noted is still valid:

> The reward system of our profession reinforces the effects of that autocriti-
> cism. Decisions that shape the career of an economic theorist are made by
> his peers. Whether they are referees of a journal or of a research organiza-
> tion, members of an appointment or of a promotion committee, when
> they sit as judges in any capacity, their verdicts will not be independent of
> their own values. An economist who appears in their court rarely ignores
> his perception of those values. If he believes that they rate mathematical
> sophistication highly, and if he can prove that he is one of the sophisticates,
> the applause that he expects to receive will condition his performance.
>
> (Debreu 1991: 5)

One may conclude that it is more promising to remodel a utility function so
that it fits the data (see Section 2.8 for a discussion), than to argue on the basis
of unordered desires to explain the unstructured phenomenon that we observe.
I do not want to contribute to the general discussion of whether there is too
much or too little mathematics applied in economic analysis. But let us face it,
desires are not always with quantities and if they are, they often do not consider
scarcity, so that the optimization calculus cannot be applied. Still, desires, and
not just pleasure and pain, also motivate action and trigger decisions.

### 2.5.2 The variety of desires and the desire for variety

After studying the Marquis de Sade's *Justine*, Airaksinen concludes that "desires
are complex, misleading, and internally challenged stories about one's happiness
and its conditions to be realized by means of real choices." However, "Sade
does not seem to accept this," conjectures Airaksinen (2013: 378). Airaksinen

observes a "calculus of desires" in the heart of Sade's narratives: Sade "casts all the issues he wants to deal with into the opposite categories, desires and virtues, and speaks as if they conflicted" (Airaksinen 2013: 374). Indeed there are frictions, i.e., counter-desires, that tend to moderate desires or even lock them away. Sade wants to get rid of these frictions. There is the "calculus of desire": a proposition, a shell, a cover, a wrapper that does not get filled up with calculations. It is a label that points out the absence of emotions and the rationality of the decision maker. As a consequence, desires can lead to self-destruction.[11] In Sade's world, "emotions complicate things and do not allow one to focus on the essence of desire. A true libertine is without emotion. He is cold, calm, and rational, an enlightened person par excellence" (Airaksinen 2013: 379). However, Sade's heroes do not calculate: they act. They want to have more and more, and more of the same. This seems to hold also for the three protagonists in Sergio Leone's *The Good, the Bad, and the Ugly*. However, there is a peculiar type of sharing towards the end of the film (see Chapter 5).

Does this urge for "more and more" contradict a standard observation subscribed to by most economists, or do we speak of two different kinds of desires? Jevons (1888 [1871]: 53) emphasizes the "great principle of the ultimate decrease of the final degree of utility of any commodity" and quotes Senior's so-called *Law of Variety*:[12]

> It is obvious . . . that our desires do not aim so much at quantity as at diversity. Not only are there limits to the pleasure which commodities of any given class can afford, but the pleasure diminishes in a rapidly increasing ratio long before those limits are reached. Two articles of the same kind will seldom afford twice the pleasure of one, and still less will ten give five times the pleasure of two. In proportion, therefore, as any article is abundant, the number of those who are provided with it, and do not wish, or wish but little, to increase their provision, is likely to be great; and, so far as they are concerned, the additional supply loses all, or nearly all, its utility. And, in proportion to its scarcity, the number of those who are in want of it, and the degree in which they want it, are likely to be increased; and its utility, or, in other words, the pleasure which the possession of a given quantity of it will afford, increases proportionally.
>
> (Senior 1854: 11f.)

11 According to Michael Wood, Orson Welles succeeded in smuggling his favorite animal fable into his movie *Mr. Arkadin*. "A scorpion, asking a frog for a lift across a river, says there is no danger in the frog's taking him on. Obviously he will not sting the frog because it wouldn't make any sense, they would both drown. Halfway across the water the scorpion stings the frog, and as they go under the frog asks why. 'It's my character,' the scorpion says" (Wood 2013: 76).

12 In fact, Senior (1854: 11) emphasizes the "love of variety," but does not point to a "Law of Variety," as Jevons submits. In *The Economics Anti-Textbook* by Hill and Myatt, we can read that "unlimited wants does not mean we want an unlimited amount of a specific thing. Rather, it means that there will always be something that we will desire. There will always be new desires. Our desires and wants are fundamentally unlimited" (2010: 10).

Here Jevons adds:

> The necessaries of life are so few and simple, that a man is soon satisfied in regard to these, and desires to extend his range of enjoyment. His first object is to vary his food; but there soon arises the desire of variety and elegance in dress; and to this succeeds the desire to build, to ornament, and to furnish—tastes which, where they exist, are absolutely insatiable, and seem to increase with every improvement in civilisation.
>
> (Jevons 1888 [1871]: 40)

This statement by Jevons reflects Adam Smith's categorization of desires:

> The desire of food is limited in every man by the narrow capacity of the human stomach; but the desire of the conveniencies and ornaments of building, dress, equipage, and household furniture, seems to have no limit or certain boundary. Those, therefore, who have the command of more food than they themselves can consume, are always willing to exchange the surplus, or, what is the same thing, the price of it, for gratifications of this other kind. What is over and above satisfying the limited desire, is given for the amusement of those desires which cannot be satisfied, but seem to be altogether endless.
>
> (Smith 1981 [1776/77]: 181)

To the latter category we should perhaps add the tastes discussed in Sade. (For those wishing to avoid reading Sade, see Airaksinen (2013).)

Perhaps we also should add to the latter the desire of distinction. Senior is quite aware that

> strong as is the desire for variety, it is weak compared with the desire for distinction: a feeling which, if we consider its universality and its constancy, that it affects all men and at all times, that it comes with us from the cradle, and never leaves us till we go into the grave, may be pronounced to be the most powerful of human passions.
>
> (Senior 1854: 12)

This of course concurs with some of the most prominent conjectures in Adam Smith's *Theory of Moral Sentiments* of 1759 and of Thorstein Veblen's *Theory of the Leisure Class* of 1899. It could be an interesting project to elaborate the status of desires in these two works. References to distinction can also be found in Smith's *Wealth of Nations*. Indeed it is the driving force for accumulating private wealth.

To conclude, again Senior:

> The most obvious source of distinction is the possession of superior wealth. It is the one which excites most the admiration of the bulk of mankind, and the only one which they feel capable of attaining. To seem more rich,

or, to use a common expression, to keep up a better appearance, than those within their own sphere of comparison, is, with almost all men who are placed beyond the fear of actual want, the ruling principle of conduct.

(Senior 1854: 12)

There is the "disposition to admire, and almost to worship, the rich and the powerful, and to despise, or, at least, to neglect persons of poor and mean condition," as Smith (1982 [1759]: 61) observes in *The Theory of Moral Sentiments*.[13]

It seems obvious that the desire of distinction cannot be modeled with the utility maximization approach suggested by Jevons unless we rely on proxies of conspicuous consumption as a means to gain and to keep the admiration of the others, suggested by Veblen (1979 [1899]). Another challenge to the utility maximization approach is Senior's "Law of Variety," if it implies an extension of the commodity space, adding new dimensions. In general, this does not allow a straightforward comparison of the alternatives with respect to preferences. Some of the new alternatives may already have existed, but others are pure desires, perhaps even of the dimensions of fairy tales. On the one hand, we know of imaginative advertisements which create the desire for commodities which are waiting to be sold. On the other, there are emerging desires for "new goods" that lack the corresponding commodities and services waiting to satisfy them. Perhaps these desires will never be satisfied because the corresponding commodities and services are not feasible. Still, these desires can have a strong impact on the choices of the decision makers, for instance, in the search of substitutes and complements. People who work with drug addicts emphasize this problem. Much of the sadness of Marquis de Sade's heroes can be attributed to this issue. Desires do not always make us happy, but still most of us try to become happy by satisfying our desires.

## 2.6 Ranking sets of desires

A possible hypothesis is that the size of the set of desires, howsoever measured, has a substantial impact on the decision behavior of people. How can we corroborate this hypothesis?

In order to answer this question and to prepare for empirical testing, the representation of desires needs further elaboration. First of all, we have to consider that often there are degrees of satisfaction that an individual can expect and, as a result of processes of execution, can experience. These degrees have to be considered in the empirical analysis whenever they seem to be relevant.

---

13 This concurs with "the desire of bettering our condition, a desire which, though generally calm and dispassionate, comes with us from the womb, and never leaves us till we go into the grave ... there is scarce perhaps a single instant in which any man is so perfectly and completely satisfied with his situation, as to be without any wish of alteration or improvement, of any kind," as stated by Smith (1981 [1776/77]: 341) in *Wealth of Nations*.

Ahlert (2014) provides a formal apparatus to explore this issue. Section 2.6.4 contains a summary. It also illustrates some editing of desires.

Of course, there are desires which are either satisfied or not, and degrees do not matter. Still, Ferejohn and Fiorina's (1975) statement, "closeness counts only in horseshoes and dancing" – the title of their rather popular article – seems somewhat exaggerated. Inasmuch as desires are related to needs, there is however an additional dimension with respect to satisfaction if we follow Herzberg's dual-factor theory. This theory allocates dissatisfaction and satisfaction on different scales (Herzberg et al. 1959; Herzberg 1966). There are *motivators* that provide positive satisfaction, arising from *intrinsic* conditions, and there are hygiene factors, identified with extrinsic conditions, that do not give positive satisfaction, though dissatisfaction results if the needs (or desires?) are not fulfilled. Herzberg studied labor relations where, in general, recognition, achievement, or personal growth are intrinsic conditions, while status, job security, salary, fringe benefits, and work conditions are extrinsic. In principle, dissatisfaction and satisfaction could coexist in this arrangement if needs are not fulfilled. Yet, this does not directly transfer to desires, as unfulfilled wishes do not always lead to dissatisfaction. But there might be a level of frustration with them which has an immediate impact on our behavior – perhaps even a strong one.

Empirical evidence shows that intrinsic motivation can be crowded out by extrinsic motivators. In his study *Not Just For the Money*, Frey (1997) gives numerous examples and a substantial discussion. He demonstrates that, contrary to the message of standard microeconomics, the price effect can be even negative inasmuch as supply shrinks when monetary compensation increases. For example, if the money reward for social helpers increases, voluntary help is likely to decrease and the total quantity (and the quality) of help will diminish.

Most individuals have more than one desire – but one of them could be a dominant one. Yet, even a dominant desire could be disaggregated in its elements and the elements then form a set of desires. Does this recommend that we consider sets of desires instead of individual ones? If so, this raises the problem of ranking sets in order to be able to specify their impact on decisions. In what follows, I will discuss three models for comparing sets of desires: counting measure, α-ordering and inclusion ordering, preparing for the testing of this hypothesis.

### 2.6.1 Three wishes and sets of desires

In Walt Disney's *Aladdin*, the genie granted three wishes with the exception of murder, romance, or revival of the dead – or the wish of additional wishes. The latter constraint keeps the set of wishes finite. Aladdin decides to use his first wish to become a prince in order to be able to legally court Princess Jasmine. His desire for Jasmine had a price: one of three wishes. In this context, wishes are the complements to desires.

There are many stories of Aladdin and many stories in which three wishes are granted. Some stories tell us that the elements of the set of desires may contradict itself from a logical point of view or, alternatively, with respect to a possible satisfaction. Contradiction of desires may either have an immediate impact of the behavior – resulting in some inconsistencies and "surprises" – or motivate the individual to edit his or her desires making them consistent and achievable. On the other hand, some desires can be very similar, even from the perspective of the individual. This could express the prominence of a particular subset of desires, but it could also result from the fact that desires derive from alternative sources and these sources overlap "to some extent." We expect that individuals take care of similarities and overlapping desires when editing their desires.

Similarities matter in the ranking of alternatives. For instance, Rubinstein (1988) discusses the ranking of risky alternatives based on similarities of probabilities, on the one hand, and of prizes, on the other. Compared to testing preferences, the information requirements of desires are easier to satisfy as completeness and transitivity are not demanded, and the cognitive problems involved are less complex as feasibility is not a constraint. There is firsthand information available: in everyday life, there are numerous references to desires including wish lists for Christmas, birthdays and weddings, or consumer reports and monthly surveys on "political preferences" which are in general listing desires, and not preferences. Pollock (2006) gives a list of arguments that support the empirical prominence of desires versus preferences. I have to confess that before I started to study economics, nearly fifty years ago, I did not even know about preferences, but I had desires and knew about desires, but, of course, I did not know what desires are.

As already said, we do not assume that (sets of) desires *cause* action, a view that is strictly rejected, e.g., in Russell (1984), but we expect that desires have an impact on decision making and thus affect behavior. We hope for correlations. Mullainathan and Shafir (2013) demonstrated that scarcity can "capture your mind"[14] and reduce the cognitive capacity of problem solving. Do desires capture our mind and in what way? There is a straightforward argument if desires trigger scarcity. A possible hypothesis could be: the larger the set of desires, the larger the experience of scarcity, the stronger is the reduction of our cognitive capacity. However, does this scarcity "capture your mind" in the same way irrespective of whether it concerns basic needs, implying limited desires, or luxuries and thus "the amusement of those desires which cannot be satisfied, but seem to be altogether endless" (Smith 1981 [1776/77]: 181). Obviously, not all desires correspond to the same category of scarcity, and some desires do not relate to scarcity at all. I may wish to be able to fly like a bird, but I know that I will not; this desire is not likely to trigger scarcity. However, one might argue that this wish is a wish – a case of a conative attitude – and not a desire (Schroeder 2014). For more details on concepts of desires, see Section 2.7 below. The next section will try to clarify the notion of sets of desire.

---

14 The review of Mullainathan and Shafir (2013) by Sunstein (2013) is titled "It Captures Your Mind." For the reduction of the cognitive capacity of problem solving, see Mani et al. (2013).

## 2.6.2 Measuring and counting measures

In order to compare sets of desires and correlate the result with quantitative empirical decision results, either gained from observations "in the field" or from experiments, it would be advantageous to have a cardinal measure of the size of the sets of desires. The analysis of the data would be straightforward and the need for interpretation could be satisfied by pointing to, more or less standard, test statistics. This raises the question whether there is an adequate way to measure the size of desire sets, i.e., attaching numbers to sets. In order to show that a measure exists and to demonstrate that there is a plausible way of attaching numbers to entities under certain conditions, we have to prove a representation theorem. According to Nurmi (1982: 260) the

> theorem says that there is a plausible way of attaching numbers to enti-
> ties under certain conditions. The conditions restrict the applicability of
> measurements by indicating the conditions which must be fulfilled by the
> entities if the measurement is to be meaningful.
>
> (Nurmi 1982: 260)

That is why we should have an understanding of desires and of what sets of desires are:

> the representation theorem presupposes a kind of "theory" of the phe-
> nomenon under study in the sense that the conditions of meaningful num-
> ber assignment refer to the properties of the phenomenon. By proving a
> representation theorem one shows that the properties of the entities inves-
> tigated can be represented by the numbers, so that the relational structure
> of the numbers preserves the rational structure of the empirical properties.
>
> (Nurmi 1982: 260)

As we will see, the latter condition is very demanding and can only be achieved by a high degree of abstraction. To demonstrate this observation, let us start with a basic model of measuring the size of desire sets. To begin with, we define X as the (finite or infinite) set of all desires, Z is the power set of X that has X, $\emptyset$ and all A, B $\subseteq$ X as elements; R is the desire set relation such that, for all A, B $\in$ Z, ARB expresses that "desire set A is at least as large as desire set B." This defines the basic model. Now we look for a "meaningful number assignment."

A seemingly trivial specification of R is to define ARB iff $|A| \geq |B|$, i.e., if and only if set A contains at least as many elements (i.e., desires) as set B. This specification defines the counting relation $R_{\#}$. Obviously, $R_{\#}$ satisfies the properties that have to be fulfilled for a cardinal measure.

Let us introduce the binary relation $I$ such that A$I$B says that "set A is as large as set B." Obviously, (A$I$B) $\Leftrightarrow$ (ARB) & (BRA). Therefore we can introduce a binary relation $P$ such that A$P$B implies "set A is larger than set B" defining (A$P$B) $\Leftrightarrow$ (ARB) & not(A$I$B). We can now borrow a set of properties and a proof from Pattanaik and Xu (1990)[15] and conclude that $R_\#$ is the only binary relation satisfying the following properties:

Property 2.1 (Simple Anonymity): For all x, y $\in$ X, $\{x\}I\{y\}$.

Property 2.2 (Simple Strict Monotonicity): For all distinct x, y $\in$ X, $\{x, y\}P\{x\}$

Property 2.3 (Simple Independence). For all A, B $\in$ Z and all x $\in$ X\ (A$\cup$B) follows $[ARB \Leftrightarrow A\cup\{x\}RB\cup\{x\}]$

Pattanaik and Xu's paper (1990) deals with "measuring" freedom of choice, i.e., comparing sets of alternatives with respect to the freedom of choice they imply. Of course, there is the underlying postulate of liberalism that more choices are better than less. Property 2.1 seems to be an essential ingredient for measuring freedom of choice, yet it captures two sets that imply no choice. It clearly indicates that only the choice setting matters, and not the choice between alternatives, and the answer with respect to choices is somewhat "negative." One might therefore argue that it is an inadequate point of departure for a theory that deals with freedom of choice. However, what is its interpretation in the case of the desire relation? Of course counting tells us that sets $\{x\}$ and $\{y\}$ are of equal size, but $\{x\}$ could represent a "big desire" while $\{y\}$ could represent a "small one." On the other hand, Property 2.2 seems more appropriate for desires than for freedom of choice: in the latter case, it compares a choice situation to a *no choice* situation; this could be interpreted as a qualitative "jump" not covered by the numerical relation $>$ or, more generally, $\geq$, i.e., "larger" and "at least as large." Claiming that $\{x, y\}$ contains twice as much freedom of choice than $\{x\}$ seems to be questionable as $\{x\}$ does not contain any freedom of choice at all. One might argue that $R$ is meant to compare two sets with respect to freedom of choice, and not a situation without choice to a situation with choice. In terms of desires, however, it could be adequate to say that $\{x, y\}$ represents twice as many desires as $\{x\}$.

There is an alternative set of properties that supports $R_\#$. There is a function f that maps Z into the space of real numbers such that for all A, B $\in$ Z we have

(1)  $f(A) \geq 0$,
(2)  $f(X) = 1$
(3)  $A \cap B = \varnothing$ implies $f(A \cup B) = f(A) + f(B)$ and
(4)  $ARB$ iff $f(A) \geq f(B)$

---

15 Pattanaik and Xu (1990) deal with "measuring" freedom of choice, comparing sets of alternatives with respect to the freedom of choice they imply. Of course, there is the postulate of liberalism that more choices are better than less.

Following Nurmi (1982: 261) we argue that a measure f(.) exists, for a finite (total) set of desires X, and A,B $\subset$ X, if the following conditions hold for the relation R:

(a)  R is transitive
(b)  R is complete
(c)  AR$\varnothing$
(d)  it is not the case that $\varnothing$RX
(e)  A $\cap$ B = C $\cap$ B = $\varnothing$ implies that ARC iff A$\cup$ BRC$\cup$B.

For readers who are familiar with power indices: Nurmi (1982) uses this set of conditions[16] to introduce the measure "is at least as probable as," on the one hand, and to show that prominent power measures such as the Shapley-Shubik index, the (standardized) Banzhaf index and the two Coleman indices, violate the additivity condition (3). For instance, they suffer from the "paradox of size," pointed out in Brams (1975: 177f.). This paradox implies that the sum of the power values of two disjoint subsets, A and B, of C is larger than the power value of C although C is the union of A and B, i.e., C = (A $\cup$ B). Therefore, if this is the case, then in terms of voting power, it seems to pay that party C splits up into subsets A and B. (For the paradox of quarreling members, see Kilgour (1974) and Brams (1975: 180f.).) However, since the corresponding power measure does not satisfy additivity, this perspective might be misleading.

There is a power measure that satisfies additivity: equalizing the seat shares with power ratios. As the seat share relation never suffers from the "paradox of size" and related paradoxes like the "paradox of redistribution" or the "paradox of quarrelling members" a measure $\xi$ that is identified with it, satisfies additivity condition (3). However, power measure $\xi$ ignores coalition formation and is therefore considered a poor proxy for measuring a priori voting power. This raises the question whether the measure $\xi$ is "meaningful" (see above), i.e., does it represent the empirical conditions in an adequate way? Obviously, there are strong doubts. But we have to see that measure $\xi$ corresponds with the counting measure $R_{\#}$ (satisfies conditions (1) to (4) above).

As coalition formation is no obvious phenomenon for desires, we can hope that $R_{\#}$ is adequate for measuring desire sets. Yet, there is a long list of arguments why the measure relation $R_{\#}$ is inadequate for measuring desire sets. Some of these arguments have to do with the equal weighting assumption implied in the counting of desires, others are more general problems implied in the listing of desires, while still others have elements of both dimensions. An often raised issue is that the set of desires may include *inconsistent* elements and the desire sets should be cleared of them before measuring. However, in general, not all desires are meant to be fulfilled. The genie granted Aladdin

---

16 Nurmi (1982: 261) referred to a publication by Niiniluoto (1975, in Finnish) for conditions (1)–(4) and properties (a)–(e).

three wishes and left it to Aladdin to choose consistent ones. Aladdin became rich and powerful and married the sultan's daughter.

If not all desires are meant to be fulfilled then *infeasibility*, a second argument brought forward, is no longer restricting the measurement of desire sets. *Infeasibility* can have several sources: one could be the just-mentioned inconsistency; a second source could be a "budget constraint." In this case, fulfillment could be an issue of degree. Note that even in the world of preferences, we ask for a pairwise comparison of elements that are not covered by the budget set. Otherwise we would get a utility representation which is constrained by the budget equation – and does not give us evaluations if the budget line pushes upward. (The indirect utility function represents such a relationship.) With respect to desires, there might be a genie offering three wishes which are not constrained by a budget. (However, consistency could be a problem as versions of the Aladdin story tell us.)

A related argument is referring to the *capability* to enjoy the fulfillment of desires. It parallels the capability argument as introduced by Sen (1985, 1989) when discussing freedom of choice. Obviously, if my 4-year-old grandson wants to drive a truck then this is limited by the fact that he cannot obtain a driver's license and, in addition, he is too small to reach the steering wheel and the gas pedal at the same time. But when it comes to discussing Christmas presents, he anyway points out that the "driving a truck" is not a "real desire," just a play – somehow qualifying his wishes by feasibility. Of course, the definition of one's capability is not always as straightforward, and, to some extent, also rather subjective. Some people overestimate their capabilities especially when it comes to desires – and suffer from their constraints of incapability when they have a chance of fulfillment.

There is a problem of counting desires if desires are not independent of each other, or if a desire $x$ is in fact a set that implies other desires that could even be considered subsets. The desire to drive a car implies a driver's license and access to a vehicle. The desire with respect to the vehicle can comprise several dimensions: color, maximum speed, brand, etc. Alternative combinations of these dimensions can represent alternative desires and create *inconsistencies of aggregation* (see Holler 2015) such that no single $x$ can be distilled by the individual $i$, but a set $\{x, y, z,$ etc.$\}$ describing alternative desires when in fact there was only the desire of driving a car. The counting relation $R_{\#}$ ignores hierarchies of inclusion, complementary and substitutional relationships among the desire alternatives. Of course, this is a serious issue for an application of $R_{\#}$. In this case, we can only hope that individual $i$ will *edit* its desires so that this issue will not prevail. (More about *editing desires* below.) It is an empirical question whether individuals edit their desires accordingly that must be tested. When it comes to the desire of "driving a truck," then my grandson is very likely to edit his list of Christmas desires. Yet, he might consider his *capability* and reckon that this desire cannot be fully satisfied – and, instead, a model railroad is a desire that could be satisfied.

Technically speaking, some of the issues which constrained the application of a counting measure of desire, or which make the application of such a measure highly questionable, can be taken care of by attaching weights. This is what we discuss in the next chapter. In the case of *The Good, the Bad, and the Ugly*, the measure $R_\#$ seems to capture the desires of all three protagonists as the sets are singletons and money is the dominant dimension. Money is additive, just like votes – purchasing power is not as power measures indicate. It seems that the desire for the treasure of $200,000 fully motivated the behavior of the three. And yet, when in the movie's final scene Blondie dedicated half of the treasure to Tuco – although Tuco has a noose around his neck and is balancing on the wooden cross of a tomb – other desires entered the scene. Whether this is revenge or an implication of fairness, we will discuss in the concluding chapter of this book.

### 2.6.3 Of α-orderings and inclusion

Discussing freedom of choice theory, Marlies Klemisch-Ahlert (1993) defines an ordering $R_\alpha$ such that for all $A, B \subset X$, we have

$$\left( \text{W} \right) \ A R_\alpha B \Leftrightarrow \sum_{x \in A} \alpha(x) \geq \sum_{x \in B} \alpha(x)$$

Here $\alpha(.)$ is a map that assigns a weight $\alpha(x) > 0$ to every x in X. More specifically, $\alpha{:}X \to \ ]0,\infty[$. An ordering which satisfies (W) is called an α-ordering. The α-ordering $R_\alpha$ satisfies properties 2.2 and 2.3, but it concurs with property 2.1 only if $\alpha(x) = \alpha(y)$, which is in general not the case. Klemisch-Ahlert (1993) demonstrates that $R_\alpha$ satisfies properties 2.2 and 2.3, and

Property 2.4. For all x, y $\in$ X, $\{x\}R\{y\} \Leftrightarrow \alpha(x) \geq \alpha(y)$.

Obviously, there is no specification $R_\alpha$ that is unique in satisfying Properties 2.2, 2.3 and 2.4. There are many α-orderings, i.e., specifications of vector α, that satisfy these properties. What α-ordering to choose? Klemisch-Ahlert (1993) discusses (W) with respect to measuring "freedom of choice" and therefore does not refer to a particular individual *i*. Accordingly, the specification of the α-ordering is exogenous to the discussed issue, perhaps imposed by a moral system or a common sense, or derived from a social evaluation procedure. A possible constraint to the α-values could be

$$\sum_{x \in X} \alpha(x) = 1$$

With this normalization, the formal apparatus is rather similar to what is discussed as weighted utilitarian welfare function and a similar question arises: what (or who) defines the α-values? But when it comes to desires, it is the individual that determines the weights. But does the individual know the weights, and how can the observer distil them from the individual's behavior or communication?

The problem of choosing $\alpha$-values can be avoided if we restrict the ranking to inclusion. We define an inclusion ordering $R\subseteq$ by

(IN) For all A, B $\in$ Z and B $\subseteq$ A $\Rightarrow$ AR$\subseteq$B.

With respect to "freedom of choice," Klemisch-Ahlert (1993) proves that $R\subseteq$ is the intersection of all $\alpha$-orderings $R_\alpha$. That is:

$$\left(\text{IN}_\alpha\right) \text{ If } B \subseteq A \text{ then } \sum_{x\in A} \alpha(x) \geq \sum_{x\in B} \alpha(x)$$

Thus, given B $\subseteq$ A and $\alpha$:X $\rightarrow$ ]0,$\infty$[, AR$_\alpha$B follows, *irrespective of the $\alpha$-weights chosen*. Obviously, $R\subseteq$ defines an incomplete (i.e., partial) ordering as it does not allow to compare two sets A and B such that A is neither a subset of B nor B a subset of A. This is definitely a serious shortcoming when measuring "freedom of choice." However, in the realm of desire, there is the possibility that an individual $i$ structures his or her wishes such that inclusion applies. Manifestations of growing or shrinking sets of wishes have been observed.

Inclusion should guarantee monotonicity in decision making and the evaluation of desires. However, people do not always recognize inclusion and when it comes to evaluating alternatives or desires, there can be effects that dominate inclusion. Tversky and Kahneman report that professional forecasters assign a higher probability to "an earthquake in California causing a flood in which more than 1,000 people will drown" than to "a flood somewhere in the United States in which more than 1,000 people will drown" (quoted in Kahneman 2003: 1467). Luckily, we do not decide whether there should be an earthquake or not. But the general feeling of uncertainty and, as a consequence, our decisions on buying an insurance or not can be influenced by such a violation of inclusion.

In the earthquake example, we can argue that the violation of inclusion simply is the result of mental laziness. However, when there is a conflict between the experiencing and the remembering selves we are somewhat at a loss if there is more than one self involved in evaluating a situation. Kahneman (2013: 382f.) gives an example that refers to two alternatives: (a) six experiences of strong pain and (b) six experiences of strong pain followed by three periods of weaker pain. The six periods of strong pain are identical. Inclusion suggests that alternative (a) is preferred to alternative (b), but this was not the case in the reported experiment. The alternatives were ranked in accordance to the remembering self and the latter was shaped by the degree of pain of the last experiences, and not by the number of painful experiences. Therefore, next time you have serious and painful tooth surgery, please ask your dentist to do some less painful drilling afterwards, irrespective of whether a tooth needs a filling or not: "Tastes and decisions are shaped by memories, and the memories can be wrong" (Kahneman 2013: 385). Are memories wrong that do not respect inclusions?

If the remembering self dominates and this is "strongly influenced by the peak and the end" (Kahneman 2013: 283), then we should expect that there is an effect on the ranking of desires. The optimal policy of giving presents should be straightforward in the case that we are confronted with a wish lists for Christmas or wedding. I still remember the silvery Mercedes 300 which I received at Christmas 65 years ago. By the standard of our family income, this toy cost a fortune.

Behavioral economists argue that welfare may increase if the opportunity set of a decision maker is decreased by a paternalistic government in case he or she has a serious self-control problem (Beaulier and Caplan 2007).[17] Does this also apply to set of desires? Do we come closer to happiness if our set of desires shrinks – perhaps to zero? Neither Blondie, nor Angel Eyes, nor Tuco see their desire shrinking for the $200,000. Inclusion seems to be guaranteed by "the more dollars the better." However, there is the movie's closing scene which does not follow this rule.

If inclusion does not work but $i$ wants to have a consistent measure of his or her possible sets of desires, then he or she might resort to $R_\alpha$-ranking and assign weights to the alternative desires. In principle, $\alpha$-weights assigned to desires by the desiring individual should be more reliable than $\alpha$-weights exogenously assigned to alternatives as implicit to the freedom of choice approach. We expect that the individual takes care of similarities and contradictions within the set of desires by appropriate choices of $\alpha$-values. Binder (2014) and, as already mentioned, Rubinstein (1988) offer an analytical treatment of similarities in preferences. It remains to check whether and to what extent it applies to desires, and whether we gain insights therefrom to improve the ranking of sets of desires when it comes to empirical testing.

Following Girard (1972), Airaksinen (2014a) maintains that desires are copies – copies of the desires of others: "People desire what other people desire." "Desires are socially scripted, in this sense we all desire/want the same things."[18] However, interpersonal similarity is a different issue, but it seems to help edit one's wishes as it is more likely to find *inconsistency* and *infeasibility* in the wishes of others than in one's own set of desires. Here Adam Smith's impartial spectator might help (or be at work) editing one's desires – i.e., making them socially adequate. I discussed Smith's impartial spectator in a series of papers (see, e.g., Holler 2006, 2007a, and Holler and Leroch 2008); I highly recommend the reading of the corresponding chapters in *The Theory of Moral Sentiments* (Smith 1982 [1759]).

---

17 Of course, elementary microeconomics tells us that this cannot happen, because all elements of the smaller set could have been chosen before. So how can an increase of welfare result from a reduction of opportunities? Yet, we do not want to smoke, and we are happy (perhaps only for some weeks) if government bans smoking.

18 Taken from a personal communication with Timo Airaksinen, April 29, 2016.

Schelling proposes

> a dynamic programming self that looks over wants and desires that continually change, anticipating preferences and attempting to satisfy them. It is as if there were a succession of momentary selves, each with its own wants and desires, all under the supervision of a timeless superself, an overall manager or referee who treats the transient selves evenhandedly.
>
> (Schelling 1982: 49)

Isn't this Freud's super-ego in new clothes, playing the critical and moralizing role? In any case, it is a close relative of Smith's impartial spectator.

### 2.6.4 Lexicographical editing and status quo

Marlies Ahlert (2014) presents a model of lexicographical editing of desires. This is a bounded rationality approach, where the alternatives are the degree of fulfillment of desires. All desires under consideration are "feasible," but choices have to be made as not all desires can be completely fulfilled – neither simultaneously nor sequentially. A desire is feasible if and only if, in principle, there is a set of actions the individual can perform in order to satisfy this desire. However, some degrees of fulfillment might be excluded by the nature of the desire or social norms. Some degrees of fulfillment of desires can be incompatible, and complete satisfaction might be impossible. It is assumed that in a first round of editing, the individual selects all combinations that are feasible. (See Holler (2013, 2014, 2015 for editing.)

How individuals select their desires and how to edit them is an empirical question. Ahlert's model is meant to serve as a point of departure. It is characterized by finitely many degrees of fulfillment of a finite number of desires. For illustration purposes, Ahlert picks two desires D1 and D2 and five degrees 0, l, m, h, and c. The latter represent levels "zero," "low," "medium," "high," and "complete." This forms a 5-by-5 grid. Here is Example 2 in Ahlert (2014).

Different types of restrictions have been applied to the set of G, i.e., the set of all "thinkable" combinations of fulfillment concerning desires $D_1$ and $D_2$.

Fulfillment degrees
of $D_2$

| | | | | | |
|---|---|---|---|---|---|
| c | | | | | |
| h | x | x | | | |
| m | x | x | x | | |
| l | | x | x | x | x |
| 0 | | | | x | x |
| | 0 | l | m | h | c |

Fulfillment degrees of $D_1$

*Figure 2.8* The set of feasible fulfillment vectors G*

G* is the resulting subset of feasible fulfillment vectors. It is the result of the editing process. The elements of G* are the feasible options. If G* contains more than one element, further evaluations must take place. If $D_1$ represents a strong(er) desire — perhaps as a result of importance or urgency — then it is plausible to assume that the individual will try to achieve a complete fulfillment c on the dimension of $D_1$. It will then opt for the pair of degrees (c,l) where l represents the level of fulfillment of $D_2$. Obviously, (c,l) dominates (c,0) in the sphere of satisfaction. If, however, $D_2$ represents the strong(er) desire, then we should expect that the individual will try to achieve (l,h) which dominates (0,h).

We can think of $D_1$ representing basic needs and $D_2$ as the desire of luxury goods. It is important that $D_1$ is completely satisfied before the individual considers satisfying his or her "desire of the conveniencies and ornaments of building, dress, equipage, and household furniture" (Adam Smith's 1981 [1776/77]: 181). Then the individual's desires should be directed towards (c,l). Figure 2.8 indicates that the desire for luxury goods seem "to have no limit or certain boundary" (Adam Smith's 1981 [1776/77]: 181) and the individual is aware of it.

Note by simple dominance the pairs the individual cannot discriminate between the pairs of fulfillment (l,h), (m,m), and (c,l). The differences in strength of wishes, represented by lexicographical editing, select the target pair of degrees of fulfillment in the example of Figure 2.8. Section 2.7 below will discuss the phenomenon of hierarchies of desires, following Maslow (1943, 1954) and his disciples and successors. Or, is it just a hypothesis? In Maslow, the hierarchy is by-and-large fixed. However, empirical evidence suggests that, to some extent, it is contextually conditioned. Ahlert (2014) argues that the status quo of the individual would be a typical influence on the ordering and this ordering is only valid for the decision of a prospective change of the status quo. To demonstrate the consequences, Ahlert introduces a status quo d in G* and assumes that the individual evaluates all choices compared to d. Here d is the state the individual i expects to emerge unless it realizes an alternative option. To illustrate the introduction of d, the combination (l,m) of Figure 2.8 is selected as status quo d. Figure 2.9 represents the case.

Fulfillment degrees
of $D_2$

| | 0 | l | m | h | c |
|---|---|---|---|---|---|
| c | | | | | |
| h | x | x | | | |
| m | x | d* | x | | |
| l | | x | x | x | x |
| 0 | | | | x | x |
| | 0 | l | m | h | c |

Fulfillment degrees of $D_1$

*Figure 2.9* The impact of status quo d* on the lexicographical editing

Note that (c,l) is no longer feasible if the editing is lexicographical, even if $D_1$ is the stronger desire. This demonstrates the possible impact of the status quo if editing is strictly lexicographical. However, a status quo $d°$ has no impact in this case if $d° = (l,l)$ represents the implied fulfillment level. Can we conclude that the lower the fulfillment of desires in the status quo the more options are available for lexicographical editing? Intuitively, this seems to be quite a plausible, perhaps even obvious, conclusion. Still, the reasoning indicates the potential behind this analysis. Of course, one could ask whether the entries in the grid of Figures 2.8 are still valid if there is a status quo d and whether they still hold if d* is substituted by d°. Desires are likely to depend on the status quo in various ways. Yet, the model demonstrates that the set of target desires can vary markedly depending on the status quo, even if evaluations are identical (and stable). There is no smoothening effect from trade-offs when editing is lexicographical. It seems that Blondie, Angel Eyes, and Tuco were dedicated to lexicographical editing. They pursued the chase for the \$200,000 treasure whenever the status quo permitted it, i.e., did not render the chase impossible.

Given d*, (l,h) and (m,m) are, in standard decision theoretic terms, weak Pareto improvements and the lexicographical ranking of $D_1$ and $D_2$ will decide whether the individual aims for (l,h) or (m,m). Of course, there might be some "weighted aggregation" such that (c,l) is still feasible (see Ahlert 2014 for a discussion), but the underlying trade-off is not consist with strictly lexicographical editing. Moreover, weighted aggregation needs to introduce some cardinality in the values of desires. I do not know whether the individual is prepared and willing to achieve this operation in a consistent way. The plethora of difficulties implied by the expected utility model, unearthed by psychology and behavioral economics à la Kahneman and Tversky (1979) allow for doubts.

## 2.7 Back to wants, beliefs, and desires

The two models just discussed describe structures for a possible editing of desires. However, it is an empirical question whether an individual *edits* his or her desires at all and whether the two models, suggested above, are useful to analyze such an editing. To prepare for empirical testing we have to gain a better understanding of what desires are and how they are related to wants, greed, wishes, needs, beliefs, and lust.

With respect to needs and wants, Maslow's motivation theory (Maslow 1943, 1954) seems to be still a valuable point of departure. However, since the theory has been extensively discussed over the last sixty years, it should be sufficient to recall that Maslow, in order to explain human behavior, proposed a hierarchy of needs starting with "physiological" followed by "safety," "belongingness/love," "esteem," "self-actualization," and "self- transcendence" at the top. This hierarchy is commonly reproduced as a pyramid, although Maslow himself did not use this illustration. However, his theory suggests that the most basic level of needs must be met before the individual will focus upon the higher-level needs – and a pyramid seems an adequate means to represent this hierarchy. (Maslow's hierarchy places sex in the category of physiological needs together with food and breathing.) This suggests, applied to the ranking of desires, that editing is lexicographical.

Critics argue that Maslow's ranking is ethnocentric inasmuch it presupposes an individualistic society. One should expect that in a collectivistic society the needs are ranked differently and allocated in other layers. Another objection is based on the empirical observation that the sequence of the love need and the self-esteem need undergo a reversal according to age; if there is a need hierarchy then, however, the hierarchy is not stable.

Maslow called the first four layers "deficiency needs": if they are not satisfied then the individual feels a shortage, something missing, and suffers of stress, frustration, and perhaps even hunger. The top-ranking needs – "self-actualization" and "self-transcendence" – are often identified with desires and, if activated, with wants. But of course these labels could be applied to lower-ranking needs, too. If so, does this imply that we can derive a hierarchy of desires from this? (Then we can further specify the set of desires discussed above and prepare for empirical testing.) In the discussion of Maslow's theory, needs and desires are often used as equivalent alternatives, but in what way do needs correspond with desires? In order to answer these questions, it seems appropriate to be more specific about the nature of desires.

### 2.7.1 On the nature of desires

In Maslow's theory, needs motivate action. Do desires induce actions? Airaksinen (2014) argues that no actions follow from desires proper. So does Russell (1984), as already mentioned. Only when a desire transforms into a want which entails a commitment, i.e., an intention, and creates need, then action follows. Wants are "looking for means" to satisfy desires. Yet, quoting Goldman (2009: 7), Airaksinen states: "Desires are not what motivates us." In fact, the corresponding action could be impossible (for us). But if we believe that the action is possible for us, then desires and beliefs create wants and wants trigger action. According to Schroeder (2014) desires "*dispose* us to action, without always bringing it about that we act" (original emphasis). So there are "idle desires," "idle wishes," perhaps we should call them "dreams." Our hypothesis is that even such dreams may have an impact on our choices, especially because it is not always obvious to us what we can do and what not, what is a dream and what can become real. This hypothesis is supported by Scanlon's attention-based theory of desire (Scanlon 1998). This theory is illustrated by Schroeder:

> desire's characteristic effect is to direct attention toward reasons to fulfil the desire. But desire has notable effects on other forms of attention, too: if Katie desires that Ohio State wins a football game, then her desire will direct her attention to information about the game, will direct her attention to opportunities to gain information about the game, will direct her

attention to people discussing the game, and so on. These ways in which attention can be directed seem, pre-theoretically, just as important to the nature of desire as the ways that are of interest to the attention-based theory of desire.

(Schroeder 2014: n.p.)

Are dreams standing desires, i.e., desires that do not motivate wants and motivate action at the moment but are ready to do so if there will be a possibility in the future? It is assumed that standing desires do not even play a role in one's psychic system. They lie quietly in the back of one's mind, "most of the time, and occasionally generate thoughts, feelings, and actions of the familiar sorts" (Schroeder 2014). This view concurs with the idea that desires are general conditions (like scientific laws). It needs particular conditions (facts, beliefs) which together with the general conditions enables actions (see Airaksinen 2014, for a discussion). On the other hand, occurrent desires are playing some role in one's psyche at the moment. However, as Schroeder points out

occurrent desires need not be in control of one's actions: my desire to laze in bed is occurrent even while I am getting up and making breakfast, for my desire is leading me to think longingly of bed, and is perhaps acting upon my mechanisms of action production in a way that would lead me back to bed if only I did not also desire to get some things done. Desires of which one is not aware, but which are current causes of one's behavior, are also occurrent on this way of thinking about things.

(Schroeder 2014: n.p.)

Inasmuch as dreams affect our behavior they involve occurrent desires.

Of course, this brief discussion of the nature of desires is not exhaustive – I expect that there is no exhaustive discussion of this issue anyway – but it should be of help when, e.g., specifying the α-values, analyzing the effects of editing and justifying measurement.

### 2.7.2 A Streetcar Named Desire

It seems that we cannot discuss desires without reference to Tennessee Williams's play *A Streetcar Named Desire* of 1947. At first sight, this seems justified: Isn't Blanche DuBois an incarnation of a multiplicity and diversity of desires and aren't her frustrated desires the reason why, at the end of the play, she is brought to a mental asylum?

Blanche was a delicately dressed Southern belle, fading, but still attractive. In her pretensions of virtue of culture and her behavior, she impersonated a society now gone. Still she desired respect and admiration in this role, especially from men, including Stanley, the husband of her pregnant sister Stella. However, Stanley Kowalski is a rough, brutish, sensual blue-collar worker, a World War II veteran, who beats his pregnant wife when drunk. Stanley and

Stella have a passionate sexual relationship – and are deeply in love with each other: they desire each other. Blanche has great difficulties understanding these feelings. Moreover, she does not accept that the society of her youth has gone and she tries to accommodate her dream world – with the help of a regular and substantial consumption of alcoholic beverages – while she stays as a visitor with Stanley and Stella in their small apartment.

Obviously, Blanche also desired to find a new home. She told her sister that their ancestral Southern plantation, Belle Reve – the "Beautiful Dream" – in Laurel, Mississippi, has been lost due to the "epic fornication" of their ancestors and she went through all sorts of troubles to find a new position in her life. She claimed that her school supervisor allowed her to take some time off from her position as an English teacher because of her upset nerves. She did *not* reveal that she was fired from the school because she had had an affair with a 17-year-old student of hers. After the mansion was lost, she was exceptionally lonely and turned to the "comfort of strangers," entertaining many gentlemen at a hotel called The Flamingo. (It was the hotel called The Tarantula Arms, corrected Blanche, when Stanley's friend Mitch asked about The Flamingo.) Her numerous amorous encounters destroyed her reputation in Laurel, and resulted in her near-expulsion from town. She wanted to keep this as a secret, but her brother-in-law Stanley learned about Blanche's past through a co-worker who traveled to Laurel frequently.

There was also Blanche's desire to marry Stanley's friend Mitch. The two fell for each other and wedding bells seemed to be waiting for them. However, Stanley informed Mitch about Blanche's past and Mitch cancelled the wedding project. But Mitch's desire for Blanche did not die with the wedding project. In a later scene, he approached Blanche asking for sexual favors. Instead, she asked him to marry her and he declined, saying "You're not clean enough to bring you in the house with my mother."

At some point it seems, more so in the film version of the play, that Stanley wanted to destroy Blanche and behaved accordingly. There are some very strong indications that he even raped her which resulted in her psychotic breakdown and, finally, her removal to a mental institution. Was this sheer sadistic lust, or revenge for Blanche's overbearingly arrogant behavior towards him? Or, did he just want to get rid of this outlandish intruder into his world, having Stella and their child again reserved for himself and enjoying some drinks and a poker game with his friends without Blanche's intervening presence? But then there is Marlon Brando, who in his movie interpretation of Stanley Kowalski "managed to turn a play about a woman's disintegration into a study of male sexual power and its collateral costs," observes Chiasson (2015: 18) in his review of *Brando's Smile: His Life, Thought, and Work*, a book by Susan L. Mizruchi. Chiasson adds that even Oscar-winning Vivien Leigh, playing Blanche DuBois, was enthralled to Brando (or was it to Stanley?) even as her character is demolished by his.

Perhaps we should not go too deep in the interpretation of the desires of the play's various characters. But there is at least a second dimension to it. Blanche represents a bygone society and still tries to inhabit it, while her sister Stella had left home to get free of its dead rules and limitations. Stella joined the modern world of Stanley, the rough, brutish, sensual blue-collar worker who openly enjoys poker, getting drunk and having sex. Blanche is highly irritated that her sister is living in a dump when they both come from such a wealthy, elite background. She remains alien to this world and becomes even more alienated (in the psychological sense) from it: she is a victim of her fixation on the past and the cruelties of today. *A Streetcar Named Desire* is both a psychological drama, focusing on the conflicting and frustrated desires of the agents, and a social drama – a requiem staging the shadows of a lost aristocracy (without aristocrats) and the emerging dominance of a modern society which is shaped by sweaty blue-collar workers, aspiring immigrants, and never-ending assembly lines.

The German title of the play is *Endstation Sehnsucht* – which can be translated as "Final Stop Desire," but this desire discharges into a longing or yearning. "Final Stop," on the other hand, expresses the "end of the line," a very adequate description of the end of the play from Blanche's point of view.

Of course, the play's original title is the choice of a genius, but perhaps it promises more about desires than we can find in the play. There is a Desire Street in the Baywater district of New Orleans and there was a Desire Line which ran from 1920 to 1948 through the French quarter down to Desire Street. In the play, Blanche is told "to take a streetcar called Desire, and transfer to one called Cemeteries and ride six blocks and get off at – Elysian Fields!" The 1975 *Encyclopædia Britannica* tells us that the Elysium (also called Elysian Plain or Elysian Fields) "was the pre-Hellenic paradise, identified by the Greeks with their own Isles of the Blessed. In Homer the Elysian Plain was a land of perfect happiness at the end of the earth, on the banks of the Oceanus River." Is this what Blanche DuBois missed after Belle Reve – the "Beautiful Dream" – was lost? Or, is it what she finally found? She followed her dreams and this brought her to the asylum.

## 2.8 Desires and the neoclassical repairshop

In order to incorporate effects of social environment in a "calculus of desires," whether reflected in the psychological dimension of an impartial spectator or the functioning of social norms, we reinterpret a Fehr and Schmidt (1999) type utility function as a "desire function," implying the possibility to trade degrees of fulfillment against each other. Let $u_i$ summarize the degree of frustration, envy, and guilt of individual i such that

$$u_i = \Sigma_k\, v_i(d_{ik} - o_{ik} \,|\, w_i) + \alpha_i \max\{w_j - w_i,\, 0\} + \beta_i \max\{w_i - w_j,\, 0\} \qquad (1)$$

Here the $d_{ik}$ represents the elements of a k-vector of i's desires and $o_{ik}$ the corresponding outcomes that are relevant for satisfying the k-many $d_{ik}$. Thus $d_{ik}$ is a particular desire k, and $d_{ik} - o_{ik}$ represents a degree of dissatisfaction, i.e., frustration, with respect to this desire. The $v_i$ function maps the differences $d_{ik} - o_{ik}$

into a (in general, positive) number space, representing degrees of unfulfilled desires, that allows, after appropriate standardization, to add up these values to a measure $u_i$ that represents frustration. $\alpha_i \max\{w_j - w_i, 0\}$ represents envy and $\beta_i \max\{w_i - w_j, 0\}$ represents guilt, both due to wealth differentials. In analogy to Fehr and Schmidt (1999), we could assume $\alpha_i \geq \beta_i$, i.e., the disutility of envy is larger than the one that results from guilt. But this is not necessarily the case. Wealth $w_i$ represents i's potential of getting his/her desires ("wishes") satisfied; this potential is of course not purely pecuniary. $w_j$ is j's potential where j is a "significant other" to i.

Instead of looking at potentials $w_i$ and $w_j$, i could evaluate the outcomes $o_{jk}$ that j has achieved with respect to the dimension k of i's desire $d_{ik}$. Then, of course, equation (1) gets more complicated as there will be more summing up and perhaps more detailed evaluation. If i knows j well enough, for instance being j's neighbor, taking $o_{jk}$ into consideration seems to be appropriate – and perhaps necessary for empirical testing. For the general self-esteem and satisfaction of i in his or her environment, a comparison of potentials, captured by money values of income and wealth, could be the relevant approach. Note that envy and guilt depend on j's potential to satisfy his/her wishes. The difference $w_j - w_i$ could be interpreted as a proxy for the case that i cannot satisfy his/her desire while j can satisfy the very same desire, at least to a higher degree than i.

Equation (1) tells us that frustration is minimized if "we get what we want" and the potentials to fulfill our desires are equal such that guilt and envy are absent. Of course, this approach could be extended to more than one significant other or generalized to represent the impartial spectator. If guilt ($\beta_i$) is larger than envy ($\alpha_i$) and $w_j < w_i$, then i's satisfaction may increase if i shifts some units into $w_j$. This could happen, e.g., in the form of monetary transfers (i.e., money presents). However, this is likely to reduce some $o_{ik}$ and thus to increase the difference $d_{ik} - o_{ik}$, i.e., frustration. Most likely, outcome $o_{ik}$ depends on wealth $w_i$ but perhaps also on the decision (and wealth) of j. Therefore, even if i has no fellow feelings, neither positive nor negative ones, his/her frustration could be reduced by enabling j to contribute to a (hopefully) more adequate outcome $o_{ik}$ through a transfer of units of $w_i$ to increase $w_j$. As a result, we might get a more even distribution of resources that can be used to achieve $o_{ik}$. In case that the values of $o_{ik}$ are fully quantifiable and the production functions $o_{ik} = o_{ik}(w_i, w_j)$ are differentiable, this transfer is beneficial if $\partial o_{ik}/\partial w_j > \partial o_{ik}/\partial w_i$.

Therefore, in order to reduce frustration, there could be a desire for equity.[19] Moreover, in this case, redistribution is likely to be welfare enhancing. But the underlying assumptions are rather rigorous. As noted, j's allocation of $w_j$ can have an impact on outcome $o_{ik}$ which is directly relevant for the level of

---

19 This corresponds to "preferences with inequality aversion," a well-documented phenomenon in experimental research. See Fehr and Schmidt (1999) for the concept and references to the literature.

frustration of i. However, we do not know how and in what direction (seen from the perspective i) j affects $o_{ik}$. So if i transfers some $w_i$ to $w_j$ this reduces guilt and increases envy (if there is envy at all), but the effect via $o_{ik}(w_i, w_j)$ is not obvious – perhaps not even to i. Does the lack of knowledge serve as a "veil of ignorance" that supports transfers from i to j?

Of course, such reasoning reflects arguments that justify taxation and the production of public goods. This is partly due to the fact that we compare wealth and not satisfaction in the case of envy and guilt. Otherwise, we might argue that we can reduce the potential of transfers to others by helping to satisfy their desires "through editing" and thereby reduce our frustration in case that guilt is larger than envy. This implication reflects much of the education which many of us enjoyed in their childhood: "Large desires are uncivilized and should be moderated. Greed and lust are bad." The assumption is that the moderation of desires is easier to achieve than a redistribution of resources which aims to make us happy.

Fehr and Schmidt's paper (1999) has been heavily criticized by Binmore and Shaked (2010). Since Fehr and Schmidt's paper is one of the most successful publications of the last two decades, measured by citations, it would be worthwhile to consider the arguments of Binmore and Shaked in detail. However, their critique refers to the utility model, i.e., social preferences, and not to desires. The pivotal argument of Binmore and Shaked (2010: 92) is that Fehr and Schmidt are engaged in "a fitting exercise, in which parameters can be changed when new data need to be accommodated." They use very different estimates of parameters (i.e., $\alpha_i$ and $\beta_i$) in different data sets. Their theory has, contrary to its claim, no predictive power and the offered empirical work is illustrative only.

To Binmore and Shaked, the "scientific gold standard is prediction." They argue:

> It is perfectly acceptable to propose a theory that fits existing experimental data and then to use the data to calibrate the parameters of the model. But, before using the theory in applied work, the vital next step is to state the proposed domain of application of the theory and to make specific predictions that can be tested with data that was used neither in formulating the theory nor in calibrating its parameters.
>
> (Binmore and Shaked 2010: 89)

This strictly follows the Popperian message of critical rationalism. Does all science follow this creed – and is it relevant for all research work all the time?

Binmore and Shaked ask the very important question:

> Should we follow those experimental economists who seek recognition of their subject as a science by adopting the scientific standards that operate in neighboring disciplines like biology or psychology? Or should we follow the tradition in policy-orientated economics of treating experimental

results as just another rhetorical tool to be quoted when convenient in seeking to convert others to whatever your own point of view may be?

(Binmore and Shaked 2010: 87)

Obviously, the above discussion does not satisfy the scientific standards mentioned in this quote, but it was not meant to give empirical evidence. It aimed to raise questions and provide possible answers. The formal model presented by equation (1) – borrowed from the neoclassical repairshop[20] – could be of help by shaping questions. Not all scientific research produces testable theories. Insights could be valuable, too. The study of desires is still a wasteland for empirical research. Or, is it a minefield?

---

20 That is, using an "enriched" utility function, but still assuming rationality. Perhaps Werner Güth was the first who used this term for critical comments on the paper of Fehr and Schmidt (1999) and related work. See van Damme et al. (2014).

# 3 Second-mover advantages

To restate, there is ample evidence of first-mover advantages and there are many cases that demonstrate the advantage of being a second-mover. What distinguishes these two diverse sequential settings is the fact that nothing may happen, and there might be nothing to observe, if there is a second-mover advantage, especially if the situation is competitive. On the other hand, if there is a first-mover advantage, a rush of too many agents can be induced and, in the end, the outcome will be catastrophic for everybody, even for the agent who had a first-mover advantage. Obviously, in both cases, time matters and in both cases it implies information. What is time and how is it related to information?

There is some economic theorizing in this chapter; however, this is not a substitute for the sophisticated modeling of market entry that we find in advanced textbooks of economics or, more specifically, in Jean Tirole's *The Theory of Industrial Organization* (1988) where limit pricing, preemptive war, war of attrition, etc. serve as analytical frameworks for the analysis of strategic market barriers. The material of this chapter is not meant to function as an illustration of this theoretical work either. It is selected and presented to demonstrate a particular choice situation characterized by a particular time structure which I think is highly relevant for understanding social interaction, including the economy. The highlight of this chapter will not be the economic analysis of market entry, innovation, and creative destruction, but the analysis of the truel at Sad Hill Cemetery starring Blondie, the Good, Angel Eyes, the Bad, and Tuco, the Ugly. Strategic time matters.

## 3.1 Of time and information

Time has a rather complicated status in movies and theater plays. There are of course the one, two, three, four hours that the audience watches what the actors present. But there is also the time that is more or less directly represented by the sequence of events performed on stage. Often time on stage is not just represented by events but also by references to the clock, time of the day, weeks, and months, the seasons, or even calendar dates. Perhaps, in order to reduce much of the possible complications which resulted from parallel times and overlaps, in his *Poetics*, Aristotle set down the principle of the unity of time: "Tragedy endeavours, as far as possible, to confine itself to a single revolution of the sun."[1] The neoclassical movement of the sixteenth and seventeenth centuries, exemplified in the works of Corneille, Racine, and Molière, added unity of place as a natural complement to unity of time. Shakespeare did not submit to this principle as, widely quoted, already Samuel Johnson (2005 [1765]) pointed out in his *Prefaces to Shakespeare*, and he praised him for this. But this did not conclude the discussion: classical drama with unity of time and place was tried again and again. On the other hand, artists experimented with the time that they presented on stage. For instance, Samuel Beckett's play *Waiting for Godot* applies various concepts of time parallel to each other. Waiting is a transubstantiation of time. Beckett shows us time on stage. For this experience, it does not matter that since the play's first performance in 1953, the universe of time as a continuum, based on the revolutions of the sun, has been largely substituted by the digital universe of 0 and 1 that produces a countable (discrete) time.[2]

The following sections focus on historical time defined by events, information, and decisions, i.e., "changes of states." Time measured with reference to the clock, the seasons, or by calendar dates is secondary. As already indicated in the trailer, the sequence of decisions and events determines the information of the decision makers and reshapes the decision situation and thereby possible outcomes. This is essential to game situations characterized by sequences of strategic interaction. In such decision situations, historical time boils down to strategic time, and a second-mover advantage can be one of its implications. In Section 3.2, we will use Sergio Leone's truel as a model case to exemplify this issue. However, for the sake of our attempt, we will see that Sergio Leone's story needs some revisions. In the sequel, we apply the implications of the purified story to the business world and submit it to economic reasoning (Sections 3.3, 3.4, and 3.5).

Second-mover advantages are often related to the information we gain by watching others. We try to avoid their mistakes and copy their achievements. The information can be hard-wired in the form of the pioneer's investments and patents. Of course, patents do not seem to invite imitation, but they signal where profits are expected. Similar signals can be derived from investments and even labor recruitment. But second-mover advantages do not always depend on information. They can be embedded in projected activity and a division of labor. For instance, in Tuco and Blondie's bounty business, Tuco did the "hanging" as the bounty was on him and not on Blondie. Correspondingly,

---

1 For example, Mishra (2014) discusses Arthur Miller's *All My Sons* with respect to Aristotle's *Poetics* and the unity of time. The latter was important to Aristotle, but about the unity of place he was "silent," writes Mishra.

2 According to Dyson (2012: 248), "Turing introduced two fundamental assumptions: discreteness of time and discreteness of state of mind. To a Turing machine, time exists not as a continuum, but as a sequence of changes of state."

Blondie has to do the "cutting." Also, more likely, he was more competent than Tuco to shoot and thus cut the rope attached to the noose around his partner's neck, but this was secondary to the sequence of moves implied by their business. And so was, in its substance, the information as the sequence was hard-wired.

I do not think that the "structure of arrangement" was unique to the bounty business. There are many partnerships in this world that have a similar structure, and marriage seems to be one of them, often giving a second-mover advantage to one of the partners. In the latter case, this is often decided by "who gets the baby?" Those who are not happy with this arrangement might try not to have a baby unless alternative arrangements are found that balance the possible second-mover advantage given by nature. Public policy tries to contribute to these arrangements if a society feels threatened by a declining birth rate, or aims to defeat a rival society by augmenting such a rate. In many situations of market entry and raisin picking, collecting information is also secondary. The market summarizes the information and shows the potentials for entry. What triggers raisin picking is the possibility of making a profit by serving a selected share of the market only. Note that I prefer the term "raisin picking" (in German: *Rosinenpicken*) to the English-language equivalent "cherry picking," because a cake looks rather bare when the raisins are gone – in analogy to the profits of the incumbent firm when a raisin-picking competitor enters its market. I do not know how a (profit) cake looks like when it experiences cherry picking.

Frequently, profitable raisin picking presupposes that the pioneer firm prepared the market to create demand that can be captured and, of course, a cost structure that allows capturing. Although the entrant has to know at least some of these details, first of all, they must exist. There has to be a market structure that invites profitable entry and then of course potential entrants have to learn about it to realize their second-mover advantage. However, if too many potential entrants are ready to make use of such a second-mover, then the market could get too crowded meaning losses to both the incumbent and the entrants. In a theoretical analysis, Sherman and Willett (1967) demonstrated that entry becomes less likely and the incumbent firm can increase its price without "fear of entry," if the number of potential entrants increases. Therefore, reducing information about raisin-picking possibilities could in fact enhance the probability of raisin picking. Limiting information can create a second-mover advantage for those who know. Hierarchies of secrets can imply a second-mover advantage, as we will see in the sequel.[3] On the other hand, secrecy and patents can be policy alternatives in order to block second-mover advantages and thereby make innovations profitable. Secrets and patents define time spaces, i.e., a then and now. In art, a cult of creativity and emphasis on the originality developed which, to some extent, protect the first-mover. In general, originality is defined along the time dimension: who is

---

3 Section 4.1.2 discusses a hierarchy of secrets.

the first and – sometimes – how much earlier? It does not matter whether a second, measured in time, knows the creation of the first. However, there is forgery, on the one hand, and successful imitation, adaptation, and elaboration, on the other, which attack this frame of originality – and there is artistic work that subverts it. Andy Warhol's silk prints are pivotal for the latter, but Marcel Duchamp's readymades are an even more radical representation of this subversion. We will come back to Duchamp's work in Section 4.3.

## 3.2 The Sad Hill Truel and some revisions

The Sad Hill Cemetery scene, also labeled "showdown" or the "end battle," starts with Tuco running through the aisles of wooden crosses desperately looking for Arch Stanton's grave and the $200,000 treasure in it. The name of the grave he got from Blondie when they prepared the treatment of bridge with explosives. (Section 4.1.2. gives details.) When he locates the grave, he starts fiercely shoveling with a wooden board; soon pearls of sweat run down his forehead. Blondie appears first as a shadow throwing a shovel into the scene. By pointing to his gun, he makes clear that the shovel is meant for Tuco. A few seconds later, another shovel comes flying when Angel Eyes enters the scene and commands Blondie at gun point to help Tuco digging: "Two people can dig a lot quicker than one. Dig." Blondie, however, kicks open Stanton's grave which contains a skeleton but no money. He makes clear that only he knows the name of the grave with the money. He declares that he is willing to write the name of the grave on the lump of stone in his hand. He adds the somewhat cryptic message: "Two hundred thousand dollars is a lot of money. We're gonna have to earn it" and places the lump of stone in the center of the arena-like stone-covered circle that forms the hub of the cemetery. Yet, this message is understood by the two other contenders. As if moved by an invisible hand, the three choose their positions forming an equilateral triangle with the lump of stone at the center. Their movements look like a rehearsal for a ballet. Is it a moral one? Once they take their positions, they stare at each other. Their looks reflect their different characters and involvement: Blondie chewing his cigar. Who will draw first? The hands move closer and closer to the guns.

To let the camera increase the visual tension by moving from the eyes of the three dualists to their hands and guns, and back again, it is of course helpful that they have three different technologies of carrying their guns. Blondie carries his gun in a classical way, elegantly next to his hip. Angel Eyes carries his gun in front of his belly, so that his right hand has to come over to it on the horizontal line of the belt which is filled with bullets. This signals deadly danger. Tuco has his gun hanging on a string. It is not elegant and looks somewhat ridiculous. But Tuco has a long list of corpses which he has produced in the course of the movie, so even this method seems to be competitive.

Who will draw first? Given the information, the audience can only guess, but not solve the logical problem implied by the given situation; it cannot form "rational expectations." (In fact, any expectation could be "rationalized" inasmuch as it can be justified by some "reasonable assumptions."[4]) The longer the scene with the three contenders watching each other, the more guessing, the more tension, and, amplified by Morricone's thrilling soundtrack – cited on the Internet as "the best theme tune ever" – the more the excitement builds up.

Suddenly Angel Eyes draws, but Blondie is faster. After Blondie places his first bullet into Angel Eyes who, heavily wounded, falls over, Tuco tries to operate his gun. However, he realizes that his gun is empty, i.e., has no bullets. He shouts at Blondie: "You pig! You want to get me killed! When d'ya unload it?" There is some irony in Tuco's protesting. It is not obvious to whom Tuco's useless gun points. Does it point at Blondie? Angel Eyes tries a desperate shot from his desperate position when Blondie's second bullet propels his body into an open grave. A third and fourth bullet from Blondie's gun moves Angel Eyes' hat and gun into the very same grave.

Blondie summarizes the outcome of the truel: "You see in this world there's two kinds of people, my friend. Those with loaded guns, and those who dig. You dig." This is an obvious truth; there are countless cases in history that confirm this truth. Some of these cases we will meet in the text below. Blondie directs Tuco to the grave next to Arch Stanton's with the name "Unknown" on it. He also lifts the contested rock and shows that nothing was written on it. He argues that this represents "Unknown." Then he makes Tuco dig the grave of the "Unknown" at gun-point.

The excitement of this showdown results from the fact that the moviegoer cannot see any solution to the problem that the three contenders face: if A shoots B, then C has time enough to shoot A. If so, then there is an obvious disadvantage for the one who shoots first, i.e., there is an advantage for the second-mover. However, it is not obvious who will be the second-mover. But this does not matter: if there is a second-mover advantage, then a likely outcome is that there will be no first-mover and nothing will happen. This is a rather general phenomenon as the discussion will show: we expect under-provision or underperformance in cases of second-mover advantages. The sequence of moves, i.e., time in its strategic form, matters. Of course, time could also matter if the environment changes and with it the decision situation. It seems that Angel Eyes becomes more and more nervous in the course of time and cannot hold back to draw first. This ruins the strategic balance of the situation, more so as he is shot by the targeted Blondie. In addition, we learn that Blondie has unloaded Tuco's gun the night before. He therefore will not face the threat of a successful second-mover if he moves first and shoots Angel Eyes. Why did he not move first? Sergio Leone wanted to demonstrate how "unworldly fast" Blondie handles his gun in direct contest with Angel Eyes.

---

4 For the game-theoretical concept of "rationalization," see Bernheim (1984) and Pearce (1984). In short, a decision (i.e., the selection of a strategy) is rationalizable if it can be justified by expectations which assume rational choices of other decision makers. Decisions that concur with a Nash equilibrium are rationalizable. But rationalizable strategies do not always concur with a Nash equilibrium.

Yet, perhaps Blondie was much faster than Angele Eyes because he did not have to worry about Tuco, while Angel Eyes had already the second shot in mind when drawing his gun for a first shot.

In principle, the danger to Blondie's shooting performance was a second-mover, i.e., Tuco. He might point his gun at Blondie after he puts his bullet into Angel Eyes. This was avoided by the unlikely story of unloading Tuco's gun. I was told by experts that you might not feel any difference in weight, etc. when your gun is not loaded. I am still hesitant to accept this answer. Another issue of course is that a gunslinger like Tuco quite regularly checks whether his gun is in good shape. There are scenes in the movie that suggest such behavior. Could Blondie rely on Tuco's gun being empty? He did. This leads us directly to further amendments to Sergio Leone's story.

Let us accept that the three contenders are just *on time* for the showdown although it seems rather unlikely that Angel Eyes appears on the scene at this very moment. Why does Blondie initiate the truel, instead of simply shooting down Angel Eyes after he put the gun back into his holster? Why should Tuco and Angel Eyes believe that Blondie writes on the rock the name of the grave which contains the $200,000 treasure? Why should he do it? If he doesn't and he is shot dead, then he has the final revenge that neither of the two will get the money. If he survives, he does not need to read the name on the rock. Why then should Tuco and Angel Eyes take part in the truel? We will come across a quite similar problem in the next chapter of this book when we discuss Nicola Atkinson's secrets.

Let us start from the fact that Blondie knows the grave's name and Tuco and Angel Eyes do not. Will he ever reveal the name? Should the two competitors expect that he will ever reveal the name? Although the rationale of initiating the truel is not very convincing, it solves a plot problem, creates a maximum of excitement – and contributed immensely to the reputation and success of the movie. In the end, it does not matter whether Blondie has written a name on the rock or not.

Interestingly, Kilgour and Brams (1997) do not refer to *The Good, the Bad, and the Ugly* when they give examples of truels referring to movies (and competing television networks). Perhaps this is the case since, from Blondie's perspective, this is not a truel but a duel, due to the fact that he knows that Tuco's gun is unloaded. Or, perhaps this is the case because in Sergio Leone's truel, the probability of each truelist hitting the chosen target does not matter, while it does matter in Kilgour (1972, 1975, 1978) and Kilgour and Brams (1997). In fact, in this literature, these probabilities are common knowledge to the truelists. They reflect the various levels of skill of the truelists. In Sergio Leone's truel, Blondie could assign a zero probability to Tuco for this purpose, but this is highly private information. Of course, we should assign a probability of one to Blondie because he never failed with his gun.

Duels and truels are not confined to shooting. Next, we will identify some stylized examples that illustrate the second-mover advantage in the business world. Then, we look at cases in which the possible underprovision is banned by a first-mover who does not follow the principle of self-interest in some form of profit maximization, i.e., who is characterized by a "deviating objective function." The government, the state, or the public agent are alternative labels for such a first-mover. If there is a second-mover advantage and agents succeed to motivate (or to capture) the government to act as first-mover, then the problem of underprovision can be mastered. Needless to say, this success is likely to trigger an uneven (by some standards, unfair) distribution of the benefits, non-productive expenditures for lobbying and even bribery, and is a challenge to a democratic political system. This is even more so, if the democratic system also faces second-mover advantages in the process of aggregating the preferences of the voters and shaping them to form the will of the people. In Section 3.6, we will demonstrate that this offers a large potential for manipulation and second-mover advantages.

## 3.3 Second-mover advantages and market novelties

In their paper "First to Market, First to Fail?" Tellis and Golder (1996) give a list of examples that demonstrate the success of a second-mover at the expense of a market pioneer. Just to give a few examples from the list: disposable diapers had already been introduced by Chux in 1935, but, after ten years of research, Procter & Gamble conquered the market with their branded product "Pampers" in the 1960s. In 1975, MITS (Micro Instrumentation and Telemetry Systems) was the first to supply personal computers, but then Apple and IBM entered this market with success, ousting MITS. The Defense Advanced Research Projects Agency (DARPA), an office created by the Pentagon in 1958, prepared the ground for the development of the personal computer:

> DARPA researcher activities take place outside of the regular government, academic, or industry research activities, providing a level of freedom and autonomy. DARPA is not about government 'picking winners and losers', it is about the government taking the lead in R&D.
>
> (Mazzucato 2014: 133f.)

Here we have the pioneering investments in R&D on which Apple and IBM built their second-mover success. The first video recorder was promoted by Ampex in 1956, priced at about $50,000. In the mid-1970s, first Sony, supplying Betamax, and then JVC, supplying VHS, took over – with JVC as market leader despite the fact that, from a technical point of view, Betamax was at least equivalent to VHS. However, it is said that VHS was more successful because of its longer recording capacity of two hours. Betamax's one-hour limit was inconvenient for recording full-length movies. In the early 1960s, Rheingold Brewery introduced "Gablinger's Lite" opening the market for low-alcohol beer, labeled "light" beer. In the mid-1970s, "Miller Lite" supplied by Philip Morris took over. Needless to say that the disposable diapers by Chux, the personal computers by MITS, the video recorders by Ampex were not the same products that Procter & Gamble, Apple and IBM, and Sony and JVC brought to the market and, according to my information, patent protection had no grip. (I confess I have no expertise about American light beers.) Still it is not obvious that Procter & Gamble, Apple and IBM, and Sony and JVC would have pioneered their products without their (less successful) forerunners. In addition to technical progress, entry was sponsored by the second-movers' particular entry strategies. Procter & Gamble aimed for a mass market for Pampers by charging lower prices and advertising an "easier-to-use" design. However, it is not unlikely that this business strategy was helped by the luxury status that Chux's disposable diapers represented earlier: Pampers did not gain a reputation of being "cheap," and, in fact, they were not cheap. Chux's luxury status might have helped Pampers to overcome the bad image of mass markets that suppliers face "especially for mature products" (Tellis and Golder 1996: 68). On the other hand, Pampers also succeeded in gaining a first-mover reputation, as the Chux brand was more or less forgotten by consumers. To be labeled a pioneer seems to be an asset – but is not always justified by the facts.

Pampers was the result of an innovative late entry. But note Tellis and Golder (1996) called second-movers like Procter & Gamble "early leaders." They point out that such second-mover companies have a low failure rate with their products. Their average market share is close to 30 percent and many of them are market leaders. In comparison, the failure rate of market pioneers is 47 percent, their average market share is 10 percent and only 10 percent are current market leaders. Of course, the numbers and shares of the pioneers and early leaders are difficult to compare as early leaders enter, on average, thirteen years after pioneers. Some technologies change dramatically, independent of the pioneer's and the early leader's R&D efforts. In general, early leaders (i.e., second-movers) are better equipped to incorporate such changes into their products.

An average of thirteen years is a long period. How can we explain this substantial time span? Either there was not enough demand in the pioneer market to nourish a second supplier with a rather similar product and innovations were a prerequisite for a successful competitive product. Or, there was a need for technological progress to reduce production costs in order to be equipped for challenging the incumbent supplier. Or, there was the threat of parallel entry (see Sherman and Willett (1967) and Section 3.5.3 below) and potential entrants tried to develop alternative products which were close substitutes to the incumbent's product before they dared to enter the market. Or, second-movers were motivated to enter a market because of changes in consumers' demand – e.g., now favoring moderately priced mass products to the luxury products of the pioneer producer. In the latter case, it could well be that entrants play an active role in changing consumers' preferences. A bundle of these arguments could explain why it took Procter & Gamble not just thirteen, but thirty years, including ten years of research, to become the market leader in disposable diapers, after Chux pioneered this market in the mid-1930s. Patents can hardly explain the thirteen-year time lag.

As pointed out by Tellis and Golder (1996: 66), it is not always obvious which supplier is the pioneer:

> Every successful, dominant firm has reached that position by doing something right. In a loose sense, that firm has 'pioneered' a new concept or a new market segment. However, such a loose definition of a pioneer based on results is circular: if successful firms are labeled pioneers, then pioneers must be successful.
>
> (Tellis and Golder 1996: 67)

In fact, Procter & Gamble claimed pioneer status, based on the success of its Pampers. Yet, Tellis and Golder applied the rather strict definition of pioneer as first to the market, which identifies Chux as the pioneer of disposable diapers despite its relative moderate success compared to Pampers. They concluded that "the passage of time, Pampers' success, and P&G's promotion of its achievement have led to a reinterpretation of the history of this market" (Tellis and Golder 1996: 67).[5] In the next section, we meet another case of reinterpreting the history of the market: the case of Gillette.

## 3.4 Public pioneers and the entrepreneurial State

In her recent book *The Entrepreneurial State*, Mariana Mazzucato gives a series of quite spectacular examples that demonstrate the pivotal impact of the State in pioneering today's living conditions and business environment.[6] For instance, Google benefitted at least in two ways from the State's activity: it makes use of the Internet and, secondly, it applies an algorithm that is based on research funded by a public-sector National Science Foundation grant.[7] Apple not only received government funding in its early stage, "but it also 'ingeniously' made use of publicly funded technology to create 'smart' products." In fact, "there is not a single key technology behind the iPhone that has not been State-funded," Mazzucato (2014: 11) concludes. She observes that

> Apple incrementally incorporated in each new generation of iPods, iPhones and iPads technologies that the State sowed, cultivated and ripened. These investments were made in part to address national security

---

5  Given the very different quality of the Chux product and the P&G's Pampers we could speak of different markets and accept P&G's claim of being a pioneer. In this case, Pampers were a *strategic substitute* to Chux. (See Bulow et al. (1985) for a reference.) Of course, it depends on where we see the borders of a specific market – i.e., where the cross-elasticity of demand is small.

6  In his review of Mazzucato's book, Madrick (2014) discusses some of these examples and adds further ones.

7  For this information, Mazzucato (2014: 20) refers to John Bettelle's (2005), *The Search: How Google and Its Rivals Rewrote the Rules of Business and Transformed Our Culture*, New York: Penguin.

concerns, and only later did it become a question of enabling the exploitation of (past) technological developments for commercial applications, and by extension, job creation and economic competitiveness.

(Mazzucato 2014: 168)

Does the State get remunerated for its pioneer investments? Mazzucato emphasizes that Apple's job creation is a myth. Most of the newly created jobs "represent no or low commitment on the part of corporations to offer stable employment, skill formation and predictable and rewarding careers" and "pay-wise the company's remuneration policy is only slightly better than Walmart" (Mazzucato 2014: 170). Of course, many of these jobs were created outside the United States. This is also where a major part of the production takes place and the largest share of the value-added is taxed at relatively low rates abroad. Even within the US, Apple prefers locations such as Reno, Nevada, and Austin, Texas, to keep tax payments on a modest level. Mazzucato (2014: 173) comments that these "facts reinforce that the tax system is not one that can be relied on for recouping investments in risky innovations." In the case of Apple, it was the State of California which was not compensated for its investments into the technologies that Apple profitably implemented.

### 3.4.1 Green technology, risk taking, and Schumpeterian destruction

In Mazzucato's "pamphlet," there are also exciting examples of state-funded research on pharmaceuticals that privately collected large profits. Mazzucato emphasized the risk-taking of the State. She claims that

> from the development of aviation, nuclear energy, computers, the internet, the biotechnology revolution, nanotechnology and even now in green technology, it is, and has been, the state not the private sector that has kick-started and developed the engine of growth, because of its willingness to take risk in areas where the private sector has been too risk-averse.
>
> (Mazzucato 2014: 13)

One may also argue that private investors are too small to assure themselves against failure. Investing in technological changes is not just *risky*, it is *uncertain* if we apply Frank Knight's categorization. (See Mazzucato 2014: 35f. and 58f., for this argument.) As we do not know the probability distribution over possible outcomes, we cannot "calculate" expectations. In fact, we do not even know the possible outcomes. This makes the writing of a business plan a work of art and the financing a game of hazard.

Risky or uncertain, the government gets involved. But, in general, it is *not* the case that the private sector is too risk-averse to engage with projects like developing the Internet. As there are obvious second-mover advantages (and externalities) related to them, it is profitable to "wait" for a pioneering first-mover — not least to avoid to be the first-mover that gets skinned by second-movers. If there is a choice between non-profitable research and investments, and profitable applications of the results, private business is very likely to choose the second alternative.

In her preface to Mazzucato's book, Carlota Perez even speaks of "a courageous, risk-taking State." However, in general, there is nothing courageous about spending public money. Politicians and bureaucrats are hardly ever made responsible for government expenditures and surely not if they result in products that prove to be very useful to the private economy, and perhaps even to the overall economic performance and the growth of GDP. The latter can almost always be concluded without strong resistance and any evidence.

Referring to the success story of private companies such as Google and Apple and the underlying public support, Mariana Mazzucato strongly suggests that the (British) State promotes green technology with pioneering investments that give the private sector a chance of a successful second-mover. She seems quite aware that switching to green technology implies a Schumpeterian destruction for the given industry structure and expects "creativity" also from the private sector:

> In the case of clean energy, it's also not just about the willingness to sustain support for new and transitional technologies until industry can 'mature' — until the cost and performance meet or exceed those of incumbent technologies (e.g. fossil power). The history of new sectors teaches us that the private investments tend to wait for the early high-risk investments to be made first by the State.
>
> (Mazzucato 2014: 196)

Germany is her model case, "a first mover among European countries" (Mazzucato 2014: 120). It "has provided a glimpse of the value of long-term support" (Mazzucato 2014: 158). Germany had a vision and policy, and private investment followed. This is not the case with the US; there the State had made "early and substantive investments in green technology," Mazzucato (2014: 120) observes, but by "proceeding without a clear vision and goal in mind, however, and without a long-term commitment to several key technologies, the US has failed to significantly alter its energy mix." Without a vision and commitment, the US government did not succeed in giving a reliable platform for second-movers to start their businesses in the green industry domain, at least not to the degree that would trigger a Schumpeterian "creative destruction" in the country. And yet, the value system in the US has changed; bigger cars are much less appreciated today than they were in the 1950s and '60s. On the other hand, we might argue that Germany experienced too much destruction, creativity is lagging behind, and the growth-effects of the supporting industry emigrated, to a large extent, to China.

There are numerous cases, not just Apply and Google that demonstrate second-mover advantages on the basis of pioneering public investments, most likely with a positive effect on overall economic performance. Inventions under the aegis of the military seem to be a major motivator for technological progress, of which the Internet is a prominent example. Of course, sometimes the share of mere redistribution from taxpayers to private business and its stakeholders is substantial. (As Blondie told Tuco: "You may run the risks, my friend, but I do the cutting." In the case of public investments, the issue is the cutting of the income cake.) Yet, the pioneering cases and their positive impact on the private sector has to be emphasized, especially for those liberal activists who see the role of the State limited to creating free markets and delivering the bare necessities of infrastructure. A step further is to ask for a leading role of the State as investor in areas of "excessive risks and uncertainty," which we identified with substantial second-mover advantages and losses to the pioneer. Clean energy is the pivotal example, and Mariana Mazzucato is very explicit on this, as indicated above. The next step, not taken up by her, is that private business will lobby for pioneering activities of the entrepreneurial State when there is a chance for a profitable second-move. In general, this implies a redistribution of taxpayers' money to the private sector. Much of what we have experienced at universities over the last two decades implies such a pattern. Private business asks (a) for larger government expenditures for higher education and (b) restructuring universities such that they become more competitive, efficient, etc. The latter means that retired or failed managers acquire an office at the university and secretarial support, and a say when it comes to allocating scarce resources on campus and defining university policy. Research contracts with the private sector are very much appreciated although – or because – they hardly ever cover the costs, including a mark-up for using university facilities. To enforce this policy, professors are remunerated and promoted in accordance to such contracts – even at State universities. Some university departments allocate their money in accordance to the sum of private money that an institute or chair succeeds in collecting. The university gets prepared for first-mover pioneering activities, in addition to its fundamental tasks of (scientific?) education and research.

### 3.4.2 Public sponsoring, patents, and business growth

Perhaps less spectacular than direct public pioneering are cases of indirect pioneering: governmental agencies support the introduction of new products by subsidy payments, technological support, or by organizing additional demand. Tellis and Golder (1996: 70) report that in 1903, "King Gillette introduced a safety razor with low-priced disposable blades," aiming for a mass market which did not exist as yet. The Gillette company succeeded in targeting the US government to buy Gillette razors and blades "during the two world wars." Details concerning World War II are difficult to find. However, it seems well documented that in 1917–18, the US government ordered 3.5 million razors and 36 million razor blades for its soldiers. Along with their uniforms and weapons, recruits were given Gillette shaving equipment. It is said that this contributed to Gillette's success, and King C. Gillette, the major owner of the company, became a rich man.

Yet, according to Tellis and Golder (1996: 71), due to the "patents on its initial products, persistent pursuit of the mass market, some new innovations, and few competitive threats, Gillette dominated the market for half a century with a peak share of 72 percent in 1962." However, Tellis and Golder did *not* tell us that in 1930, Gillette "imploded" when

> Auto Strop, a much smaller competitor led by inventor Henry Gaisman, cleverly wedded patent and trademark law in an effort to lock-in the blade aftermarket for its razor handles and introduced a new blade and blade format that was backward compatible with the existing stock of Gillette razors. Gillette responded by introducing a new razor, a new blade, a new blade format and a new top price of $1. But . . . Gillette had not secured its patent position at the time of the launch, and Gillette immediately found itself on the defensive when Auto Strop filed a patent infringement action alleging that the new razors and blades violated Auto Strop's patents.
>
> (Picker 2010: 5)

By the end of 1930, the patent litigation was settled by merger: "The Gillette insiders were swept from the executive committee of the board, and by the end, only one razorman was on the executive committee, Henry Gaisman, formerly of Auto Strop" (Picker 2010: 5f.).

Talking about patents and their power to limit second-mover advantages, I cannot resist referring to the story of the Opel 4/15PS car, called "Laubfrosch" ("Treefrog"), produced in Germany from 1924 onwards. It seemed to be a perfect copy of the Citroën 5CV with the one exception that it was delivered in an intense green color while the Citroën was lemon yellow. Citroën filed a suit against Opel, but German courts found other differences between the two cars besides their color. However, the German language was enriched by the frequently used expression *"dasselbe in grün"* – literally translated as "the same in green" – which acknowledged the infringement of Citroën's first-mover rights.

The case of Gillette clearly demonstrates an essential limit to a rigorous test of second-mover advantages. The power to manage might change inside a company dramatically, or a company might merge with competitors so that its identity radically changes: "it is no longer the same company." Is Henry Gaisman's Gillette a second- or a third-mover? Another limit to testing second-mover advantages are substantial modifications in the products – as with Chux's and Proctor & Gamble's disposable diapers. Thus, the success rates of second-mover advantages given above with reference to Tellis and Golder (1996) should be interpreted as estimates that represent a qualitative illustration, rather than a quantitative one.

The Gillette company continued its career, but mainly as a wrapper and not in its essence. But the new arrangement also faced competition. For instance, in 1962, the British company "Wilkinson Sword introduced a stainless steel blade that lasted three times longer than Gillette's carbon blade" (Tellis and Golder

1996: 71). Interestingly, there were imitators of Wilkinson that also entered the market. As a consequence, Gillette's market "share fell to 50 percent in a little over a year." Gillette's response triggered a sequence of innovations: Trac II twin-head razors in 1972, Acra pivoting head razors in 1977, followed by the Good News twin-blade disposable razor, and, in 1989, by Sensor, "a razor with twin blades that move independently . . . The atmosphere at Gillette reveals how it succeeds at innovation. There is a passion for the product, while innovation is almost an obsession" (Tellis and Golder 1996: 1). And Gillette went on innovating:

> After disposables lost their luster, Gillette introduced the two-bladed Sensor in 1990, then the three-bladed Mach3 in 1998, then the six-bladed Fusion line in 2006. By then its market share figures exceeded 80% in the lucrative U.S. market, and yearly sales of replacement blades and razors were approaching $1 billion.
>
> (Cendrowski 2012: n.p.)

Creating a mass market for razors and blades surely was an important precondition for Gillette's success; however, one might argue that Gillette's innovative powers were somewhat lulled to sleep by the support it received from the US government during World War I. Another dimension worth pointing out is the entry of Wilkinson and its imitators. Unfortunately, details about imitators are not available. It has been argued that, to some extent, King Gillette himself was an imitator, i.e., a second-mover, in the design of his product and the business model. However, King Gillette is widely credited with inventing the so-called "razor-and-blades" business model, where razors are sold cheaply to increase the market for blades. In fact, he only adopted this model by copying his competitors. The separation and combination of razor and blade was not his innovation either. As early as the 1870s, the Kampfe brothers, Frederick and Otto, introduced the Star Safety Razor. They obtained their first US safety-razor patent on June 15, 1880 (Picker 2010). The Star Razor had a removable blade but the blade still required re-sharpening. Gillette added the disposable blade. This novelty necessitated an adequate reconstruction of the razor.

Gillette received his original patents on November 15, 1904, which were valid for seventeen years. However, there was no patent on disposability, and serious competition emerged in 1906: the Ever-Ready blades sold by the American Safety Razor Company, and Gem Junior sold Gem Cutlery Co, "which came with a razor, seven blades – one for each day of the week – and a separate stropping handle all for $1.00" (Picker 2010: 17). The latter also offered to exchange old blades for new ones for 25 cents. However, Gillette prevailed, protected by its patent and "pampered" by the US government. Gillette is a story of a series of second-mover advantages and substantial public support for one of the market players. But there is also a story of patents that were issued to protect first-movers, which had earlier used their second-mover advantages to establish themselves.

Heidrun Hoppe (2000) proposed a theoretical framework that allows us to identify sources of market failure in the innovation process justifying public intervention. Her study models the uncertainty involved in this process. It builds on work by Jennifer Reinganum (1981) and Fudenberg and Tirole (1985). While Reinganum derived a first-mover advantage for the equilibrium of the entry game, Fudenberg and Tirole offer a model such that any first-mover advantage is completely dissipated by preemptive adoption. Related work is Jensen (1982, 1992) and Hendricks (1992). Hoppe derives a second-mover advantage from the fact that "once a firm adopts the new technology and thereby reveals its true value, the rival firm will be able to revise its adoption decision based on the knowledge as to whether adoption will be profitable or not" (Hoppe 2000: 316). However, if there are many adopters, then the profits decrease in the number of adopters – and a first-mover advantage may prevail. The model of Sherman and Willett (1967), discussed below, represents an extreme case of such a model result, based on the (strategic) uncertainty of market entry. The conclusions of Reinganum, Fudenberg and Tirole, Hoppe, Jensen, and Hendricks could be used to interpret and to evaluate much of Gillette's history. However, we will not go further into the details of this highly technical literature.

## 3.5 Raisin picking and the Sherman–Willett trap: a theoretical excursus

Some cases of (non-profit) State entrepreneurship, discussed in Mazzucato (2014), invite free-riding. Most obviously, this applies to the Internet. However, there are second-movers that make use of the Internet to offer services in a way such that exclusion works and customers pay. The benefits do not accrue with the Internet provider but with the service providers that make use of the Internet. Although the providers of services are second-movers with respect to using the Internet, they are pioneers for their particular product for which they try to create a monopoly position, blocking a next generation of second-movers.

There seems to be a virulent relationship between monopoly and second-mover advantages. In the sequel, we will discuss some models that elaborate on this. The models demonstrate that the profits of the incumbent do not always invite entry. Barriers to entry can be strategic, as proposed by the Sherman–Willett trap outlined in this section.

### 3.5.1 The monopoly case and contestable markets

The standard illustration of a first-mover advantage is a monopoly that is protected by barriers to entry at least long enough to accrue larger profits than any second-mover entering the market, with discounting taken into account. If such barriers exist (e.g., a patent is effective such that entry is not relevant), then the textbook monopoly model applies. This model is familiar to every student who did first-year microeconomics. Yet, in order to introduce some basic concepts, here are some details.

The profit-maximizing monopoly faces two constraints: its cost function and the demand of the buyers. The cost function summarizes second-order constraints, such as the production technologies and the input prices under the precondition of cost minimization. The latter implies technological efficiency, i.e., maximizing productivity for a given output. The cost function assumes that the monopoly uses inputs that are traded on perfectly competitive markets, i.e., it buys at given prices. The demand of the buyers is captured by a demand function $q = q(p)$ which reproduces their maximum willingness to pay. It answers the question what price $p$ the monopoly can charge if it wants to sell $q$ units of the product. If it sells $q$ at a price $p$, then $R = pq$ is the revenue and its first derivative $R' = p + p'(q)q$ represents marginal revenue. Note that $p = p(q)$ is the inverse of demand function $q = q(p)$; it represents average revenue $R/q = p(q)$. In case of a standard downward sloping demand curve, the marginal revenue $R'$ related to a quantity $q°$ is smaller than the willingness to pay expressed by price $p = p(q°)$ for this quantity.

Since a firm's profits are revenues minus costs, "marginal revenue = marginal costs" is the first-order condition of profit maximization. It determines the profit-maximizing quantity $q*$, and $\pi* = R(q*) - C(q*)$ is maximum of profits. Of course, we can think of market data and costs such that $\pi*$ is negative – for instance, if fixed costs are extremely high and demand is relatively low, but, in general, textbook monopoly models either show a horizontal average cost curve, implying an identical marginal cost curve, which intersects with the marginal revenue curve $R'$ for positive prices, or the average cost curve is assumed to be U-shaped, which implies that the marginal cost curve intersects with the average cost curve in its minimum and from below. In almost all cases, average cost curves are sketched such that positive profits result. In these cases, a second-mover may be tempted to enter the market at lower price and capture the demand and the profits. If the market is perfect and no barriers to entry exist – i.e., no patents, no secrets concerning the product, its production and its marketing, no brand fidelity, no constraints on the input markets, etc. – then it suffices that the price offered by the entrant is marginally lower than the incumbent's price in order to eliminate the incumbent, or to force the incumbent firm to decrease its price to the level of the competitor or even lower. The theory of the homogeneous price duopoly (the Bertrand case[8]) tells us that in the equilibrium, prices will be equal to average costs and therefore profits will be zero, i.e., being equal to the "normal rate of profits" which is a "natural rate" defined by the equilibrium.

---

8 Bertrand (1883) criticized the assumption that oligopolies compete by choosing quantities as assumed in the Cournot duopoly model and suggested a price adjustment model.

However, an equilibrium in pure strategies does not always exist in this environment of ultra-fast entry and exit. For instance, in the case of U-shaped average cost curves, it could well be that "4 are too few and 6 are too many," to borrow from the title of Reinhard Selten's (1973) seminal paper. There will be a mixed-strategy equilibrium, i.e., there will be entry and exit, and no stability. However, if average cost curves are horizontal (and identical), then the Bertrand model has a zero-profit equilibrium (with an indeterminate number of firms). Yet if reactions are immediate, without loss of time and without chances of making profits outside of equilibrium, why should an entrant be attracted to enter such a market? The threat of a zero-profit equilibrium could be sufficient to suggest to a second-mover not to enter the market. It seems that in this case there is a substantial first-mover advantage, honored by positive profits, as forward-looking second-movers will not enter. So why patents, business and trade secrecy, investments in brand loyalty, and R&D for new products?

A quick answer is: markets are not perfect and can be made even more imperfect by patents, secrecy, investments in brand loyalty, R&D for new products and their introduction. Even the underbidding of prices needs time and informed buyers who do not suffer from (substantial) transaction costs when switching sellers. The theory of contestable markets demonstrates that it needs very little – or is it too much? – in order to derive a zero-profit result for the monopoly case.

The theory of contestable markets has been summarized in William Baumol's Presidential Address to the American Economic Association (Baumol 1982) and in a treatise by Baumol and co-authors (1982). In earlier publications, Baumol (1977) and Baumol and co-authors (1977) analyzed the multi-product case. The technical apparatus for this analysis is rather demanding, and the issue seems to be highly relevant for a *detailed* analysis of joint products like Gillette's razor and (disposable) blade. But let us keep the argument as simple as possible and stick to the one-product case.

The contestable-market model assumes that there are no barriers to entry – more specifically it proposes a market "into which entry is absolutely free, *and exit is absolutely costless*" (Baumol 1982: 3; original emphasis). Consequently, there are no fixed costs to the firms. However, it adds the assumption of hit-and-run: an entrant can enter the market at a price marginally lower than the price of the incumbent, capture profits, and leave the market before the incumbent reacts by lowering the prices. Any market price p above marginal (and average) costs "constitutes an irresistible entry opportunity for hit-and-run entry in a perfectly contestable market, for it promises the entrant supernormal profits even if they accrue for a very short period of time" (Baumol 1982: 5). But if the time period goes to zero, profits should also have a zero-profit limit. Moreover, will the incumbents suffer from losses if there is entry and they do not sell because their prices are too high? Note that there are no fixed costs.

But these are not the only problems that this theory faces. Again, U-shaped average cost curves are a challenge. The equilibrium suggests that prices will be equal to the minimum of the average costs and thus equal to marginal costs.

In the case of U-shaped average costs, again, it could well be that "4 are too few and 6 are too many." (See Holler, 1985, for a discussion.) Baumol is aware of this problem. He cites empirical research indicating that average cost curves typically have a flat range, rather than being characterized by a unique minimum point. On this assumption, there will be "a *range* of outputs over which MC pricing yields zero profits. Moreover, the longer the flat-bottomed segment the better the matters are for existence of equilibrium" (Baumol 1982: 9; original emphasis). Then, of course, the industry structure, i.e., the number of firms, is generally not determined, which violates one of the promises given by contestable-market theory.

The theory of contestable markets assumes a second-mover advantage which, however, is only potentially profitable, i.e., if markets are not in equilibrium. Since, by definition, there are no fixed costs if markets are contestable, then time does not really matter. However, in strategic terms, measured by events, it determines which firm is on the market and which is not. But since profits are zero, even this does not really matter. Yet, if we somewhat vary the assumptions and assume that time is measured by the clock and economic agents discount benefits, then the "length of time" matters. Despite second-mover advantages, it can be profitable to act as a pioneer firm if the expected period of adoption of the entrant is long enough to assure revenues that cover total costs, including the "equilibrium profits." There is an advantage to first-movers if the expected life of a product category is short, because the benefits of a later entry could be low due to lack of time and block entry. This applies if the market for a (very) durable product is limited and cannot be extended even by an innovative second-mover. For instance, when copyright for books did not exist and copying was expensive and time-consuming, the first-mover publisher hurried to exhaust the market for a specific publication. Authors were paid by the page in order not to issue information about sales and thus not to reduce uncertainty for potential second-movers. "Germany's greatest poet" Johann Wolfgang von Goethe invented the second-price sealed-bid auction, also called a "Vickrey auction," to collect information about the market value of his epic poem "Hermann and Dorothea," according to Moldovanu and Tietzel's (1998) interpretation.

Alternatively, one might argue that Goethe fixed a lower limit of the price for his epic poem to improve his bargaining position vis-à-vis the publisher.

Secrets are a barrier to entry inasmuch as they contain uncertainty for a second-mover. The next chapter of this book will discuss this issue. But the example of the book market demonstrates that secrets can be productive as they can motivate a first-mover (e.g., a publisher) to accomplish a pioneering project, even when there is the potential threat of entry.

But let me come back to the zero-profit equilibrium in the Bertrand duopoly case and the contestable-market model with "prices equal to marginal costs." Microeconomics tells us that this result implies efficiency if this condition holds for all markets. Yet, in the next section, we will learn that in the case of natural monopolies (with increasing returns to scale production) marginal cost prices imply losses and efficiency requires a violation of "prices equal to marginal costs." However, efficiency is not our focus – and yet, it might be a possible result if there is a potential of second-mover advantage, e.g., because of the hit-and-run arrangement, that suggests marginal cost prices to the first-mover.

### 3.5.2 Natural monopoly, raisin picking, and the core

In Baumol's theory, a natural monopoly is defined by subadditivity of costs (Baumol 1977). Costs of a firm are (strictly) subadditive if $C(y^1,...,y^m)$ < $C(y^1)+...+C(y^m)$ for any output factor of goods $(y^1,...,y^m)$ that the firm can produce. $C(y^1,...,y^m)$ implies that total output is produced in one production unit, while the right-hand side of the inequality suggest that production is split up into at least two units. For instance, if Gillette produces razor-and-blade sets in two plants 1 and 2, then the strict subadditivity of costs implies that costs will be smaller if the two plants merge into one production unit. Given this definition, whether a firm is a natural monopoly does not depend on market demand. Yet it is possible that for some output vectors a firm will have subadditivity of costs, while for others it will not. In such a case, we have output-specific subadditivity. This means that a particular output vector y* is produced more cheaply by one firm than by any combination of smaller firms.

Note that the subadditivity of costs parallels the superadditivity of the characteristic function – a game-theoretical instrument used to assign values to coalitions, already proposed by John von Neumann in his pioneering paper "Zur Theorie der Gesellschaftsspiele" of 1928 (Von Neumann 1959 [1928]).

Obviously, subadditivity of costs applies if a (one-product) firm satisfies increasing returns to scale with the consequence of average costs and marginal costs decreasing. Such a firm is a natural monopoly. With average costs larger than marginal costs – otherwise average costs do not decrease – marginal cost prices imply losses. If the market is contestable, the market equilibrium is characterized by price p* that equals average costs, i.e., zero profits, and an output quantity y* which is determined by the intersection of the curves of market demand and average costs. This result is locally efficient, but causes problems in an environment of marginal cost prices on directly or indirectly connected markets. The second-mover, i.e., the potential competitor, only serves to guarantee the described equilibrium inasmuch as a different market behavior is not profitable to the incumbent if there is the threat of "contestable entry."

The situation is remarkably different if costs are subadditive, but the natural monopoly is not sustainable as entry can be profitable. Then there is a second-mover advantage if there is no third-mover, given that the incumbent tries to avoid losses. Figure 3.1 illustrates such a market situation. In Berz and Holler (2014), this figure represents an electricity network. But we can also think of a telecommunications network, characterized by high fixed costs, zero variable costs, and capacity constraints. Let us stay with the telecommunications (TC) example in what follows. The necessary investment for a network imply (fixed) costs of 10. For a demand $D_0$, a single switch can cover the market,

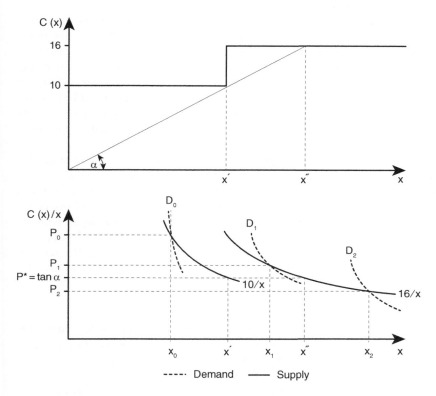

*Figure 3.1* Nonsustainable natural monopoly

asking for zero-profit prices without inviting entry. This applies to quantities $x \leq x'$. However, if demand increases and a curve $D_1$ holds, then an additional network is required to satisfy demand. Demand can be covered if either the incumbent extends its network – which implies an extra investment of 6 units – or a second supplier enters the market. If the incumbent extends its network and asks for a zero-profit price $p_1 = C(x_1)/x_1$ for quantities $x$ in the interval $x' < x < x''$, an entrant could deliver the quantity $x'$ at a price $p^\circ = p_1 - \varepsilon$, with $\varepsilon$ very small, if markets are perfect, snatch customers from the incumbent and thereby accrue profits. Note that $x' < x_1$, so there will be no market clearing at price $p^\circ$, but profits waiting for the entrant. These profits and the quantity $x'$ are the raisins that the entrant is "picking."

Of course, one might think that the incumbent charges a lower price than $p^\circ$ and (re-) conquers $x'$. But there will be entry as long as the incumbent's price is above $p^* = C(x')/x'$.

However, at a price $p^*$, the incumbent firm makes losses if it supplies quantity $x_1$. Consequently, in order to avoid losses, it offers $x'$ at a price $p^*$, and does not extend its TC network, although $D_1$ represents total demand. Some buyers will get frustrated as they are willing to pay p* "just like the others," but they will not get any offer. In fact, there are buyers who are willing to pay more than p*, but they will not get an offer either. A situation of rationing prevails. A quantity x − x' will not be served. As the price mechanism does not work, we do not know whether these are buyers with a higher or lower willingness to pay or a mix of both. An entrant could take care of the frustrated buyers and even gain profits from selling the amount of $x^+$ at a price above average costs $10/x^+$, if the buyers' willingness to pay is large enough. Note that $D_1$ illustrates total demand and not the residual demand that the entrant faces.

TC clients with low willingness to pay, who were successful with the incumbent, may offer their contracts to TC clients with high willingness to pay. If this is possible from a technical and legal point of view, then all kinds of bargaining solutions can pop up which means a large variety of prices for identical services. We can expect that, in the end, those with a higher willingness to pay will be served; however, not all the rent will go to the TC suppliers, as TC clients with a low willingness to pay participate in sharing the rent, of course, at the expense of not having TC services themselves. Is this how the invisible hand works?

Let us review Adam Smith:

> As every individual . . . endeavors as much as he can both to employ his capital in the support of domestick industry, and so direct that industry that its produce be of greater value; every individual necessarily labours to render the annual revenue of the society as great as he can. He generally, indeed, neither intends to promote the publick interest, nor knows how much he is promoting it.
>
> (Smith 1981 [1776/77]: 456)

The preference for the "domestick industry" is due to the additional risk and even uncertainty that investments in foreign industry meet. In the words of Smith: "By preferring the support of domestick to that of foreign industry, he intends only his own security." Adam Smith's reference to the invisible hand follows:

> and by directing that industry in such a manner as its produce may be of the greatest value, he intends only his own gain, and he is in this, as in many other cases, led by an invisible hand to promote an end which was no part of his intention. Nor is it always the worse for the society that it was no part of it. By pursuing his own interest he frequently promotes that of the society more effectually then when he really intends to promote it.
>
> (Smith 1981 [1776/77]: 456)

Those who welcome this dictum enthusiastically celebrating the efficiency of competition and the market economy often ignore Smith's qualification implied by "frequently." However, Smith himself gave several examples in which the invisible hand tends to fail to promote the interest of the society, e.g., when discussing money and the banking sector (Smith 1981 [1776/77]: 286ff.).[9] Raisin picking in the case of a nonsustainable natural monopoly is another example demonstrating that the invisible hand can fail to promote the interest of society if this interest implies efficiency. It is a case of Schumpeterian competition "which commands a decisive cost or quality advantage and which strikes not at the margin of profits and the outputs of the existing firms but at their foundations and their very lives" (Schumpeter 2010 [1942]: 74).

Needless to say that, in the above TC toy example, neither a market outcome with frustrated buyers nor with two suppliers concurs with efficiency. The cost structure of the TC market illustrated by Figure 3.1 implies subadditivity of costs and thus represents a natural monopoly which is, however, not sustainable. If efficiency should be achieved for a demand of quantities in the interval $(x',x'')$, then the regulator, e.g., the State, has to ban entry. Then the monopoly could establish a monopoly solution. However, the regulator might insist on zero-profit price $p_1$ (which includes "normal profits") as a compensation for protecting the incumbent from entry. If this is the case, the demand in the interval $(0,x']$ cross-subsidizes the demand in the interval $(x',x_1]$, as TC clients in the interval $(0,x']$ could be served at a lower zero-profit price than $16/x_1$ while TC clients in the interval $(x',x_1]$ had to pay a much higher price if not served by the joint network. In other words, the joint network would not pass the stand-alone test.[10]

Of course, the cross-subsidization always implies a second-mover advantage if entry is possible – and not barred by regulations, patents, law, etc. In game-theoretical terms, the core is empty: if demand is $D_1$ then there is no pair $(p, x)$, such that the corresponding allocation of benefits is (a) individually rational, (b) Pareto efficient, and (c) coalitional rational. In our case of the TC network, *individual rationality* implies that firms do not enter the market or leave the market, if they have to expect losses, while TC clients will not buy services, if the price is larger than their willingness to pay represented by the demand curve. *Pareto efficiency* presupposes that all buyers that are willing to pay the zero-profit price of the one (natural monopoly) firm will be served. *Coalition rationality* is satisfied for $(p, x)$ if no subset of buyers can be profitably served by an entering supplier under the pretext of individual rationality.

The zero-profit solution of a *sustainable* natural monopoly is in the core. *There is no second-mover advantage if the market outcome $(p,x)$ is in the core.* However,

---

9 "[F]or Smith the question was not whether or not the banking trade ought to be regulated: the answer was a resounding yes. The question was rather which regulations would look after 'the security of the whole society' and at the same time leave enough room for the pursuit of self-interest and allow banks to provide the needed credit for doing so" (Kurz 2016a: 633). Smith's reasoning "supports a kind of dynamic and open second-best liberalism" (Sturn 2010: 266). For further discussion, see Kurz (2016b: 32f.).

10 For cross-subsidization and stand-alone test, see Faulhaber (1975).

if the core is empty, then there is a second-mover advantage implying a threat of entry, but, without further barriers, the first-mover could successfully counteract, turning the "second move" into a failure. Under the label of bargaining sets, cooperative game theory offers a rich set of solution concepts that are based on the idea of objection (e.g., threat of entry) and of counterobjection (see, e.g., Owen 1995, Ch. XIII). They vary, e.g., on details such as whether an incumbent has to give the same price to the client as offered by the entrant, to keep his or her fidelity, or whether in the case of counterobjection, the incumbent has to offer more than the entrant. The general principle is that of stabilizing an outcome (which is not in the core), threatened by objection (e.g., entry), by the threat of counterobjection. A competitor might not make use of a second-mover advantage if the incumbent is likely to make a competitive offer such that the buyers are motivated to stay with the incumbent. In general, it is not necessary that all buyers stay with the incumbent. There can be a sufficient amount such that the incumbent can avoid losses and cause troubles to the entrant.

We will come back to these game-theoretic concepts that may help us to get a better understanding of what is going on if demand increases from $D_0$ to $D_1$. If demand increases such that at a price $p < p*$ a quantity $x > x"$ is sold, raisin picking is no longer possible, as entry involves losses. Demand $D_2$, price $p_2$, and quantity $x_2$ describe such an outcome. Note if no further capacity constraint is met, then the natural monopoly is sustainable for all quantities larger than $x"$ if demand is adequate. If a public authority wants to support a monopoly either because it shows subadditivity of costs or because of an "industrial policy reason," e.g., to protect national production against foreign raisin pickers, it may create additional demand that assures an $x > x"$ outcome. As mentioned above, in 1917–18, the US government ordered 3.5 million Gillette razors and 36 million Gillette razor blades for its soldiers. In the early 1950s, BMW produced two very expensive luxury car models: the BMW 501 and the V8 Super BMW 501. Sales were moderate and implied losses. Interestingly, these luxury cars (with some resemblance to a Rolls Royce) became the standard vehicles of the Munich police and were used by the police all over Bavaria. BMW's headquarter is in Munich and Munich is the capital of the State of Bavaria which is a member state of the Federal Republic of Germany. (In addition, Munich is my home town.) The close relationship between BMW and the State of Bavaria is mirrored in the BMW logo. It shows the blue and white panels of the Bavarian national flag at its center, and the name of the company: *Bayerische Motorenwerke AG*. However, selling luxury cars to the police did not solve BMW's financial problems, which were mainly the result of a rather peculiar selection of products in the 1950s – and of distortions and interruptions due to World War II.

It is not obvious that Gillette and BMW enjoy subadditivity of costs, but the two cases demonstrate how public agents could expand demand such that entry is not profitable, as the incumbent is helped by the public agent, i.e., through tax money. Faulhaber (1975) analyzed the efficiency conditions for a water supply system. Each neighborhood can have its own well, storage tank, pump, and local distribution system but neighborhoods can cooperate sharing a well, a storage tank, and even a pump. Yet, sharing these facilities presupposes also sharing the corresponding costs. The cost-sharing arrangement decides whether cooperation prevails or not on a voluntary basis. But if the core is empty, then there is no sharing rule that does not motivate the entry of an alternative water supply system. An efficient supply system, making use of the subadditivity of costs, thus necessitates regulating entry, i.e., blocking it, if one cannot rely on the effects of possible counterobjections (which are not modeled in Faulhaber (1975).) The latter can block entry if the agents think strategically, in the sense of game theory, and expect that the others do the same. These expectations are a decisive element, making the threat of counterobjections effective. The following section will discuss a case of mutually strategic thinking and the resulting barrier to entry – making second-mover advantages void.

### 3.5.3 Strategic barriers to entry

There is an immense literature on strategic barriers to entry.[11] I have selected the work of Sherman and Willett (1967) because it describes an interesting scenario with somewhat disturbing results. In a note of four pages, the authors present a model which demonstrates that (a) the potential of a multiple entry can forestall entry and (b) an enlargement of the number of potential entrants will not lower the incumbent's limit price, blocking entry, but raise it. If these results hold, then the second-mover advantage of a raisin picker in a nonsustainable natural monopoly crumbles into dust. Despite the fact that this note has been published in the prestigious and widely read University of Chicago's *Journal of Political Economy*, this paper has been only infrequently quoted. I conjecture that this can be explained by three reasons: (1) the model is based on very abstract assumptions, some would call them "extremely unrealistic," (2) the authors are somewhat "weakish" in the modeling of expectations and (3), correspondingly, do not discuss the mixed-strategy Nash equilibrium. In fact, they abstain from using game-theoretical parlance although they use a game-theoretical model to discuss strategic barriers to entry that result from "putting oneself into the shoes" of potential fellow entrants. Here I want to mend these shortcomings.

But let us start with (1), the abstract assumptions of the model. Arguments (2) and (3) will be discussed in the course of the elaboration of the model. With reference to papers by Modigliani (1958, 1959) and original work by Bain (1956) and Sylos Labini (1962), Sherman and Willett introduce the Sylos postulate:"potential entrants behave as though they expect existing firms to adopt the policy most unfavourable to them, namely, the policy maintaining

---

11 For instance, Tirole (1988) contains an overview (and reinterpretation) of models of limit pricing and predatory pricing. For limit pricing, Milgrom and Roberts (1982) is the "classical paper."

output while reducing the price" (Modigliani 1958: 217), such that this output can be sold. So, for example, if demand is described by the function $x = 100 - p$ and the incumbent charges a price $p = 60$ which corresponds to sales of $x = 40$, potential entrants expect that the incumbent firm will lower its price such that it still will sell $x = 40$ after entry – obviously, irrespective of costs and possible losses. Implicitly, it is assumed that it will keep the buyers with a willingness to pay of "60 and above" for itself so that for the potential entrants the residual demand function $x = 60 - p$ applies. Further, it is assumed that all producers, the incumbent and the potential entrants, are able to supply units of an identical commodity at identical costs. But there are some fixed costs (or, alternatively, exit is not costless). Information is assumed to be perfect inasmuch as all producers know the market situation (i.e., the decisions of the incumbent, market demand, production technology, etc.) and potential entrants know that all other potential entrants also know.

In game-theoretical language, the information is not perfect, but complete: "players" know the game. Sherman and Willett give a two-by-two payoff matrix for the game of two potential entrants. Note that in the case of firms' profits ("money payoffs"), these are quite acceptable proxies for utilities (i.e., equalized with payoffs per se in modern game theory). In Figure 3.2, which corresponds to Figure 1 in Sherman and Willett (1967), p is the price of the incumbent before entry and $p_1$ is the price that would forestall entry by a single potential entrant if charged by the incumbent. Implicitly, it is understood that p and $p_1$ are large enough to cover average costs and avoid losses to the incumbent. $f(p - p_1, 1)$ is the profit of an entrant if there is a single entrant only. If the incumbent's price p is larger than the blocking price $p_1$, i.e., $p > p_1$ holds, then $f(p - p_1, 1) > 0$. However, if two second-movers enter simultaneously then p is assumed to determine a residual quantity such that the payoff of an entrant is $f(p - p_1, 2) < 0$. Note that Figure 3.2 assumes that there are two potential entrants. More general, $f(p - p_1, n)$ is the profit of an entrant if n potential entrants actually enter. Zero profits are assigned to firms that do not enter.

As Sherman and Willett assume that utilities are linear in profits, we can read Figure 3.2 as the payoff matrix of 2-by-2 market entry game. The set of players is $N = \{A,B\}$ with cardinality $n = 2$. Each player has two pure strategies "Do not enter" and "Enter."

Obviously, if the game in Figure 3.2 is played sequentially – if, e.g., A succeeds to enter before B enters, and B learns about A's entry – then there is a

| A's strategy \ B's strategy | Do not enter | Enter |
|---|---|---|
| Do not enter | 0,0 | 0, f(p – p₁,1) |
| Enter | f(p – p₁,1),0 | f(p – p₁,2), f(p – p₁,2) |

*Figure 3.2* Strategic barriers to entry

first-mover advantage. As a result, a single entrant will challenge the market position of the monopoly and make profits as $f(p - p_1, 1) > 0$ if $p > p_1$. A first-mover advantage in the entry game may trigger a second-mover advantage on the market if the entrant is more successful than the incumbent. But if entry is sequential, the incumbent is likely to choose $p = p_1$ to block entry.

However, the game in Figure 3.2 and the story told by Sherman and Willett does not imply a sequential structure, but a simultaneity of entry decisions. Sherman and Willett analyze various forms of behavior within the context described by the matrix in Figure 3.2. If a player $i$ chooses a maximax behavior, then $i$ chooses "Enter" irrespective of what the other player chooses – in fact, $i$ will not form any expectation with respect to the strategy choice of the other player; $i$ ignores the strategic relationship illustrated by Figure 3.2. Either $i$ is not aware of this relationship, or $i$ expects that the other player, $j$, expects that $i$ ignores the strategic relationship. Perhaps $i$ thinks that $j$ thinks that $i$ is not smart enough to recognize the strategic dilemma illustrated by Figure 3.2 and does not enter to avoid losses. Then $i$ enters and earns $f(p - p_1, 1) > 0$. However, if both potential entrants choose maximax and decide to enter, then their payoffs are $(f(p - p_1, 2), f(p - p_1, 2))$ with $f(p - p_1, 2) < 0$.

As long as the incumbent's price satisfies $p > p_1$, maximax players will enter irrespective of n, the number of potential entrants. Thus, n has no effect on p; $p_1$ is the limit price. However, n will affect p if players follow the maximin rule trying to avoid any payoffs below 0, i.e., the value which an entrant can guarantee itself by not entering. Sherman and Willett (1967: 402) motivate maximin behavior by the well-known dictum that a player assumes the worst from his fellow players: "a firm anticipates a malevolent opponent and seeks a best response to the opponent's most harmful action." However, all we have to assume in the given case is that a potential entrant expects the same behavior of its fellow entrant that it will choose itself. Given the assumption that all entrants are equal, i.e., have access to the same technology and same information, then this expectation does not seem implausible. Therefore, if potential entrants want to avoid losses they will enter only if the incumbent's price p is high enough to allow for the profitable entry of all potential entrants. If the price p is not high enough to allow for the entry of all n entrants then none of them will enter and the incumbent can enjoy the fruits of its pioneering position. This defines a limit price $p°$, which is the largest entry-blocking price the incumbent can ask for without risking entry under the maximin hypothesis.

A given number n of potential entrants thus necessitates a large enough price p of the incumbent to allow for entry. Thus the limit price $p°$ increases with the number n of potential entrants. However, the limit price $p°$ is not likely to be profit maximizing. If $p°$ is larger than the profit-maximizing price $p*$ then the incumbent can choose $p*$ and realize monopoly profits which do not depend on n. Sherman and Willett do not consider this possibility.

If the limit price $p°$ is smaller than $p*$, it could be profitable for the incumbent to create potential entrants. It is a well-known strategy of established firms to announce forthcoming new products to keep potential entrants out of the market. Such new products can be understood as potential entrants, especially as some of them will never be realized.

Sherman and Willett (1967) offer a third solution to the entry problem summarized in Figure 3.2, which actually includes maximin and maximax as special cases. In what follows we present this solution in its original notation, only to remold it in more "conventional terms" afterwards when we give a game-theoretical interpretation of this solution. In other words, I will make use of my second-mover advantage discussing Sherman and Willett (1967). They define P(E) to be the subjective probability of the other firm's entry and assume this probability to be the firm's own entry decision. The expected utility of a firm will be $E(U) = P(E) f(p - p_1, 2) + (1 - P(E)) f(p - p_1, 1)$ if it enters and 0 if not.

Since $f(p - p_1, 2) < f(p-p_1, 1)$, E(U) will reach a maximum when P(E) = 0. In this case, the limit coincides with $p_1$.which is the same limiting price as in the case of maximax. Indeed, an expectation of P(E) = 0 thus yields the same result as in the case of maximax, if shared by all potential entrants, but expectations should not be confused with decision rules – in this case, maximax. This also applies for P(E) = 1 that brings about the same result as the maximin decision rule.

Of course, there can be expectations in the interval 0 < P(E) < 1. Sherman and Willett (1967) do not discuss the forming of expectations. Expectations are therefore external to their model analysis. Given that potential entrants have no exogenous information about the behavior of their fellow entrants, they could try to apply game-theoretical thinking to "rationalize" their assumptions on P(E). The following analysis, however, demonstrates that the gain from applying game-theoretical reasoning to the strategic decision situation described in Figure 3.2 is rather modest, even in the case of two entrants only. For this case, we can simplify the game matrix. Assuming a > 0 > b, Figure 3.3 is equivalent to Figure 3.2.

The solutions discussed in Sherman and Willett (1967) are (1) maximax with the choices (Enter, Enter) and the resulting (negative) payoffs (b,b), (2) maximin with the choices (Do not enter, Do not enter) and the payoffs (0,0), and (3) expected utility maximization with $u_i(Enter) = rb + (1 - r)a$, where r is subjective probability of the other firm's entry, i.e., a belief, which is considered exogenous. An application of game theory tells us that the game in Figure 3.3 has two Nash equilibria in pure strategies and one in mixed

| A's strategy          B's strategy | Do not enter | Enter |
|---|---|---|
| Do not enter | (0,0) | (0,a) |
| Enter | (a,0) | (b,b) |

*Figure 3.3* Decisions of two potential entrants: a > 0 > b

strategies. For the latter, we have $r* = a/(a - b)$ for both players. As the game is symmetric, this equilibrium looks promising – more promising than the two asymmetric equilibria in pure strategies with choices (Do not enter, Enter) and (Enter, Do not enter). However note that player $j$ is indifferent between "Do not enter" and "Enter" if $i$ chooses "Enter" with probability $r*$ and "Do not enter" with probability $1 - r*$. In fact, it is enough that $j$ assumes that $i$ chooses randomly with probability $r*$ between the two pure strategies. This assumption makes $j$ indifferent between all possible alternatives, including mixing "Do not enter" and "Enter." To conclude, if $j$ expects $i$ to randomize in accordance to $r*$, then all his choices are equivalent, i.e., best replies. Of course, the same holds for $i$ if $i$ expects $j$ to randomize according to $r*$. Thus, the mixed-strategy pair $(r*, r*)$ is a Nash equilibrium as neither of the two players can improve their payoff by choosing an alternative strategy, given the equilibrium strategy $r*$ of the other. However, it is a weak equilibrium as deviating does not hurt, if the other player chooses the Nash equilibrium strategy. If he does not, then there are anyway better strategies than "Nash" to choose from.[12]

It should be added that the mixed-strategy Nash equilibrium is inefficient, i.e., the resulting payoff vector (0,0) is not Pareto optimal – and it is equal to the maximin outcome. If the two entrants agree to let a perfect coin decide whether A or B will enter and the other will stay out, the expected payoff of the two potential entrants is $a/2$ for each of them – which is larger than 0. However, agreements are not enforceable in this market game; in fact, they could be even illegal. Economists and perhaps market regulators might worry about the inefficiency of the mixed-strategy equilibrium, market entrants and the incumbent monopoly will not.

### 3.5.4 *The Volunteer's Dilemma and market entry games*

The Nash equilibrium solution concept is the standard instrument to form expectation about the players' choices in a strategic decision situation. However, the example of the market entry game shows that it does not always help the players to select best strategies. There are two problems involved: (a) the multiplicity of equilibria and (b) the weakness of the mixed-strategy Nash equilibrium. In fact, one of the two problems could be enough to disqualify the Nash equilibrium as a recipe for selecting optimal behavior.

The game in Figures 3.2 and 3.3 is a two-person version of the Volunteer's Dilemma introduced by Diekmann (1985, 1986). The focus of Diekmann's analysis was to study social phenomena like the murder of Kitty Genovese. A description of this case, illustrating Diekmann's Volunteer's Dilemma, we find in Weesie (1993). Kitty Genovese was

---

12 For details of the mixed-strategy equilibrium, see, e.g., Wittman (1985, 1993); Holler (1986a, 1986b, 1990, 1993), Tsebelis (1990), Andreozzi (2002a, 2002b, 2004), and the analysis of the Inspection Game in Section 3.8.2. The pioneering paper is Aumann and Maschler (1972).

a young woman brutally attacked and stabbed to death in New York. The attack happened in front of a building block. At least 38 people witnessed the crime, but nobody came to help her or phoned the police to report the incident. Given a helper's risk of being hurt oneself, it is not surprising that people were reluctant to step in. The fact that people seemed unwilling to apply the minimal resources to phone the police triggered a public response that condemned the indifference of people in our modern anonymous society with respect to the affairs of their fellow citizens.

(Weesie 1993: 569)

An alternative explanation is of course that, given the large number who witnessed the crime and many were seen witnessing the crime, people did not get involved because they believed others would contact the police. It seems that the larger the number of witnesses (i.e., second-movers), the less likely it is that somebody will phone the police, i.e., produce the public good. This concurs with the empirical results offered in Diekmann (1985, 1986) which suggest a decline of cooperation with increasing group-size. "This mechanism is well known in social psychology as the effect of 'diffusion of responsibility', which is confirmed by a large bulk of experimental data" (Diekmann 1993: 84). The results support Olson's (1965) "Logic of Collective Action" as well as the theoretical conclusions in Sherman and Willett (1967), derived from the highly stylized monopoly entry game. Obviously, the strategy "to help" in the responsibility games corresponds to "Do not enter" in the market entry games.

The Volunteer's Dilemma does not only show a conflict of interest among the players, but also a serious coordination problem as highlighted by the two asymmetric equilibria in pure strategies and the mixed-strategy equilibrium.[13] One could argue that the coordination is due to the symmetry of the decision problem. Isn't the assumption of identical payoffs for the two players in the various outcomes highly questionable and very unrealistic? Indeed, but if we assume that the potential entrants do not know the details of the other potential entrants – e.g., their cost function and the quality of management – isn't it an acceptable hypothesis for a decision maker that the competitors have the same possibilities and constraints? If we accept this reasoning, then the symmetry in the payoff matrices in Figures 3.2 and 3.3 is the reflection of a somewhat perverted "principle of insufficient reason." The assumption of complete information, underlying these games, seems rather paradoxical, if symmetry is the result of a complete lack of information with respect to the other player's payoffs. But "not to know" is also information and the symmetry derived from "principle of insufficient reason" is a possible solution for a player to structure his/her decision problem.

---

13  Raub and Voss (2017) use the Volunteer's Dilemma to illustrate James Coleman's micro-macro model which relates "micro" and "macro" to "individual rationality" and "collective outcome."

If we interpret the payoff matrices as a modeling from the point of view of the individual player, then symmetry seems adequate, if the player does not have additional information about the other player's payoffs. In the entrant game, payoffs summarize the efficiency, constraints, etc. of the potential entrants. If entrant A has specific information about entrant B, this can be captured by the payoffs. For instance, let us assume that A knows that B is more successful than itself in case that only one of them enters the monopoly market and competes with the incumbent. This could be due to the fact that B's management is better qualified to handle this market situation. For instance, a member of B's board of directors was the head of the sales department of the incumbent before she joined firm B. In Figure 3.4, this qualification is expressed by a payoff $a° > a$. Figure 3.4 also tells us that this "advantage" of B should not matter to B. If we assume that Figure 3.4 represents A's interpretation of the entry game, then we can easily find a story that justifies this expectation. However, it might be more challenging to discuss how A will decide in case A assumes $a° > a$. Compared to the symmetric case, is it more likely that A enters or less?

A possible answer is: as $a° > a$, it seems straightforward that A expects B to be more likely to enter the market. As a consequence, A is less likely to enter and the asymmetric Nash equilibrium ("Do not enter", "Enter") is better qualified to describe the outcome, as in the symmetric case. Equipped with payoffs $a° > a$, it may also serve as a focal point to solve the coordination problem of the given entry game. But there is still the mixed-strategy Nash equilibrium as a possible road map to solve the strategic problem. However, its implications are somewhat bizarre. It implies (a) that entrant B does not change its behavior and (b) A chooses strategy "Enter" more often than in the symmetry case, i.e., with a probability $r° = a°/(a° − b) > r*$, although A's payoffs do not change. The intuition behind this "counter-intuitive result" (see Wittman 1985) is the following: in the mixed-strategy Nash equilibrium, agent A is assumed to randomize with probability r over its strategies "Enter" and "Do not enter" such that B is indifferent between choosing its strategies "Enter" and "Do not enter." If the payoff for the strategy pair ("Do not enter", "Enter") increases from a to $a°$, then A has to take care that the outcome ("Do not enter", "Enter") becomes less likely by choosing with a higher probability $r°$ "Enter" than in the case of payoff a.

Again, this is a thought experiment for forming expectations; it does not (necessarily) imply that the game's participants randomize over their pure

| A's strategy \ B's strategy | Do not enter | Enter |
|---|---|---|
| Do not enter | (0,0) | (0,a°) |
| Enter | (a,0) | (b,b) |

*Figure 3.4* Decisions of two potential entrants: $a° > a > 0 > b$

strategies. Here the problem is that A has to do both the calculation of B, which leads to no change of behavior for B, and the calculation for its own behavior which results in $r°$ ($> r*$). A's reasoning is vacuous if B becomes attracted by the higher payoff $a°$ and chooses "Enter" with a higher probability than r. (Is this a framing effect?) If A expects such a behavior, then it is better staying out of the market in order to avoid losses, i.e., a negative payoff. There is some experimental evidence for such a result with respect to the Volunteer's Dilemma (Diekmann 1993, Weesie 1993).

It seems that the mixed-strategy equilibrium is not a convincing model to forecast behavior (see Høst and Holler 1990, Holler et al. 1992). This is not surprising when we take into consideration that this solution concept is meant to rationalize the forming of expectations but does not assume that players actually throw a coin or a dice selecting their pure strategies. Another issue is how to test for mixed strategies on the level of an individual decision maker? Do we have relative frequencies that approximate a probability indicating randomization? In general, the answer is "No." To come closer to such an approximation, in Høst and Holler (1990) and Holler and co-authors (1992), a homogeneous population was chosen and the relative frequencies of the pure strategies were counted as a substitute for probabilities. To summarize:

> we do not know whether actors really have employed mixed strategies. . . . the experimental test allows for potential falsification on the group level. Whether or not subjects employ mixed strategies on the individual level, aggregate results on the group level clearly falsify the mixed Nash-equilibrium hypothesis.
>
> (Diekmann 1993:81)

We could argue that in the case of market entry the simultaneity of choices implied in the matrix representation is inadequate. Flukes apart, there will always be an entrant who is faster than the other(s). The larger payoff $a°$ can be the result of B being more competent or efficient and thus likely to be first in the "race to the market." Since A shares B's evaluation $a° > a$, it is likely that A will refrain from entering the market and let B collect the benefits. The game acquires an endogenous sequential structure. Thus, the pure-strategy equilibrium ("Do not enter", "Enter") describes the outcome and the mixed-strategy equilibrium and its peculiarities becomes irrelevant.

To some extent, this result has been corroborated by Diekmann's (1993) experimental results. However, A might still try to be faster to overcome its disadvantages expressed in payoffs $a < a°$ just like Angel Eyes tried to shoot Blondie by drawing first. Although B seems to have a larger potential, it does not necessarily mean that it makes use of it in rushing to entry. Weesie (1993) discusses the potential of waiting and rushing in a Volunteer's Dilemma under the label of "Volunteer's Timing Dilemma." The following story nicely connects the potential to act with waiting time and information:

I was once walking along a bridge over a canal in Amsterdam when I heard cries for help from below. It took a few seconds to realize what was going on. Being a relatively poor swimmer and given the bad smell from the canal, I would much rather have someone else jump in. A number of other bystanders and I found ourselves looking at one another, silently: Who was to blink first? I was relieved to find that someone else was a better citizen.

(Weesie 1993: 588f.)

So somebody jumped and a life was saved. But this is not the end of this story. Weesie, being social scientist, asked himself: "What was going on here?" He reflected:

With hindsight, I was looking at the other bystanders to estimate their inclination to jump in. Does one of these people behave like a friend or acquaintance of the drowning person? Does one of them look like a sportsman? In theoretical terms, we had incomplete information about the costs and benefits of each other. By observing each other, we estimated these. The fact that we had to wait provided additional information. A good friend would jump immediately. The fact that this didn't happen made it more likely that my costs and benefits were among the more favorable for a rescue attempt. Had we had to wait long enough, I probably would have jumped; luckily for me, someone else jumped and saved the drowning person.

(Weesie 1993: 589)

## 3.6 Fair shares and second-mover advantages

Jeroen Weesie's report demonstrates that there are second-mover advantages which imply that we do not move, and still get the benefits – *if there is a first-mover*. The benefit is in enjoying the result, but not in contributing to it. This of course is a version of free-riding and a handicap to the production of a "public good." There are, however, decision problems in which the first-move presupposes the second-mover's action. In some cases, the first-move predetermines a second-move. Given such an intimate relationship, there is the question whether the sharing of cost and benefits is fair. If the answer is no, first-movers might be absent and second-movers cannot enjoy benefits – and people would drown in the presence of a multitude of potential rescuers.

Costs and benefits out of collective actions are difficult to compare and even more difficult to share. Participation and utilization are here the catchwords. But of course there are first-movers and second-movers in joint production who have to decide on the division of the surplus. If they do not agree, because at least one party thinks the sharing rule unfair, the production is in danger. Here is an example full of danger.

### 3.6.1 Tuco and Blondie's bounty business

Sergio Leone's *The Good, the Bad, and the Ugly* gives a rather informative introduction into the head-hunting and gunslinger business, however with no historical pretension. There is Angel Eyes who executes killing orders on the basis
of a $500 payment. If he is paid the sum, he will kill irrespective of the specific
circumstances. Implicit to his efficiency in killing, he has to look for a new job
every time he has satisfied his customer. Because of his competence with the
gun and his "cold blood," he does not need a partner in his business.

Tuco and Blondie run quite a different version of the head-hunting business. Blondie delivers Tuco to the Sheriff, submitting Tuco to the well-earned
punishment by hanging, and cashes the bounty which is on Tuco's head, i.e.,
sums of $2,000 and $3,000. When Tuco is under the hanging tree with the
noose tightening duly on his neck, Blondie will cut the rope with a perfect
shot from his perfect rifle. This division of labor looks perfect, but sharing the
bounty can be a problem. Tuco asked Blondie for a larger share in their business of collecting the head-hunting money: he considered his input more risky.
Blondie's response is somewhat ambiguous and irritating to Tuco: "You may
run the risks, my friend, but I do the cutting. If we cut down my percentage –
liable to interfere with my aim." Of course, the cutting and the aim have at
least two meanings in this context. One of them is cutting the "money cake."
The other is cutting the hangman's rope by a perfect shot. If Blondie fails, then
the noose will tighten. Tuco's response to Blondie's sphinxian statement was
straightforward: "if you miss, you had better miss very well. Whoever double-
crosses me and leaves me alive, he understands nothing about Tuco." The
movie shows that Blondie did not take too much heed of this warning.

Angel Eyes observed one of the business events of the Blondie-Tuco partnership commenting: "People with ropes around their necks don't always
hang. Even a filthy beggar like that has a protecting angel. A golden-haired
angel watches over him." The golden-haired angel is Blondie, and he does a
good job by shooting the rope again, however, less than perfectly: this time he
needs three bullets to cut the rope. Tuco feels the rope tightening more than
expected. This experience made Tuco reason: "You never had a rope around
your neck. Well, I'm going to tell you something crazy. When that rope starts
to pull tight, you can feel the Devil bite your ass." So he asks for a larger
share. The result is that Blondie keeps all the head-hunting money for himself
and dumps Tuco in the desert seventy miles away from the next settlement.
Blondie finds himself a new partner who "takes the risk." However, this risk
taking will end deadly for the risk taker named Shorty, due to an intervention
by Tuco, who had survived the seventy-mile march through the desert and
came back with a gun in his hand. He stopped Blondie from cutting the rope:
"Sorry Shorty." Then we see Blondie marching in the desert, directed by
Tuco's gun, suffering exhaustion and dehydration almost to the point of death.

There is a natural second-mover advantage of the one who does the cutting in the bounty business as designed by Tuco and Blondie. The value of
this advantage increases with an increase in head-hunting money – and the

risk of getting hanged, and not be cut off, may also increase, while the risk of the second-mover is not directly affected. The analogy with many asymmetric business relationships and labor relations is obvious.

A fair solution could be created by taking turns in risk taking. However, there is no bounty price on Blondie so far and Tuco is perhaps not as competent in cutting the rope. He seems to be a genius with his Colt, measured by the quantity and quality of people he shoots in the course of this movie, but we never see him shooting a rifle, and only a rifle can make the perfect shot that cuts the rope. We can see that the division of labor into a first-mover and second-mover is "hard wired" in this case. A fair solution cannot be implemented by taking turns. Most likely, there is only one round if the cutting job is allocated to Tuco, and Blondie is not likely to submit himself to this division of labor. Moreover, there is still the problem that Blondie has first to earn a bounty on his head before somebody wants to hang him.

Sergio Leone comes back to the sharing issue and the hanging business in the final scene of the movie. We will see this in Chapter 5.

### 3.6.2 The median voter equilibrium

There are decision settings in which turn taking is embedded, at least in the model world. By this means, the first-mover advantage is balanced, fairness is approximated, and stability is assured. The toy model of public choice theory, i.e., the median voter model, shows neither a first-mover nor a second-mover advantage. Voters are assumed to have single-peaked preferences with respect to a one-dimensional political (or ideological) space, say Left to Right. They can be identified by their most preferred political position in this space, as a voter will vote for the political party (or candidate) whose platform represents a political position closest to his or her preferred position. Voters will not abstain: they are not alienated by the size of the distance to the "closest" platform or because the platforms are identical. There are two parties, A and B, free to choose positions of their platforms in this one-dimensional space defined by the voters' preferences, A being the incumbent, B being the opposition. It seems somehow natural that A chooses its platform first, also because of its previous performance. B will choose a best reply. Both parties aim to win the election by a majority of votes. This implies that they will maximize votes by choosing their platforms. A will choose the median voter position for its platform which is characterized by 50 percent of voters to its left and 50 percent of voters to its right. B, maximizing votes, has no other alternative than to choose the median voter position as well.

This position defines the outcome, but does not determine the winner of the election. In general, it is said that there is a 50 percent chance for each party to win. But this presupposes that voters throw a coin or apply an alternative randomizing tool when they face identical platforms. (Note that the model excludes abstentions.) In any case, A and B choosing the median position constitutes a strict Nash equilibrium. If one of the two parties proposes a platform different from the median position, then it will lose the election. However, long before John Nash introduced his solution concept, Harold Hotelling proposed the described median voter result as a byproduct of his "Stability in competition" (Hotelling 1929). He discussed the theoretical result, which he derived from his spatial duopoly model, with respect to the empirical observations which he made with regard to the interplay of Republican and Democrats in the United States:

> The competition for votes between the Republicans and Democratic parties does not lead to a clear drawing of issues, an adoption of two strongly contrasted positions between which the voter may choose. Instead, each party strives to make its platform as much like the others as possible. Any radical departure would lose many votes, even though it might lead to stronger commendation of the party by some who would vote for it anyhow.
>
> (Hotelling 1929: 54)

Hotelling points to elements of obfuscation that allow politicians to keep competition low – which, in practical terms, means "less risk, less work."

Black (1948) presented a proof of the median voter equilibrium and Downs made it popular, however, with "very strange" arguments. If you want to see his arguments, please look at his Figure 1 (Downs 1957: 117) and its interpretation. Downs refers to Hotelling (1929) but not to Black (1948), which is somewhat puzzling as he thanks Kenneth Arrow in the acknowledgment and Arrow referred to Black already in his first edition of *Social Choice and Individual Values* (1951). Since Black (1948) was published in the University of Chicago's *Journal of Political Economy*, his results should have been common knowledge within the group of scholars working on the aggregation of preferences. Perhaps Black was too British to have his work acknowledged on the other side of the Atlantic. And yet, Arrow quoted him. In view of Black (1948) and Hotelling (1929), Downs (1957) is a second-mover, but he ranks as a pioneer of the spatial modeling approach.[14] Indeed, his book opened the discussion to a wider academic audience – somehow just like Procter & Gamble, and not Chux, opened a wider market for disposable diapers. The case of the "Downsian model" nicely illustrates Stigler's law of eponymy: "No scientific discovery is named after its original discoverer" (Stigler 1980: 277). As an example, Stigler referred to Robert K. Merton who, according to Stigler, may claim priority with respect to "Stigler's law." Of course, Stigler's law of eponymy is assisted by the fact that nobody calls it Merton's law.

Given the median voter equilibrium, it does not matter in the two-party case whether A or B selects its platform first, or whether they present their platforms simultaneously. It is a version of the equilibrium of the divide-and-choose model that results from sharing a homogeneous cake between two agents: one cuts the cake, the other chooses. If both are interested in maximizing their share, half-and-half will be the equilibrium outcome. Thus it does

---

14 See, e.g., Merrill III and Grofman (1999: 4). Of course, the two authors know of Duncan Black's work.

not matter who divides and who chooses. There is neither an advantage for a first-mover nor for the second-mover.

This median voter equilibrium is rather robust. Likely this is the reason why it is often used in model building when a two-party system is a close proxy for the relevant political environment. Yet, there are hardly any "pure" two-party systems "in the real world." Unfortunately, there is no equilibrium in pure strategies for the case of three parties when platforms are chosen simultaneously. In the case of sequential choices, there are many constellations possible. For instance, two parties A and B can always choose platforms such that the third party C will not get a majority of votes. Yet, party C will decide whether A or B will get a relative majority. Since none of the parties will get an absolute majority coalition formation might be relevant and the roles of incumbent and opposition have to be redefined.

If there are four parties and there is a unit distribution of votes over the interval of 0 to 100, an equilibrium exists such that two parties choose position 25 and two parties choose 75 (see Selten 1971). In the case of simultaneous choices of platforms, there is a serious coordination problem given by the symmetry of the equilibrium. It does not seem unlikely that three instead of two parties will choose one of the equilibrium positions, and one of the parties might even hope for a coordination failure and choose a position for its platform different from 25 and 75.

In the case of sequential platform choices, it needs additional "efforts" to identify the incumbent party (or parties) and the opposition: "Who is the divider, and who chooses?" There is a second-mover advantage waiting in case there are more than two parties. However, if there are more than two parties, then there is more than a single possible move structure.

### 3.6.3 The pie-slicing model of politics

The equilibria of the spatial model of party competition looks even more bizarre if the number of parties is larger than four. However, the policy space does not always match with a single dimension and corresponding multi-dimensional models propose a high degree of instability (even in the case of two parties, only).[15] More specifically, there is no one-dimensional preference space if the voting is on the distribution of an "income cake" as, e.g., implied by the introduction or revision of a particular tax or the reconstruction of the public transfer system. In fact, in general, we cannot design any spatial model for such a policy issue. If the voting is on sharing a constant sum, any platform that the incumbent presents can be defeated by a platform offered by the opposition in majority voting. (The core of such a voting game is empty.) Obviously, there is a second-mover advantage if winning a majority is the sole objective of the political agents. This is the point of departure of Donald Wittman's pie-slicing

---

15 See Schofield (2008, 2009) and the references given in these two books. Pioneer papers are Plott (1967), Kramer (1973), McKelvey (1976, 1979) and Schofield (1983).

model presented under the label "Parties as utility maximizers" (Wittman 1973). Again, there are two political parties, A and B – party A representing the incumbent and B serving as opposition party. There are three disjointed groups of voters: A° and B° represent the party partisans of parties A and B, respectively, and there is C, a group of voters C who are not affiliated with any political party. We assume that none of these groups represents a majority of votes. This is captured by assigning one vote to each of the three groups. More generally, we assume that there are n groups of voters and n is an odd number. However, we will first look at the case of n = 3.

Parties present platforms that propose the sharing of a fixed cake among the voters. In the version of the model that is presented here – a further simplification of Wittman (1973) – the size of the cake is standardized to 1. Wittman assumes that party A is aware of the fact that it cannot win the election if B selects a majority platform – and such a majority platform always exists for B, irrespective of A's platform. To motivate (and determine) A's decision, it needs an alternative objective: maximizing the share of the cake for its partisans A°. Correspondingly, it is assumed that B will maximize the share of its partisans B°. In general, there are many majority-winning platforms for the opposition party B. The equilibrium under the share-maximization hypothesis will select exactly one of them.

Figure 3.5 gives the optimal strategies of A and B and the shares offered to A°, B° and C. The strategy of B is the winning platform. Thus the vector $(\frac{1}{2} - d + e, \frac{1}{2} + d - e, 0)$ expresses the winning cutting of the pie. The d and e are marginal shares of the cake. Does this vector present the equilibrium and why? Figure 3.5 illustrates the reasoning of A and B that determines this result.

Incumbent A's reasoning behind its optimal strategy listed in Figure 3.5 is:

(1) Do not make any offer to B°, i.e., the partisans of B, since B will make a larger offer to B° unless A offers all of the pie to B°, but this leaves A° without. (Note that if A offers B° all of the pie, then A has a chance that B will let A win the election.)

(2) Offer shares to (n–1)/2 voters that are larger than the offer to A° so that they become more expensive votes to B than the votes of A°, and (n–1)/2 voters (including B°) a share of 0.

B's reasoning is simple: make an offer to (n–1)/2 voters and to its partisan voters B°. This implies an offer "close to zero" for (n–3)/2 voters who were offered nothing by A, and an offer to A° slightly larger than what A offered to A°. The rest of the pie will be earmarked for the B° voters. If we abstract from

| Proposition presented by | Shares offered to | | | |
|---|---|---|---|---|
| | A° | B° | C | Total |
| A | ½ – d | 0 | ½ + d | 1 |
| B | ½ – d + e | ½ + d – e | 0 | 1 |

*Figure 3.5* The pie-slicing equilibrium for n = 3

| Proposition presented by | Shares offered to | | | | |
|---|---|---|---|---|---|
| | A° | B° | C | D | E |
| A | 1/3 – d | 0 | 1/3 + d/2 | 1/3 + d/2 | 0 |
| B | 1/3 – d+e | 2/3 + d–2e | 0 | 0 | e |

*Figure 3.6* The pie-slicing equilibrium for n = 5

the marginal slices d and e, then the shares of A° and B° will be $2/(n+1)$ and $(n-1)/(n+1)$. Obviously, the larger the number of groups of voters, the smaller will be the share received by A° and the larger will be the share gained by B°. Figure 3.6 shows the result for n = 5 groups of voters.

This model tells us that it is in the interest of the incumbent A to keep the diversification in the electorate small. However, this is a very abstract model, especially with respect to creating and satisfying partisan voters. Still, it demonstrates a second-mover advantage growing with n. Yet, it is embedded in the model that parties will take turns in carrying the burden of being a first-mover. Of course, the turn-taking has less drastic consequences and promises more stability for the political system, if the numbers of group of voters are small. In case of n = 3, the outcome is close to equal shares if d and e are marginal, i.e., a distribution which is considered fair whenever there is no (substantial) differentiation and the division problem is "symmetric" (as, e.g., defined in Nash 1950a). For n > 3, the turn-taking will balance the second-mover advantage given in each period if discounting is zero, i.e., if there is no preference for today's shares of the pie compared to future ones. Given an infinite time horizon, A° and B° will enjoy equal sums of benefits. Note that, in general, political systems assume infinite time horizons or "unforeseeable ends."

However, if discounting is substantial, n is relatively large, and there is a "foreseeable end," then today's second-mover advantage of the opposition will not be fully balanced. Another issue is the size of d and e. They should be infinitesimal if voters have complete information and are highly sensitive to income differentials, i.e., to each crumb of the pie. However, if this assumption does not hold, then an information policy that keeps d and e low, is profitable to the parties. Manipulation of information or obfuscation, or both, could help the parties to satisfy this objective. Already Hotelling (1929: 54f.) observed that each candidate of the Democrat and Republican parties "replies ambiguously to questions, refuses to take a definite stand in any controversy for fear of losing votes. Real differences, if they ever exist, fade gradually with time though the issues may be as important as ever." Hotelling's observation is based on the concept of a one-dimensional model of voters' preferences; however, this behavior is also relevant in cases that seem closer to the pie-slicing model world.

### 3.6.4 Condorcet cycles

The pie-slicing issue is a special case of Condorcet's cyclical majority result, i.e., the well-known "Condorcet Paradox," also called "Voting Paradox."[16] If the preferences of the (groups of) voters A, B, and C on the alternatives u, v, and w are ordered as in the matrix of Figure 3.7 and none of the voters represents a majority of votes, then, in a two-party system, the opposition party that is second in choosing an alternative, can always reach a majority, irrespective of which platform the incumbent party selected before. However, if there is a third-mover party, then it can choose a platform that beats the platform of the second-mover, but this platform will be defeated by the platform of the first mover, and so on. No Condorcet winner exists, i.e., no platform that beats any other on pairwise comparison.

For instance, in Figure 3.7, u will be defeated by w, and w will be defeated by v, and v will be defeated by u. Thus we have a majority cycle. The transitivity of the individual preferences does not carry over in social transitivity under the majority rule. Intransitivity of social preferences results. However, it would be misleading to speak of social irrationality as there are different decision-making bodies, i.e., groups of voters that support the various outcomes. Alternative u will be defeated by w by the votes of {B, C}; w will be defeated by v by the votes of {A, C}, and v will be defeated by u by the votes of {A, B}.

This result is quite a challenge to democratic decision making. However, what should we expect from an aggregation of individual preferences if they are as extremely diverse as assumed in Figure 3.7? The majority cycle reflects this diversity, and does not gloss it over: "Where there is no will of the people, there is no will of the people," i.e., no *volonté générale*. (See Chapter VII of Arrow's *Individual Value and Social Choice* (1963 [1951]). However, in real-world voting, we will only see the winning platform (of the opposition), if there are two parties, and no immediate indication of a pell-mell in the individual preferences.

|                   | A | B | C |
|-------------------|---|---|---|
| First preference  | u | w | v |
| Second preference | v | u | w |
| Third preference  | w | v | u |

*Figure 3.7* Condorcet cycle

16 This phenomenon was introduced by (Marquis de) Condorcet in his *Essai sur l'application de l'analyse à la probabilité des décisions rendues à la pluralité des voix* (1795). (The first edition of this book is still available in public libraries.) For the text in English (trans. and ed.), see Condorcet (1989).

With the help of his ranking-wheel model, Saari (1995, 2011) gives general conditions for the existence (and non-existence) of a majority cycle. From this analysis, we conclude that the Voting Paradox illustrated in Figure 3.7 is a rather common phenomenon afflicting the aggregation of individual preference orderings.

The majority cycle and the intransitive social outcome presuppose that the political agents are only interested in winning the majority and thus incumbency, and have no political preferences of their own. The pie-slicing model demonstrates that there could be other alternatives. Some features of this model also apply if we introduce party preferences in the decision situation described by the voter preferences in Figure 3.6 and the majority rule. There is a series of papers that analyze the decision making of parties (or candidates) and voters if the agents that propose platforms have both (a) an interest in winning a majority and (b) preferences on the available alternatives.[17] However, this material has thus far not gained in popularity. As I consider the related questions rather important for the understanding of democratic decision making, a more extensive treatment is added in Section 3.8.1 below. An obvious shortcoming of this analysis is that the underlying model is rather specific, but I hope for a generalization. For the specific model, follows: "it may be stated that being the first to present a program can never be preferred to being the second" (Holler 1982: 41). The second-mover advantage survives, but there are situations, depending on the preference profile,[18] in which it does not matter whether one is a first- or second-mover.

## 3.7 Creative destruction and second-mover advantages

The small selection of second-mover advantages give an indication of how Schumpeter's creative destruction may work. This is not to say that I want to uplift the explanatory power of the second-mover advantage to the level and status that creative destruction asserts in Schumpeter's theory of the business cycle, of capitalism and the replacement of capitalism by socialism. The analysis of the second-mover advantage does not deliver a "general theory," and does not pretend to do so, although it is a very general phenomenon with a substantial impact on the functioning of the society, economy included, irrespective of whether capitalism or socialism is its label. However, I want to argue that some of the theoretical and empirical material that we unearthed by discussing second-mover advantages is a valuable amendment to Schumpeter's

---

17 For a recent publication, see Holler (2010), published in 2012. One root of this model is the Holler-Steunenberg model discussed in McNutt (2009: 282ff.) and applied to European decision making in Holler and Napel (2007) with reference to Holler (1994) and Steunenberg (1994). Another root is Holler (1982). In this paper, I tried to find a way out of the Voting Paradox.

18 A preference profile is a complete listing of the preference orderings of the individual members of a group (or society).

theory. One might well argue that it is not innovation, based on invention or "realization of new combinations," but excess imitation that drives the economy into "destructions" with the potential of creating novelties. Schumpeter (2010 [1942]: 83) specifies: "The fundamental impulse that sets and keeps the capitalist engine in motion comes from the new consumers' goods, the new methods of production or transportation, the new markets, the new forms of industrial organization that capitalist enterprise creates." More specifically, the "new does not simply grow out of the old, but replaces it" (Kurz 2012: 877). Of course, if there is no first-mover, then there is no second-mover, and the evolutionary process does not get started. In many cases, as we have seen above, it is the second-mover who decides on the success of the new product, whether it conquers the market or vegetates in a niche and then, in the end, dies out. The first move might be spontaneous and prevail without assistance of economic reasoning, however, the second move often concurs with textbook economics.

The second-mover story could get support from economic history showing us the very successful development of those economies that were able to imitate and follow that strategy. Germany (in the nineteenth century), Japan, and China are candidates for such studies. Of course, Schumpeter (1983 [1934]: 64) is right in his observation: "Add successively as many mail coaches as you please, you will never get a railway hereby." The Stockton and Darlington Railway (S&DR) was the world's first public railway to use steam locomotives. It opened its operation on September 27, 1825; its gauge of 1435 mm became a "world standard," though not always applied. Soon there were competitors like the York, Newcastle and Berwick Railway threatening to take over S&DR, and there were companies taken over by S&DR. In 1863, S&DR was acquired by the North Eastern Railway but continued to operate as the Darlington section for more than another decade. The network expanded by "merger and acquisition" – and by imitation. Schumpeter is right in his observation that adding mail coaches will never make a railway. But a locomotive and some coaches are not sufficient to get a railway (network) either.

### 3.7.1 Schumpeter's entrepreneur and the need to innovate

In *Capitalism, Socialism and Democracy*, Schumpeter (2010 [1942]) hypothesizes that capitalism will come to an end because of its success and will finally transfer into a sustainable socialism. Major driving forces behind this process are creative destruction and entrepreneurship. Innovations, i.e., the bringing to the market of inventions and the implementation of new combinations, are the ingredients, and the Schumpeterian entrepreneur is the executor. Schumpeter already elaborated this dynamic scenario in his *Theorie der wirtschaftlichen Entwicklung* (*Theory of Economic Development*) of 1912. I have neither the competence to contribute to the discussion of this oeuvre – I strictly rely on the presentation (and translation) in Kurz (2012) – nor does it seem that such a discussion is indispensable when confronting the general reading and interpretation of

Schumpeter's "creative destruction" with the results of the second-mover perspective. I simply behave like a second-mover challenging some of the implications of Schumpeter's theory – and propose some destructions. Yet, not all destructions are creative.

Schumpeter's entrepreneur is a "somewhat" heroic character, not a profit-maximizing bookkeeper, not an owner of wealth waiting for getting invested, but he is looking for power, success, and reputation. He feels the need to innovate. There is the spirit for the new. When, in 1858, Abraham Lincoln toured the US, he gave a talk on "Discoveries and Inventions" to the Young Men's Association at Bloomington, Illinois. He exclaimed that the country had "a great passion – a perfect rage – for the new."[19] Schumpeter saw some of this passion when, in 1932, he arrived in America and settled there for the rest of his life. According to Kurz, already in his *Theorie der wirtschaftlichen Entwicklung* of 1912, Schumpeter emphasized:

> that what we may call the 'entrepreneurial gene' is present in many people, to a smaller or larger degree, and as the economic system develops and innovations become a permanent part of the economic process and obstacles to them dwindle, entrepreneurship becomes ever more widespread in society.
>
> (Kurz 2012: 882)

To some extent, this seems to contradict his hypothesis that capitalism will mutate into socialism. But this hypothesis applies to the long run, whatever the long run is, and hinges on Schumpeter's rather specific definition of capitalism as we will see.

Where does the type of entrepreneur, suggested by Schumpeter, come from? It seems that some of these agents jumped out of Veblen's panopticon that populates his *Theory of the Leisure Class*. Veblen (1899: 233) observes that the

> employment of the leisure classes in modern industry are such to keep alive certain predatory habits and aptitudes. So far as the members of those classes take part in the industrial process, their training tends to conserve in them the barbarian temperament.
>
> (Veblen 1899: 233)

The robber-barons and Keynesian "animal spirit"[20] reflect this "barbarian temperament" that characterizes Schumpeter's entrepreneur. In fact, Schumpeter's entrepreneur seems to be a close relative to Machiavelli's *Il Principe*, looking

---

19 For reference and quote, see Phelps (2016: 6).
20 In his *General Theory*, Keynes (1936: 161) refers to the "animal spirit" as a rather civilized feature of entrepreneurial decision making, but still it implies "a spontaneous urge to action rather than inaction, and not as the outcome of a weighted average of quantitative benefits multiplied by quantitative probabilities."

for success, dominance, and, in the end, for glory, relying on the helping hand of *Fortuna* in a world of risk and uncertainty.[21] Like the Prince, Schumpeter's entrepreneur destroys in order to create something perhaps more successful. However, Schumpeter's entrepreneur is less heroic, indeed "industrial and commercial activity is essentially unheroic in Knight's sense" (Schumpeter 2010 [1942]: 113);[22] he is part of an evolutionary process "that increasingly revolutionizes the economic structure from within, incessantly destroying the old one, incessantly creating a new one. This process of Creative Destruction is the essential fact to capitalism" (Schumpeter 2010 [1942]:73).[23] Therefore, when capitalism is successful and succeeds to protect itself against destruction (and innovation), capitalism dissolves itself and Schumpeter's entrepreneurs will die out. As Schumpeter identifies "stability" with "lasting," his discussion in "The Instability of Capitalism" (Schumpeter 1928) is about the end of capitalism. In a stationary state, "capitalism, being essentially an evolutionary process, would become atrophic" (Schumpeter 2010 [1942]: 116). "The true pacemakers of socialism were not the intellectuals or agitators who preached it but the Vanderbilts, Carnegies and Rockefellers" (Schumpeter 2010 [1942]: 119). It is the success of capitalism which undermines the social institutions which supported and protected it. But note Schumpeter "wishes to confine the words 'capital' and 'capitalism' exclusively to situations in which new combinations are carried out by means of credit provided to innovators by banks" (Kurz 2012: 885). This is quite an unorthodox exercise and invites some confusion.

I do not want to add to this confusion but do point out that the entrepreneur might be heroic in Schumpeter's sense, daringly ignoring uncertainty and risk when following his calling, but there are the banks that will check the expected profitability of the various projects. They will give the credit to those projects that promise profits. This is where the profit-maximizing target sneaks into Schumpeter's innovation process. Creativity and destruction might not be convincing enough to induce a bank to give the necessary credit.

In a non-Schumpeterian world, entrepreneurs may own money to invest and finance their innovation. These entrepreneurs, however, care about earning

---

21  There is a long list of publications and a substantial industry applying Machiavelli to the business world. In general, the work of Machiavelli is cut down to the hundred pages of *The Prince*, and quite often it serves an image which was introduced by Shakespeare as Machiavellian – then it was meant to be negative, today it is rubber-stamped by its perspective of success in management and business.

22  Keynes's entrepreneur is perhaps even less heroic, but still very effective to the performance of the economy: "if the animal spirits are dimmed and the spontaneous optimism falters, leaving us to depend on nothing but a mathematical expectation, enterprise will fade and die; – though fears of loss may have a basis no more reasonable than hopes of profit had before" (Keynes (1936: 162). "Even apart from the instability due to speculation, there is the instability due to the characteristic of human nature that a large proportion of our positive activities depend on spontaneous optimism rather than mathematical expectations, whether moral or hedonistic or economic" (Keynes (1936: 161).

23  For the evolutionary aspect of creative destruction, see Metcalfe (1998).

profits in general. They hate the idea of their wealth melting down. We have argued above that if there is a second-mover advantage, they are likely not to invest – and inventions will never mutate into innovations if there is no heroic first-mover or a public investor who does not have to be afraid of losses, i.e., costly investments that do not earn money. However, is the Defense Advanced Research Projects Agency (DARPA), which prepared the ground for the development of the personal computer, an innovator and Apple and IBM are just imitators, or is the bringing to the market, successfully exercised by Apple and IBM, the innovation and DARPA is responsible for the invention only? One may give Apple and IBM the credit for innovation. But how is it with Apple making use of technologies in each new generation of iPods, iPhones and iPads that the State developed and made available? (See Section 3.4 above). To repeat Mazzucato's quote: "there is not a single key technology behind the iPhone that has not been State-funded" (Mazzucato (2014: 11). Where is the creativity located? What is destroyed by whom? Indeed, Apple's mastership is the implementation of new combinations. Again, we can give Apple the credit of innovation – simply because the State agencies did not bring their novelties to the market. But the identification of invention, innovation, and imitation might not always be so simple and often it is the imitation of a novelty that is destructive, and not the innovation.

### 3.7.2 Creative innovators and destruction by imitation

Can we identify Schumpeter's entrepreneur with the first-mover? In Tellis and Golder's study (1996), first-movers introduced novelties to the market, but many of them failed inasmuch as second-movers entered the market and became the dominant player. When, in 1975, MITS (Micro Instrumentation and Telemetry Systems) offered the first personal computer, it did not destroy the dominance of mainframe computers and drive their suppliers out of the market. It was only later, when Apple and IBM entered the market of personal computers, ousting MITS, that the balance shifted and Microsoft and Intel conquered the computer market. This example demonstrates that novelties, i.e. creativity, do not necessarily lead to destruction. Large-scale imitation caused the destruction. Creativity and destruction do not always come as a package.

Of course, Schumpeter was aware of the power of imitation. One of its consequences is that "the profits of the entrepreneur and also his entrepreneurial function as such perish in the whirlpool of the competitors that are at his heels" (Schumpeter 1983 [1934; in German 1912]: 286). But our discussion shows that a second-mover advantage is a rather common phenomenon. Of course, one might argue that Apple and IBM represented "combinations" quite different from MITS. But the ideas behind the product were very similar, not to say, the same – yet the marketing strategies differed quite substantially, and also between Apple's and IBM's strategies.

Is there enough novelty in Apply and IBM to call them innovators instead of imitators? If so, then we have two cases in which there is destruction without creativity. The discussion of entry in a nonsustainable natural monopoly and raisin picking – see Section 3.5.2 above – could show us the way to look for digging out such cases. What did UPS contribute to the distribution of parcels when it took over this branch of service from the public postal services, as happened in Germany? From the consumer's point of view, the difference is hardly noticeable. The postal worker still brings letters and smaller parcels to the door. The consumer cannot see that the postal worker's position is no longer a tenured one, and is perhaps based only on a half-year agreement (and relatively lower payment). The consumer might wonder why an increasing number of letters end up at the wrong address, but will only notice this if their address invites such mistakes and the corresponding letters are numerous. The latter is not very likely in a world of e-mails and iPods.

For many private consumers, mailing and receiving parcels became more complicated (and confusing), additionally because the public postal service closed down many branch offices as business slowed, or because of restructuring. The situation became even more confusing when the public postal service created its own subsidiary, the DHL, to compete with UPS, and the core of the postal service mutated into the "Postbank," emphasizing the service's banking business. One result of this is that if you want to buy stamps in one of the fewer branch offices of the Postbank you might be disappointed by the small selection it offers, and frustrated if they do not even have the stamp values they charge, e.g., for international mail, even by adding up smaller values. The postal clerk behind the counter will point to the "slot machine for stamps" fixed to the wall outside the building – and comment that the Postbank is now a bank, and no longer a post office. The stamp dispenser is, of course, a rather cumbersome alternative, for, e.g., a small publishing company which might have nearly a hundred mailings per month. To sum up, the arrangement we find today is certainly inefficient, should subadditivity of costs apply. For at least some ranges, this is quite likely because of network effects. Of course, one might argue that previously the public postal services, which included some banking business, was inefficient and subadditivity of costs did not apply. We do not know this. What we *do* know is that the postal service was not sustainable as a monopoly, when the government destroyed the barriers to entry and opened up the market for competitors – inviting raisin picking. Today, the market looks completely different from what it was twenty years ago. The "all-embracing" public postal service no longer exists: there was destruction but the results of creativity are hard to trace.

The model in Section 3.5.2 is in the back of my mind when I look at what happened to the public postal services in Germany and many other European countries. It demonstrates that one can expect a breakdown of the market equilibrium when the market's growth invites an imitating entry. Whether this breakdown leads to the exit of the incumbent or to price differentiation and rationing cannot be said without considering further details of the market. Shall we relate this breakdown of market equilibrium to destruction? If so, then there is no creativity involved. Note that market entry leads to inefficiency because a subadditive cost structure is assumed in this model world.

Monopolies like to argue with subadditivity of costs when they ask the regulator to protect them from entry in order to assure efficiency. Clearly, not all monopolies have subadditive costs, and monopolies tend to lose this valuable property, if they had it before, once they are protected by the regulators erecting barriers to entry for competitors – and, on the macro level, the economy may experience a slowdown of innovation, as Edmund Phelps argues in his note "What is wrong with the West's economies?" (2016).[24] He observes that "taking concrete actions" against this slowdown and loss of dynamism "will not help much without fresh thinking: people must first grasp that standard economics is not a guide to flourishing – it is a tool only for efficiency" (Phelps 2016: 10). By flourishing, he understands the experience of a "good life" involving "using one's imagination, exercising one's creativity, taking fascinating journeys into the unknown" (Phelps (2016: 5). The above model discusses efficiency, and says nothing about "good life,"[25] and yet it demonstrates that there can be destruction through imitation instead of by innovation. If so, there will be disequilibrium, but not necessarily growth and "flourishing."

The threat of such a scenario can lead to a "non-start," although there is creativity waiting. Are we on the way to socialism if the State acts as first-mover, inventor, and perhaps innovator in such a case? Obviously, this is no longer Schumpeter's capitalism – but Schumpeter's capitalism is a rather narrowly defined world. For example, it seems that the heroic Schumpeterian entrepreneur has been successfully substituted with the hedge fund manager, at least when we consider the financial success stories. To some extent, hedge funds have taken over the controlling function from the banking system, as proposed in the Schumpeterian world. However, hedge funds do not give credits.

The following section is meant to illustrate this epochal change. But note this is only a draft and not the result of extensive reading and a careful check of data and discussion. If no other references are given, then this is what you find on the Internet.

### 3.7.3 The hedge fund managers' second move

It is easy to model, and I conjecture there is some truth to it that the enormous income shares gained by hedge fund managers over the last decade is due to their second-mover advantage. Starr refers to an analysis by Kaplan and Rauh (2013) which shows that "the average pay (in 2010 dollars) for the twenty-five highest-paid hedge fund managers climbed from $134 million in 2002 to an

---

24 Phelps's note has been republished, together with eight comments, in *Homo Oeconomicus* 33(1/2), 2016 from *The New York Review of Books* with the permission of the author. Another set of eight comments on Phelps's note has been published in *Homo Oeconomicus* 33(4), 2016.

25 For a recent publication on "Humor and the good life in modern philosophy," see Lydia Amir (2014). The issue is discussed with respect to Shaftesbury, Hamann, and Kierkegaard. This is what philosophers call "modern."

astonishing $537 million in 2012" (Starr 2014: 33). Given this size, I wonder whether "climbing" is the right word. Note these are *averages*. David Tepper, founder of hedge fund firm Appaloosa Management, made $2.2 billion, to top the 2012 list. "In every year since 2004, those twenty-five hedge fund managers alone have received more income than all of the chief executive officers of Standard and Poor's 500 companies combined – and, of course, those CEOs haven't been doing badly" (Starr 2014: 33). However, in a way, these CEOs and their companies only delivered the material that the hedge fund managers needed to gamble with.

Typically, hedge fund managers earn an annual management fee, based on the assets of the fund, and a performance fee as a percentage of the increase in the fund's net asset value, i.e., the value of an entity's assets less the value of its liabilities, during the year. Some hedge funds manage several billion dollars of assets, and a 1 percent management fee seems not exceptional. Does this explain the large payments to the hedge fund managers?

It seems that there are neither third-movers nor market conditions that constrain hedge fund managers' earnings. In addition, "the marginal rate on the top federal income tax bracket, which was 70 percent during the 1970s, has been reduced below 40 percent" (Starr 2014: 33). This seems to explain why rich people become richer and richer, but it does not explain the differences in remuneration between the CEOs and the top-earning hedge fund managers.[26] Of course, there is competition among hedge fund managers to capture the most profitable arrangements, but none are interested in "price competition" that lowers income. Moreover, low demands are likely to signal low expectations with respect to the success of a particular fund.

I do not want to describe the business of hedge funds here. The general view is that it is a very risky one, and textbook descriptions suggest that it is complicated and, measured by the textbook's fuzzy explanations and incomprehensible language, its rules and tools should be kept a secret. It is therefore not surprising that hedge funds cannot be offered or sold to the general public. By restricting its cliental to "assorted investors," hedge funds avoid direct control and licensing requirements that other investment companies must accept – and thereby gain flexibility. The emergence and success of the hedge fund business, however, is generally attributed to the revolutionary new information and communication technologies that generated global markets. In this way, they are, like Apple and Google, second-movers that benefit from public investments in the development, extension, and upgrading of the Internet and related technologies. In his *Economics of Superstars*, Rosen already hypothesized that

---

26 As pointed out by Kaplan and Rauh (2013: 40), in 2010, the twenty-five highest-paid hedge fund managers combined earned roughly four times as much as the CEOs of Standard and Poor's 500 firms.

secular changes in communications and transportation have expanded the potential market for all kinds of professional and information services, and allowed many of the top practitioners to operate at a national or even inter-national scale. With elastic demands there is a tendency for increasing concentration of income at the top as well as greater rents for all sellers as these changes proceed over time.

(Rosen 1981: 856)

Of course, the CEOs of Standard and Poor's 500 firms also make use of new information and communication technologies and global markets, but their actions and reactions are constrained by the rules of the business in which they perform (and by the markets in which they do business). These rules are more or less binding, depending on the branch of business. The rules of the hedge fund business are, however, most flexible. Without the tight constraints of legal regulations that govern the stock market, and free from the chains of contracts and laws that restrict the CEOs of Standard and Poor's 500 firms in their policies, hedge funds managers can literally react at the speed of light. As their business is based on the changes of values (of the net assets), they can even accrue large earnings when the economy suffers from a crisis and firms go bankrupt. This suggests that there is a second-mover advantage. We know too little of the "secret details" of the hedge fund business, but it is difficult to explain average earnings of \$537 million per year by means of Rosen's superstar theory.

The background of the hedge fund scenario is a substantial increase in the top 1 percent's income share over the last twenty-five years as observed in the English-speaking countries United Kingdom, Canada, and, most prominently, the United States.[27] Piketty and Saez (2006: 204) emphasize that the "rise of top income shares is due not to the revival of top capital incomes," that characterized the pre-World War II period, "but rather to the very large increases in top wages (especially top executive compensation)." They discuss three groups of arguments that are brought forward to explain why top wages have surged in English-speaking countries, but not in continental Europe or Japan. The first group of arguments refers to technological progress, but other countries such as Japan and France "have gone to similar technological changes." The second group of arguments focuses on the "impediments to free markets due to labor market regulations, unions, or social norms regarding pay inequality," which "have been largely removed in the United States, but still exist in Europe and Japan." The third group of arguments points "to the increased

---

27 "Over the period 1980 to 2007, when the top 1 percent share rose by some 135 percent in the United States and the United Kingdom, it rose by some 105 percent in Australia and 76 percent in Canada ... The experience is markedly different in continental Europe and Japan, where the long pattern of income inequality is much closer to an L-shaped than a U-shaped curve ... There has been some rise in recent years in the top shares in these countries, but the top 1 percent shares are not far today from their levels in the late 1940s, whereas in the United States the share of the top 1 percent is higher by more than a half" (Alvaredo et al. 2013: 5).

ability of executives to set their own pay and extract rents at the expense of shareholders." It seems that there is another second-mover advantage embedded in this result. In this case, the CEOs of Standard and Poor's 500 firms are likely to profit from it. Shareholders are quite aware of it, however, because of ongoing low interest rates and a lack of profitable alternatives, they do not leave the stock market in larger numbers. Low interest rates of course also fuel (financial) investments, and augmented capital justifies larger remuneration of both the CEOs of Standard and Poor's 500 firms and David Tepper and his hedge-fund colleagues.

### 3.7.4 What is wrong with the West's economies?

A possible answer to Edmund Phelps' question "What is wrong with the West's economies?" (Phelps 2016) could be found in what we just discussed: the fact that an industry which is built on pure competition and speculation, without a key to innovations that enhance productivity, pays maximum income – "wages" that are ten times or even hundred times higher than the income of the CEOs of leading manufacturing companies. For Phelps, an uneven income distribution which grows more uneven every year is not the only problem: People

> need an economy that is good as well as just. And for some decades, the Western economies have fallen short of any conception of a 'good economy' – an economy offering a 'good life' . . . The good life . . . typically involves acquiring mastery in one's work, thus gaining oneself better terms – or means to rewards, whether material, like wealth, or nonmaterial – an experience we may call 'prospering'.
>
> (Phelps 2016: 5)

Phelps points out that the slowdowns in productivity and the globalization "that have spread over the West" during the last four decades, dragging down "both employment and wage rates at the low end . . . has cost the less advantaged not only loss of income but also a loss of . . . *inclusion* – access to jobs offering work and pay that provide self-respect" (original emphasis). The loss of inclusion is multiplied by the fact that, different from what was in the past, the children of those who suffer from it "have virtually no chance of climbing to a higher rung in the socioeconomic ladder" (Phelps 2016: 4). The "good life" can be the result of innovations and it can trigger inventions and innovations. According to Phelps, this is what the West experienced in the nineteenth century. However, a large share of the population, e.g., in Germany, were unskilled and day laborers. There was no inclusion and straightforward discrimination, e.g., of the Jews. But there was also a substantial share of skilled craftsmen and technicians who loved their job and looked for inventions and implemented innovations. Productivity increased substantially. However, in the second half of the twentieth century, this dynamism was lost, with much of the "good life" gone and a remarkable narrowing of innovation. Phelps (2016: 9) offers two classes of explanations that "have the ring of truth": (a) vested interests and (b) the repression of potential innovators by families and schools. The argument in (b) is somewhat surprising but indeed, schools do not prepare children for adventures and parents try to prevent their children from taking risks. It seems that John Dewey's vision of "education by experience" is no longer popular. If we subscribe to Phelps's idea, then we are back to the "traditional scheme" which "is, in essence, one of imposition from above and from outside. It imposes adult standards, subject-matter, and methods upon those who are only growing slowly toward maturity" (Dewey 1979 [1938]: 18f.). This teaching does not produce Schumpeterian entrepreneurs, but agents who are afraid of challenging second-movers.

In order to illustrate the retarding effect of the vested interest, Phelps submits an interesting illustration:

> Invoking the corporatist notion of solidarity, companies hurt by innovators – as GM was hurt by BMW and Toyota – have been able to obtain federal government bailouts to help them regain positions. As a result, fleeting innovators – BMW and Toyota in my example – often lose money in their attempts. So would-be innovators will think twice before trying again to innovate in America's automobile market.
>
> (Phelps 2016: 9)

This quote takes up issues that we discussed above. The threat of a bailout can be interpreted as a possible second move, i.e., a possible reaction on the entry of innovator. Expecting this second move and the advantage to the second-mover, there will be no first-mover, i.e., no entry of an innovator. As a result, the incumbents do not have to worry about the entry of innovators. The vested interest is protected by a second-mover advantage that refers to a first move that will not happen.

The inertia and prevalence of vested interest is just a specific outcome related to the problem embedded in second-mover advantages. Can we generalize Phelps's answer to the question about the causes of narrowing innovation by pointing to the second-mover advantages that block first moves? If such situations are numerous and substantial, we cannot expect increases of productivity and economic growth, but instead stagnation. And how does economics deal with this? According to Phelps, it

> makes no room for economies in which people are imagining new products and using their creativity to build them. What is most fundamentally 'wrong with economics' is that it takes such an economy to be the norm – to be 'as good as it gets'.
>
> (Phelps 2016: 7)

These are harsh words, especially because Phelps himself is a brilliant representative of mainstream economics, whose work was distinguished with a Nobel Prize. Many economists would not subscribe to them. But even in the development of economics, there are second-mover advantages and innovations have great difficulties gaining acceptance. Imitations peppered with incremental variations are more promising for lighting up a career.

## 3.8 Strategic secrets, hiding, and the second–mover advantage

One of the advantages of being a second-mover is the information he or she deduces from the success of the first-mover. A second-mover can identify the choices of the first-mover and the reaction of the environment, e.g., the impact on market demand, and then decide whether to compete or copy the first-mover, and in what way or to what extent. In Sections 3.3 and 3.5, we have listed several examples that show this pattern. Some of them demonstrate an obvious disadvantage for the first-mover. It has been argued that there will be no first-movers if second-mover advantages are prominent, i.e., substantial, evident, and easy to cash in. However, first-movers might have means (a) to prevent a second-mover from cheaply copying and (b) to obfuscate facts that reflect the reaction of the environment. For instance, a first-mover may keep secret sales figures and the effects of marketing campaigns. Or, they may either seek patents for their products or production processes, or maintain secrecy of the recipes of their products, or try to follow both paths. If successful, secrecy and obfuscation become the engine that overcomes the second-mover advantage and innovations can prevail. There will be a product on the market, although a second-mover advantage hangs like a sword of Damocles over the first-mover that supplies it to the market.

A substantial amount of literature discusses the alternatives of seeking a patent or of creating a secret to avoid exploitation of an invention (and possible innovation) by a second-mover imitation.[28] Kultti and co-authors (2007) analyze a situation of simultaneous innovation with, more or less, the same innovation independently emerging at the same time. History shows that this is not unlikely, as earlier innovations pave the path of future innovations. The concomitant standardization and fixed installations (and network inertias) reduce variety and thereby the range of expectations. In this context, the main function of patents is to spread information and to block second-mover advantages. Yet this is costly. There are the direct costs implied in the patenting procedure. Perhaps more importantly, however, valuable information must be disclosed. In principle, patent applications contain sufficient information so that competitors can reproduce the particular product. Secrecy seems to be cheaper and, most likely, more efficient to assure a first-mover advantage, if the probability that a competitor comes up with the same innovation and patents is sufficiently small. If not,

---

28  See, e.g., Arundel (2001), Cohen et al. (2000), Gallini (2002), and Kultti et al. (2006a, 2007).

it pays to apply for the patent even if it confers only weak protection because, otherwise, someone else gets it, and the innovator risks infringement if she tries to capitalize her innovation . . . In other words, when innovators contemplate patenting, the typical choice is not between patenting or keeping the innovation secret but between patenting or letting the competitors patent.

(Kultti et al. 2007: 23)

There is, however, still another problem with the secrecy policy which may support patenting. Once the product is on the market, and thus has left the *hortus* of secrecy, it could be analyzed by a second-mover in order to reveal its innovative part and to make use of it for a similar product. Of course, there might be a substantial time lag involved, depending on the product and, most likely, its complexity. A possible hypothesis is that the more complex a product is and the more difficult it is to distill the innovative part from it and to use it for a competitive product, the more successful a secrecy policy of the innovator could be. Another aspect that could matter is whether the innovation relies on upstream products that are difficult to purchase. Modeling such properties and relationships would of course need further sophistication. But not to consider such aspects means that we tell only half the story. Consequently, an innovation policy based on secrecy only could look more favorable compared to patenting as it really is. It definitely depends on the product.

Another feature that favors patenting is that, in most cases, it is easier to exchange patents than secrets. *The Good, the Bad, and the Ugly* contains many examples that demonstrate the difficulties in exchanging secrets. We will discuss a selection of them in Chapter 4. The exchange of patents often takes the form of cross-licensing, which invites collusive behavior as it typically can be found between similar firms with similar products (Kultti et al. 2006b).

So far we have not considered welfare aspects. Is it better for society if innovations are protected by secrecy or patents, or both? Again, the answer is likely to depend on the kind of innovation we're considering and on the transaction costs of secrecy policy and patenting, respectively, related to it. Not all innovations are socially beneficial either. Moreover, creating and keeping secrets is not an easy affair, and often bound to fail, as we will see in Chapter 4. In addition, it can be very costly. Nevertheless, the creation of secrets, directed to resist potential second-mover advantages, is a major social and economic activity. It is also a prominent component in crime and war. Cryptography and the games of coding and decoding are the most obvious realization if the activities of the first-movers necessitate communication. This is almost always the case if they are the result of social decisions and actions as in modern production, on the one hand, and the interaction with the clients, subcontractors and third-party services provider, on the other. Increasing division of labor and globalization tend to intensify the need for communication – and the demand for strategic secrets. Cryptography is a lively business. Its focus is on information security, i.e., data confidentiality, data integrity, authentication, and non-repudiation. The Zimmermann Telegram, discussed below, illustrates a historical case of cracking a code and its strategic consequences. Both were of eminent importance, if not decisive, for the victory of the Allies in World War I.

### 3.8.1 The Inspection Game

Randomization is a particular form of the shaping of strategic secrets. If the first-mover introduces a random decision mechanism – and thus does not know the outcome – the second-mover cannot have the information either and thus does not profit from the advantage that, in principle, the sequential structure implies. This can be illustrated, e.g., by an *Inspection Game* if played sequentially. Figure 3.8 represents a possible payoff matrix of such a game if we assume that

(IG) $a > b$, $a > c$, $d > b$, $d > c$ and $\alpha < \beta$, $\alpha < \gamma$, $\delta < \beta$, $\delta < \gamma$.

The payoffs in (IG) are assumed von Neumann-Morgenstern utilities. Therefore they are unique "up to an order-preserving linear transformation."[29] Any transformation of the type $v_i = ru_i + t$ with $r > 0$ and $u_i$ and $v_i$ representing von Neumann-Morgenstern utilities of player i (i = 1, 2), will leave the game in Figure 3.8 "unchanged."

Note that Figure 3.8 still represents an Inspection Game if we substitute ">" with "<" and "<" with ">" in (IG). These conditions guarantee that both Nash equilibrium and maximin solution imply mixed strategies if decisions are simultaneous. In fact, for an Inspection Game it suffices to assume $a > c$, $d > b$, $\alpha < \beta$, and $\delta < \gamma$. These inequalities are covered by (IG); they do however not guarantee that the maximin solution is in mixed strategies.

| Inspector (player 1) \ Polluter (player 2) | Pollute $s_{21}$, q | Not pollute $s_{22}$, 1 − q |
|---|---|---|
| Enforce $s_{11}$, p | (a,α) | (b,β) |
| Not enforce $s_{12}$, 1 − p | (c,γ) | (d,δ) |

*Figure 3.8* Inspection Game – if IG holds for the payoffs

29 Mathematicians call this transformation isotone. Note that a von Neumann-Morgenstern utility function satisfies the expected utility hypothesis: individual i's utility of a lottery (A, p; B, 1 − p) thus equals $pu_i(A) + (1 − p)u_i(B)$, where $u_i(A)$ and $u_i(B)$ are i's utility values of the "sure outcomes" A and B, and p is the probability of A. Payoffs are von Neumann-Morgenstern utilities; therefore there are no qualifying differences between expected utility and the utility values of sure outcomes.

Because of the rather general condition (IG) it should be clear that, in what follows, we speak of a large class of games, and not of a more or less unique case. For instance, there are no constraints with respect to the size of a in relation to d or of $\alpha$ in relation to $\delta$. This implies that there is no specific relation between c and b and between $\gamma$ and $\beta$.

A possible story could be: there is an inspector in a nature resort who has the choice to patrol the forest with the possibility to catch a polluter and bring him to the court for punishment, i.e., to "enforce." If there is no polluter to catch, then "enforce" boils down to controlling. The second choice of the inspector is the strategy "not enforce," i.e., to stay in his lodge and watch TV. However, he could also randomize and choose "enforce" with a probability p and "not enforce" with probability $1 - p$. In this case, what we, and perhaps the polluters, will observe is a relative frequency of "enforce" that approaches p. Similarly, the polluter has the choice between "pollute" and "not pollute" and a randomization over these two pure strategies captured by the probability q for selecting "pollute." Note we will call player 2 polluter not by the fact that he or she pollutes but because of his potential to choose "pollute." This inclination makes a polluter.

An alternative story is "fare evasion," on the one hand, and "ticket checking" on the other, in which the fare dodger slips into the role of player 2, the polluter. I introduce this story because it seems to have practical relevance for the City of Munich, Germany, and its enforcement policy. I will come back to this. Other examples are tax evaders and their interaction with the tax inspector – see Frey and Holler (1997, 1998) for "tax compliance policies" in Inspection Games – or principal–agent settings in labor relations. Labor contracts are "incomplete" because not all details are foreseeable that the employee has to cope with. "Controlling" and "enforcing" is implied in the hierarchical structure that characterizes firms in contrast to plain contractual arrangements. (See Williamson's seminal study, *Markets and Hierarchies* (1975).)

In what follows, I will refer to the polluter story, but also speak in more general terms of the transgressor or the violator facing the inspector. To speak of an inspectee would be even more general, and in any case, more neutral, of course. What is a transgressor who gets inspected, but did not transgress – and a violator who did not violate?

### 3.8.2 Mixed-strategy equilibrium and maximin solution

Obviously, the game in Figure 3.8 has no Nash equilibrium in pure strategies: there is no pair of pure strategies such that no player can achieve higher payoffs by choosing an alternative strategy, given the strategy of the other player. For instance, take the pair $(s_{11}, s_{22})$. Then player 1 can "improve" by choosing $s_{12}$ instead of $s_{11}$, given $s_{22}$. Since the game is finite, i.e., has a finite number of pure strategies, we know because of Nash's proof (Nash 1950b, 1951) that there has to be at least an equilibrium in mixed strategies.

Already Aumann and Maschler (1972) analyzed this equilibrium.[30] They pointed to the fact that

a)  the payoffs of the players in the (mixed-strategy) Nash equilibrium (p\*, q\*) and in the (mixed-strategy) maximin solution (p°, q°) are identical, and
b)  the "behavior" prescribed by the underlying strategies are, in general, different. They also pointed to the particularity that
c)  the Nash equilibrium strategy of player 1 is exclusively determined by the payoffs of the other player, i.e., player 2, and vice versa.

As a consequence of (c), if player 1's payoffs increase or decrease, this has no impact on the decision of 1, but on the decision of player 2, as long as the conditions in (IG) hold. In fact, for this peculiarity it suffices that one of the weaker conditions $a > c$, $d > b$, $\alpha < \beta$, and $\delta < \gamma$ or $a < c$, $d < b$, $\alpha > \beta$, and $\delta > \gamma$ is satisfied for the bi-matrix in Figure 3.8. The same applies to player 2 given player 1 chooses p\*.

It seems that Aumann and Maschler (1972) were somewhat irritated by this result and proposed choosing the maximin strategy for the case that Nash equilibrium and maximin solution are both mixed. Their proposition was based on plausibility. This plausibility argument was repeated by Harsanyi (1977: 125) and Aumann (1985). On the one hand, playing the mixed maximin strategy p° guarantees the same payoff value which 1 will achieve if player 2 chooses the mixed Nash equilibrium strategy q\*. On the other hand, if player 1 chooses his mixed Nash equilibrium strategy p\*, 1 determines the payoff of player 2, but not his or her own. So why should players 1 and 2 choose their Nash equilibrium strategy at all?

Moreover, technically speaking, (p\*,q\*) is a weak Nash equilibrium and deviating does not hurt, given the equilibrium strategy of the other player. The probability p\* guarantees that player 2 is indifferent between his first and his second strategy, and all randomizations (i.e., linear combinations) between the two, while q\* assures that player 1 is indifferent between his first and second strategy, and all randomizations between the two.[31]

Here are the values of the mixed-strategy equilibrium (p\*,q\*) of the Inspection Game in Figure 3.8:

---

30  However, their results did not become common knowledge. There is a series of more recent publications discussing the Inspection Game – without reference to these results. See, e.g., Wittman (1985, 1993); Holler (1986a, 1986b, 1990, 1993), Tsebelis (1990), and Andreozzi (2002a, 2002b, 2004).

31  For calculating p\* and q\*, see, e.g., Aumann and Maschler (1972), Tsebelis (1990), Holler (1993), Cheng and Zhu (1995), and Andreozzi (2002a).

$$p^* = \frac{\delta - \gamma}{\alpha - \beta - \gamma + \delta}$$

$$q^* = \frac{d - b}{a - b - c + d}$$

Here are the corresponding values of the maximin solution $(p^\circ, q^\circ)$ of the Inspection Game in Figure 3.8:

$$p^\circ = \frac{d - c}{a - b - c + d}$$

$$q^\circ = \frac{\delta - \beta}{\alpha - \beta - \gamma + \delta}$$

Obviously, the strategy pairs $(p^*, q^*)$ and $(p^\circ, q^\circ)$ describe different behavior for the players unless there is some symmetry in the payoffs. They are identical for the case of zero-sum games first analyzed in depth in von Neumann (1959 [1928]). Since von Neumann and Morgenstern's *Theory of Games and Economic Behavior* (1944) also focuses on zero-sum games, there was no "need" for the Nash equilibrium in the early days of game theory. However, the Inspection Game, as presented here, is not of the zero-sum type.[32] Yet, it is strictly competitive: (IG) implies that what is good for player 1 is bad for player 2, and vice versa. As reminiscence of this property, the payoffs of Nash equilibrium and maximin solution are the same for each player, i.e.,

$$u_1(p, q^*) = \frac{ad - bc}{a - b - c + d} = u_1(p^\circ, q) = u_1^*$$

$$u_2(p^*, q) = \frac{\alpha\delta - \beta\gamma}{\alpha - \beta - \gamma + \delta} = u_2(p, q^\circ) = u_2^*$$

This result is rather robust. It also follows if players do not think strategically but try to maximize their expected utility in the decision situation described by Figure 3.8. (See Holler (1990) for this approach and its results.) The expected utility of player 1 is

---

32 Binmore (1992: 257ff.) discussed a zero-sum version of the Inspection Game which is, of course, less complex than the game presented here.

$$u_1 = apq + bp(1 - q) + c(1 - p)q + d(1 - p)(1 - q)$$

The variable p captures the possible decision of player 1. The first derivative $u_1$ with respect to p is

$$\frac{\partial u_1}{\partial p} = qa + (1 - q)b - qc - (1 - q)d$$

Since $u_1$ is linear in p, the first derivative, $\frac{\partial u_1}{\partial p}$, does not depend on p, i.e., player 1 has no tool to maximize his/her expected utility. However, given (IG), there is a value of q so that $\frac{\partial u_1}{\partial p} = 0$. It turns out that this value is the q* that we calculated for the Nash equilibrium above. On closer inspection, this does not come as a surprise. The value q* made player 1 indifferent between his/her pure strategies and all linear combinations of the two. Thereby it fixed the payoff value of player 1. This is what $\frac{\partial u_1}{\partial p} = 0$ stands for.

### 3.8.3 Inspection Games with sequential moves

Arguments and results are different if the Inspection Game is played sequentially assigning, e.g., a first move (in fact, it is the choice of a strategy) to player 1 (inspector) and the second move to player 2 (polluter), assuming that player 2 can see what player 1 has chosen. There is a second–mover advantage if pure strategies are available only. Player 2 will get his "best results," i.e., either β or γ, while player 1 will get his "worst results," i.e., either b or c. Thus, if player 1 prefers b to c, then players 1 and 2 will choose "enforce" and "not pollute." Payoffs (b, β) will result which is a rather unfavorable outcome to player 1. Player 1 can assure itself a higher payoff than b (or c) if he chooses the mixed-strategy maximin strategy p° given that player 2 learns p°, but does not observe $s_{12}$ or $s_{22}$, i.e., the realization of the corresponding random mechanism. The corresponding payoff is $u_1(p°, q)$.[33] This demonstrates that randomization is profitable: *it reduces the disadvantage of the first player facing a second-mover advantage.*

Is p° an optimal randomization? If player 1 chooses a p' which is "slightly" larger than p*, then player 2 chooses "not pollute" and the expected payoff of player 1 will be

$$u_1(p',0) = p'b + (1 - p')d = p'(b - d) + d.$$

---

33  The corresponding payoff is $u_1(p°, q) = (ad - bc)/(a - b - c + d)$. Condition (IG) implies that $u_1(p°, q) > b$ and $u_1(p°, q) > c$.

Since $b - d < 0$, $u_1(p',0)$ is decreasing in p'. If player 1 choose a p" which is "slightly" smaller than p*, then player 2 chooses "pollute" and the expected payoff of player 1 will be

$$u_1(p'',1) = p''a + (1 - p'')c = p''(a - c) + c$$

and thus increasing in p" as a > c. We can conclude that irrespective of whether $u_1(p',1) > u_1(p'',0)$ or $u_1(p',1) < u_1(p'',0)$ holds, the corresponding values of p' and p" should be as close as possible to p* (see Andreozzi 2004). As we assumed complete information, players knowing their payoffs and the payoffs of the other player, this can be "very close." Expecting that player 2 is rational and maximizes his or her payoff, the maximin strategy p° is no longer attractive to player 1.

This result demonstrates that there is a means to counter the second-mover advantage inherent to the leader-follower version of the Inspection Game, here assumed. However, the inspector has to stick to the randomization and the transgressor has to know about the randomization and expect that the inspector randomizes – and does not decide to choose a pure strategy after the second-mover has made his decision. Indeed, the latter would imply that the inspector can react on the choice of the inspectee and put himself in an advantageous second-mover position. Of course, the randomization will select a pure strategy, but it is the randomization and not the inspector that decides which pure strategy will be selected. It needs some mechanism that guarantees a particular randomization, e.g., assuring p*, and convinces the other party that this randomization, i.e., p*, is at work. The next section discusses some examples.

Note that for the Inspection Game, we cannot conclude that payoffs of the second-mover, i.e., the transgressor, are larger or smaller than the payoffs of the first-mover, i.e., the inspector. Von Neumann and Morgenstern's utilities do not allow interpersonal comparison. This is immediate from the fact that the payoff function is unique "up to an order-preserving linear transformation." All we can say is that it is profitable for a first-mover to randomize if there is a second-mover advantage in a strategic decision situation as given by the Inspection Game – or a zero-sum game without equilibrium in pure strategies. The result for the zero-sum game follows from the maximin theorem which is the core of von Neumann's (1959 [1928]) pioneering paper.

### 3.8.4 Some applications

How relevant is this result? How do mixed strategies prevail and enter the strategic considerations of the decision makers? We can think of a series of interaction of the inspector with the public, including a number of polluters, so that the polluters can learn the randomization p, or we can think of an agency of inspectors, known to the polluters, that suggests a relative frequency of (control and) enforcement which implies an estimated probability p for future interactions. An increase of the agency's membership could be interpreted as an increase of p. Here, statistical and game-theoretical analysis meet.

There is pioneer work on mixed-strategy equilibria by Dresher (1962) and Maschler (1966). Dresher's paper models the problem of arms control agreements as a two–person zero–sum recursive game which is of course less general than the game in Figure 3.8. The paper has been published by the RAND Corporation, based in Santa Monica, California, a hotspot for the application of game theory to military problems. Maschler (1966) defined the Inspection Game (the "inspector's game") as a non–constant-sum two–person game as described by Figure 3.8. He discusses a sequential setting which allows the inspector, being the "leader" (following von Stackelberg's leader-follower duopoly model),[34] to choose mixed strategies. It seems that essential consulting work with reference to the Inspection Game has been accomplished but not necessarily published.

In 1997, the game theorist Rudolf Avenhaus published a study on the control of ticketing in public transportation modeled as an Inspection Game. In the introduction and numerical example, he referred to the City of Munich and its activities to reduce fare evasion. The results come very close to what most users of the public subways ("S- and U-Bahn"), busses, and tramways experience. Ticket checking is rather frequent. On some lines, especially, on the one to the airport, I estimate that there is a 20 percent chance of getting controlled (which is rather high, given my experience in other cities). The city administration does not hold back information when it hires additional personnel for checking tickets or discovers a more efficient method to catch fare dodgers – or those who could not handle the ticket machines correctly. With a 20 per cent chance of inspection, it seems advisable to buy a ticket in almost all cases. Of course, deterrence is a goal of high priority in sequential (or even repeated) Inspection Games. However, there is still the chance that a customer buys the wrong ticket or forgets to punch it, or punches it the wrong way, or tries to punch it but this very ticket is not for punching, etc. There are good reasons why Avenhaus (1997) analyzes effects of unintended illegal behavior on equilibrium behavior. For his modeling, he assumes that costs will be lower if the misbehaving can be shown to be unintended. This is the case, e.g., if you paid for a monthly ticket but forgot it at home. But if you did not punch your ticket, because you simply forgot to do so, then you pay the full punishment fee of €60.00 – even if you forgot "unintentionally." This can also happen if the punching machine does not work properly. One can also ask the question why the customer has to pay for the complications of the ticketing systems, if he or she manages to prove that "deviation" was unintended.

In this context, it seems interesting to point out that the equilibrium derived in Avenhaus (1997) implies that the costs of control are equal to the income

---

34 I am hesitant to speak of a Stackelberg leader-follower model. In his 1934 volume *Marktform und Gleichgewicht*, Heinrich von Stackelberg uses the term "Führer" (which translates as to "leader") for a very different institution.

from punishment. So if we forget to punch the ticket and we get caught as a fare dodger, the City of Munich can afford more controlling – in the equilibrium. Is this a pleasant perspective for your local transportation system? There are incentives for designing a ticket system which is more complicated than it should be – again, in the equilibrium.

The control and penalty system puts the traffic agency in the shoes of a second-mover: the customer has to perform and to prove performance. But let us come back to arms control. From 1963 to 1968, prominent mathematicians and game theorists analyzed problems of arms control and disarmament (ACD) as members of Mathematica, Incorporated of Princeton, New Jersey. According to the first contract (Mathematica, 1963), the objectives were

> to identify and explore potential applications of statistical methodology to the inspection aspects of arms control and disarmament; to develop and analyze techniques from the disciplines of sampling, decision theory and the theory of games for application to inspection in connection with arms control and disarmament planning and negotiation; and to evaluate the adequacy of the statistical methodology and the techniques developed as bases for determining if and how desired levels of verification can be achieved in connection with various arms control and disarmament measures.
>
> (quoted in Avenhaus et al. 1996: 385)

The list of authors contributing to the Mathematica project reads like a Who's Who in game theory. For instance, the research in Maschler (1966) was performed in part for Mathematica, as a footnote on the first page of the published version says. But, in the shadow of the Cold War, many results of this research program were classified and kept secret: they were considered "relevant information." About three decades later, in an invited review paper, Avenhaus and co-authors (1996) unearthed some of the once secret material.[35] But obviously the secrets of the inspector in the Inspection Game is of a different nature than the veil put over the research work on the inspection problem. These secrets belong to a different world of secrets, however, both imply hiding. Is hiding a form of creating a secret? Are there other forms of creating a secret? We will come back to these questions in the next chapter.

We also find applications of the Inspection Game in experiments and survey data. In the already mentioned studies by Holler and Høst (1990) and Holler and co-authors (1992), it is tested whether the mixed-strategy Nash equilibrium or the mixed-strategy maximin solution is a more convincing solution concept in an Inspection game as described in Figure 3.8. A rather exciting test of the mixed-strategy equilibrium is reported in Walker and Wooders (2001). They tested whether the service in tennis follows the game-theoretical

---

35 In Section 4.4, we will meet again the Cold War as an "agent of secrecy."

prescription. They found that players on the tennis court fared better than students in the laboratory, but there is still more "switching-up of serves" than theory predicts. Wiles (2006) further refined the underlying model. The implications of the refined model came closer to the data, and yet a substantial rest of deviating behavior remained. In any case, in these studies, tennis is modeled as a zero-sum game, and not as an Inspection Game, which seems appropriate, and I do not play tennis so I'd better not go into details. Yet, the little I know suggests that doing a service is a first-mover advantage anyhow, and adding randomization to it increases the disadvantage of the second-mover.

### 3.8.5 Hiding, anonymity, and the cult of creativity

Randomization is a particular form of the shaping of strategic secrets. If the first-mover introduces a random decision mechanism – and thus he or she does not know the outcome – the second-mover cannot have the information either and thus does not profit from the advantage that, in principle, the sequential structure implies. However, randomization creates two-way secrets, as nobody knows the truth. It simply destroys information or does not create information where information could be created. In order to avoid conflicts, classical Athens and medieval (and early Renaissance) Italian-city states took refuge in lotteries when selecting people for public offices.[36] Hiding is a one-way secret, which however means that the truth can be found out. This is what we meant when we discussed secrets versus patents as alternative policies of protecting innovations.

Today, many people use the Tor Network to keep their computer address hidden from the recipient of a message. Its core idea is that a message passes through a randomly selected chain of "voluntarily" connected servers within the network. The recipient can only identify the last server in this chain, but not the computer of the original user. Step by step, the user's software builds a circuit of encrypted connections through servers on the network. Each server knows only which server gave it data and which server it is giving data to. No individual server ever knows the complete path that a data packet has taken – and the path has been chosen randomly by the Onion Proxy program on the user's computer.[37]

In his "Defying the assassin's veto," discussing the massacre of *Charlie Hebdo*, Timothy Garton Ash asks the question: "If anonymity can be used to cloak evil, why not to employ it to guard good?" There is the proposition to establish a website

---

36  Manin (1997) offers a series of historical examples and an extensive discussion of the use of the lot in political decision making.

37  Tor is short for "The Onion Router." The Onion Proxy program connects the user's computer with the Tor network.

specifically dedicated to republishing and making accessible to the widest readership offensive images that are of genuine news interest, but which, for a variety of reasons, many journals, online platforms, and broadcasters would hesitate to publish . . . There would be a case for keeping the site's staff anonymous, and perhaps even its board, since otherwise they too would attract the assassins' attention.

(Ash 2015: 6)

Ash observes that it "might be still risky for publications in Turkey, the Middle East, Pakistan, Indonesia, or even India to link to this site, but it would be less dangerous than for them to publish the material themselves" on this very site.

At the first glance, this hiding strategy seems a rather convincing instrument to undercut the second-mover advantage of those who react with wrath and, possibly, with violence and even murder. But who decides what will be published on this site and how? Legality cannot serve as a measuring rod. There will be material that violates the law at least in some countries. Is it likely to see material that violates legal rules of the West? Can we tolerate children pornography, Nazi propaganda, or severe violations of personal rights on this site? What are its constraints, obligations, and boundaries? We might define human rights as a selection criteria, but the interpretation of human rights is culturally dependent – in fact, there are several human rights catalogues in this world – and the application is burdened with inertia. Ash's (2015: 6) verdict is that there "is no reason for us not to use reason, and a standard of reasonableness, when we reasonably can." We try to apply reason also in this case, but there are handicaps to deriving standards of reasonableness.

There are many ways to create anonymity as a means of protection to avoid a second-mover advantage. Sharks may have great difficulty catching an individual herring, as herring swim in schools (i.e., shoals). There is even the term "schooling fish" for species such as herring, that shoal for life in such schools. The school serves as defense against predators and increases "hydrodynamic efficiency." The school members swim in the same direction in a coordinated manner and at a constant distance to each other, all resembling one another, as any deviating from the norm are likely to stand out and be pre-dated. In like manner, in Australia, large flocks of nicely colored lovebirds give a hard time and often no food to hunting hawks.

Similarly, voters hide behind a veil of anonymity in order both to avoid sanctions for their decisions and to evade those competing for their vote. The anonymity of competitive markets gained its notorious representation in Adam Smith' concept of the "invisible hand." Selling and buying is the only activity in this model world and there are no particular characteristics of the agents – just as in a school of herring or flock of birds. The anonymity of the agents guarantees that there is no second-mover advantage, neither for the buyers not for the sellers, nor within each group. But where are the secrets? For secrets, see the following chapter.

We have seen that there are many ways and methods to circumvent or sub-vert a second-mover advantage. In art, the cult of creativity and emphasis on the originality that developed over the centuries has protected the first-mover. However, this protection is rather imperfect. There is forgery, on the one hand, and successful imitation, adaptation, reinterpretation, and elaboration, on the other. In the Middle Ages, the common understanding was that origi-nality was not an issue because artists only revealed what the Creator has cre-ated (Eco 1986). All artists were second-movers. Artists were craftsmen; some were more skilled than others, but, in principle, all were anonymous. This changed with the dawn of the Renaissance: A Giotto painting was painted by Giotto, or by members of his workshop or imitated by a competitor. However, the mastery related to skill was sufficient to discriminate between Botticelli, Michelangelo, Titian, and their imitators. It seems that discrimination was more difficult in the case of Leonardo da Vinci, because he tended to leave paintings unfinished and workshop members contributed much to the final result. In addition, Leonardo did not always use material and apply produc-tion methods for his artwork which lasted. Even during his lifetime, his fresco work vanished or had to be restored by others.[38] Step-by-step, the masters' workshops became dominant and it was down to the skill and art of the master to organize the production of the painting such that they demonstrated their mastery of the genre. The selection of the subject, the composition of artwork, the skill of the workshop members and the organizational and social talents of the master defined creativity and originality. Peter Paul Rubens is a prime example of such a master. His position and performance were impossible to copy, and this carried over to his paintings as they became immediately notori-ous as "Rubens" when they left his workshop. Yet, many masters copied their own work, at least in parts.

When skill perfection became less important for the quality of a painting, a cult of creativity and emphasis on originality emerged, with a focus on the idea and concept of the artwork. In the end, art boiled down to the represen-tation of ideas and to extensive discussions of their values and origins. Now and then, the representation is, however, still very skillful. In any case, art-ists try to find representations which are original. Andy Warhol's *Brillo Box* and Marcel Duchamp's readymades (see Section 4.3) are notorious solutions to this problem. Both invite second-movers, but the ideas and concepts are

---

38 For his large fresco *The Battle of Anghiari*, meant to decorate the Hall of Five Hundred in the Palazzo Vecchio at Florence (in competition with Michelangelo), Leonardo applied hot wax painting which uses heated beeswax to which colored pigments are added. The heated liquid couldn't be spread evenly over the fresco and the artwork was irreparably damaged before it was finished. But it seems that the remains were so impressive that many painters studied and copied it. It has been said that Peter Paul Rubens (1577–1640) was one of them, how-ever, Giorgio Vasari (1511–74) already transformed and redecorated the Hall of Five Hundred which contained the damaged fresco. Ruben's drawing of 1603 is either taken from a prepara-tory study by Leonardo or based on an engraving of 1553 by Lorenzo Zacchia.

sheltered by the originality status. In fact, without second-movers, the first-mover outcome remains pale. Often, second-movers are necessary to make the first-mover prominent and to demonstrate how perfect the first-mover is. This holds not only in art, but perhaps also for Rolls Royce. There is a short way from Warhol's factory to Keith Haring's factory store and back again.

## 3.9 Who is a second-mover? Akira Kurosawa, Sergio Leone, or Bob Dylan

In art, it is not always clear who is a second-mover and who is the first one; who inspired whom, what is plagiarism, and what is not. The case of Gillette illustrates that this problem is highly relevant in business as well. In fact, there is an entire industry devoted to finding out who was first and who just copied. There are patent offices and well-paid patent lawyers who work for this industry. In academia, over the years we have developed the habit of citing quotations. In his *Wealth of Nations* (1776/77) but also in his *Theory of Moral Sentiments* (1759), Adam Smith was still rather miserly in his use of quotations. A particular case is Thorstein Veblen. In his *Theory of the Leisure Class* of 1899, he proposes for his readers that

> premises and corroborative evidence as are drawn from remoter sources . . . are also of the more familiar and accessible kind and should be readily traceable to their source by fairly well-read persons. The usage of citing sources and authorities has therefore not been observed.
>
> (Veblen (1979 [1899]: xii)

It is no longer a habit to rely on the "fairly well-read persons." Perhaps they no longer exist in large enough numbers. Or, are we just very keen on references? Some readers read articles and books by looking only at the references. Recently, the economic profession discussed with great concern and deep emotions the issue of self-plagiarism, i.e., when authors make use of their own published material either by republishing a slightly revised version or by incorporating chapters of earlier publication into newer ones – without quoting their earlier publication "adequately," or not at all. In my understanding, most arguments that deplore or regret this "laxity" of the author ignore the rights of the first-mover, i.e., the author, the originator, the creator. These rights are even stronger than the "right to repeat oneself."[39]

I don't want to go deeper into this discussion – also in order to avoid plagiarism. Anyhow, there is a lot of self-plagiarism in this book and I am not

---

39 For further discussion, see, e.g., Nentjes's. "On the Right to Repeat Oneself" (2012) and the comments in *Homo Oeconomicus* 29(3) and the following issues of this journal. To be precise, comments are published in *Homo Oeconomicus* 29(3) and 29(4), published in 2012 and 2013, respectively, and *Homo Oeconomicus* 30(2) of 2013

always sure that I gave the original sources. Sometimes I do not remember that I have already written down my thoughts and observations. Moreover, in some cases, I do not recall that I've already published them, i.e., sent them to a journal, waited six months for the reports of the reviewers and the reaction of the editors, revised and resubmitted the submission after two months, waited another six months before I received the information that the paper will be published, and then, after a year or two, I find reprints of my articles in my mail (the old version) or news from the publisher on my computer that I can download my article from the net, or just the publisher's information that the article is now available for downloading (the new version). I remember a case that the publisher, the editor, and the author forgot about one of my papers after acceptance. It was a one of little importance, published many years later and, I expect, never quoted.

I am sure that there is also plagiarism in this book. We all make use of valuable ideas that we find in the literature. Isaac Newton famously said "If I have seen further, it is by standing on the shoulders of giants." Was he the first to say this? Probably not. I am not Newton, yet I stand on many shoulders and not all are shoulders of giants. Some ideas just conveniently fit into the patchwork of my thoughts.

Does the condemnation of plagiarism and the potential legal consequences imply a first-mover advantage, and does this first-mover advantage possibly balance second-mover advantages that derive from imitation and further elaboration?

It has been reported that in a letter to Sergio Leone, Akira Kurasawa expressed his admiration for Leone's *A Fistful of Dollars* of 1964: "I've seen your movie. It is a very good movie." Leone may have been be pleased, but Kurasawa added: "Unfortunately, it's *my* movie." Consequently, Kurosawa's studio Toho sued Leone. In the legal dispute that followed, it has been argued that *A Fistful of Dollars* was a remake of Akira Kurosawa's 1961 film *Yojimbo* and this remake, as it was unlicensed, infringed Kurosawa's copyright. Eventually, the case was settled out of court. The Kurosawa party received 15 percent of the worldwide receipts of *A Fistful of Dollars* plus 100 percent of the receipts in Japan, Korea, and Taiwan.

In fact, Leone had sent all his friends and collaborators to see *Yojimbo* before he started working on *A Fistful of Dollars*. He had even asked the producers of his movie (Colombo and Papi) to obtain the rights, but they didn't. In defense, Leone admitted that Kurosawa had a strong influence on his movie, but argued that the main sources were Dashiell Hammett's novel *Red Harvest* (1929) and Carlo Goldoni's eighteenth-century play *The Servant of Two Masters*,[40] whereby the thematic source of Hammett's novel can also be seen in Goldoni's play. He believed that Kurosawa's *Yojimbo* was influenced by *Red Harvest*. Had this

---

40  The influence of Goldoni's play on Sergio Leone's *A Fistful of Dollars* is confirmed by (the eminent professor of film studies) Peter Bondanella (2001: 255).

argument been accepted, then the common roots and of course the high quality of the movie directors were the reasons for the similarities between the two movies. Then Leone's second-mover advantage brought the theme and style of the two films to the audience, but it was not a case of plagiarism or a violation of copyright. In fact, it seems that the legal case and the success of *A Fistful of Dollars* made *Yojimbo* much more popular than it was before. However, Leone's arguments did not convince at that time. Most likely, Sergio Leone was more interested in completing his "Dollars Trilogy", than in the legal business involved in this law case. *The Good, the Bad, and the Ugly* was still waiting to be filmed. To be honest, I could not verify the sequential structure of the lawsuit and the out-of-court settlement with the completion of the *Trilogy*.

In an April 2014 Internet article, entitled "Rampant Remakery: *Yojimbo* vs. *A Fistful of Dollars*," Kyle Anderson argues that

> in many respects the two films could not be more different. Aside from the obvious setting and country of origin, the tone and cultural politics of essentially the same actions are worlds apart and the motivations of the films' respective 'heroes' are equally different.
>
> (Anderson 2014: n.p.)

Then he gives a list of details which make the two films so different. Most of them are really convincing. But do substantial differences in details exclude a successful charge of plagiarism? Where is the borderline between quotation and plagiarism? Is it sufficient just to refer to the "first-mover"? One argument was not aired during the legal process or in the corresponding references – perhaps because Leone was not even aware of it: *A Fistful of Dollars* was the first of a completely new genre of films, i.e., the "Italo Western," also called "Spaghetti Western."

While rereading this section, I had to muse about Bob Dylan and his being awarded the 2016 Nobel Prize for Literature. He deserves it. His work is very original, inspiring, filling a substantial space for people who listen to his ballades either performed by himself, or performed by other artists, making Dylan a best-selling song-writer. But there is also his strong inclination for copy & paste production – i.e., making use of a second-mover position. It seems that the album with the tale-telling title "Love and Theft" of September 2001 contained lyrics which were strongly related to Junichi Saga's book *Confessions of a Yakuza*, a biography of one of the last traditional Yakuza bosses in Japan: "However, when informed of this, author Saga's reaction was one of having been honored rather than abused from Dylan's use of lines from his work."[41] Dylan claimed that these quotations were material to him to "enrich" folk and jazz music.

41 These lines I copied from the Internet. However, I cannot recover the original source, but see Deley (2013) on "Bob Dylan and Plagiarism" subtitled "To Catch a Master Thief." As the subtitle indicates, Deley is rather critical towards Dylan's collage technique, especially as applied in his memoir *Chronicle: Volume One* (Dylan 2005). I enjoyed reading the *Chronicles*.

There are many other lines in Dylan's work which can be traced back to other authors. For instance, it has been claimed that "Beyond here lies nothin'/ Nothin' but the moon and stars" we can find in Ovid. Obviously, there are some problems finding these words in Ovid, and if so, to use these lines in modern folk-rock is a creative act, and Ovid would not object (perhaps, however, he would ask for a share of the cake).

In the next chapter, we will briefly discuss Marcel Duchamp's readymades, products of industrial production which could be bought in department stores and ironmongeries. In contrast, Bob Dylan's readymades had authors; we often know them at least by name. Therefore, the sequence of first-mover and second-mover and possibly third-mover often has its names. Bob Dylan was not always winning in this sequence. His debut album of 1962 contained a version of "The House of Rising Sun"; earlier versions of this song had been recorded by Pete Seeger, Joan Baez, and Miriam Makeba only a few years or months before. But Dylan presented a new version of this song which was performed, but not recorded, by Dave Van Ronk.

In 1984, also based on Van Ronk's version, but with Dylan's recording as blueprint, the British rock group The Animals recorded this song in a London studio and made it a world-wide success story – one of the most played and sold songs of the decade which was dominated by supergroups like The Beatles, The Rolling Stones, and The Beach Boys. It has been said that Dylan stopped performing this song because he was afraid of being accused of plagiarism. If we accept this argument, then it seems that a first-mover lost his position because of a more successful second-mover. To me, a more convincing argument, however, is that Bob Dylan sounds like Mickey Mouse compared to the strong Newcastle voice of Eric Burdon supported by the vibrating organ play of Alan Price. Since The Animals' version of the song was widely heard and appreciated, Dylan was well advised to drop this song from his repertoire.

# 4 Secrets

## How to create and how to deal with them

*Secret de Deux, Secret de Trois, Secret de Tous,
and Secret de Dieu.*[1]

When, in 1738 or 1739, David Hume published the first volume of his *Treatise of Human Nature* anonymously, this "was as much a conventional expression of modesty as an attempt to escape the consequences of censure" (Gottlieb 2016: 68). In addition, it allowed the author to react on critical comments and allegations from a third-person point of view. Hume made use of this possibility. Later, he regretted that he rushed into print too soon, as he did not agree with the book, but despite anonymity it became clear who was the author.

Writers of the late Middle Ages and early Renaissance such as Boccaccio and Chaucer dwelled on secrets: secrets were the engine of their "tales."[2] Secrets seem to be everywhere, not just in detective stories. The creation and revelation of secrets is a major human activity. But do we understand what secrets are and what they do? This chapter will discuss some of the puzzles related to secrets. However, it will not deal with secrecy as a marketing strategy. (There is a growing literature on this issue.) I will discuss, only in passing, the status of secrets in religious cults or fundamental questions such as: is God a secret, and, if so, is there revelation and how does it work? Or, borrowing one of Steven Brams's superb book titles, *Superior Beings: If They Exist How Do We Know?* (Brams 1983): is truth a secret and, if so, how can we disclose it? Do secrets presuppose that there is a truth? In these times of "alternative facts," a discussion of the relationship of secrets and truth is highly topical. A better understanding of the notion of secrecy is a necessary prerequisite. Of course, a particular event can be described by alternative sets of facts and these sets can be ranked, quite similar to the ranking of desires discussed in Section 2.6. But desires and facts are different – perhaps. Desires can determine the selection of facts, thereby obfuscating reality, destroying truth, and creating secrets – even where there is no truth (left).

---

1 Found in the men's room of the Isabella Stuart Gardener Museum, Boston, Massachusetts.
2 See Geoffrey Chaucer's *The Canterbury Tales,* written in the 1380s.

## 4.1 A variety of secrets

Are there secrets that can help us to find the truth? We can hope for an uncorrelated and sincere vote if the ballot is secret, voters cannot be punished for their decision, and votes are difficult to sell and buy. The larger the number of votes the more likely is secrecy for the individual vote – and the stronger is the protection of the individual voter from being harassed because of his decision. Only then we can hope that the majority of voters selects the alternative, out of two, that is closer to the "truth" as suggested by Condorcet's jury theorem. Then it holds: the larger the number of voters, the closer we get to the truth.[3]

Condorcet (1785: xxv) pointed out that there are objects for which an immediate personal interest will light the spirit: the maintenance of safety, freedom, and property. On such issues a direct democratic vote can be taken by a large assembly, i.e., the nation, without damage. But if the ballot is not secret then there are all kinds of possibilities to influence the votes. Most prominent there are bribing ("buying votes") and threatening the voters. Voters have to be "unbiased" by bribes and threats, and they have to be experts otherwise large numbers do not approximate truth, but disaster. For issues of some complexity the condition of expertise, assumed by the jury theorem, puts constraints and limitations on the democratic process and the application of Jakob Bernoulli's principle of large numbers. Recent experience with referenda suggests that the alternatives have to be well defined and understood and should not at all be subject to political propaganda and party competition if the outcome should be reasonable from the point of view of Condorcet's aspirations of truth finding. "With boundedly rational voters and politicians, democracy is no guarantee against political catastrophe" (Glaeser 2006: 142).

In general, secret ballots are a constituent element of referenda. They are meant to assure anonymity serving as a shelter. But the impact of a vote is small when the number of voters is large, and secrecy invites "sloppiness" as rewards to the individual vote are negligible or even "insignificant"[4] and, behind the veil of secrecy, individual responsibility is nil.

We will see that large numbers do not always guarantee secrecy – on the contrary. Larger numbers are the conspirators' entry ticket to the torture chamber.

---

3  However, Condorcet argued that the larger the number of decision makers, the lower will be their competence, in general, and therefore collective decisions resulting in useful reforms of the administration or of law making, will become less likely, the larger the number of voters (see Condorcet 1785: xxv). On the other hand, the larger the number of votes, the more likely is secrecy for the individual vote – and the stronger the protection of the individual voter from being harassed because of their decision.

4  This refers to Hartmut Kliemt's "veil of insignificance" in voting when the number of voters is large (Kliemt 1986). Expressive voting is a possible consequence. (See Hillman (2010) for a review of expressive behavior in economics and politics.) On the other hand, experimental research shows that decision makers become "rational" if rewards increase (Smith and Walker 1993). However, the "expected utility model" hardly applies if the number of voters is large and the ballot is secret – then individual responsibility is zero.

Less dramatically, larger numbers can signal where the honey is, where profits can be made. It can be beneficial to suppress such signals. Here is a story. On the eve of dropping of the atomic bomb which destroyed Hiroshima and Nagasaki and killed most of the inhabitants of the two cities, the Princeton members of the Los Alamos team which constructed the bomb were asked not to buy their train tickets to Albuquerque, New Mexico, at the Princeton railway station which was rather small and there was not too much traffic. However, in his autobiography *Surely You Are Joking, Mr. Feynman* (Feynman 1985), Richard Feynman tells us that he bought his ticket at the Princeton station. He was a member of the Princeton crew. Later he became a Nobel Laureate. He studied for his Ph.D. at Princeton University's Institute of Advanced Studies which housed a cyclotron laboratory in a basement; at age 22, in 1940, he was hired by Robert Oppenheimer to work on developing the atomic bomb. He figured out that if everybody bought their tickets somewhere else, buying his ticket at Princeton station would not arouse suspicion. When he went to the station and asked for a ticket, the man at the counter said. "Oh, so all this stuff is for *you!*"

Feynman (1985: 111) comments on this reaction somewhat smugly: "We had been shipping out crates full of counters for weeks and expecting that they didn't notice the address was Albuquerque. So at least I explained why it was that we were shipping all those crates; *I* was going out to Albuquerque." Perhaps this coverage was not very convincing. Most likely this secrecy game did not matter too much anyway, since the Russian spy Klaus Fuchs was added to the Los Alamos team in 1943. Fuchs lent Richard Feynman his car so that he could visit his wife who was in the hospital with TB.

The world of fairy tales and myths is plastered with secrets: "For little knows my royal dame that Rumpelstiltskin is my name!" When Oedipus meets the Sphinx at the crossroads on his journey to Delphi, Oedipus must answer the Sphinx's riddle correctly in order to pass, and not meet death: "What walks on four feet in the morning, two in the afternoon and three at night?" In one version of the fairy tale, Rumpelstiltskin tore himself into pieces when the "royal dame" found out his name. The Sphinx killed herself by throwing herself into the sea when she heard Oedipus' correct answer. Often those who know the secrets are either threatened with misery, or they threaten others with eternal pain or painful death. There are cases which suggest that it is dangerous to have secrets – see Tuco's experience with Angel Eyes – and there are cases that suggest that it is dangerous to initiate the revelation of secrets. Some cases suggest that it is profitable to keep a secret, while others suggest it is better to reveal or disclose a secret. Issues become more complicated, at least from a strategic (i.e., game-theoretical) point of view, if it is profitable to reveal the information contained in a secret, but the cost might be extremely high if others learn that a secret was disclosed. The Zimmermann Telegram – an important keystone of World War I, presented and discussed in Section 4.2 below – is a case that demonstrates this problem; it leads directly to the question of how to deal with secrets.

In fact, the Zimmermann Telegram reads like a fairy tale, but it describes a rather dramatic historical event. It shows that a story does not need the supernatural power of Greek gods and Northern witches to produce surprising results with a touch of the supernatural. More worldly implications of secrets are discussed in Section 4.1.2 with respect to our pivotal story *The Good, the Bad, and the Ugly*. If, in the end, The Good succeeds in saving the treasure for himself, then this not only confirms his competence in dealing with secrets and, perhaps more so, handling his gun, but it also illustrates the various qualities of secrets, especially their hierarchical dimensions. However, why he shares half of it with The Ugly also has the touch of a secret.

It is not just by degree of secrecy that distinguishes the decision situations of the three protagonists, i.e., the Good, the Bad, and the Ugly. The variations in their modes of behavior suggest that there is a moral dimension to secrets. Section 4.6 explicitly deals with this dimension in discussing George Orwell's notebook. The discussion of Machiavelli's conspiracy paradoxes in Section 4.5, however, suggests one should discard one's moral concerns and fellow feelings when conspiring.

By its very nature, conspiracy is accompanied by a creation of secrets. Our study will also unearth other mechanisms that produce secrets. The production of secrets is also topical to Section 4.4. It unravels the use, perhaps even exploitation, of artists in the cultural warfare immanent to the Cold War that dominated world politics from the end of World War II to the break-up of the Soviet Union and the dissolution of the Communist bloc. Abstract expressionists, such as Jackson Pollock, Mark Rothko, and Willem de Kooning, and members and participants of the Congress of Cultural Freedom operated as agents of the "Free World," but in secrecy. Some of them knew their role in this game, others did not. Our discussion of Orwell's notebook reflects the dilemma of many artists and intellectuals in which the Cold War placed them.

Humankind spends a lot of time and energy creating (and keeping) secrets and perhaps even more resources unraveling them — see our Secret Services in both roles — but often the question of what to do and how to use the dearly achieved knowledge is not answered, and in many cases the question is not even asked. Modern societies enjoy many private and public institutions that collect data and a large proportion of these data are in fact secrets "from some point of view." But the use of these data is still in its infancy and hardly understood. How can data become a secret and what kind of secret are they? A related issue is the creation of "alternative facts" making truth, information, and secrets obsolete.

In a recent publication, Arruñada (2017) discussed a notable relationship between secrecy, move structure, and property rights. He gives the example of a landowner O who sells, in period $t_1$, his property to B. In period $t_2$, O and L agree on a secret lien to L. In period $t_3$, L seizes the parcel of land to satisfy the lien. If there is the possibility of a secret lien, then of course B will pay a lower price to O — the market value of O's property is lower than in case secret liens are impossible or not enforceable, e.g., by law. In fact, without any legal constraint on contracting secret liens, the value of all assets will be lower than in the case where there is a law that bans such contracts. A consequence could be that agents are less inclined to invest in their property. Moreover, if secret liens become standard expectation, then the market for these properties will break down – or reduce to a "market for lemons" à la Akerlof (1970). The externality of free and secret contracting on liens is non-contractable and leads to market inefficiency.

This result illustrates the dilemma of matching liberty, i.e., unconstrained contracting, with market efficiency. We already came across this dilemma when we discussed Adam Smith's "invisible hand" (see Section 3.5.2). His conclusion is: "The obligation of building party walls, in order to prevent the communication of fire, is violation of natural liberty, exactly of the same kind with the regulations of the banking trade" (Smith (1981 [1776/77]: 324). Arruñada's (2017) analysis suggests that a law banning secret liens on property is such a party wall.

Arruñada (2017) gives the above example to demonstrate that the move structure matters in social relations of more than two agents. The property right problem, introduced in Coase (1960), focused on two agents and a single-exchange framework only. Therefore, move structure and secrecy do not have the form and relevance of the example above, and are more or less neglected. But Arruñada shows that zero transaction costs and well-defined property rights are not enough to guarantee efficiency in case of externalities,[5] if there are more than two agents and contracting is not constrained to one transaction only. Secrecy connects the transactions which cannot be separated as long as secrecy prevails – and is not banned by an exogenous agent, i.e., the lawmaker.

### 4.1.1 Personal, private, and public secrets – and the Emperor's new clothes

The creation of secrets is a key dimension of Nicola Atkinson's work. She uses this tool to seduce people to participate in her experimental work, and she is most curious to learn how people react. The reaction is part of her artwork – in fact, it is the pivotal part of her work as we will see in Section 4.3. Her "Secrets of the World" has stirred substantial discussion. In 1996, I had the pleasure to organize a *Oberseminar* at the University of Hamburg when Atkinson asked the participants to write down their personal, private, and public secrets. Identifying the secrets in these categories was part of the project and a challenge to the participants, as we will see. Public secrets are defined as secrets that everybody knows – and everybody knows that everybody knows – but nobody admits this knowledge in public. It is said that, during World War II, every adult German knew that concentration camps (KZs) existed and that

---

5 This is what the Coase Theorem says. Most likely, it was the "second-mover" George Stigler who was the first to call this result Coase Theorem. See Stigler (1966: 133).

people were tortured and killed there because of their political affiliations and convictions, their Jewishness, or because they belonged to the nation of Roma, or because they were part of the political opposition, etc. But people did not dare to talk about the KZs because they were afraid that they were turned in to a KZ themselves when betrayed by their neighbors, friends, or enemies. Although they did not talk about it, they assumed that everybody knew. This assumption was justified, although there could be exceptions.[6]

A popular example of a public secret is Hans Christian Andersen's fairy tale "The Emperor's New Clothes." Everybody saw that the emperor was naked, and everybody expressed admiration for the new clothes, with the exception of a little child who exclaimed, "But he hasn't anything on!" One whispered to another what the child had said, and "at last" the "whole town" cried out: "But he hasn't anything on!" (quotes taken from Andersen's fairy tale).

In contrast with the tentative definition of public secrets above, in Andersen's tale, people did not know that the others saw the Emperor naked as well – on the contrary. The secret was sealed by the clothes' (postulated) property – i.e., the garments were invisible to anyone who was unfit for the office he held, or was incorrigibly stupid.

This *revelation rule* was coined by two rogues who were stranded in the imperial city and gave themselves out as weavers. They declared they could weave the finest fabrics imaginable. They enjoyed their days with laziness while weaving the invisible clothes for the Emperor, and were generously remunerated by him. Everybody knew about the peculiar quality of the material embedded in the revelation rule. Everybody kept silent when they saw the Emperor naked, not to make their incompetence public. They did not know that all the others, including the Emperor, shared their observation.

It was a little child that broke the spell. The young whistleblower was not submitted to the revelation rule as it had no office and did as yet not know what stupidity is. The child made the secret public, but was it a public secret? Under the revelation rule, even the Emperor considered his secret – the fact that he did not see his new clothes – a private one. He remained silent about the fact that he saw himself naked, and he rightly assumed that others would also remain silent who saw him naked, in order not to reveal that they were unfit for the offices, or incorrigibly stupid. The revelation rule made the secret a private one to each individual that believed in it and accepted it, and was subject to it because he or she had an office or a reputation to lose. Since the rule referred to each individual on a personal basis – you see the new clothes or you don't – it also implies a personal secret, i.e., a secret that has to do with you as an individual person. Obviously, not all private secrets are personal secrets, and

6  It is said that Winifred Wagner, a daughter-in-law of Richard Wagner and a personal friend of Adolf Hitler from 1925 onwards – she brought writing paper to Hitler in the Landsberg prison so he could write *Mein Kampf* – claimed that even Hitler did not know about the mass killings of Jews in Auschwitz. On the other hand, it was reported that she was "disgusted" by Hitler's persecution of the Jews, but it seems that she loved him.

personal secrets can have a public dimension, e.g., if everybody can see that a politician is hit by Alzheimer's disease but nobody dares to say it.

Sofia Blind (2002: 566) rightly observes that

> political issues can be private secrets, as well, if they only concern those who know the secret. Private secrets may be shared by several people: Many families hide secrets, ethnic groups keep secret knowledge on ritual or religious traditions, and corporate employees possess information on secret production processes.
>
> (Blind 2002: 566)

In ancient societies, families had their own gods that derived from their ancestors. All ceremonies were kept strictly secret, "secrecy was necessary" (see Fustel de Coulange 2006 [1864]: 37). However, if "the keepers of a secret know about each other, sharing it openly," then we have the case of a public secret – "Sometimes, however, people secretly share their hidden knowledge: I know it, you know it, but I don't know you know, and you don't know I know" – then the secret is private – it is made a private secret.

As in the case of Andersen's fairy tale, many secrets have the three dimensions of personal, private, and public secret, however, not necessarily in the same state of aggregation of the story. Figure 4.1 illustrates the field of combinations that result from combining the three dimensions under the assumption. It is no coincidence that this figure resembles the triangle in Figure 1.1 in Chapter 1 and the same qualification applies here: the triangle should not be read as a simplex, as the three components do not satisfy a Cartesian measure. In this figure, distances cannot be added up or divided; they only illustrate a monotonic relationship. The three nodes are meant to illustrate the dimensions of the secret of the Emperor's new clothes, starting with a heavy load of public secret melting down to a state with a high degree of private secret, when the Emperor understood that he is naked, and transforming into a state

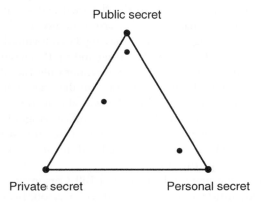

*Figure 4.1* Private, public, and personal dimensions of a secret

of low public and private secret, but substantial personal secret. The latter state became valid in the processes of unraveling the secret after the child cried out that the Emperor "hasn't got anything on!"

There is this proverb: "Children and fools speak the truth." It worked in Andersen's fairy tale. People believed what the child said, also because it cried out what they saw. But the child could have been silenced, for instance, upon the order of the Emperor, who had a strong interest in preserving his private and personal secret as a public secret, such that everybody knows the truth but nobody admits to know it. The two rogues would have helped the Emperor to maintain the secret – somehow silencing the children or closing the others' ears.

Of course, the distinction of personal, private, and public secrets is not the only possible categorization. There are many more, as we shall see from what follows. However, Nicola Atkinson's art experiment demonstrates that the distinction can be a rather disturbing one, though with minor consequences. In Atkinson's experiment, the process of creation is constrained by writing down some lines on a piece of paper; this can be cheap, at no cost whatsoever. But it also can involve high emotional costs. In fact, there are situations in which the creation of secrets can be very costly and its consequences can be deadly – not just for people who know of Bill Carson's secret in *The Good, the Bad, and the Ugly*.

### 4.1.2 "The Good," "The Bad," and the hierarchy of secrets

*The story, part I:* Bill Carson and his partners had stolen $200,000 in gold, the war chest of the 3rd Cavalry Unit of the Confederate Army. Only he knew where this treasure was buried. Angel Eyes, "The Bad," played by Lee Van Cleef in Sergio Leone's *The Good, the Bad, and the Ugly*, learned about Bill Carson and the treasure while doing his job as professional killer. So he already knew about Carson and the treasure before Tuco, "The Ugly," played by Eli Wallach, presented himself as Bill Carson. Tuco, wearing a Confederate uniform, was detained as a prisoner of war in a Union Army camp. Coincidently, Angel Eyes served as a Union sergeant in this camp. He had used his position to rob the already scarce property that was left to the detained and sell it to "human vultures." When he heard the name of Bill Carson, he invited Tuco to his office and arranged for a very rough interview, having Tuco tortured by a heavyweight subordinate. In the end, the blood-spitting and tooth-gnashing Tuco disclosed that the gold is buried in Sad Hill Cemetery, but only Blondie, "The Good," played by Clint Eastwood, knew the name on the grave where the treasure was buried. It just happened that Blondie was also in this very Union prison camp, so he too was invited to Angel Eyes's office. Angel Eyes considered Blondie to be smart and expected that he would not reveal the name on the treasure grave, even when severely tortured and threatened with death. Angel Eyes offered Blondie a partnership.

Blondie learned the name of the grave when the real Bill Carson was on the verge of dying of thirst, exhaustion and loss of blood. Bill Carson, heavily wounded, was in a runaway carriage, together with a heap of dead corpses, that

Tuco halted. Promising Carson some water, Tuco learned about the $200,000 buried at Sad Hill Cemetery. While Tuco was away fetching water for the dying Carson, in order to persuade him to tell Tuco the name on the grave, Blondie talks with Carson and extracts from him the name on the treasure tomb before Carson dies. Previously Tuco had forced his former partner Blondie on a brutal, dehydrating march across the desert, and was ready to kill him when he found Carson dead and Blondie next to him. But the exhausted Blondie babbles that Carson had told him the name of the tomb, and then he passes out.

When Blondie recovers, Tuco becomes very friendly. He has realized that he needs Blondie's information to find the treasure. On the other hand, Blondie does not know the name and location of the cemetery where the $200,000 in gold is cached. This state of affairs forces Tuco and Blondie to become reluctant partners. But is their partnership balanced? Do they have equivalent power? Are their secrets of equal value?

*The story, part II*: On their way to seeking the $200,000 treasure, Blondie and Tuco were nailed by members of a troop of Union soldiers who held a position on one side of Branston Bridge, ready to fight the Confederates, who were stationed on the other side of the bridge, "twice a day." To avoid possible misunderstandings, Blondie and Tuco claimed that they wanted to join the Union troops as volunteers. The commanding captain accepted their story. Loosened by the consumption of large quantities of liquor straight from the bottle, he described the craziness and cruelty of the situation to Blondie and Tuco. Twice a day, accompanied by heavy shooting of machine guns and artillery, the two squadrons met on the bridge to slaughter each other in a bloody ritual. The high commands of both sides have declared that the bridge is important and should not be damaged. The intoxicated captain spoke of serious doubts about the bridge's military significance and confessed his daydream of blowing up the bridge after an attack when the two sides collect their wounded and dead.

During another round of shelling, gunning and slaughter, Blondie and Tuco came across a wooden case with explosives and, when the violence came to a halt for the day, they went to fix its contents to the poles of the bridge, perhaps as a consequence of the captain's story. However, to get to the treasure it was by now obvious that Blondie and Tuco would have to cross the river, which was impossible as long as there is a bridge and hostile combatants occupying either shore.

While fixing the explosives under the bridge, Tuco suggested that he and Blondie exchange their secrets. After some debate regarding who should dare the first move, Tuco revealed that Bill Carson had told him that the treasure was located in Sad Hill Cemetery. In exchange, Blondie stated that the tomb carried the name of Arch Stanton. Did we experience an exchange of secrets? Or was there a second-mover advantage at work?

After the bridge was blown up and the military personnel left, the two reached the other side of the river where Tuco mounted an abandoned horse to rush to Sad Hill Cemetery, quitting the partnership. He managed to find

Arch Stanton's grave and started to dig with the help of a wooden board. Before he could finish his digging job, Blondie arrived, delivered a shovel and, pointing to his gun, supervised Tuco's further digging. Next, Angel Eyes appeared on the scene, with a second shovel. Pointing to his gun in the right hand, he wanted to make clear that this second shovel was meant for Blondie. However, he had to put his gun back after Blondie, kicking open the coffin lid, showed that there were only bones in the coffin. Blondie still had his valuable secret.

Furiously, Tuco turned to Blondie; he felt cheated. Blondie reacted with a "You thought I trust you?" Indeed, there were serious problems of trust. Tuco realized that it is difficult to hold back the cemetery's name when you have to give directions after the crossing of the bridge. Perhaps his "confession" was affected by the fact that he had already given the cemetery's name to Angel Eyes when tortured in the Union Army prison camp. But still, one way or the other, the cemetery's name seems less valuable to him than the name on the actual grave – otherwise he would have probably not proposed the exchange of secrets and been the first to volunteer any information. On the other hand, he should have considered that Blondie's information concerning the identity of the grave could not be trusted. But he trusted this information since he was greedy to find the grave and the gold, without Blondie's company if possible.

Perhaps it is surprising that Blondie gave Tuco a name on a grave next to the grave labeled "Unknown." I think we have to leave it to psychology or to Sergio Leone to explain this correspondence. With some intuition and second thoughts, Tuco could have concluded that the treasure might be buried in the grave dedicated to the "Unknown." There were so many unknown dead in this war who were shuffled into mass graves: why should an unknown soldier be buried next to Arch Stanton's grave? But first he tried Stanton's grave. He had no chance for a second trial before Blondie and, in the sequel, Angel Eyes arrived. On the other hand, Blondie must have learned from the dying Carson that there is a grave for "Arch Stanton." This was the ID of the "Unknown." But he could not know that he would be in place before Tuco had second thoughts about the Arch Stanton grave, having found no gold in it. The reference to Arch Stanton contained some information which was, however, ignored in what followed.

*The story, part III*: The next scene introduces the notorious shoot-out three-way duel, i.e., the truel. Blondie lifts a stone and claims that he has written down on the back of it the name of the grave that holds the treasure. He puts the stone in the middle of the stone-paved circle that forms an arena where the agents now take their positions, forming a equilateral triangle with the stone laying in the center where the three bisectors cross. However, why should Angel Eyes and Tuco trust Blondie that he wrote down the correct name on the stone? As the story goes, it is not likely that Blondie is shot and either Angel Eyes or Tuco will lift the stone – so he should be indifferent to whether or not he writes down the name. On the other hand, Goddess Fortuna may play her trembling hand and dismisses the particular weak Nash equilibrium that suggests Blondie bequeathing the name of the grave to his rivals. Or, his fellow-feelings for either might not be strong enough to let them have the gold. Neither Angel Eyes nor Tuco checked whether there was a name written on the stone, and of course they could not check whether it was the correct name either.

*The story, part IV*: After Blondie had literally shot Angel Eyes's body, hat, and gun into an open grave and Tuco discovered that his gun had no bullets – because it had been emptied by Blondie in due time – Blondie lifts the stone and shows to Tuco (and the audience) that nothing was written on its base. He explains to Tuco that the missing name on the stone symbolizes "Unknown," showing how smart he is. Tuco is not likely to understand this twist to the story, but Blondie makes him dig the grave of the "Unknown" next to Arch Stanton's grave – unearthing the 200,000 gold dollars. The secret of the treasure is lifted.

All the secrets are gone, but still there is a puzzle. Why had the heroes of our movie been so sure that Bill Carson told them the truth? Of course, when he was dying, it did not really matter for him what happened to the treasure. But he told his secret – first part to Tuco, second part to Blondie – hoping that he will be given some water and the chance to survive. If not, why should he tell the secret at all?

*The comment*: What, at first glance, looks like a partnership between Tuco and Blondie is biased by some asymmetry in the structure of their secrets, which creates a hierarchy. First of all, this is due to the fact that Tuco's and Blondie's secrets are interrelated: one cannot make use of one without the other. Yet, there is an inherent sequential structure: before Blondie's secret becomes relevant and its disclosure can be tested, Tuco's secret must be disclosed and "tested." Tuco tried to overcome this dilemma by trying to be faster than Blondie, hoping that Blondie had disclosed his secret to him – which was not the case as Arch Stanton's grave contained only bones, not dollars. Clearly, this is a case that one cannot beat the power of strategic time by relying on time as measured by the clock. Blondie had a second-mover advantage by the nature of his secret.

*Hierarchy of secrets*: Given the sequential structure, the early secret cannot keep its status if the later one should be unveiled. There is a structural dependency in the story that creates an intertemporal hierarchy. Below, we will come across a strategic hierarchy of secrets that derives from the effort to create a secret out of the dissolution of a secret. This hierarchy is essential to the story of the Zimmermann telegram and to the application of the knowledge derived from the breaking of the Enigma code.

### 4.1.3 Good and bad secrets

In the course of dealing with secrets, I came across the opinion that all secrets are bad. I also learned that this opinion is widely shared even within the academic community. However, it is not always obvious what is understood by a secret. In fact, the given examples often reflect some moral deficiencies or inefficient outcomes. In her article, "Shall I Sell You My Secret?" Sofia Blind proposes the following definition of a secret:

> A secret is a statement known to a finite set of people which, if revealed to one or more people outside this set, changes the utility levels of one or several people in this set. The set can be a singleton.
>
> (Blind 2002: 565)

The reference to utility points out that this definition is meant to serve for economists. Blind continues with an illustration:

> the contents of my pocket are not a secret. I would not mind revealing them, and no one would profit from knowing, so no one's utility changes. If I had a freshly stolen diamond ring in my pocket, though, things would be different: I would not want to show it, and the police might be keen to know.
>
> (Blind 2002: 565)

The example demonstrates that secrets are "referential": there must be another one *potentially involved* and the secret-monger benefits from this relationship:

> the utility of keeping the secret is identical to the disutility caused by its disclosure . . . Blackmailers are very good at estimating these utilities: They earn their living by demanding as large a portion of the economic value of a secret as they can get; ideally, close to 100 per cent.
>
> (Blind 2002: 566)

The gains of blackmailers could be identified with the internalization of direct externalities of secrets. Secrets imply externalities. There are direct benefits to the one who holds the secret. There can be positive or negative benefits to those "who do not know." The benefits can be rather general and indirect: "classified information on military defence strategies can be a good secret, protecting the general public. The keeper of such a secret increases the utility of others" (Blind 2002: 566). The discussion of the Zimmermann Telegram and the case of Alan Turing below will illustrate such cases. However, at least Turing's case demonstrates that there can be substantial individual costs related to the creation of social benefits that derive from secrets. The economic argument is as follows:

> The incentive to keep such secrets is systematically too low, or inversely: the temptation to divulge them is too high. To attain an optimal supply level, good secrets should be protected by paying their keepers for staying silent . . . The large rewards for traitors, who procure other countries' military or political secrets, also prove their high external benefit. Capital punishment for traitors is a mirror image of these benefits and rewards.
>
> (Blind 2002: 566)

Economics textbooks suggest that, as in all cases of externalities, the outcome will be inefficient if decision makers are rational and internalization is excluded. Positive externalities lead to underprovision, i.e., secrets will not be kept to the level and the degree which are good for the society under consideration.

Of course, there are bad secrets, too, with negative external effects in abundance. Paying traitors, using inspectors, spies, and secret agents, are just some means to unveil them. However, whistleblowing is not always welcome, as the case of Edward Snowden illustrates. What is a bad secret for the one side can be a good one for the other, and vice versa. Often it is not even clear whether the secret is good or bad, but some secrets should not be disclosed at all – especially if the secrets are part of a bundle that represents power and authority. On the one hand, the "prestige enjoyed by doctors, priests or lawyers partly stems from their professional obligation to keep secrets. In politics and administration, keeping state secrets is a main part of the job" (Blind 2002: 568). On the other hand, "knowledge may be dangerous to those who know . . . Giordano Bruno was burned at the stake in Rome in 1600. Galileo was harassed by the church" (Airaksinen 2011: 431).

There is a close relationship between religion, mystery and secrets. We already asked the question: is God a secret? In his discussion of Bacon's *New Atlantis*, Airaksinen (2011: 416) claims that religious mysteries

> are secrets which cannot be known by any human mind however elevated they are; for instance, the reasons and causes of miracles as well as the true and ultimate purpose of God's plans and designs. Perhaps the priest's secret is that he does not know what these propositions mean, although he should. How can he be a priest if he does not know the key truths, the esoteric mysteries? Of course he knows them – not the truths but the texts. He knows them, but he cannot explain them. Be this as it may, the priest is a guardian of such mysteries in the sense that he has something to offer in relation to their interpretation, use, and promotion.
>
> (Airaksinen 2011: 416)

To many religions, confession is part of these mysteries. It transfers secrets to the confessor such that they are no longer private to the penitent.

If there is a seal of confession, there is still a secret. But the quality of the secret changed as the following, rather popular story, illustrates (as I cannot remember where and when I read the story and people who confirmed the story obviously suffered from a similar lack of reference, I have chosen a rather abstract wording): "There is a good-bye party for the priest of village A; the priest retires after many years of serving God and the villagers. Looking back at his career he tells the shocking story that in the first confession he was listening to, he learned that the penitent committed a murder. Several minutes later, jolly Mr. X enters and proudly reports that he was the first to confess his sins to the priest. The case of a murder was solved."

Is this a model of cryptography? There are two pieces of information that are rather "innocent" because no consequences follow as long as they are separated. Once they meet, the informational contents change rather dramatically. The murderer is found.[7] I will not go into details of cryptography in this text, although it is highly relevant when it comes to secrets. However, it is the driving force behind the Zimmermann Telegram, which was an essential building block in the history and course of World War I. And, of course, the breaking of the code of the Enigma machine was decisive to World War II and to the life of Alan Turing. We will try to learn from both cases.

## 4.2 The Zimmermann Telegram and Alan Turing's dilemma

This chapter deals with submarines, Mexico, and Room 40. Its heroes are people who unraveled secrets or have the power to do so. Some people create secrets; others decipher secrets; others have a pile of secrets in their cupboard.[8] Almost all of them, directly or indirectly, face a problem: how to make use of a secret that is no longer a secret to you, without letting others know that you know the secret? The latter condition could be paramount in case of war, as the story of the Zimmermann Telegram illustrates. You do not want the enemy to know that you can decipher his messages. The safest way to achieve this is not to use the information. But then what good is reading the enemy's messages? We will see that this issue is also relevant for Alan Turing's decision of how to make use of the breaking of the Enigma code – at least if we trust the story offered in the movie *The Imitation Game*, i.e., the movie that reveals Turing's "top secret life"[9] to us. First, however, I will tell the story of the Zimmermann Telegram and add a somewhat unusual interpretation to it. I call it story, as history has not yet decided.

### 4.2.1 The Zimmermann Telegram story

Most secretly:

> We intend to begin on the first of February unrestricted submarine warfare. We shall endeavor in spite of this to keep the United States of America neutral. In the event of this not succeeding, we make Mexico a proposal of alliance on the following basis: make war together; make

---

7  This is in marked contrast to the so-called "Epimenides paradox," or liar paradox. Epimenides was a Cretan who made the statement: "All Cretans are liars." The sentence is informative as long as we do not add the information about the one who said it. Then the system becomes self-referential and the information is gone. (See Hofstadter 1980: 15ff.) See also 4.6.1 below.

8  In her "Secret of the World" project, Nicola Griffith-Atkinson collects secrets and puts them in a cupboard, see Section 4.3.1 below.

9  This refers to the subtitle of the German version of the film which is "*Ein streng geheimes Leben.*" It seems that the marketing managers did not fully trust the attraction of the title *The Imitation Game* for the German version – especially as the film is dubbed and actors speak German. References to secrets, i.e., *Geheimnisse*, are an attractive marketing tool.

peace together; generous financial support and an understanding on our part that Mexico is to reconquer the lost territories in Texas, New Mexico, and Arizona. The settlement in detail is left to you. You will inform the President of the above most secretly as soon as the outbreak of war with the United States of America is certain and add the suggestion that he should, on his own initiative, invite Japan to immediate adherence and at the same time mediate between Japan and ourselves. Please call the president's attention to the fact that the ruthless employment of our submarines now offers the prospect of compelling England in a few months to make peace.[10]

It was January 17, 1917, when the transcript of a German wireless landed on the desk of De Grey's desk in Room 40, the locus of decoding situated in the vicinity of the British Admiralty. The decoders unearthed first the sender's name: Arthur Zimmermann, the Kaiser's Minister of Foreign Affairs. Then they found "Most Secret" and "For Your Excellency's personal information." Since the wireless was directed towards Washington, a very plausible hypothesis was that the German Ambassador Count von Bernstorff was the Excellency in question. Further scrutiny uncovered that the German will resume "unrestricted" submarine war by February 1 and that the German Minister in Mexico, von Eckhardt, should convince the Mexicans and possibly the Japanese to make war against the US *if the United States does not remain neutral*. In her best-selling book, *The Zimmermann Telegram* (1971), Barbara Tuchman followed the traces of this telegram which, in the end, became a decisive factor which made President Wilson to give up the policy of neutrality and bring the United States into war against Germany. This chapter explores Tuchman's book with a focus on the working of secrets, secret messages, and their decoding.

However, before we dive into this swamp, it must be told that, at the beginning of 1916, the perspective of Mexico making trouble for the United States and Japan joining the war, was not as unrealistic as it seems today. In fact, General Pershing commanded 12,000 American soldiers operating within Mexico's borders. It is not obvious whether this activity was meant to support President Carranza against the growing band of competitors, or to teach the Mexicans an adequate interpretation of the Monroe Doctrine – i.e., to accept the dominance of the United States. In any case, this action added to the Mexicans' hostile feelings towards their mighty northern neighbor. The promise of plentiful guns and ammunition fueling the dream to regain the old borders which included Texas, New Mexico, and Arizona could motivate the Mexicans to consider threatening the southern border of the United States.[11] The promise and the fuel for the dream were contained in Zimmermann's memo.

---

10  This is considered as the ultimate English version of the so-called "Zimmermann Telegram" (quoted after Friedman and Mendelsohn (1994 [1938]: 1). Also see *Collier's Encyclopedia* (1969: 761). Bauer (2013: 185ff.) gives a summary of the Zimmermann Telegram story.

11  California was not mentioned. Perhaps it was reserved to bribe Japan.

The relationship between the United States and Japan was even more delicate. On the one hand, Japan was an ally of England, France, and the other enemies of the Axis. Japan declared war on Germany on August 9, 1914, and by November that year it had harvested the Marshall and Caroline Islands and taken over Tsingtao on the Chinese mainland which was formally leased by China to Imperial Germany as a naval base, but in fact was treated as a colony and functioned to control major areas of the host country. On the other hand, the Americans were more than irritated when the *Asama*, a Japanese battle cruiser, together with a fleet of smaller units, was grounded in the mud of Turtle Bay on the coast of Mexican Lower California. Many Americans felt that the "Yellow Peril," a term made popular by the Kaiser, had come close. Barbara Tuchman observed that

> Japan was not displeased by the universal suspicion of her intentions. The greater the doubts of her loyalty, the higher the price the Allies would pay to keep her loyal. She did not mind letting it be known to the Allies that she had been approached by the enemy.
>
> (Tuchman 1971: 59)

In any case, the Germans were strongly convinced that the Japanese had chosen the wrong side in this war. Step by step, they promoted the Japanese from "Yellow Peril" to the "Prussians of the East." This conviction might look peculiar in the early twentieth century, but the future demonstrated its implementation, at the expense of millions of lives.

There was a somewhat bizarre argument which, in the view of the Germans, connects the fate of Japan with that of Mexico, and vice versa. The Germans considered the Mexicans and the Japanese "alike races" and, strangely enough, not only more and more Mexicans and Japanese, but also Americans and Germans, drew their political conclusions from this peculiar message. Obviously, the Zimmermann Telegram and its interpretation were partly a result of it. Thus, the Telegram fell on fertile ground and so did its publication.

By some highly unlikely coincidence, my wife and I had the chance to read the so far unpublished memoirs of Wilhelm Freiherr von Schoen – "Zeitzeuge Deutscher Außenpolitik 1908–1944" (A Witness of German Foreign Policy 1908–1944) – written in 1945 after the end of World War II. During 1908–44, von Schoen served as a German diplomat. In 1914, after Japan declared war on Germany on August 23 and the German diplomats had to leave the country, von Schoen arrived in Seattle on September 13. Then, until December 26, 2016, he was a member of the German Embassy at Washington. On December 26, he left for Mexico to fill his new position at the German Embassy at Orizaba, halfway between Veracruz and the Highlands. (The Mexican government of President Carranza had to leave Mexico City in the turmoil of the civil war.) In fact, von Schoen writes that it was rumored that he had brought Zimmermann's telegram from Washington to Mexico, but lost the message on his way. Von Schoen clarifies that he arrived in Mexico on January 5, whereas Zimmermann's telegram was issued on January 19.[12] Of course, after the telegram was published, guesswork circulated as to whether the information in the telegram was made public by treason or by negligence. According to von Schoen, the simplest and most obvious answer was that the "rather primitive" code was read by the enemy's secret service. The telegram's contents he considered "extremely ridiculous," as the Government of Mexico had not even the financial and military means to end its own civil war. He is sure that Zimmermann did not write the telegram, but he acknowledged Zimmermann's responsibility for this blunder.

### 4.2.2 How Admiral Hall managed the secrecy of the secret

Admiral Sir William Reginald Hall, Director of Naval Intelligence and head of Room 40, was "seized by the agonizing problem that always haunts the cryptographer: how to make use of the information without revealing that he knows the code" (Tuchman 1971: 7). Hall was sure that he held the instrument that would puncture American neutrality – if it could be used. To bring the United States into war was vital to the Allies, exhausted as they were in men, morale, and money. It was not only the Germans who expected that the unrestricted submarine war could strangle Britain and the unoccupied rest of France by cutting the delivery of the necessities to resist the German war machinery – and ultimate defeat loomed. However, it "had taken years, the genius of a few men, the lives of others, the long patient month" (Tuchman 1971: 8), to break the German code and the prospect that the Germans could switch to another code was not promising at all.

One of the first activities of the British after declaring war on Germany on August 4, 1914 was to cut the German transatlantic cables and thus to seal Germany off from direct cable communication. The Germans were constrained to wireless communication that allowed the British to pick German secrets, commands, and gossip out of the air, or the Germans sent their messages on detours via neutral information channels. Supportive Swedish government officials allowed a large number of German messages to be sent via Stockholm–Buenos Aires to America. In 1915, the British protested against this practice. However, the

> British government must have realized soon after this protest . . . that the information they were gleaning from the study of these messages was too valuable to lose, even taking into account the fact that the messages were of considerable use to the enemies. It is more than likely that the information was at least as useful to the British as it was to the Germans themselves. In some cases there is no doubt that it was even more useful.
>
> (Friedman and Mendelsohn 1994 [1938]: 18)

---

12 Also in the literature (see above), there is the date January 17.

Of course, these secrets were coded and thus needed decoding. This gave birth to Room 40. When the Zimmermann Telegram was intercepted, Room 40 was staffed by eight hundred wireless operators and up to eighty cryptographers and clerks. Without going through the intricacies of deciphering, it has to be said that it was of great help to the Room 40 team that the Germans sent out their messages in duplicate and triplicate, thus producing several versions of the same message in alternative cryptographic codes. This, of course, helped breaking the codes and reading the messages: "The sending of a message in more than one code is a capital crime in cryptography. True, it was a crime that we know the Germans to have committed" (Friedman and Mendelsohn 1994 [1938]: 43). The Germans committed a similar violation of a basic principle of cryptography in World War II, as we will see below.

This procedure also was of help to Admiral Hall to solve his secrecy problem. As the "very secret" Zimmermann Telegram was sent over various channels, Hall could design a story which made it difficult, if not impossible, for the Germans to trace back the leaking to Room 40 or to even think that their code was broken. However, what was even more substantial was German hubris, which made Admiral Hall think that "the Germans were clever . . . but just that fatal inch short of being clever enough to suspect that their enemy might be clever too" (Tuchman 1971: 7). He actively supported this perspective also at the occasion of the Zimmermann Telegram. When President Wilson arranged its publication in the US press, Admiral Hall "was very anxious that there should be no suspicion in the German mind" that the British "had anything to do with it." At Admiral Hall's own request, the *Daily Mail* "published a stinging leader passing severe reflections on the British Intelligence Service" (Friedman and Mendelsohn 1994 [1938]: 47). The Germans never thought about changing the code. Even when the Zimmermann Telegram was published, they still used the very same code and sent messages in duplicate and triplicate to find out where the Telegram was leaked. But where was it leaked?

Room 40 produced *alternative facts*, preparing a version of the Telegram which suggested that it was stolen from the desk of von Eckhardt, probably by a spy, after it reached Mexico via Washington with the help of US communication installations. If the make-up was believed then there was no hint that the code was broken – and that the British had a routine of reading the telegrams transmitted over the US communications installations, generally sent and received by US government agents. This version of the Telegram was shown to the US ambassador in London and then transferred into the hands of President Wilson. The latter, "perhaps the most tragic figure of the day,"[13] not only saw his edifice of peace break down, but seemingly became very angry when he learned that the Germans used the US communications hardware to look for partners in the pending war against the United States: "the German Foreign Office used the American Government as an errand boy for

---

13  This is how (George) Bernard Shaw (1964 [1919]: 45) ranked the American President.

the transmission of a document that contained a plot against its own territorial integrity" (Friedman and Mendelsohn 1994 [1938]: 20). In his biographical work on Walter H. Page, the wartime US ambassador to Great Britain, Burton J. Hendrick commented:

> Humor of any kind the Germans seldom displayed at crises of this sort, yet the mechanism adopted to make certain that this plot against the American people would safely land on Bernstorff's desk evinces an unmistakable gift – even – though an unconscious one – for the sardonic.
>
> (quoted from Friedman and Mendelsohn 1994 [1938]: 19)

Lewis reports that Wilson

> pushed through Congress in 1917 an Espionage Act that criminalized not only espionage but speech critical of the government. Wilson proposed to include, but the Congress struck out, a provision for censorship of news-papers. In 1918 Congress passed an amendment, known as the Sedition Act, that made it a crime to use 'disloyal' or 'profane' language that might encourage contempt for the Constitution or the flag.
>
> (Lewis 2009: 44)

Lewis concludes that Wilson was a reformer on economic issues "but on civil liberties he was a disaster" (Lewis 2009: 47). This is strongly confirmed by Hochschild (2017) in his review (headlined "When Dissent Became Treason") of Margaret E. Wagner's *America and the Great War: A Library of Congress Illustrated History*, Michael Kazin's *War Against War: The American Fight for Peace, 1914–1918*, Nick Fischer's *Spider Web: The Birth of American Anticommunism*, and *The Great War*, a three-part television series produced by Stephen Ives and Amanda Pollak for PBS's American Experience. Recently, "at Princeton, students of color have contended that, because of Woodrow Wilson's racist views, the school should remove his name from a residential college and from the university's school of public policy" (Cole 2016: 4). However, one cannot remove his name from America's history. Nevertheless, having these details in mind, I felt somewhat irritated when in June 2016 I bicycled over Pont Wilson at Lyon crossing the Rhône river and walked the Wilsonova in Prague in November 2016 to reach the Central Station.

### 4.2.3 Grapes of wrath and naivety

Still at the beginning of 1917, Wilson was hoping and rallying for a "'peace without victory." He thought this could only be achieved if the United States acted as a mediator. This mediator role made it necessary that the US maintain its neutrality. However, both sides of the European War insisted on victory and the ultimate defeat of the other side. But Wilson was firm in his policy, which was supported by a majority of US citizens who had just elected him to a second term. Most Americans thought that the Europeans should solve their troubles on their own. Although this opinion was quite different from Wilson's motivation, it gave his presidency a majority.

Wilson was especially furious about the Telegram because it was he who agreed that the German Embassy could receive messages in code. He expected that the exchange of messages was about conditions for peace, and not about finding allies that would keep the US busy at home. Wilson felt cheated, humiliated, and betrayed.

Now, after he had read the Telegram and its text was widely published in the press, whatever the original motivation for neutrality had been, the US's neutrality transformed into disgust and hate for the *Huns*. Even the American West, thus far absolutely disinterested in the European War, saw itself attacked by a German policy which invited the "Yellow Peril" to come ashore. More or less within a day, public opinion swung from neutral position that even allowed some sentimental ties with Germany (not surprising with a large portion of the US's population being of German origin), to the call for joining the Allies in the fight against the German aggressor. Most likely, the "cry of wrath" would have been even louder if it had been made public by what channel Zimmerman had transmitted his instructions. But the US government kept its silence on this and many other details – a silence which was readily supported by Admiral Hall and his office.

In the US Senate, there were still members who doubted the authenticity of the Telegram and proposed that it could be a fake, deployed by the British to bring the United States into the war. These doubts were strengthened by the fact that President Carranza had categorically denied that he had received any offer from the Germans, and had confirmed his and his country's neutrality. Confirming the Telegram's authenticity looked like a rather complicated problem. For a solution, Admiral Hall pointed out that there was at least one copy of the Telegram in the records of the US telegraph system, although still coded. He offered some hints that the transcript on President Wilson's desk was a deciphered version of this copy. However, "standing on federal law protecting the contents of telegrams," Western Union "would not let its files be searched" (Tuchman 1971: 165). It needed some government pressure on Western Union's president to overcome this barrier. Still, Room 40 kept some degree of ambiguity about how much of the German code the British could decipher. This did not help President Wilson to make a decision. He was very angry but still hesitant, while most of his voters now cried for some sort of revenge, especially when information arrived that several US ships had been torpedoed and sunk by German submarines, and American lives lost.

Rather unexpectedly, Admiral Hall received support from an absolutely reliable source that unambiguously confirmed the Zimmermann Telegram. In a press conference in Berlin, Arthur Zimmermann said he could not deny the veracity of the Telegram. "It is true," he said. Why Zimmermann did not deny the Telegram's authenticity – which would have left the authenticity discussion pending, and given German intelligence a chance to obtain further information of how the Telegram was leaked – remains one of the great secrets of history. Perhaps Zimmermann relied on a reading of the Telegram as a listing of possible measures which the United States must expect if it entered the war. Perhaps he even hoped that potential threats from south of its border and from the other side of the Pacific could make neutrality even more attractive to the Americans. However, this is just guessing: there is no evidence. Five weeks later, the United States joined the Allies in the war against Germany.

A series of other questions are related to this case that remain unanswered. Admiral Hall continued to play cat-and-mouse after his retirement, and the tons of deciphered documents which he left for the public only demonstrate that Room 40 was extremely skillful and highly efficient. But they do not answer why the British waited till the end of February 1917, to let President Wilson know the German plans in the case that his government declared war, while the Telegram had already been deciphered in Room 40 on January 17, 1917. Friedman and Mendelsohn (1994 [1938]) suggest a mix of quite convincing arguments for this "delay." Firstly, the British could not admit that they received the information by decoding messages sent via American channels. Secondly, Room 40 had problems with deciphering; in order to fill the gaps, British had to resort to time-consuming crosschecks with information contained in the duplicates and triplicates sent by the Germans. Thirdly, Admiral Hall could have been hoping that the reopening of the unrestricted submarine warfare would bring the United States onto the British side. In fact, "diplomatic relations between the United States and Germany were severed. But as the weeks went by there was no declaration of war . . . Something had to be done to stir up the President and the people of the hinterland beyond the Mississippi" (Friedman and Mendelsohn 1994 [1938]: 45).

Perhaps Admiral Hall was not convinced that the Telegram could have a decisive effect at all. Releasing information which would signal that the British could read the German code could be too high a price. In fact, from a careful reading of the Telegram, the Americans could have learned about German measures, *if the US enters war against the Axis*. They could also read that the Germans will "endeavour . . . to keep the United States of America neutral." This does not sound like looking for a fight.

In his book *Road to War, America 1914–1917*, Millis (1935: 407) pointed out that the headlines of the American press commenting the Zimmermann Telegram, or what was given to them by the US Government

> were not always precisely accurate. Germany had not actually sought an alliance as yet . . . It was not a proposal for an aggression against the United States, but merely a conventional, though rather blundering diplomatic preparation against a probable American attack upon Germany.
>
> (Millis 1935: 407)

Obviously, Zimmermann was too naïve to make this point clear to the Americans and their president. It seems that he relied too much on careful reading. What made the telegram particularly shocking, of course, was the suggestion that the Japanese . . . should be invited to the American Continent, or that the principle upon which many Americans had demanded the restoration of Alsace-Lorraine (because they had been acquired by force) should be applied to California and Texas, which we had forcibly detached from Mexico. Informed Americans understood perfectly well that the Allies had bribed Japan, Italy, and Rumania into war with the promise of slices from the enemy carcass.

(Millis 1935: 407)

But even informed Americans felt threatened by the perspective that was drafted in the Telegram. Zimmermann did not try to clarify that this was a draft that would become relevant only if the Americans joined the Allies in the war against Germany. Somewhat ironically Millis concludes that there

is no doubt that President Wilson was profoundly shocked by this revelation of the fact that one could not go to war with Germany without having the Germans fight back. It did never even occur to him to question the authenticity of the document or the motive for the production of a month-old telegram at just that moment.

(Millis 1935: 407)

Indeed, there was no need to question the document's authenticity after the published text was confirmed by Zimmermann. However, the political evaluation of the telegram was not based on careful reading, but on strong resentments triggered by the possibilities indicated in its text and the scandalous circumstances of its transmission. Moreover, from reading Millis (1935), one could conclude that "America" was on the Road to War anyhow. There are alternative interpretations why it entered so late – even after the German government had declared unrestricted submarine warfare: "According to Thorstein Veblen, the United States had entered the war, belatedly, only to ensure that the transnational interests of the industrialists would be protected against any social upheavals that peace in Europe might unleash" (Dyson 2012: 20).

### 4.2.4 The Telegram Game

The need for information and communication, which is an important feature of modern wars, forced the Germans into wiring coded messages after the British had cut the German transatlantic cables at the beginning of the war. However, the creation and use of information implied thinking in terms of "putting oneself into the other's shoes" when making decisions. This is the essence of a game situation and, indeed, most of the involved agents acted strategically, in a game-theoretical sense. Applying game theory might be a key to a deeper understanding of the problem that Admiral Hall faced after reading the decoded message of the German Ministry of Foreign Affairs to Mexico.

The envisioned game had various players: the United States represented by their president, the members of the Congress and of the political elite, the Germans, the governments and military of the Allies including Hall's own superiors, and Admiral Hall and his staff. However, these players were relatively unconnected to each other and coalitions can be the *result* of the game but not a *precondition* at the outset. If we take this into consideration, then we can look at the game that Admiral Hall and his office played with the US under the constraint that the Germans should not find out about Britain's capacity for decoding. As the above story tells us, the Germans did not behave strategically in a game-theoretical sense and therefore can be considered a part of nature in the telegram game: they never thought that somebody could ever decode their messages. They even committed the blunder of sending a message in more than one code, as already noted. Therefore we can reduce the strategic decision making to two players: Admiral Hall and his office, in short "Hall." and President Wilson and his staff, in short "Wilson." Although the behavior of President Wilson seemed to be dominated by his emotions, and not by strategic reasoning, the strategic acting of the British side indicates that Wilson entered Hall's reasoning as a strategic agent, i.e., a player.

Having identified the players, what are their strategy sets? As we want to keep the game simple, we restrict ourselves and consider two pure strategies for each player only. Hall can deliver the contents of the telegram, inasmuch as it is deciphered, but keep the source fully covered. We will label this strategy as "keep covered." Alternatively, Hall can admit to Wilson and his staff that the British can read the German code and that they followed communication on US information channels. In this case, the secret of the decoding is fully disclosed and the fact that the British spy on US information channels is uncovered. However, Hall can choose degrees of (incomplete) disclosure and this is what he did by making up the story of the stolen documents. In what follows, the variable p indicates this degree: p = 1 indicates that no reliable information about the source is given while p = 0 implies full disclosure.

President Wilson and his staff

|  |  | Not publish $(q = 1)$ | Publish $(q = 0)$ |
|---|---|---|---|
| Admiral Hall and his office | Keep covered $(p = 1)$ | (0,2) | (1,1) |
| | Disclose $(p = 0)$ | (1,1) | (-5,2) |

*Figure 4.2* The Telegram Game

President Wilson can decide to publish the information that Hall gave, or not. In order to convince the public, Wilson will also give information on the source if he chooses the pure strategy "publish," conditional on the information that Hall delivers. Of course, there are also degrees of how much to publish. These degrees are expressed by q, with q being a value between 0 and 1; q = 0 indicates that Wilson publishes the information that Hall delivered on the issue of the Zimmermann Telegram without further qualification; q = 1 means to be absolutely silent about the source of the Telegram.[14]

Note that the matrix representation implies that Hall does not know the strategy choice of Wilson when he is to choose his strategy, and vice versa, i.e., players are assumed to have imperfect information. This also implies that Wilson will decide on publishing before he can see Hall's decision. The assumption that the President has informed the press before it has been verified whether Hall has disclosed the information's source, or to what degree, might seem somewhat peculiar. However, this is what happened. But to take care of possible objections, we will analyze also a sequential model which suggests that the degree of disclosure is known to Wilson before he decides to "publish" the source of the information, or not.

To give a complete description of the game, we have to know the outcomes that result from the various strategy combinations and, most importantly, the values – i.e., payoffs – which the two players assign to these outcomes. Of course, the latter are the most debatable entries of the matrix in Figure 4.2.

But let us first talk about the outcomes that do not show up in the matrix, but are in the background of the matrix's entries. The assumption is that in the case the source of information contained in the Telegram is fully uncovered and the source will be published, then the Germans know that the British can read their coded messages. It is assumed that the Germans will stop wiring information if this information is meant to be secret, and look for a new code. Both consequences are expected to have damaging effects for the Allies (but are also costly to the Germans, because the latter will have to revise their information network which is rather difficult in a war situation). This justifies a value of -5 for Admiral Hall and his office, while President Wilson and his staff can convincingly argue that the US must enter the war against Germany. The latter is evaluated by an entry of 2. However, the same value is assumed for President Wilson and his staff if the source is kept covered and nothing is published. Then, at least so far, the US will not enter the war. We should not forget that Wilson was looking for peace, as long as he was not forced by hostile actions to become active against the German Reich.

Compared to the two outcomes just described, less favorable results are expected for President Wilson if his agents support the publication of

---

14 Alternatively, q can also be interpreted as the probability that the given information will not be published. Then q describes a mixed strategy and q ∈ [0,1] is Wilson's set of mixed strategies with the pure strategy q = 1 and q = 0 as extreme cases. Similarly, Hall's p can be identified with the probability of "keep covered" (p = 1) and "disclose" (p= 0).

the Telegram but the source remains fully covered – then Wilson's payoff is assumed to be 1 – or, alternatively, the source is fully disclosed, but the information is not published. Again, Wilson's payoff is assumed to be 1. Corresponding values for Hall are shown in the matrix. We assume that Hall's payoff out of (keep covered, not publish) is 0, i.e., strictly lower than for the outcomes of (keep covered, publish) and (disclose, not publish). Of course, the payoff values are open to be debated. For the arguments that follow, it suffices that we accept the ordinal ordering of these values. Obviously, "not publish" is not a best reply for Wilson if Hall chooses to "disclose" how successfully his office works (which he did not intend per se). However, the strategy "disclose" is a best reply to the strategy "not publish" – i.e., there is no risk in giving information if it is not published – but not vice versa. Therefore, the strategy pair (disclose, not publish) is not a Nash equilibrium as the strategies are not mutually best replies to each other.

In fact, there is no pair of pure strategies in this game that represents a Nash equilibrium. Whatever strategies Admiral Hall and President Wilson choose, one of the two decision makers can do better by choosing an alternative strategy, *given the strategy of the other*. Obviously, the game has the structure of the *Inspection Game* discussed in Section 3.8.1. We can straightforwardly apply the results of this section to the game in Figure 4.2. We get the equilibrium values $p* = 1/2$ and $q* = 6/7$. The corresponding payoff values are $u_1(q*) = 1/7 = 0.143$ and $u_2(p*) = 1.5$.[15] Of course, these values imply a cardinal interpretation of the payoffs given in Figure 4.2. For the interpretation of the Telegram Game, these values are not essential, but the fact that the equilibrium is mixed should matter. If we interpret p and q as levels and degrees, then neither will Hall fully disclose its source, nor will Wilson publish all details. Perhaps it is more realistic that Hall expects Wilson to randomize on "publish" and "not publish."

The equilibrium interpretation assumes that the players know the matrix in Figure 4.2. However, alternatively we could define Figure 4.2 as representing the reasoning of Admiral Hall. The payoffs, his own and those of Wilson, are his estimate. In this case, the cardinal values $p*$ and $q*$ are his estimates of the equilibrium values – and the assumption of cardinality might be even justified. But if Hall expects that Wilson chooses $q*$, then any p is a best reply, and Hall cannot derive any specific plan of action from this form of reasoning. In a way, he is "free to choose" as any choice is "rationalizable."

However, is the simultaneity of action implicit to the matrix in Figure 4.2 justifiable? It could be argued that Wilson and his adviser cannot decide on publishing the information contained in the Zimmermann Telegram before Hall and his office disclose the message. History tells us that Wilson gave a preliminary text to the press before the conditions to verify the information was clear. Of course, Hall made the first move in this game by letting the US

15 For details of the calculation, see Holler (2009a).

government have a preliminary version of the Telegram's text. But does this already imply disclosure? Or, does it necessitate that the British will have to produce a story that makes the Telegram booty trustworthy? Does it matter whether Hall decided first on disclosure and Wilson followed, or is the simultaneous-move story, implied in Figure 4.2, a good approximation?

In order to prepare for an answer to these questions, we assume a sequential game such that Hall decides first on "keep covered" ($p = 1$), "disclose" ($p = 0$), or any other degree of p. Wilson can observe Hall's decision, even when p is more complex than $p = 1$ and $p = 0$, and will choose a best reply to p, selecting either "not publish" or "publish" or a linear combination of these two strategies, characterized by $q \in (0,1)$. As Hall expects such a reaction, the following reasoning derives from simple backward induction.[16]

The indifference properties of $(p*,q*)$ suggest that if Hall chooses $p° > p* = \frac{1}{2}$, then $q = 1$, i.e., Wilson will choose the pure strategy "not publish." In this case, Hall's payoff will be $u_1(p) = p°0 + (1 - p°)1 = 1 - p°$. Assuming $p° = p* + \varepsilon$ and $\varepsilon > 0$, then $u_1(p°) = 0.5 - \varepsilon$. This result shows that the payoff to Hall will be the larger the smaller $\varepsilon$ is. This suggests minimizing $\varepsilon$. Of course, $\varepsilon$ has to be large enough so that Wilson is no longer indifferent between "not publish" and "publish," but will choose the pure strategy "not publish" for sure.

If Hall chooses $p° < p* = \frac{1}{2}$, then Wilson will react with $q = 0$. Accordingly, Hall's payoff will be $u_1(p) = p°1 + (1 - p°)(- 5) = 6p° - 5$. Assuming $p° = p* - \varepsilon$ and $\varepsilon > 0$, then $u_1(p°) = -2 - 6\varepsilon$.

A comparison of the payoff $u_1(p°)$ for $p° > p* = \frac{1}{2}$ and $p° < p* = \frac{1}{2}$ indicates that Hall should choose for $p° > p* = \frac{1}{2}$ if he wants to maximize his payoff. For any $\varepsilon > 0$, obviously $\frac{1}{2} - \varepsilon > -2 - 6\varepsilon$ holds. The more sensitive Wilson is to variations of degrees of disclosure, the smaller $\varepsilon$ will be. If $\varepsilon$ approaches 0, that is, if Wilson is very sensitive and Hall knows about this, then Hall's payoff will be close to $\frac{1}{2}$. This, of course, is larger than the payoff $u_1(q*) = 1/7 = 0.143$, i.e., the value corresponds to the mixed-strategy equilibrium of the simultaneous game in Figure 4.2. Note that the (subgame perfect) equilibrium of the sequential game, $(p°, q = 1)$, presupposes that Hall cannot change the strategy $p°$ after Wilson opted for "not publish." This assumption is essential because $p°$ is not a best reply to $q = 1$ as we know from the discussion of the simultaneous game.

In order to complete the picture, Wilson's payoff in the sequential game will be $(\frac{1}{2} + \varepsilon)2 + (\frac{1}{2} - \varepsilon)1 = 1.5 + \varepsilon$, while his value in the equilibrium of the simultaneous game will be $u_2(p*) = 1.5$. Since $\varepsilon > 0$, also Wilson will get a higher payoff in the sequential game. The result shows that it pays for Wilson not to be too sensitive and to have a larger $\varepsilon$, given that Hall knows about this fact. For Hall, however, it is advantageous if $\varepsilon$ is small and Wilson reacts on

16 Here we follow the reasoning already applied in Section 3.8.3. See Andreozzi (2004) and Holler (2009a). In Andreozzi, $p°$ is a probability (representing a share of the population), but no degree.

minor variations of p. The sensitivity of Wilson may depend on the facts disclosed, on the reliability of the source, but also on political convenience. In any case, the American publication policy and the British information policy were such that the Germans did not conclude that their messages were decoded. This result is consistent with our game-theoretical analysis.

### 4.2.5 The Turing solution

Winston Churchill said that Turing made the single biggest contribution to Allied victory in World War II. Captain Jerry Roberts, who worked with Turing at Bletchley Park, even claimed that without Turing's contribution, the Allies would have lost the war.[17] More conservative estimates claim that Turing's contribution shortened the war by at least two years and thereby spared 2–3 million lives. Bletchley Park, some 55 miles northwest of London, was the home of an organization called the Government Code and Cypher School (GC&CS), which was responsible for deciphering the military codes that secured the enemy's communications. There was a team in charge of breaking the Enigma code of the German Navy. This code was used by the U-boats which were engaged in the large-scale sinking of Allied ships bringing vital arms and provisions from North America. However, Roberts emphasized that Turing was pivotal to the success of the team – without Turing, the team at Bletchley Park would not have succeeded.

The success had three conditions. Two are obvious: breaking the code, and sending ships and airplanes to fight the U-boats. The third one is not to let the Germans know that Enigma had been deciphered. If condition three is not satisfied, then the Germans are likely to change their code and the problem of decoding starts again. Or the Germans will reduce reliable communication and flood the decoding office with fake information. Alan Turing faced a similar problem as Admiral Hall: how to make use of the information after breaking the code without letting the enemy know that the secret is no longer a secret? We do not know what happened behind the gates of Bletchley Park, but there is a scene in the movie *The Imitation Game* that suggests that Turing proposed a mixed strategy – and implemented it. This strategy did not always mean making use of the decoded information one had regarding German U-boats attacking the Allied convoys. The price of such a strategy of course

17 See "Churchill: Turing made the single biggest contribution to the war effort," *Days to Centenary: 248*, posted on October 19, 2011, by *nashedron* – https://theturingcentenary. wordpress.com/2011/10/19/churchill-turing-made-the-single-biggest-contribution-to-the-war-effort/ [accessed April 1, 2018]. The collection (Turing 2004: 338–340) contains a letter of October 21, 1941, addressed to then British Prime Minister Winston Churchill, signed by Alan Turing and three other members of the Bletchley Park team, pointing out the shortage of staff and the possible delay in reading Enigma. Turing's signature is on the top, not considering the alphabetical order of signing addressors. The historical facts on Turing, referred to in the following, are taken from this report and of Jack Copeland's biography (2012).

was sunken ships and lost lives; the benefits were that the Germans did not change the code and thus many ships and lives could be saved and the share of food and armament supplies arriving by sea was augmented substantially.

The price had to be costly enough that the Germans would not become suspicious or alarmed. That is, the price that had to be paid implied large sacrifices of "men and materiel." Most likely, this was not easy to implement. In one scene in *The Imitation Game*, Turing is called a "monster." In the scene, at the moment the Enigma code is deciphered by the Bletchley Park team, one of its members realizes that the German U-boats are heading to attack a convoy which included a ship on which his brother was doing service. He begs Turing to quickly pass on the information so that the convoy can be warned and counter-measures taken, a plea echoed by the other team members. However, the Turing of the movie rejects this plea, explaining that the Germans might conclude that the secrecy of their messages is lost. His arguments suggested a mixed strategy. Indeed, this is what decision theory suggests for this case. But this strategy does not imply that you should never use the information that you gain by reading your competitor's (or enemy's) secret messages. Obviously, if you never use it then your decoding success is worth nothing. So why shouldn't Turing start "mixing" by trying to save the brother's life and much of the convoy? Or did he want to reserve the first post-decoding action for the saving of a more valuable convoy? The movie is silent about this possibility. Actually, Caryle (2015: 20) reports that "the British secret services covered their growing success against German U-boats, for example, by strategically strewing rumors of ultra-powerful new sonar systems." Indeed, again and again, the story of this sonar system is told in stories and histories of the "Battle of the Atlantic."

In fact, there *were* new and quite successful sonar systems. However, sonar systems rely on acoustics and are not very helpful in identifying positions of enemy ships over a long distance. (Sonar is an acronym for Sound Navigation And Ranging.) Before Enigma could be read, the U-boat's transmissions were used to identify the enemy's position. "The U-boat transmissions provided the British and, later, American listeners with the direction-finding 'fixes' which determined where dangerous areas in the Atlantic lay and so how convoys should be routed to avoid them," explains Keegan (1990: 286) in his book *The Price of Admiralty*. He also made clear that

> radio intelligence lay at the heart of the waging of the U-boat campaign by both sides. The theory of U-boat pack operations (Rudeltaktik) . . . was based on the principle of massing U-boats against a convoy target by control from a central, shore-based headquarters. It required transmission from headquarters to captains; it equally required transmission in the opposite direction, and it was those which presented the U-boats' enemies with the raw material of the radio war.
>
> (Keegan 1990: 286)

Of course, once the British could read the messages they were in a much better position to organize their convoys to avoid the "wolf-packs" of German submarines. They learned about the intention of their enemies and not just about their location. According to Keegan (1990: 288), "for long and significant periods of the war the German-B-Dienst could read the Royal Navy's codes, sometimes when the reverse was not the case." Moreover, like the British, like Turing's team, the Germans faced the problem that they "were obliged to forego the use of much valuable information out of prudent concern to protect the secret of their cipher-reading success," Keegan (1990: 289) points out. There are serious restrictions to the use of secrets when secrets should be treated as secrets – after secrecy is gone.

The Royal Navy code was broken in February 1942 while the German Navy's Shark key was not broken before December of the same year. The latter was achieved by Turing's Bletchley Park team and the "bomb," but only after the destroyer HMS *Petard* captured the U 559 in the Mediterranean in October 1942 and collected the codebook of Enigma-M4, the most complex member of the Enigma family. Turing's bomb was an electro-mechanical calculating device that helped to reduce the complexity of the Enigma machine. It took care of characteristics of the Enigma machine, inasmuch as they were known, thereby reducing the number of possible combinations that the decoders had to deal with. Using this principle and a corresponding machine, the codes of the German Army and Air Force were already deciphered in 1940. To a large extent, decoding was an "imitation game."[18] In his biography of Turing, Leavitt (2006) has chosen title "The Imitation Game" for the chapter dealing with Turing's work at Manchester University from 1948 onwards.

### 4.2.6 Imitation games

Christian Caryle's "Saving Alan Turing from His Friends," a review of *The Imitation Game* movie and of two books on Turing, gives a list of interpretations and unconfirmed details which attest that the movie shows Turing in a rather unfavorable light – "reducing him to a caricature of tortured genius" (Caryle 2015: 19). He adds: "In perhaps the most bitter irony of all, the filmmakers

---

18 It happened that the German operators repeated messages without changing the settings of the wheels of the coding machine. Of course, if "the repeated message was identical to the original, the codebreakers were not better off ... But if the sender made a few typos the second time around, or used different punctuation, the depth consisted of two, not quite-identical plaintexts, each encrypted with exactly the same letters, a codebreaker's dream" (Copeland 2012: 90). Another codebreaker's dream must have been the standard formula "Heil Hitler" that ended many of the messages coded in Enigma and Tunny. Tunny was technologically more sophisticated than Enigma with a high degree of automatic operation. (See Copeland (2012: 86) for details.) It did not become as popular as Enigma, perhaps because the "story of Tunny and Turing's contribution to breaking it were kept secret for almost sixty years" (Copeland 2012: 86).

have managed to transform the real Turing, vivacious and forceful, into just the sort of mythological gay man, whiney and weak, that homophobes love to hate" (Caryle 2015: 20). Moreover, they presented Turing as a traitor even in two layers. First, we learn about the secret story at Bletchley Park from an interrogation that Turing had with a police officer. This was in the very early 1950s, when there were still draconian security restrictions on this issue. Secondly, and even more hilarious, the filmmakers put John Cairncross, who was spying for the Soviet Union at Bletchley Park, into Turing's team: "When Turing discovered his true allegiance, Cairncross turns the tables on him saying that he'll reveal Turing's homosexuality if his secret is divulged. Turing backs off, leaving the spy in place" Caryle (2015: 20).[19] However, Caryle observes, there is no evidence that Cairncross "ever crossed paths with Turing."

Caryle stresses that the filmmakers' errors are not random; they want to present Turing as a martyr of the homophobic establishment and relate his early death to the therapy, involving female hormones, that followed his conviction on homosexuality charges in 1952. The therapy ended in 1953. A full year later, he was found dead, of cyanide poisoning. The filmmakers concluded that this was suicide – as the standard interpretation tells us. In his speech pardoning Turing on September 10, 2009, Prime Minister Gordon Brown refers to the suicide alternative as a fact (Brown 2009). But Turing had been conducting experiments with cyanide and his death could have been an accident, the alternative subscribed to by Turing's mother. There was no evidence that Turing was particularly depressed in the days before his death, and there was no suicide letter either. Referring to Copeland's book (Copeland 2012) that is also a subject of his review, Caryle (2015: 20) hypothesized that Turing's homosexuality was regarded as a security risk and "he knew a lot of secrets, in the postwar period as well." Or, as Copeland (2012: 233) hypothesized: "Some may have considered that Turing knew too much about much too much."[20]

Alternatively, we could theorize that Turing was a victim of the notorious Cambridge Five, which possibly included John Cairncross and was headed by Kim Philby. The latter was a high-ranking member of British intelligence who worked as a double agent with a clear preference for the KGB. By late 1944, he had even become head of counterintelligence. In 1963, he defected to the Soviet Union where he died in 1988. In his review of Ben Macintyre's book *A Spy Among Friends: Kim Philby and the Great Betrayal*, Xan Smiley

19  This relates Turing's "personal secret" (see above) to the fundamental conservatism of British society and its corresponding legal system. For more on the relationship between conservatism and secrecy, see Gylling (2009).

20  See also Leavitt (2006: 278) for this hypothesis (although he seems to favor the suicide explanation.) As Copeland (2012: 233) pointed out, the notorious Senator Joseph McCarthy was very explicit in declaring "that homosexuals who were privy to national secrets threatened America's security." Copeland continues to ask the quite rhetorical question: "Did the secret services carry out covert assassinations in Britain?"

(2014: 46) reports that Philby, after the war, handed to the Russians "a list of several thousand anti-Nazi agents, mostly Catholics, who had survived the war in Germany but were rounded up and presumed to have been shot by the Russians after they conquered what became East Germany." Also, it is "probable . . . that Philby was responsible, across Europe, for the torture and deaths of hundreds of other agents." So Turing could well have been one of Philby's victims executed in favor of the Soviet Union – to make him stop thinking. Perhaps it is a coincidence that Smiley's review has been titled "Kim Philby: Still an Enigma."

Smiley (2014: 46) suggests that, to some extent, Philby's success was due to the fact that he succeeded to sow

> poisonous discord[21] . . . within and between the intelligence services of America and Britain. The dogged FBI and its British equivalent, MI5, were long convinced that Philby was a traitor but were prevented from nailing him by the often snobbish members of the CIA and MI6, who looked down on the domestic services.
>
> (Smiley 2014: 46)

Of course, this calls to mind Graham Greene's novel *Our Man in Havana* which builds on the rivalry of MI5 and MI6.[22] This should not come as a surprise: Kim Philby was Greene's supervisor at MI6 which he had joined in 1941. Greene even contributed an introduction to Philby's 1968 memoir, *My Silent War*, published five years after Philby's defection to Moscow. There is a lot of imitation in this story.

There is an imitation related with Turing's work, not mentioned in the movie, which nevertheless might even have a more substantial impact on our lives than the Enigma decoding: the stored-program computer, i.e., the universal programmable computer: "Every one of the smart devices that populate our lives today – every smartphone, tablet, and mainframe – owes its origins to Turing's original vision of the stored-program computer" (Caryle 2015: 19). Today, the concept of the stored-program is connected with the name of John von Neumann – one even uses the label of "von Neumann architecture" when referring to this principle – while Turing's pioneering contribution was for a long time only known to the academic world, partly covered

---

21 Smiley borrows this expression from Ben Macintyre's *A Spy Among Friends: Kim Philby and the Great Betrayal* (New York: Crown Publishers, 2014) – the book that he reviewed.

22 The novel is set in Havana. The vacuum-cleaner retailer James Wormold is approached to work for the British secret service MI6 and he accepts. When he has no information to send to London, he decides to submit sketches of vacuum-cleaner parts, telling his handlers that the sketches depict a secret military installation in the mountains. This interpretation is gladly accepted by the MI6 officers. When the sketches are uncovered as fake, Wormold is awarded a "Most Excellent Order of the British Empire" (OBE) as a bribe for his silence. The Service could not be allowed to lose face.

by the veil of secrecy that covered his person and his work for many years. John von Neumann acknowledged that the central concept of the modern computer was due to Turing's work – but this acknowledgment remained more or less in the private domain. There is a letter by Stanley Frankel to Brian Randell, 1972, quoted by Copeland (2004: 22) in which the author testifies: "von Neumann . . . firmly emphasised to me, and to others I am sure, that the fundamental conception is owing to Turing – insofar as not anticipated by Babbage, Lovelace and others."[23] In a footnote, Leavitt (2006: 6) mentions that "Martin Davis must be credited with setting the record straight on this account," confirming Turing's path-breaking contribution to the development of the modern computer. In the text, Leavitt (2006: 216) gives further details, also with reference to Martin Davis (who is the author of a study, published in 2000, on the prehistory of computers: *Engines of Logic: Mathematicians and the Origin of the Computer*).

Alan Turing was born in 1912 and died in 1954. In 1936, he came to Princeton to earn a Ph.D. in mathematics, at least partly under the supervision of the more senior John von Neumann who had a professorship at the Institute of Advanced Study. He studied a very general and highly philosophical problem that was already proposed by Leibniz and pointed out by David Hilbert in 1928 as *Entscheidungsproblem* (a problem): "Could reasoning be reduced to computation . . . is there some automatic procedure that will decide whether a given conclusion logically follows from a given set of premises?" (Holt 2012: 33). Turing gave a mathematical demonstration that no such automatic procedure and thus no algorithm could exist.[24] He suggested an idealized machine that defined the limits of computability: the Turing machine was born.

Here is a short introduction to this marvel

> A Turing machine designed for some special purpose – like adding two numbers together – could itself be described by a single number that coded its action. The code number of one special-purpose Turing machine could even be fed as an input onto the tape of another Turing machine.
>
> (Holt 2012: 33)

23  This reference is to the mathematician Ada Lovelace (1815–52), the only legitimate child of Lord Byron. She worked on Charles Babbage's early mechanical general-purpose computer, the "Analytical Engine."

24  In his seminal article "On Computable Numbers, with an Application to the *Entscheidungsproblem*," published 1936 in the *Proceedings of the London Mathematical Society*, Turing "proves the existence of mathematical problems that cannot be solved by the universal Turing machine. There he also advances the thesis . . . that any systematic method for solving mathematical problems can be carried out by the universal Turing machine. Combining these two propositions the result is that there are mathematical problems which cannot be solved by a systematic method – cannot, in other words, be solved by any algorithm," Jack Copeland, in Turing (2004: 576).

This was the stored-program. Turing was thinking of

> a universal machine: one that, if fed the code number of any special-purpose Turing machine, would perfectly mimic its behavior. For instance, if a universal Turing machine were fed the code number of the Turing machine that performed addition, the universal machine would temporarily turn into an adding machine. In effect, the 'hardware' of a special-purpose machine could be translated into 'software' (the machine's code number) and then entered like data into the universal machine, where it would run as a program.
>
> (Holt 2012: 33)

Did we see the universal machine in *The Imitation Game* movie decoding Enigma? It seems straightforward to think of the Turing machine as a self-referential system in terms of Hofstadter (1980), and the relationship to Gödel's proof seems obvious. Indeed, in 1936, Turing submitted a paper "On Computable Numbers, with an Application to the *Entscheidungsproblem*," in which he demonstrated an alternative to Gödel's proof of 1931 on the limits of proof and computation, already applying a conceptual frame that became known as the "Turing machine." It is said that this marks the birth of artificial intelligence.

Most likely von Neumann knew about Turing's paper.[25] Did von Neumann inspire Turing? Perhaps von Neumann's game-theoretical work led Turing to pick the mixed strategy which was hinted at in *The Imitation Game*. On the other hand, the idea of a mixed strategy was around long before von Neumann did his proof of the minimax theorem. Moreover, during the time when both Turing and von Neumann were at Princeton, it seems that the latter was not very interested in game theory and the path-breaking volume *Theory of Games and Economic Behavior* (authored with Oskar Morgenstern in 1944) was not even in the state of planning. In fact, von Neumann and Morgenstern did not meet before 1939 and it took some time before collaboration on *TGEB* started. In 1938, during a visit of Morgenstern to Princeton University, after Hitler's Germany overran Austria ("Anschluss Österreichs"), he decided not to return to Vienna, but to stay in the United States and to become a member of the faculty at Princeton.[26]

I do not think that such an ingenious brain as Turing's needed an introduction into game theory to find out that randomization over types of behavior can be a suitable means to save a secret. In summer 1938, after Turing completed

---

25 According to Holt (2012: 33), when Turing arrived at Princeton as a graduate student, von Neumann made his acquaintance. "He knew all about Turing's work," said a co-director of the computer project. "The whole relation of the serial computer, tape and all that sort of thing, I think was very clear—that was Turing."

26 See Morgenstern (1976), Leonard (2010), Holler (2009c, 2016) for details on the cooperation of John von Neumann and Oskar Morgenstern.

his Ph.D., von Neumann offered him a salaried job as his assistant "at $1,500 a year – roughly the same amount as his King's fellowship –" (Copeland 2012: 30). But "with war seemingly imminent, Turing decided to return to England instead" (Holt 2012: 33).

My father, Joseph Holler, born in 1924, was one of the 12,000 U-boat crew members out of 40.000 who survived: "28,000 had gone down with their boats, a casualty rate of 70 per cent, unapproached by that of any branch of other service in any country" (Keegan 1990: 315). Indeed, my father was lucky. As he told us, the commander of his boat was a merchant ship's captain before he was ordered to take over a submarine: he knew how to navigate and to organize the crew – and had no intention to become a (dead) hero. I was often told that I shared the luck of my father and should be happy that he survived. Being born in 1946, I have no conclusive answer so far.

Hastings observes:

> As late as September 1944 Bletchley Park read only 18 percent of German army traffic. What was done by the codebreakers was indeed miraculous, but they could not walk upon all the water all the time. A nuanced interpretation suggests that even such excellent intelligence as was secured by the Western Allies did little to diminish the operational difficulties of defeating the Wehrmacht, although it played a critical part in overcoming the U-boat.
>
> (Hastings 2016: 28)

Indeed, *The Imitation Game* focused on the U-boat.

### 4.2.7 Apple's encryption and "going dark"

In this text, I will not deal with whistleblowing, although it is a substantial by-product of secrecy. In his book *Secrets and Leaks: The Dilemma of State Secrecy* (2013), Rahul Sagar[27] argues that leaks play an important role in checking secrecy abuse. The lives of Edward Snowden, Julian Assange and Bradley (now Chelsea) Manning) demonstrate that this service to the public can incur extremely high private costs. Instead, I want to briefly discuss a case in which the public authority wants to gain excess to private secrecy. This case combines secrecy with second-mover advantages, or the blockage of the latter. The issue at stake seems of utmost importance to our society and to the way we live in the future.

In February 2016, the US District Court for the Central District of California ordered Apple to create and provide software that would allow the FBI to read the iPhone 5C which was used by Syed Rizwan Farook. On December 1, 2015,

---

27 See Sagar (2013) for full reference. Cole (2014) reviewed this book and added a substantial discussion of the issue of whistleblowing.

Farook and his wife Tashfeen Malik, claiming allegiance to the Islamic State, had attacked a holiday gathering of Farook's colleagues in San Bernardino, California. Fourteen people were killed and twenty-two injured. The two attackers died in a shootout with the police. Subsequently, the police tried to find out whether the two attackers might have had assistance and if so who these persons were. Their personal phones had been destroyed, but Farook's work phone was recovered intact. However, it could not be read because it automatically encrypted all of its stored data, using Apple's new operating system that protected the user's password. So, in principle, only the user could read the messages on their phone. It had been "going dark."[28] This is where the case of Apple versus FBI has its origin. FBI director James Comey made the claim that

> Encryption isn't just a technical feature; it's a marketing pitch. But it will have very serious consequences for law enforcement and national security agencies at all levels. Sophisticated criminals will come to count on these means of evading detection. It's the equivalent of the closet that can't be opened. A safe that can't be cracked. And my question is, at what cost?"
>
> (Halpern 2016a: 20)

My first reaction on this was: what is wrong with a safe that cannot be cracked? Comey would say: the police cannot look into it. But isn't this the reason why people buy a safe, in the belief that it will not be cracked? Perhaps they are afraid of burglars. Next comes the "closet": it can be opened by the one who has the key. This seems appropriate for most closets, and can't be too bad for iPhones either, one should think. We prefer closets that can be locked and safes that cannot be cracked, although criminals might "come to count on these means of evading detection." FBI director Comey is right: encryption is a marketing pitch for iPhones. But it is also an iPhone property which is important to some users; it is not just a marketing pitch, but a distinctive feature of the product which makes the product what it is. If you take away the marketing umbrella, this feature is still there. Some people are likely to buy this product only because it has this feature. Are they all criminals?

Is it a marketing pitch if the supplier tries to augment its potential of trustworthiness by investing in trustworthiness?

> Apple's move to encrypt its phones was both a way to reassure customers that it was not partners with American intelligence agencies and a way to make largely impossible for the company to cooperate with agencies, at least with the newer models of the phones.
>
> (Halpern 2016a: 21)

---

28 "Going Dark" is the title of the review article by Sue Halpern (2016a) of four books on cyberphobia, privacy and surveillance in a digital age, the hacked world order and the secret history of cyber war. But, in fact, the review focuses on the case of Apple versus FBI.

Giving the key to the customer was a way of self-binding. To win back the trust of customers – and make them buy the new iPhones – this self-binding policy was an appropriate arrangement, and a necessary one. It has been leaked that all the major US Internet companies, including Google, Apple, Yahoo, and Microsoft, sent data such as e-mails, photographs, videos, calls, and chats directly to the NSA and "millions of American tax dollars were being spent to reimburse these companies for their compliance" (Halpern 2016a: 21).

Apple declined to create the software for reading Farook's iPhone. On February 16, it issued a statement from its CEO Tim Cook:

> The United States government has demanded that Apple take an unprecedented step which threatens the security of our customers. We oppose this order, which has implications far beyond the legal case at hand. This moment calls for public discussion, and we want our customers and people around the country to understand what is at stake.[29]

Apple pointed out that the request might establish a precedent that the US government could use to force any company to create software that could undermine the security of its products. Although "the FBI was insisting that it was asking only for a single phone to be unlocked, once it had been cracked, other requests would be forthcoming" (Halpern 2016a: 22). Indeed, as the immediate history shows, the request for disclosure was not limited to the case of Farook's phone. Halpern (2016a: 22) reports that the New York district attorney "made a public display of the 175 iPhones he needed to have unlocked in order to search for evidence in his office's criminal investigations." Most of these cases, if not all, have nothing to do with terrorism and the "war" against it.

On March 28, the government announced that with the help of a "third party," the FBI had unlocked Farook's iPhone and withdrew its request as it no longer needed Apple's assistance. Estimated fees for hiring unnamed helpers were $1.3 million – to be paid by the public. These were the direct costs, but what were the indirect costs? What were the costs to those iPhone users and their partners in communication who relied on encryption? What were the costs to Apple because it can no longer guarantee secrecy for the messages on its iPhone?

What was perhaps not understood was that the breaking of the encryption of a single iPhone can have tremendous negative spill-overs – i.e., negative externalities, network effects, etc. – not just in telecommunication but in every corner of the society where trust matters – which is basically everywhere. If Apple cannot protect its encryption promise, who can guarantee secrecy? Of course, there might be answers, but these answers imply costs and limitations, and will not balance the general loss of trust that resulted from the Apple iPhone case and the spying of NSA, etc., into private and business secrets. Knack and

---

29 "A Message to Our Customers," Apple Inc.

Keefer (1997) and Zak and Knack (2001) identified a positive relationship between social trust and economic growth. The argument is that by trusting people, they do not have to spend time verifying potential business partners to the same degree. They can use their time more productively. With a low degree of trust, some business projects could even be too costly to implement, e.g., because a partner might exploit second-mover advantages. A decrease of social trust is likely to have a negative effect.[30] Social trust, as defined and measured by the World Values Survey (WVS) (see note 31) – does not refer to secrecy, but to the uncertainty of expected behavior. Of course, the claim of the FBI and the treatment of Apple's case increases uncertainty and is likely to reduce the general level of social trust.

In principle, growth can be measured, but, unlike injustice, it is not directly felt (or perceived) by the individuals.[31] As a consequence, welfare effects of a loss of trust are difficult to verify. But this does not mean that they do not exist. Correspondingly, the welfare effects of the loss of privacy due to spying into the iPhone, made possible by FBI policy, cannot be measured. But to most people, the psychological and social effects of losing secrecy are negative. There is a lot of information which you want to be secret which is not related to any criminal action – more specifically, to terrorism. You do not want an FBI officer to have the ability to trace your sex life. (You might fear being blackmailed.) Nor do you want to share your innovations with competitors. Spying in business is very popular and it has been surmised that much of the unauthorized scrutiny of computers and cell-phones is the result of spying. Even if none of this were happening, we know that the revealing of secrets has psychological costs. It seems that we need a corner where we put our secrets. The spoken confession and the possibility to share one's secrets with the priest explains much of the attraction of the Catholic Church. The confessional secret is an essential element of this arrangement.

Sharing secrets can have many forms. There was King Midas's barber who could not keep his master's secret of his "long ears": Midas had not sided with Apollo in a musical competition with Marsyas, so Apollo gave Midas donkey's

---

30 Berggren and co-authors (2008) demonstrated that, from an empirical point of view, the relationship between social trust and growth is "shaky" if we apply more sophisticated econometrics and a larger data set. However, there is a problem with the measurement of social trust in these studies. It is measured by the share of people in different countries who answer 'yes' to the first part of the following question: "In general, do you think most people can be trusted or that you can't be too careful?" Social trust was measured by counting the answers "most people can be trusted" as offered by the World Values Survey (WVS). (See Inglehart et al. (2004) for detailed references.) It would be interesting to know whether the people who answer "yes" expect that other people trust them. Is there a "trust equilibrium" in this society? What kind of social trust do we observe, if almost everybody answers that most people can be trusted, but they do not expect that many people trust them? And what will be the growth effect of this kind of trust? I conjecture that it will be much smaller than in a society in which people trust others *and* expect that they are trusted.

31 See Holler and Leroch (2010) for this observation and some consequences therefrom.

ears as a punishment. The barber went into a meadow, dug a hole in the ground and whispered: "King Midas has an ass's ears!" and as a result felt much better afterward. However, a bed of reeds grew in the meadow and began to whisper "King's aaaass ears! King's aaaass ears!", which was soon echoing through the entire kingdom and thus everyone learned the king's secret.

Most likely you do not want such an echo for your secrets. You do not want a barber who can read your e-mail account and distill unpleasant interpretations. You want to feel safe. But this of course is an illusion, quite similar to the illusion that Orwell's Winston Smith of *Nineteen Eighty-Four* (1981 [1949]) had when he scribbled in his diary in a corner of his room which was not covered by the two-way telescreen which received and transmitted simultaneously. It was not illegal to write a diary, since laws did not exist, but Smith knew that if his diary was discovered he would be punished by death, or at least by twenty-five years in a forced-labor camp. (How does this relate to whistleblowing?) Of course, this "dark corner" was a trap.

Earlier we have argued that secrets were a means of blocking second-mover advantage and thus making first moves profitable – and possible. If there is no "dark corner," then this possibility is lost. However, one might experience a permanent process of creating such dark corners: new technologies of information protection will be designed, only to trigger new technologies of decryption. There are substantial high privacy and social costs involved. One consequence will be that sharing of secrets is risky or impossible. Not only criminals are interested in sharing secrets. Perhaps we ourselves also want to win confidants and allies by sharing secrets. This dimension can also be significant for the creation of secrets in art.

## 4.3 Creating secrets as a work of art

"The artist is the creator of beautiful things." This quotation is taken from the preface of Oscar Wilde's *Picture of Dorian Gray*. But, considering Dorian Gray's portrait, the novel itself shows that this is not necessarily the case. Alternatively, the artist is the *creator of secrets*. In 2002, the quarterly journal *Homo Oeconomicus* published a symposium that containing eight commentaries discussing, more or less explicitly, an art project undertaken by Nicola Atkinson-Griffith entitled "Secrets of the World," introduced and edited by myself (Holler 2002a).[32] In what follows, I will use Atkinson instead of Atkinson-Griffith as Nicola Atkinson nowadays does. Moreover, her project will be addressed as Nicola's game. The reviewers – Sofia Blind, Leonard Dudley, Petra Grüning, Joanna Hoffmann, Karola Koch, John Sedgewick, Ben Spencer, and myself – were selected, or selected themselves, from a network which gravitated around the Institute of SocioEconomics of the University of Hamburg and the ARTS&Games Academy. The latter is still in status nascendi.

---

32 This section makes substantial use of material published in Holler (2002a, 2008).

Perhaps it needs explaining why *Homo Oeconomicus*, a journal which focuses on economics and the social sciences, should be interested in addressing such a subject. One argument is that although the concept of the secret has been, by and large, neglected by the theoretical literature in economics and the social sciences, or not given the attention it deserves, in the real world, secrets seem to be an important phenomenon, e.g., in the business world, in politics, and in daily social interaction. Of course, when it comes to discussing secrets, economists would immediately point to the bulk of literature on asymmetric information, signaling, moral hazard and adverse selection, literature which has been honored by awarding the 2001 Nobel Prize in Economics to three of its pioneer contributors: George Akerlof, Michael Spence, and Joseph Stiglitz. Indeed, these concepts could be applied to analyze secrets as phenomena. Yet, the eight contributions to Holler (2002a) and Nicola Atkinson's art project "Secrets of the World" made clear that there is more to a secret than just asymmetric information. Secrets can be dangerous, beautiful, exciting, immoral, etc.; they can hurt and please, they can be shared.

Since secrets are produced, sold, and bought, they should be accessible to economic analysis. However, secrets are rather strange goods and, as pointed out in Blind (2002), the incomplete definition of property rights seems to be part of their nature. I may hand you a secret in a sealed envelope and you may carry this envelope to the other side of the globe. Still I can destroy this secret by publishing the information which is sealed in the envelope. But it could also be that there is no information in the envelope and you merely think that you are carrying a secret with you.

Integrating the secrecy phenomenon with an art project seemed a promising perspective. Artists have a long and intensive tradition of working with secrets and many artists have made a secret out of their art. Nicola Atkinson has chosen a rather direct approach: she made use of the myth of the secret by asking people to write down their personal, private, and public secrets, and put the information into an envelope which is then sealed.

There is the dimension of participation and sharing the experience in this work. In fact, as Spencer comments:

> The work is participatory on a global scale and begins to explore the notion that work does not need to be based in any particular location. It is not the secret which is of interest, but the act of participation itself to create a shared, unified community which underpins this project. Crucial to this process is the trust invested in the artist that the secrets will not be disclosed.
>
> (Spencer 2002: 564)

The creation of secrets is a means to install this participation. Secrets create communities of those who know and those who do not know. However, there are also those who *think* they know.

Indeed the thread running through Atkinson's projects is the creation of temporary communities, existing or fabricated, in order to pursue the links that bind established, or disparate, worlds together. She establishes an idea to explore a particular community and then works intimately with its members to elicit contributions to the project – perhaps an object, a likeness, or a memory. Making use of secrets seems to be an extremely adequate, but also exciting lever to achieve this end. To Atkinson, it is important that this participation in the project is not coerced but is entirely voluntary. The process of gathering is itself seen as an artwork; it is fundamental to Atkinson's practice. It concurs with her "artist's statement":

> My work questions people's perception of their environment. I produce frameworks of ideas which enable the public to contemplate other views of the world. I present thoughts, questions and concepts which gently challenge the safe and familiar cocoon within which we each tend to embed ourselves. The human need to feel protected can limit our outlook and blind us to the remarkable aspects of life which surround us.
>
> (Atkinson-Griffith, 2002)

In her "Secrets of the World" project, Nicola Atkinson asked the participants in Hamburg, Los Angeles, and Karachi to write down their personal, private, and public secrets on a piece of paper and hide them in identical grayish envelopes. She promised to keep the secrets secret "for all her life."

Qualifying the secrets as public, private, and personal was part of the project. At the University of Hamburg, it triggered a vehement discussion among participants. Even months later, participants were discussing the idea of creating secrets and the various categories offered by Atkinson. Are all personal secrets private? Is a public secret a collective secret, or is it still an individual issue? What happens to the secrets if, contrary to her promise, Atkinson discloses (or has to disclose) the contents so far concealed in the envelopes?

I took the liberty to replicate Nicola Atkinson's work at the occasion of a seminar on "guru management," which I gave to students of jewelry making at the Teknisk Skole, Copenhagen. I also asked for the secrets of the participants in a company seminar on interactive decision making, which I organized for the marketing managers of Unilever/Germany, a major European ice cream producer. I must confess that I did not ask for Atkinson's permission to replicate her work but I did not feel guilty. Pieces of art belong to the public – at least, the ideas, questions, and experiences which they provide. More specifically, a constituent element of Atkinson's work is the discussion which it stirs and the questions which it induces. Replications are a means to find answers to the questions and new arguments for the discussion. Of course, I always referred to Atkinson as the inventor of the original experiment – and, of course, she had read my contribution to the issue of *Homo Oeconomicus* (Holler 2002a). In what follows, I will present some corresponding facts and interpretations, beginning with some observations related to the Hamburg experiment. I then discuss the Copenhagen replication and the experience at Unilever and conclude with an interpretation of the results.

### 4.3.1 Nicola Atkinson's Hamburg experiment

There were close to forty participants at the *Oberseminar* which I organized in 1996 at the University of Hamburg when Nicola Atkinson was the guest speaker. This was at least double the number who would usually attend the regular seminar sessions on economic theory, or, more specifically, on economic model building and game theory. More than ten participants were attracted by the fact that an artist was presenting some material; they would not have attended the *Oberseminar* on economics issues. Another ten participants were doctoral economics students from various institutes. They were coaxed into participating by the expectation of spending two hours working with problems which do not have an obvious relation to their regular work. They were drawn in by their curiosity – the curiosity which is at the heart of research work. The rest of the participants were people connected as members, guests, external or former Ph.D. students to the Institute of SocioEconomics which was responsible for the *Oberseminar*'s program. It might be important to consider the heterogeneity of the participants for the interpretation of what follows.

First, Atkinson lectured on some of her previous art work, which was supported by a somewhat senile slide projector. Most of her work was related to a social, if not public space, mobilizing and connecting people within the context of an artistic idea. This confirms what a website (sadly no longer available) said about her work:

> [she] works to question people's perception of their environment through producing frameworks of ideas which enable the public to contemplate alternative views of the world. The work intriguingly warps the everyday to disturb the status quo and to alert audiences to remarkable aspects of life around them . . . This approach is based upon the idea of art as a form of communication through which the artist can influence (and be influenced by) as wide a range of people as possible.

After this introduction to her work, Atkinson distributed a sheet of paper to each seminar participant with the three categories "personal," "private," and "public" secret, typed on it, together with a grayish-green envelope. The envelopes had been donated by the Institute of SocioEconomics and looked very bureaucratic. Immediately, discussions started between neighboring participants as to the difference between public, private and personal secrets. After a while, bilateral discussions turned into multilateral discussions and in the end there was a general discussion which ended with asking Atkinson for a resolution. Most participants appeared satisfied by her response.

Only then did the discussion begin to ask whether the secrets were safe with Nicola Atkinson. There were no doubts expressed that she would try to keep the envelopes sealed and the secrets secret; however, does she have the ultimate *power* to do so? What if she is robbed on her way back to Scotland, or if somebody broke into her home while she was visiting California, which she very often does? The general conclusion was that Nicola Atkinson might guarantee that the secrets will be kept secret, but that there was a very small probability that she might fail to protect the envelopes. But if complete strangers open the envelopes, will they (a) understand the project and (b) be able to verify the secrets? Not very likely. Still, this principle stood that secrets should be kept secret if secrecy is promised.

The discussion then moved on to the nature of the request for secrets. Isn't the question brought forward tasteless, impolite, or even immoral? Why not ask for something else? However, nobody – even days and weeks after the session – could think of something equivalent to secrets. Ask yourself this question and, most likely, you will have the same experience.

The discussion led some participants to think about the nature of information as complementary to secrets. For example, it was argued that one can destroy the secrets in the grayish-green envelopes, as locked away in a steel box in Glasgow, by making the information in the envelopes public knowledge. (I was thinking of exam questions which are a secret only up to the exam day – then the secret is destroyed.) Discussion about asymmetric information and private information, which are basic concepts of modern microeconomics, continued to dominate lunch conversations for several weeks – in connection with questions of trust and power. Has Nicola Atkinson gained power by collecting the secrets? No and yes.

Slightly more than half of the participants returned a sealed envelope to Atkinson. Some of the others claimed that they abstained because they could not resolve the classification into public, private, and personal secret. Others felt as though they'd had a shock: they could not cope with being asked to write down their secrets. I had the impression that the number of abstentions and the arguments which supported this reaction could not be differentiated between a group of economists, trained in rational choice modeling, and the other participants with no similar training. However, I have to admit that I did no survey analysis on these reactions and cannot claim scientific status for this observation. I felt myself much too involved. Moreover, some arguments only became clear days later. Needless to say, my curiosity was not satisfied and I took the next opportunity, albeit five years later, to replicate Atkinson's work on secrets.

Commenting on the above result, Sofia Blind observed that those who refused to return the envelope

> thought the idea pointless, they did not trust the artist to keep their secrets, or they questioned the categories of secrets offered. But not a single one refused to participate on the grounds that he or she did not have a secret to offer! Can this be true – do we all have secrets?
>
> (Blind 2002: 565)

The Copenhagen replication and the result of the company seminar, both discussed in the following section, seem to corroborate that we all have secrets – at least we tend to behave like we have secrets. We may voluntarily admit or pretend that we have secrets, but we are not inclined to disclose them. Why? We will come back to this question.

### 4.3.2 The Copenhagen replication and a company seminar

Sten Bülow Bredsted (a Danish artist and prominent member of the ARTS&Games group) arranged that I give an eight-hour seminar on guru management with Master's students of jewelry making at the Teknisk Skole at Copenhagen on February 20–21, 2001. At that time, Bredsted himself was studying for a Master's degree in jewelry making at this school. He felt that he and his fellow students should become aware of the interactive relationships in which they and their work are embedded and gain some training to succeed in their social nexus. During the seminar sessions, we discussed the concepts of strategies, players, and preferences and looked for Nash equilibria in Prisoners' Dilemma games and the Battle of the Sexes. We learned that it was Johann Wolfgang von Goethe (1749–1832) who invented the sealed-bid second-price auction (see Moldovanu and Tietzel (1998)[33] – and that its remarkable properties were first analyzed by the late William Vickrey, who was not only awarded a Nobel Prize for Economics in 1996 for this work, but also gave his name for this type of auction. The Teknisk Skole students were interested in auctions (perhaps also for practical purposes). We discussed the creation of secrets involved in sealed bids. Studying Brams and Taylor (1996) for rules and recipes, we also learnt how to share property when we divorce, or when we inherit a house, a garden, a model T car, and a dog, jointly with brothers and sisters. Trust, reputation, morality were reduced to rational choices and the forming of corresponding beliefs (i.e., assessments). It seemed that all the participants were quite happy with this perspective – at least, in a classroom.

Things changed dramatically when, after more than seven hours of the seminar on rational thinking, I asked the students to write down their personal, private, and public secrets. Of course, I promised not to look into the grayish envelopes, and to defend the sealed envelopes with all my strength until my last day. In the end, only four of the eight seminar participants gave me their sealed envelopes. All of them argued that this was a real challenge and some of them considered it an immoral act asking them for their secrets.

It took quite some time until emotions calmed down and we could start to discuss a game-theoretical approach to analyze the various strings of expectations, mistrust, and rejection related to this experiment. In the end, it was felt that situations of conflicting interests and expectations tended to be less threatening to friendly social interaction when interpreted as a game and transformed into game models. Did this act of rationalization transform the situation into a non-conflicting game? Do rational arguments push emotions to the back of our mind?

---

33 In fact, the auction proposed by Goethe was a second-price auction only for one of the two parties. See Chapter 13 of Holler and Klose-Ullmann (2018) for details.

The experience with replicating *Nicola's game* in the company seminar at Unilever/Germany was quite different. In contrast to the seminars in Hamburg and Copenhagen, all of the about twenty seminar participants wrote down something on their sheets of paper, sealed their envelopes and handed them over to the interviewer without much hesitation and delay. Scarcely any discussion about the request arose in this group. No participant "volunteered" to question whether asking for secrets – personal, private, or public – is appropriate and morally justifiable in a business environment.

It is straightforward to conclude that the respondents saw their dealing with the envelope as part of their job and applied business routine. Answering questions about public, private, and personal secrets is perhaps not considered part of the business domain, but since the envelopes are still sealed we do not have any answers, based on the experiment as such, to this issue. Perhaps all twenty envelopes are filled with incoherent doodling. Karola Koch (2002: 560) concludes that "the given arguments indicate that *Nicola's Game* cannot be seen separate from the environment where it takes place. And this fits quite well with the artist's own intentions." Moreover, the

> choice of profession is a biographic factor with direct impact on experiences, standards, values, attitudes, etc. The importance of professional impact on our lives allows [us] to draw certain conclusions that apply to reference systems. Individualistic behaviour in a heterogeneous seminar context or a higher conformity with its demands to adapt to company standards contribute to different mimetic effects and the emotional incentives are different as well in the two environments. For example, master students of jewelry making at the Technisk Skole in Copenhagen are trained to go into a personal discourse in their creative art-work. The creation process is not only self-expression but also self-experience. A business context trains to disregard personal emotions and to act strategically to gain advantages.
>
> (Koch 2002: 558)

### 4.3.3 Towards a game-theoretical interpretation

In its most abstract form, a game is defined by the set of players, by the sets of strategies from which each player can choose their plan of action, and by the payoffs of the players which express their interests in the outcomes of the game. The outcomes are determined by the strategy choices. At first glance, the strategic relationship in *Nicola's Game* seems to be straightforward: There is the interviewer who asks for the secret and there are the various respondents who either hand over a sealed envelope or abstain. The interviewer may open the envelopes, keep the information as a private secret, or make them public. In the second case, a large variety of actions and reactions are possible, perhaps bringing in new players if, e.g., a respondent feels cheated and turns to a legal adviser, or even initiates legal proceedings. Moreover, making a secret known may imply bringing new players indirectly into the game, e.g., through activating those agents who share the secret or even are objects of the secret, i.e., playing a "role" in it.

By the design of the game, it is not clear what the interviewer will do with the secrets. Will they exhibit the secrets in a public space, or incorporate them in their art work, or just simply lock them in a steel box? Is it in their interest to inform others that they have the secrets or will they open the envelopes one day in a dark room – or destroy them unopened?

The respondents' payoffs and interests are even less obvious. For those who have decided to return a sealed envelope, the social pressure of the situation causing them to obey an instruction or to support science or art seems to be a major motivation. Yet, some participants confessed that they enjoyed writing down their secrets and that they felt better afterward. Remember King Midas's barber who could not keep his master's secret of the "long ears." One must be very careful with secrets.

There is no guarantee that those who contributed a sealed envelope actually wrote a secret on their sheet. There is no proof at all that they contributed a secret or that the secret they contributed was not a lie. This has to be considered when we discuss the strategies of the respondents. The contents of their writing cannot be controlled before sealing *and* hence for as long as the envelope is sealed. This is implicit to asking for secrets and promising to keep them secret. All that could be observed, depending on the setting of the experiment, is whether a respondent contributed a sealed envelope or not.

It seems that the sets of strategies for the interviewer and the respondent are very large and difficult to define. There are, however, prominent strategies which are candidates for a Nash equilibrium, such that no player can improve his position by choosing an alternative strategy, *given* the strategy choices of the other players. Note that this definition of an equilibrium implies that the strategies are mutually best replies to each other. Obviously, to write down yesterday's weather report, or another low interest, low-info story and the decision not to open the sealed envelopes are such mutually best replies. The strategy pair constitutes a (subgame-perfect) Nash equilibrium which, in addition, has the nice property that it does not invite new players.

Of course, if a game invites new players and creates additional strategies, then it can no longer be guaranteed that this Nash equilibrium still exists. If we abstract from this possibility, then writing down "nothing," or nothing that contains information, is a weakly dominant strategy. There is no better reply to the interviewer's decision on the envelopes if the respondent does not want to give away any information or does not feel the urgent need to express their secret as did King Midas's barber. Therefore, writing down "nothing" is a rational way to defend oneself and one's secrets against the interviewer's intrusion.

As soon as this solution was accepted by the participants in the Copenhagen seminar, they were less critical of me asking for their secrets. They admitted that it takes more than an eight-hour seminar to internalize interactive thinking in such a way that it cannot be challenged by "immoral" demands such as writing down secrets. They told me that when they made their decisions they were not aware of this possibility. (Whether I believe this remains a secret.)

In his critical comment, Sedgwick (2002) rightly asked the question whether *Nicola's Game* is a game at all, in the game-theoretical sense. He argues that players behave independently of one another. Yet, it seems that the respondents at the *Oberseminar* and at the Teknisk Skole saw themselves connected not only with the interviewer (the *principal* in terms of Sedgewick), but also with the other participants as the discussion indicated: handing over a sealed envelope, or not, depended on what other participants said and did. And they saw themselves in a strategic decision situation with the interviewer: can we trust her (or him)? Will she (or he) be careful enough to protect our secrets? Most likely, in case of the experiment at the Unilever business seminar, the strategic relationship was more on the surface: it seemed to be determined by the benefits of conformity and a result of social training. The interviewer was not necessarily considered a player in this game. Perhaps I should open the envelopes to find out whether that seminar's participants wrote down any secrets at all.

Spencer (2002: 563) stated that his "reaction to 'Secrets of the World' is primarily as an artwork and not a game as rationalized by Holler." I fully agree with this interpretation inasmuch as Atkinson's work is considered and, of course, including the game's original design. She is an artist. What I did was not art – I am not an artist – but the consequence of my interest in human behavior, especially when it comes to decision making in strategic situations that can be described as games (in a game-theoretical sense). For instance, I concur with Dudley's (2002: 550) suggestion that it "would be very interesting to observe whether responses to the experimenter's provocation differ across societies. To function . . . societies require trust. The Secret game might provide a possible measure of this trust." Spencer (2002: 564) points out that Atkinson's work is participatory on a global scale and it

> is not the secret which is of interest. Nor is collecting secrets an end in itself. It is the act of participation to create a shared, unified community which underpins this project . . . The key point for Atkinson-Griffith is in building trust with those who participate in the work and not in playing games. Crucial to this process is the trust invested in the artist that the secrets will not be disclosed. Trust her – your secrets will be safe.
>
> (Spencer 2002: 564)

Inasmuch as the participants believe that Nicola Atkinson will keep their secret, they will profit from writing down their secrets if they feel that they benefit from this. If there are these benefits and the benefits increase by trusting Atkinson to treat the secret as a secret, then the "Secrets of the World" game has the structure of a trust game: Player 1 decides how much of a given "cake" he will hand over to player 2. Typically, this share x will be multiplied by an exogenous agent or by means of production and sales if player 2 runs a company. Then player 2 decides how much of the augmented cake he will give to player 1. Of course, player 1 hopes for a piece of cake larger than x. However, if player 2 is rational and loves cake, and he is not interested in good relations with player 1 or a good reputation, he will give nothing to player 2. Note that the efficient outcome implies that player 1 maximizes x, i.e., the share of the cake that he hands over to player 2. Yet, giving back a crumb of the cake, however small it is, is not subgame perfect. If player 1 expects that player 2 is rational and believes in subgame perfectness, then x = 0, and there will be no multiplication. Again, the second-mover advantage will hamper individual gains from social interaction.

Games of this type, i.e., trust games, belong to the standard toolkit of experimental game theory (see, e.g., Bolle 1998, Ortmann et al. 2000, Dufwenberg et al. 2001, Güth et al. 2001). Nicola Atkinson's "Secrets of the World" can be interpreted as belonging to this category – of course, depending on how strongly participants evaluate trust and the writing-down of secrets as an expressive act. (Effects of social trust, e.g., on economic growth, were already discussed in Section 4.2.7.)

### 4.3.4 Art, games, and Duchamp's perfect secret

When discussing Nicola Atkinson's "Secrets of the World," Joanna Hoffmann (2002: 552), an eminent artist herself, asks "Is art a game?" Her response to this question is "It is difficult to answer positively to that question. Nevertheless this term can help us to understand how art and mechanisms which manipulate it function." For some artists, the relationship between art and game seems to be more straightforward. Indeed, Marcel Duchamp was a great chess player and perhaps the most influential artist of the first half of the twentieth century. His discovery of the readymades and the assemblages offered for many artists the chance of a successful second move – and he produced secrets. The most obvious secret was his last piece of work: *Étant donné* or *Given*. The full title of this assemblage was – translated from French – "Given: 1. The Waterfall, 2 The Illuminating Gas, 1946–1966," the years indicating that he worked twenty years with this. Yet, as we know from his interview with Pierre Cabanne (published 1967), that during this period his work consisted mainly in doing nothing, or playing chess. In fact, even his friends were not aware that he was still actively pursuing an art project. The general notion is that *Given* was found in his New York studio only after he died on October 2, 1968, having enjoyed a dinner with his friends Man Ray and Robert Lebel and his second wife Alexina, called Teeny, in his French home at Neuilly. However, Nobel literature laureate Octavio Paz (1978: 209) notes that, in 1968, prior to his departure to Europe, Duchamp took the painter Bill Copley "to see the completed *Given* in his secret studio and expresses the wish that it will join the large group of his works already in the Philadelphia Museum of Art," which it did. He also shared this secret "and some of the work" with Teeny (Haladyn 2010: 4).

When, in the early 1950s, Louise and Walter Ahrensberg donated their art collection to the Philadelphia Museum of Art, a section was reserved to form the Duchamp Gallery. It includes many of Duchamp's important works, e.g., *The Green Box*, and an authorized version of the *Fountain*. Duchamp's life-long collector, friend, and patron Katherine Dreier contributed *The Large Glass* to this collection.

Duchamp assisted in installing the collection, and he succeeded in reserving a small room, accessible via a floor that looked like an emergency exit, just outside "his" gallery. This was the secret of the empty room – a room kept empty for more than ten years, which was made known to the art world only after Duchamp's death in 1968. Buried in France in the family tomb at Rouen Cemetery, Duchamp's epitaph, "D'ailleurs, c'est toujours les autres qui meurent" ("By the way, it's always the others who die"), is another result of his passion to create paradoxes (and secrets) by means of self-reference. Also, *Given* is self-referential inasmuch as it makes the visitor, i.e., the viewer, an essential part of it. He "draws back from the door feeling that mixture of joy and guilt of one who has unearthed a secret," Paz (1978: 96) observes in his extended discussion of *Given*.[34]

Are joy and guilt typical emotional experiences of unearthing a secret? Paz reports that when looking for the work *Given* in the Philadelphia Museum, the visitor first faces a dead end: a wooden door,

> worm-eaten, patched, and closed by a rough crossbar made of wood and nailed on heavy spikes . . . A real condemned door. But if the visitor ventures nearer, he finds two small holes at eye level. If he goes even closer and dares to peep, he will see a scene he is not likely to forget.
>
> (Paz 1978: 95f.)

It is the peeping into a secret world, in a hidden corner of the museum, that creates a relationship between the viewer and the object, augmented by the fact that the object represents sexuality, perhaps violence, perhaps . . . in fact, the viewer does not know what he sees even if he peeps into the hole. In its essence, the secret remains a secret, as the viewer cannot solve the puzzle that he or she faces: "The question 'What do we see?' confronts us with ourselves" (Paz 1978: 98). In fact, it mutates into "What do we want to see?"

Haladyn (2010) points to the artistic voyeurism embedded in this work and the observation of shame and guilt of visitors who peeped through the eyeholes to face the female nude. The scene is illuminated by a Bec Auer gas lamp which the nude carries in her left hand. (Is its light flickering?) Queuing up for having a look through the eyeholes can be a challenge; it needs some self-confidence. The challenge also works when there was no queue: somebody might enter the room with somebody already peeping through the two holes in the door. Even entering the room that allowed us to peep through the holes could be experienced as an act of shame. Was this challenge intended by

---

34 Octavio Paz's text is the major source of the following interpretation.

Duchamp? In any case, it puts the spectator in a rather specific relation with the work of art. This is discussed in depth by Haladyn (2010). Note that the relationship between the artist and the audience was of paramount importance to Duchamp. To him, it defined art. Here, however, our focus is on the secrecy of Duchamp's work, especially of *Given*.

The more experienced visitors remember interpretations of the assemblage by art critics and through reports of skillful commentators that make them think that they hold the key to the secret space in front of them. Here follows Paz's description of *Given*:

> First of all, a brick wall with a slit in it, and through the slit, a wide open space, luminous and seemingly bewitched. Very near to the beholder – but also very far away, on the 'other' side – a naked girl, stretched on a kind of bed or pyre of branches and leaves, her face almost completely covered by the blond mass of her hair, her legs open and slightly bent, the pubes strangely smooth in contrast to the splendid abundance of her hair, her right arm out of line of vision, her left slightly raised, the hand grasping a small lamp made of metal and glass.
>
> (Paz 1978: 96)

In his description, Paz does not mention of what material the naked girl is crafted. In fact, in general, descriptions of the work are not straightforward on this issue, however. One hypothesis is that the figure was made with plaster casts and parchment, painted to look like skin. However, the museum plaque mentions "leather stretched over an armature of metal and other material" (Haladyn 2010: 44), and does not mention plaster and parchment. According to Paz (1978: 179), an earlier version of the naked girl is of "painted leather over plaster relief, mounted on velvet." Yet, does the material matter? The worm-eaten wooden door prevents the viewer from making a closer examination anyway. First what we see of this girl through the peephole looks very realistic, even the twist of her body. Perhaps we are shocked by her nakedness. But then we realize that her genitalia are misshaped or misplaced or – "the depiction of the vagina in *Given* is not simply abstract or unrealistic, it gives the visual impression that the woman has undergone some traumatic form of physical castration" (Haladyn 2010: 66). Is she dead? But then there is the outstretched left arm with a relatively strong hand carrying the "illuminating" gas lamp.

The lamp

> glows the brilliant light of this motionless, end-of-summer day . . . our glance wanders over the landscape in the background, wooded hills, green and reddish; lower down, a small lake and a light mist on the lake. An inevitably blue sky. Two or three clouds, also inevitably white. On the far right, among some rocks, a waterfall catches the light.
>
> (Paz 1978: 96)

Here we find *1. The Waterfall, 2 The Illuminating Gas*, as announced in the title. Note that there is no reference to the naked girl in the title; it is kept as a secret, perhaps to augment the emotional experience that waits for the viewer when peeping through the holes in the worm-eaten wooden door that Duchamp acquired when visiting Spain. Is it to amplify a shocking surprise or to camouflage the "queen"? She "dominates the installation with the unabashed and blatant exposure of her body, controlling the board . . ." (Haladyn 2010: 67). Haladyn refers to Duchamp's passion for chess, when searching for the meaning of the female nude, and his notion of art as a discourse between the artistic object and the audience: "*Given* depends upon a conceptual commitment by the viewer, who projects the reality of the vagina where there is none" (Haladyn 2010: 80). In both fields, art and chess, interactive elements are prominent.

Paz interprets the female nude as a reincarnation of the *Bride* of *The Large Glass*. This iconic work is shown in the neighboring Duchamp Gallery. It is titled *The Bride Stripped Bare by Her Bachelors, Even, 1915–23* ("La Mariée mise à nu pas ses célibataires, même") and carries the qualification "finally unfinished."[35] In 1923, Duchamp stopped working on it. The *Bride* is an apparatus, a complicated piece of machinery. "It is a symbol machine" (Paz 1978: 36) attached to a "large glass" together with items that represent, e.g., bachelors. This object is perhaps even more complex than the *Given*. For most viewers, it is beyond secret; it is simply not accessible even after reading the notes in the *Green Box*, a compilation of scraps of paper slips published in a limited edition of (perhaps) 320 copies that Duchamp offered in order to explain the *Large Glass* and the process of creating it. We will not try an interpretation here, but note that art can be puzzling without constructing a secret. I know this does not give *The Large Glass* the credit it deserves. It was not meant to be a puzzle or a secret, but a representation of ideas. Until after his death, many friends considered it as the final artwork of Duchamp who seemed to prefer playing chess, and studying this game in some depth. To Paz (1978: 106) "the machine of the *Large Glass* is the representation of an enigma, in the nude of *Given* is the enigma in person, its incarnation." Enigma combines secret with machine. It characterizes Duchamp's cryptography – a dominant feature of his work. To him, ideas are secrets and can only be represented by secrets and unearthed through irony.

For a long time, the empty room in the Philadelphia Museum of Art was such a secret although we do not know whether it aroused any interest. (Is there a secret if nobody is interested in it? There are secret secrets waiting to be unearthed.) Its "measurements were integral of the final stage of planning the installation, allowing Duchamp to produce elements specifically for that space while keeping the project secret" (Haladyn 2010: 12). Obviously, *Given*

---

35 A reconstruction of the *Large Glass* executed by the Swedish multi-talented artist Ulf Linde and authorized by Duchamp at the occasion of his visit to Sweden in 1961, can be seen in the Moderna Museet, Stockholm. A later reconstruction by Richard Hamilton is part of the collection of the Tate London. When Duchamp came to London in 1966, he acknowledged the four glass studies produced by Hamilton as "faithful replicas."

was created specifically to be in the museum.[36] When *Given* was finally opened to the public, there was no formal act, no private ceremony, or press release to announce the event. This concurred with Duchamp's will and his will was honored.

Haladyn concludes:[37]

> Taken in conjunction with the assemblage's having been a twenty-year-long covert project, it transforms the experience of viewing 'into decipher-ing, a game, a more complex undertaking, more disturbing, more anxious than when' one views a simple work of art 'for the pure pleasure of it'.
>
> (Haladyn 2010: 14)

And he conjectures: "Perhaps Duchamp has made the secret meaning of his work and *Given* – in this case a literal secret – definitive through the strategic release of the assemblage after his death" (Haladyn 2010:16). Is *Given* Duchamp's reaction to Edouard Manet's *Le Déjeuner sur l'Herbe* ("The Luncheon on the Grass")?[38] In its artistic status, it is like a mirror image to *Given*. *Déjeuner* shows two young men sitting in the grass, fully dressed, in conversation which each other, a chemise-wearing woman who bathes in a river in the background and, together with the two men, a second woman. She is nude. Her cream-white body and the face are fully lit by an imaginary sun that seems to function as a spotlight. She is very close to the two men, but does not interact with them. She gazes out of the picture. Her dress is in front of her in the grass together with a basket of fruits and round loaf of bread, creating a bizarre still life in the painting's foreground.

Manet's *Déjeuner* was rejected by the jury of the Salon de Paris of 1863, and exhibited in the Salon des Refusés of the same year. Even in this alter-native show, it was rated as scandalous. Arguments ranged from criticizing that the painter's brush strokes are uneven to the indecency of the depicted scene. Of course, many negative comments were regarding the nudity of the woman in front and her shining body, in contrast to the darkish exposure of the fully dressed men. Inappropriate or just plain immoral? As Zola (1867) pointed out in his eulogy on Manet's work, in the Louvre, the *Pastoral Concert*, painted either by Giorgione or the young Titian around 1510, showed two nude women in the forefront and two dressed men just behind them. We can be sure that Manet has seen this picture. In the Academia at Venice, we can admire Giorgioni's *The Tempest* with a fully-clad, well-dressed young man in the forefront looking at a nude woman with a baby in her arms, only covered by a small blanket around her shoulders. It is not considered indecent, but a puzzle. It is the puzzle that irritates the viewer and transforms it into an icon.

---

36  Duchamp compiled a "Manual of Instructions for *Étant donné*" to be used should his work be moved from the studio to the museum.

37  Also quoting Foucault (2004: 183).

38  Manet painted this "oil on canvas" in the years 1862–63. Today it is one of the icons shown at Musée d'Orsay at Paris. There are many works of art that refer to it.

Did Manet's scene point to the flourishing prostitution in Bois de Boulogne – which was common knowledge but treated as a (public) secret? Was there something like the Emperor's new clothes involved? Or was it the nude's gazing out of the picture – her staring at the viewer that was scandalous? The nude irritated the spectators, triggering shame and aggression – also because in the open environment of the gallery, others could see what one is looking at. By the staring gaze of the nude the spectators become aware of what they are looking at and, in their imagination, other visitors become sort of accomplice to her: "Look what he or she is looking at!" As in *Given*, and claimed by Duchamp for art in general, the audience becomes part of the *Déjeuner* by looking at it, trying to cope with the challenge of the nude's direct gaze. Neither in the *Pastoral Concert* nor in *The Tempest* is the viewer directly addressed by the gaze of a nude woman or of a fully clad man.

Although in *Given*, the nude does not address the onlooker, the installation's arrangement creates a similar tension between the spectator, the work of art, and the other visitors, as with the *Déjeuner*. Again nudity is a challenge. In the *Déjeuner*, it is because of a "looking out" while in *Given*, it is the looking in and the way it is arranged – i.e., staged – that creates the challenge. You do not peep through the holes in the door of rotten wood just by passing by, but you might be drawn into peeping through the holes without knowing what you will see – and then find yourself irritated, offended, and ashamed, especially if you see that others have seen you peeping.

In both *oeuvres*, the sexual dimension is obvious, but we cannot see how it is directed. We can interpret both works and find stories, but we do not know whether our interpretation holds. In fact, we cannot find any conclusive evidence for our interpretation of the presented scenario, irrespective of our interpretation. This is the secret. Perhaps it is true, as Monet's great admirer Emile Zola, claimed, that "the nude woman . . . is only there to furnish the artist the occasion to paint a bit of flesh."[39] But we do not know.

Duchamp's *Given* is a prominent example of the creation of a secret and the making use of it, but also of how to deal with it. It is a perfect secret: whenever

---

39  This conjecture is part of a more comprehensive observation by Emile Zola in his "Une nouvelle manière en peinture: Eduard Manet," published in the *Revue du XIX^e siècle* of January 1, 1867: "Les peintres, surtout Édouard Manet, qui est un peintre analyste, n'ont pas cette préoccupation du sujet qui tourmenta a foule avant tout; le sujet pour eux est un prétexte à peindre, tandis que pour la foule le sujet seul existe. Ainsi, assurément, la femme nue du Déjeuner sur l'herbe n'est là que pour fournir à l'artiste l'occasion de peindre un peu de chair. Ce qu'il faut voir dans le tableau, ce n'est pas un déjeuner sur l'herbe, c'est le paysage entier, avec ses vigueurs et ses finesses, avec ses premiers plans si larges, si solides, et ses fonds d'une délicatesse si légère; c'est cette chair ferme, modelée à grands pans de lumière, ces étoffes souples et fortes, et surtout cette délicieuse silhouette de femme en chemise qui fait, dans le fond, une adorable tache blanche au milieu des feuilles vertes; c'est enfin cet ensemble vaste, plein d'air, ce coin de la nature rendue avec une simplicité si juste, toute cette page admirable dans laquelle un artiste a mis les éléments particuliers et rares qui étaient en lui" (Zola 1867).

we find a meaning, there is another meaning. There is this *"possibility of possibility"* as a result of "Duchamp's never defining the work but rather allowing it to be reconciled or created through the experience of individual viewers" (Haladyn 2010: 62). Since the creation of art and its interpretation depends on the viewer, there is an infinite space of possibilities. However, the viewer's experience is restrained to what can be seen through the peepholes in the wooden door and the hole in the brick wall. Is this a general experience with secrets? We see, we hear, we smell, but reality is either missing or inaccessible for us, because we find ourselves behind a wooden door. But there are also gaps and paradoxes that contribute to this infinity of possibilities. *Given* creates a gap, perhaps even an antithesis, to Duchamp's previous work inasmuch as it strongly relies on what we see – by looking through the holes in the wooden door we experience the installation and become part of it. In his previous work, Duchamp rejected the retinal dimension: a snow shovel bought in a hardware store does not offer much for us to see, quite different from what is waiting behind the wooden door. As a consequence, there is this antagonism between *Given* and his previous work that invites (or urges) people to rethink the latter, to redo their interpretation, to admit that there are new possibilities and then to see that these possibilities are unlimited. In this way, the secret of *Given* captures the total of Duchamp's *oeuvre*. Given that Duchamp worked twenty years on *Given*, we can be sure that he was aware of this effect: leaving us with a perfect secret.

### 4.3.5 The growth of Duchamp's world of secrets

In his younger years, Marcel Duchamp painted, first in an impressionist style, then following the paths of cubism and futurism. In 1913, his painting "Nu descendant un escalier no. 2" ("Nude Descending a Staircase No. 2") was shown, together with some of his other paintings, at the Armory Show in New York. It has been said that this painting was strongly influenced by Eadweard Muybridge's photo series, especially by "Woman walking down stairs."[40] Duchamp's painting caused a scandal. It could well be that visitors to the show expected to see a nude, probably a female, going down a staircase. Instead, they saw variations of a puppet made out of tubes painted in a yellow-brown color stepping down a staircase indicated in the dark-brown background of the picture. What they saw was a cubist painting that represented in a rather abstract way rhythmic movements. This was not a human body, but more a machine,

---

40 A selection of twenty-two works by Muybridge (1830–1904) were exhibited at the Pinakothek der Moderne, Munich, April 24–October 4, 2015, demonstrating the movement of men, women, and, e.g., a horse in the form of a sequence of photos. There was a reference to Marcel Duchamp and his *Nude Descending a Staircase No. 2* posted in the exhibition space of the Muybridge show. The Moderna Museet at Stockholm presents photo series by Muybridge together with artwork by Duchamp.

as Paz (1978: 10) notes. The visitors were trapped into an interpretation of a painting which came as a shock to most of them. It represented a secret, and this secret implied irritation.

To Octavio Paz, Duchamp was a painter of ideas who never accepted the interpretation that painting is a manual activity producing art subject to visual experience only. Duchamp was fascinated by language. He considered language a perfect instrument to both create meaning and destroy it (Paz 1978: 5). Both elements we find in Duchamp's readymades. Duchamp reports:

> In 1913 I had the happy idea to fasten a bicycle wheel to a kitchen stool and watch it turn . . . In New York in 1915 I bought at a hardware store a snow shovel on which I write 'In Advance of the Broken Arm'.
> (Sanouillet and Peterson 1989 [1973]: 141)

It should be noted that these objects were meant to be private experiments, as Duchamp refrained from showing them to an audience or exhibit them in a gallery. In a 1959 radio interview, he clarified that an object can only become a piece of art if it is noticed and acknowledged by an active audience.[41] Later, his object *Fountain* transgressed this line of privacy. He smuggled this porcelain urinal, signed with "R. Mutt," into an exhibition organized by the Society of Independent Artists in 1917, staged at The Grand Central Palace hotel in New York. Although he was a member of the jury of this event, this object was rejected for getting displayed and banished into a dark corner.

Recently it has been argued that Duchamp did not create *Fountain*, but only assisted in submitting the piece for a friend. This concurs with a letter which Duchamp wrote to his sister Suzanne, telling her that Richard Mutt was the masculine pseudonym of a female friend who had sent him the urinal as a sculpture. He never identified this friend. The adapted urinal was a readymade to him, and he made use of it. When the show was over, *Fountain* reemerged, a sale was enacted, and the object was brought to Alfred Stieglitz's studio to be photographed. The photo was published together with comments in the Dadaist magazine *The Blind Man*. There were rumors that Duchamp himself was the author of these comments, which claimed that "R. Mutt" wanted to introduce a new idea for this object, extending its relevance to the world of art by demonstrating that it is not just for use as a urinal.

Danto (1999: 73) argues that Duchamp anticipated Warhol's proclamation that everything can be art and prepared the way for Beuys's dictum that everybody is an artist. In this spirit, no wonder, seventeen replicas of

---

41 Kosuth (1974: 148) confirms: "Art 'lives' through influencing other art, not by existing as the physical residue of an artist's ideas." He further claims: "The 'value' of particular artists after Duchamp can be weighed according to how much they questioned the nature of art; which is another way of saying 'what they *added* to the conception of art' or what was not there before they started" (Kosuth 1974: 146; original emphasis).

*Fountain*, authorized by Duchamp, exist today. (The original object has been lost.) Most of them are items in the collections of rather prominent art galleries. Duchamp might argue that it does not matter that the original object no longer exists, as long as the replicas convey his idea and disseminate it over the globe. (Then of course it does not matter whether he submitted the urinal or whether he just arranged the submission.) Most likely this is the main reason why he authorized so many replicas. But he was also aware that objects must be scarce to be considered as art and have a corresponding impact. This is why he signed readymades and insisted on authorization of the replicas. He also realized "the danger of repeating indiscriminately this form of expression and decided to limit the production of 'readymades' to a small number yearly." He "was aware . . . that for the spectator even more than for the artist, art is a habit forming drug" and he wanted to protect his readymades "against such contamination" (Sanouillet and Peterson 1989 [1973]: 142).

Yet, it took quite some time until the message of the readymades spread: not the object but the process is art. The difference between art and other objects can no longer be discovered by just looking at them: "the differences are not of a kind that meets or even can meet the eye" (Danto 1992: 95). Indeed, over many years, Duchamp did not produce art objects at all, but dedicated himself to playing chess. He was a competent chess player, and became a member of the French national team, competing at the unofficial Chess Olympics at Paris in 1924 and four official Chess Olympics thereafter. It has been argued that his dealing with art, and the concepts and strategies he developed therein, were just an apprenticeship for his playing of chess. But his secret work with *Given* somehow falsifies this observation.

His dedication to chess, which was established in his parental home and shared by his brothers and sister, was also evident in his pictorial work; for example, the game of chess in *The King and the Queen Traversed by Swift Nudes* of 1912, which is a graphite drawing on Japanese laid paper, and foreshadows the *Nude Descending a Staircase*: It is difficult to see the King and Queen without knowing Duchamp's passion for chess, and the Nudes are even more difficult to identify. Its structure is very similar to another pencil work of the same year, *La Mariée mise à nu par les célibataires*, which can be seen from its title as a blueprint of *The Large Glass*. But there was still a long way to go. The oil painting *Portrait de Joueurs d'Échecs* of 1911 is more explicit: one can see the two players in their cubist contemplation over some chessmen in the center of the painting. In 1910, Duchamp painted a post-impressionistic "oil on canvas" titled *Chess Game* depicting his elder brothers bent over a chessboard. A comparison of two oil paintings demonstrates not only a substantial change in style, but also a pivotal interest in chess. Chess was a lifelong passion for Duchamp. He is (very) often quoted saying: "I have come to the personal conclusion that while all artists are not chess players, all chess players are artists." To Duchamp, chess demonstrates that the value of creative activity lies in the process, in the act of making, rather than in the esthetic significance of the thing made. In the end, the chessboard is "stripped bare."

This artistic perspective also shows up in his theoretical work with chess. With the Ukrainian-born chess champion Vitaly Halberstadt, Duchamp authored a book in French, German, and English (Duchamp and Halberstadt 1932), Even the title of the book is in three languages: *L'Opposition et Cases Conjugees, Opposition und Schwesterfelder, Opposition and Sister Squares* describing its subject. But the title is extended – also in three languages: *Opposition and Sister Squares are reconciled by Duchamp et Halberstadt*. In this book, the two authors dealt with endgame problems which are, as Duchamp himself admitted, of no interest to chess players as they are extremely unlikely (Cabanne 1967: 146). According to Duchamp, only three or four people looked at these problems, in addition to him and his co-author. In spite of this observation, Strouhal (2012) gave – in German, English, and French – a rather extended analysis of the problems and the solutions offered by Duchamp and Halberstadt.

If *Opposition and Sister Squares are reconciled* is not a book for chess players, is it a book for artists? Or, is it art?

## 4.4 The artist as a secret agent

Artists work with secrets and, to a large extent, art itself is a secret. Who has the key? What is the interpretation? It should not come as a surprise that art and artists are used in the realm of politics when politics chooses secrecy and obfuscation as strategies. This is very often the case, as some prominent examples in this section demonstrate.[42] But the matching of art and politics is not always without conflict, as the rise of Abstract Expressionism and its career in the period of the Cold War illustrates. During the Cold War period, which followed World War II, the CIA (Central Intelligence Agency) supported art and made, of course secretly, Abstract Expressionist painting the dominant aesthetic culture of the West carrying its political message of freedom directed against socialism and communism. According to Eva Cockroft (1974: 40), in "the world of art, Abstract Expressionism constituted the ideal style for these propaganda activities. It was the perfect contrast to 'the regimented, traditional, and narrow' nature of 'socialist realism'."

### 4.4.1 Conflicting perspectives in the political arena

In hindsight, it is not obvious that the CIA's secret cultural policy was a "bad thing" whereas its more or less transparent counterpart at the government level, often attacking modern art with disdain, was the better alternative. For example, "America's pre-eminent liberal historian," Arthur Schlesinger ranked the CIA leadership as politically enlightened and sophisticated. Indeed, most

---

42 Subsections of this section are reprinted – by the permission of the publishers – from Holler (2007c) "The Artist as a Secret Agent: Liberalism Against Populism." See also Holler (2002b) and Holler and Klose-Ullmann (2010) for closely related material.

of them *were* well educated. This "view of the CIA as a haven of liberalism acted as a powerful inducement to collaborate with it, or, if not this, at least to acquiesce to the myth that it was well motivated" (Saunders 2000: 3). This paved the way for artists to contribute their art as a tool to be used in the culture race of the Cold War.

The linkage of this artistic "weapon" with the CIA remained secret for a long time and is still an object of discussion. But there is ample evidence that the CIA gave, directly and indirectly, financial and logistic support to modern art. Abstract Expressionism became the vehicle for the United States's imperial burden and this vehicle needed fuel. However, why did the support of modern art and the corresponding cultural policy depend on covert fuel? Why covert?

US President Harry Truman did not think much of modern art and even less of the artists who produced it. This evaluation was shared by many politicians, at least when they talked in public. George Dondero, a Republican Congressman from Michigan,[43] attacked modern art as an instrument of Communist subversion. He declared that "modernism to be quite simply part of a worldwide conspiracy to weaken American resolve" (Saunders 2000: 253). Modern art became emblematic of "un-Americanism" – "in short, cultural heresy" (de Hart Mathews 1976: 763).

More specifically, Dondero succeeded in his war against modern art, forcing the withdrawal of a State Department exhibition called "Advancing American Art." This exhibition had been shown with great success in Paris and Prague. In Congress, however, it was denounced as subversive and "un-American." The State Department issued a directive ordering that in future no American artist with Communist or fellow-travelling associations be exhibited at government expense. These associations were rather generously defined to include many leading artists in the Abstract Expressionist crowd. In the period of the McCarthy witch-hunts, this meant that politicians who, in principle, took a benevolent view of modern art hesitated to become officially involved.

Hauptman (1973) gives details on cultural policy during the McCarthy decade from the mid-1940s to the mid-1950s. In general, this was an unpleasant period for the creative industry, including artists. However, it was the rich, well-educated, adventurous, and liberal East Coast elite who (a) had the insight that Abstract Expressionism could be an excellent weapon in the Cold War, and (b) had the financial means and the social connections to do this on their own account. Some, like Nelson Rockefeller, had strong personal connections to the CIA, partly as a result of earlier wartime intelligence work. In addition, this group had the conviction that they had to fight oppressive Russian Communism in order to defend freedom – and that Abstract Expressionism was a most exciting art project, which chimed with their liberal taste.

---

43 While there is some uncertainty regarding George Dondero's home state – Eva Cockroft (1974) and Jane de Hart Mathews (1976) connect him with Michigan, while Frances Saunders connects him with Missouri – he did serve as a member from Michigan in the US House of Representatives from 1953 to 1957.

This set the stage. On the one hand, we had the politicians, constrained by their desire for majority support, popular assistance, and the benevolence of their peers; and on the other, we had the East Coast elite, determined to use modern art to defend American liberalism against the Russian Communist threat, and, to some degree, also against the corruption of the political establishment and "redneck" ideas about art, advocated by a Republican from Michigan (which is of course not a "redneck" state).

### 4.4.2 Pawns, kings, and queens in the Cold War game

At the time, the scene very much looked like a contest of "liberalism against populism."[44] Yet, what appeared to be a fundamental conflict was solved through recourse to obfuscation and secrecy – private political action under a public umbrella, and state interventions in the guise of private organizations. The major players of this "secret game" were the CIA, the Museum of Modern Art (MoMA), and the Congress of Cultural Freedom (CCF). The relationship among these players was the result of historical ties, personal links, and ongoing collaboration.[45] Figure 4.3 illustrates the links between the intermediate agents in the "American battle against Russian Communism."

It does not seem far-fetched to understand the Cold War situation as a game, and many participants in fact saw it as a two-person zero-sum game: the gains of one party are the losses of the other one. This implies, of course, strict conflict. Here, however, we deal with a game played within the Western bloc characterized by changing coalitions, secret payoffs, conflicts of interest, and also coordination problems. It is not obvious, and also subject to the chosen perspective: how to identify the players and their positions in this game? There were many pawns in this game, and also knights and bishops. But who were the kings and queens? A short characterization of the major players could help us to identify the kings and queens.

The CIA was created by the National Security Act of July 26, 1947 in order to coordinate military and diplomatic intelligence. Although the Agency was not explicitly authorized to collect intelligence or intervene secretly in the affairs of other nations, the Act mentioned "services of common concern," which was used to move the CIA's activities into espionage, covert action, paramilitary operations, and technical intelligence collection. Saunders (2000: 32f.) points out that "the terms under which the Agency was established institutionalized the concepts of 'the necessary lie' and 'plausible deniability' as legitimate peacetime strategies." The CIA's officers were dedicated

---

44  This reflects the title of Riker (1982). Although Riker's book has been motivated by theoretical results of social choice theory, it refers to the same basic dilemma which was already discussed in Alexis de Tocqueville's *Democracy in America* (1956 [1835 and 1940]).

45  The following "portrait" of the three organizations summarizes the corresponding material in Saunders (2000). In parts, the description is very close to Saunders's text and quotation marks could be adequate.

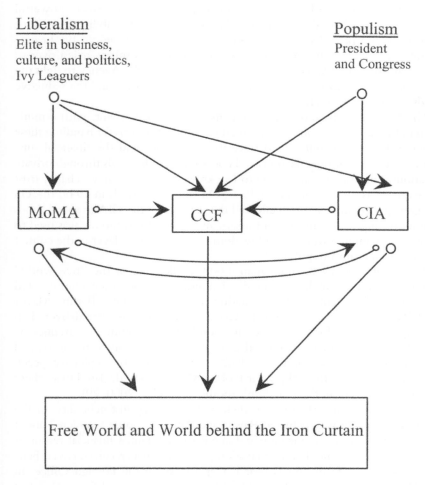

*Figure 4.3* The major players in the Cold War game

to the mission to save "western freedom from Communist darkness," a mission resulting from their training in solid Christian morality, the principles of a robust intellect which most of them had enjoyed at some Ivy League school, and the spirit of the Declaration of Independence which they had inhaled in their social environment.

Some CIA officers had already engaged in intelligence work for the Office of Strategic Service (OSS) during wartime. The OSS counted members of the Vanderbilt, DuPont, Archbold, Weil and Whitney families in its ranks, as well as a son of Ernest Hemingway and J.P. Morgan's two sons. To some OSS members, the Service was an exciting adventure. Working with secrets can be very attractive and working secretly can be pleasurable, and create powerful and amazing social bonds. In any case, the OSS offered a possibility to enhance reputations and provided another network in addition to the old Ivy League school ties. Some of the OSS mentality and most of its spirit carried over to the newly created CIA. Young Ivy Leaguers flocked to the Agency to fight the threat of Communism and to enjoy the privileges of power and the seductive bonds of a secret brotherhood.

The CIA had substantial finances at its disposal to be spent, with a minimum of bureaucratic control; and it used various institutions for handling these resources to make it difficult to trace its transactions and the financial support it gave to other organizations and cooperating individuals through private donations. For instance, according to Cockroft (1974), Whitney's charity trust was exposed as a CIA conduit in 1967. On the other hand, in 1949, the US Congress passed an Act which allowed the director of the CIA to spend funds without having to account for disbursement. Some of this money was used to support the Congress of Cultural Freedom, another major player in the contest of "liberalism against populism."

At end of June 1950, more than 4,000 intellectuals of the "free world" gathered in Berlin, which was then divided into four zones, each administrated by one of the four "Allies." The invitation committee included Berlin's Mayor Ernst Reuter and several prominent German academics. Reuter delivered an opening speech in which the word "freedom" appeared with great frequency. Over four days, participants moved from one panel session to the next, and discussed issues such as "good" and "bad" nuclear bombs. In his plenary speech to the invited intellectuals, the actor Robert Montgomery declared that "there is no neutral corner in the Freedom's room!" (Saunders 2000: 79).

Not everyone subscribed to this rhetorical crusade against neutrality, or the option of a middle way between Russia and America. Some wondered about the independence of the meeting and about the substantial financial resources that made the event and their participation possible. Others received covert benefaction via the Information Research Department of the Foreign Office. In a 1994 interview, Tom Braden, OSS officer in his youth and former head of the International Organizations Divisions (IOD), the greatest single concentration of covert political and propaganda activities of the CIA, reflected on the event's financing in Berlin: "We've got to remember that when we're speaking of those years that Europe was broke . . . There wasn't any money. So they naturally looked to the United States for money" (quoted after Saunders 2000: 82). Delegates who speculated about who was footing the bill concluded that this was not quite the spontaneous event its organizers claimed. Simple common sense was enough to find out who financed the Berlin congress and who was behind it.

Despite some irritations, the Berlin congress was celebrated by US government officials and the CIA as a great success. Following the event, the Berlin congress was institutionalized as the Congress of Cultural Freedom (CCF), which became a precious instrument in the CIA toolbox. Its principle task: winning over the waverers:

It was not to be a centre of agitation, but a beachhead in Western Europe from which the advance of Communist ideas could be halted. It was to engage in a widespread and cohesive campaign of peer pressure to persuade intellectuals to dissociate themselves from Communist fronts or fellow traveling organizations. It was to encourage the intelligentsia to develop theories and arguments which were directed not at a mass audience, but at the small elite of pressure groups and statesmen who in turn determined government policy. It was not an intelligence-gathering source, and agents in the other CIA divisions were warned not to attempt to use it as such.

(Saunders 2000: 98f.)

The CCF managers were answerable to Tom Braden, then head of the CIA's IOD. Its activities were either directly financed by CIA's Farfield Foundation or, indirectly, by one of the many foundations that were more than willing to transfer CIA money to CCF officials or to contributors to CCF projects, e.g., museum directors, gallery owners, art critics, journalists, or artists. The CIA's undercover activities were generously subsidized by Marshall Plan money. Recipient countries were asked to deposit an amount equal to the US contribution in its central bank. Ninety-five percent of the currency funds remained the legal property of the recipient country's government, while 5 per cent became the property of the US government – and were made available as a war chest for the CIA (Saunders 2000: 1005f.). Lashmar and Oliver (1998) report that, at its height, the resulting organization of the Congress of Cultural Freedom would employ 280 staff members, and have representatives in 35 countries organizing conferences and seminars, as well as a network of sponsored journals: "During the early 1950s . . . the CIA budget for the Congress of Cultural Freedom . . . was about \$800–\$900,000, which included . . . the subsidy for the Congress's magazine *Encounter*."[46] We will come back to *Encounter*.

Some contributors to the US's cultural activities were supported by their own foundation, and thus did not depend on CIA money. This did not hinder them in closely cooperating with the CCF. Nelson Rockefeller was such an "independent supporter," and also was the president of the Museum of Modern Art (MoMA) in 1939–41 and 1946–53. His mother was one of the museum's five founders in 1929. MoMA represented the "enlightened rich," the future of American culture.

During World War II, Nelson Rockefeller was in charge of all intelligence in Latin America. His organization sponsored touring exhibitions of "contemporary American painting" of which nineteen were contracted to MoMA.

---

46 Information given by Tom Braden in an interview in 1994, quoted in Lashmar and Oliver (1998: 132). Tom Braden was an OSS (Office of Strategic Services) officer in his youth and head of the International Organizations Divisions (IOD) of the CIA. He confirmed the CIA financing of the Berlin meeting (see Saunders 2000: 82).

Rockefeller was not involved in the OSS but his close friendship with Allen Dulles compensated for this shortcoming. Dulles, in charge of OSS wartimes operations in Europe, was the younger brother of Secretary of State John Foster Dulles and held the position of CIA director in the period 1953–61. He and Tom Braden delivered briefings on the CIA's covert activities on a regular basis. In 1954, Nelson Rockefeller was appointed as Eisenhower's special adviser on Cold War strategy. He was also chairman of the Planning Coordination Group which controlled the National Security Council and CIA's covert operations. Thus was closed the circle of secrecy.

Similarly, the various engagements of William Burden,[47] a great-great-grandson of Commodore Vanderbilt, illustrate the connection between the CIA, the CCF and MoMA. During the war, he worked for Nelson Rockefeller's intelligence service. After the war, he became director of CIA's Farfield Foundation and thus decided on the financial support to CCF, sat as chairman of an advisory committee of the MoMA, and became MoMA's president in 1956. In his book, Saunders (2000) introduced us to several other high-ranking officials, who held similar links to at least two of these institutions. However, in the case of MoMA's activities, "unlike those of CIA, it was not necessary to use subterfuge. Similar aims as those of CIA's cultural operations could be pursued openly with the support of Nelson Rockefeller's millions" (Cockroft 1974: 41).

By 1956, the International Program of MoMA hat organized thirty-three exhibitions, including the US's participation in the Venice Biennale. As Cockroft observes:

> The State Department refused to take the responsibility for U.S. representation at the Venice Biennale, perhaps the most important international-cultural-political art event, where all European countries including the Soviet Union competed for cultural honors. MoMA bought the U.S. pavilion in Venice and took the sole responsibility for the exhibitions from 1954 to 1962. This was the only case of privately owned (instead of government-owned) pavilion at the Venice Biennale.
>
> (Cockroft 1974: 40)

The US government's difficulties in handling the delicate issues of free speech and free artistic expression, generated by the McCarthy hysteria of the early 1950s, made it necessary and convenient for MoMA to assume this role of international representation of the United States. This was consistent with the neoliberal principle that there is nothing to prevent an individual from exerting as much influence through his work in a private foundation as he could through work in the government (Saunders 2000: 139).

When MoMA contracted to supply the works of art for the CCF's 1952 Masterpieces festival in Paris, "it did so under the auspices of trustees who were fully cognizant of the CIA's role in that organization" (Saunders 2000: 268)

---

47 See Saunders (2000: 137) for this short portrait and further details illustrating William Burden's political and cultural role.

and of its propaganda value. On the other hand, the collaboration with the CCF brought MoMA and its favored Abstract Expressionism access to many of the most prestigious art institutions in Europe, whose directors were sitting on the Arts Committee of the CCF.

During 1953–54, MoMA organized a tour of Europe, dedicated exclusively to Abstract Expressionism. The show, entitled "Twelve Contemporary American Painters and Sculptures," had its opening at the *Musée National d'Art Moderne* at Paris. This was achieved with the help of the American Embassy in Paris (which acted as a quiet liaison between MoMA and its French hosts) and with the financial support of the Nelson Rockefeller Fund, which was partly conducted through the *Association Française d'Action Artistique*. This association was a donor to the CCF. Its director, Philippe Erlanger, was a designated CIA contact at the French Foreign Office (Saunders 2000: 270).

Eva Cockroft (1974), when discussing the relationship between the CIA's cultural apparatus and MoMA's international program, observed that the functions of both institutions were similar and "mutually supportive." Saunders (2000:264) concludes that "there is no *prima facie* evidence for any formal agreement between the CIA and the Museum of Modern Art. The fact is, it simply wasn't necessary." The motivations of both institutions, being at least functionally divergent, converged in the support for Abstract Expressionism and its advance throughout the "free world" and to some dissident circles behind the Iron Curtain. Why Abstract Expressionism? Was it not that precisely this form of expression that had been rejected by America's silent majority and by some of its very outspoken politicians?

### 4.4.3 Individualism and universalism

If the CIA, the Museum of Modern Art, and the Congress of Cultural Freedom were major players in the cultural warfare game, then the Abstract Expressionist artists were the pawns. In fact, the major players did not really care about the individual artists, but focused on their works and the ideology behind. This was, in a sense, paradoxical because individualism was one of the cornerstones of Abstract Expressionism and a major reason why this art was supported as an alternative to the "collectivistic art of socialism." The art works showed substantial variety, but the variation among the artists themselves seemed even greater and "most of them were people who had very little respect for the government in particular and certainly not for the CIA," observed Donald Jameson in an interview in Washington in June 1994, reproduced in Saunders (2000: 260). Jackson Pollock was said to be a drunk; he was killed in a car crash. Mark Rothko and Adolph Gottlieb were committed anti-Communists. Barnett Newman "was painting for America,"[48] while Robert Motherwell and

---

48  However, he "clung throughout his life to the independent anarchistic views he had formulated in youth" and even "wrote a foreword to a new edition of Kropotkin's memoirs" (Golding 2003: 32). His paintings were meant as a challenge to the observer and to the art world. His *Who's afraid of red, yellow and blue III* triggered vandalism and overpaint (see Schinzel 2012).

the Dutch-born Willem de Kooning did not think highly of a national context for their work. Ad Reinhardt participated in the March on Washington for black rights in August 1963. It seems that nothing remarkable has been said about Clyfford Still's life and political orientation. There were times when he refused to be co-opted by the museums and the critical establishment, directed by art critic Clement Greenberg, but he still wished to be perceived as spiritual leader of the Abstract Expressionist movement. To some extent, he was the mentor of color-field painters such as Barnett Newman and Mark Rothko and, unlike Pollock, Motherwell, and de Kooning, Still rejected Freud and Surrealism and "all cultural opiates, past and present" (Cox 1983: 51).

These artists formed the "essential eight" of Abstract Expressionism. Others who were added to this group are William Baziotes, Arshil Gorky (who hanged himself), Philip Guston, Hans Hofmann, Fritz Kline, Richard Pousette-Dart, Mark Tobey, and Bradley Walker Tomlin (see Gibson 1997: xx). Instead of going deeper into the individual history and political beliefs of these people, I will follow the strategy of the three major players and focus on the ideology of art which made Abstract Expressionism.

Danto summarizes the essence of Abstract Expressionism

> with its celebration of the self, of the inner states that painting allegedly made objective, and of paint itself as the medium par excellence through which these inner states were externally transcribed. In a certain sense, abstract expressionist painting was a kind of private pictorial language, a turning away from the public and the political in the interest of producing an art that was, in the words of Robert Motherwell, 'plastic, mysterious, and sublime'.
>
> (Danto 1999: 75)

The focus on color instead of form or narrative expressions represented the abstract dimension. The discovery of the unconscious with the help of color contained the expressionist dimension. The two dimensions met in automatic drawing and painting, doodling, gesture and action painting, and Jackson Pollock's dripping method. The "fluid space, lack of closed shapes, a deliberately unfinished quality, and an 'overall' composition that diffused any notion of focus" of Abstract Expressionist work – complex, cosmopolitan, and ever-changing – "was intrinsically at odds with the need for certitude and control" (de Hart Mathews 1976:785), which were actively looked for by many Americans during the Cold War.

"Marxism gave way to psychiatry" (Guilbaut 1983:165). Quite a few Abstract Expressionists had political roots in the Marxism of the 1930s. As a consequence, their analysis of the new political situation and their own position in it bore the imprint of the Marxist tradition. However, in the 1940s, there was an important shift away from critical studies of the social and political environment and of alienation in the capitalist society. Gottlieb and Rothko were dedicated readers of Freud and Jung. This concurred with the focus on creativity (or originality) as one of Abstract Expressionism's core principles: "Originality, like abstraction, was an important way predicated on the denial of politics" (Gibson 1997: xxviii). Alienation became a purely individualistic (psychological) phenomenon which, according to Clement Greenberg – self-appointed prophet and spokesman of Abstract Expressionism – made the American artist the "most modern" of all artists and enabled him to express the spirit of the modern age. However, Abstract Expressionists, different from Marinetti's futurism, rejected machine imagery and industrial and urban landscape. They "entered into a pastoral world that was primitive and elemental" (Cox 1983: 48). On the other hand, abstraction made it possible to engage in an active dialogue with the age, and private material could be treated as a public declaration. However, to art historian Serge Guilbaut (1983: 197), "the freedom of expression and existential violence that leap to the eye in the work of abstract expressionists were in fact products of fear and the impossibility of representation, of the need to avoid the literary expression."

"The American problem," Robert Motherwell emphasized, "was to find a creative principle that was not a style, not stylistic, not an imposed aesthetic" (quoted in Danto 1999: 23). Many Abstract Expressionist artists were followers of Carl Jung. As Jungians, they believed that the collective unconscious was universal and "self-identical" in all human beings (Gibson 1997: 48). The function of art was considered as the invention of codes to transpose universal, rather than local, meaning into visual form. It was seen as a means of decoding – a key: "Turning . . . to private visions, insights, and most especially the subconscious, the abstract expressionists plumbed the depths of their own experience for metaphors and symbols that would somehow possess universal meaning" (de Hart Mathews 1976: 783). This was the spiritual-intellectual basis for the claim on universalism and a retreat from pre-war America's isolationist spirit – a pre-condition for applying art to cultural warfare.

Paradoxically, to some extent Abstract Expressionism contained a turning-away from the market. Before it was discovered as an instrument of the Cold War, its main representatives were not very much of a success in the art market. By the simple fact that this art often used immense formats – different from its European predecessors – it urged museums, mostly public ones, to provide adequate space which, consequently, was made available in the course of Cold War cultural policy. In principle, this conflicted with the private pictorial language of Abstract Expressionism, its "artistic free enterprise" strategy and non-political attitude, and made its dissemination dependent on semi-public (political) entrepreneurship as developed by the CIA, MoMA, and the CCF.

There are many paradoxes embedded in Abstract Expressionism; some are embedded in the inconsistency of its claim of individualism and freedom, on the one hand, and its policy effects which focus on the dominance of ideas, ideology, and power on the other. Eva Cockroft (1974: 41) concludes that "attempts to claim that styles of art are politically neutral when there is no overt political subject matter are as simplistic as Dondero-ish attacks on all abstract art as 'subversive'."

Paradoxically, the discriminatory edge of Abstract Expressionism was its claim for universalism. And it was this claim, together with its individualistic ideology that made this style and the artists a focus of interest for Cold War strategists. Does not Communism also make a universalistic claim? To Cockroft, it is evident that

> rich and powerful patrons of the arts, men like Rockefeller and Whitney, who control the museums and help oversee foreign policy, also recognize the value of culture in the political arena. The artist creates freely. But his work is promoted and used by others for their own purposes. Rockefeller . . . consciously used Abstract Expressionism, 'the symbol of political freedom,' for political ends.
>
> (Cockroft 1974: 41)

This had also enduring side effects on the cultural landscape. In March 1948, Clement Greenberg was the first to declare that New York had achieved international status as a cultural center and even replaced Paris as the cultural symbol of the Western world: American art was the foremost in the world. After Paris was occupied by the Germans in 1940, many artists had fled to America. Sandler (1970: 31) lists André Breton, Marc Chagall, Salvador Dalí, Max Ernst, Jacques Lipchitz, Matta, Mondrian, Amédée Ozenfant, Kurt Seligmann, Yves Tanguy, Techlichew, and Ossip Zadkine. Perhaps it is somewhat overdone to argue that "by an act of war, New York became the international art capital" (Sandler 1970: 31). New York needed the Cold War and the ascendancy of Abstract Expressionism and the New York School to consolidate its dominant role in the art world for the next decades.

### 4.4.4 Basic questions on "why secrecy?"

Saunders (2000: 5) raised a number of questions which could serve as a starting point for evaluating the CIA's engagement in the cultural warfare. The first question addresses the issue of freedom: "Clearly, by camouflaging its investment, the CIA acted on the supposition that its blandishments would be refused if offered openly. What kind of freedom can be advanced by such deception?" Of course, this question was relevant for the Free World and its frontier states near the Soviet Empire. However, it was also of interest to the political, economic, and social life within the US's borders. A preliminary answer to this question is: a liberal freedom controlled by an elite and the elite's principle. For instance, with respect to the contribution of MoMA and the various private foundations which supported the cultural warfare, as already stated, liberalism implies that there is nothing to prevent an individual from exerting as much influence through his work in a private foundation as he could through work in the government. Obviously, keeping this influence and corresponding interventions secret from the public and even major parts of the political establishment, does not invalidate this principle and its application.

It is seen as a corrective to parliamentary decision making and, more so, to majoritarianism. However, it violates the accountability inherent to the model of democracy which refers to the competition of the candidates for incumbency (see Riker 1982).

The Founding Fathers, and more specifically James Madison, wanted to refine the voice of the people in government, not replicate it. They proposed various restraints to majority voting which were thought to shelter the governing elite from direct popular impact. Voting was considered a method of controlling officials by subjecting their tenure to periodic electoral tests, but not a method for citizens to participate directly in making law, expressing the "Will of the People." To create and to use a policy frame which is independent of majoritarian support is a natural consequence of this principle of American liberalism as soon as the elite finds the elected representatives too narrow-minded, and too close to popular values, to collaborate in the pursuit of the grand scheme.

More specifically, Saunders (2000: 5) asks: "Did financial aid distort the process by which intellectuals and artists were advanced? . . . Were reputations secured or enhanced by membership of the CIA's cultural consortium?" *Ex post*, one can conclude that most of the writers, film-makers and artists selected for CIA sponsorship were of extremely high quality. The Abstract Expressionists such as Jackson Pollock, Willem de Kooning, and Mark Rothko have re-defined the art world of their period and are still prominent in museums of modern art around the globe. (See Mark Rothko's expressive room at the Tate Modern in London.) But it seems impossible to answer whether they could have done this without the support which they derived, directly or indirectly, from the resources invested by the CIA in their secret cultural warfare. We have to see that Abstract Expressionism entails a high degree of exclusivity and of cartelization and its support had a substantial discriminating effect on American art – with precarious consequences for those who were not members of the cartel. Abstract Expressionism "was sealed inside a bell-jar and protected from infection by any unwanted Germs, from intrusion by any outsider who might disturb the cherished harmony" (Guilbaut 1983: 10). There was no (gallery) space left for Byron Browne, Carl Holty, Karl Knath, and Charles Seliger, painters who had been successful before the Abstract Expressionists conquered the stage; but their works were too European, too close to Paris, and too un-American to be enlisted by governmental agencies and private organizations in the fight against the expansion of Communism. The threat of Communist expansion was palpable. On February 25, 1948, Czechoslovakia joined the Soviet bloc after the Czech Communists succeeded in out-maneuvering the divided Social Democratic Party.

Gibson summarizes:

> To the extent that the work of an artist who is not in the canon looks like that of one who is, the noncanonical artist's work is derivative. To the extent that the noncanonical work does not resemble that in the canon, the contending work is not Abstract Expressionist.
>
> (Gibson 1997: xxxi)

This sounds like *Catch 22*, doesn't it? Paradoxically, the discriminating effect resulted from the focus on universality. This excluded artists whose identity did not generalize "in a postwar society whose standards were racist, misogynist, and homophobic" (Gibson 1997: xxii). The mechanism of this society functioned to reinforce the power of European (i.e., Caucasian), male, heterosexual identity and discriminated against artists who did not fit this pattern. The CIA was grateful for this pre-selection of artists and their work; it made it less cumbersome to transfer Western values to the rest of the world. Not only in America were the standards of the postwar society racist, misogynist, and homophobic.

However, as Saunders inquired:

> was there any real justification for assuming that the principles of western democracy couldn't be revived in post-war Europe according to some internal mechanism? Or for not assuming that democracy could be more complex than was implied by the lauding of American liberalism?
>
> (Saunders 2000: 5)

Indeed, democracy is a complex concept. Left to its internal mechanism, it is not obvious that a democratic equilibrium evolves. Perhaps such an equilibrium does not even exist, or it cannot be unearthed by majority voting, as Condorcet (1785) had already pointed out in his "*Essai sur l'application de l'analyse à la probabilité des décisions rendues à la pluralité des voix.*" From a theoretical point of view, coordination on a democratic equilibrium, if it exists, seems to be easily resolved by the implementation of American liberalism, arranged by the American way of life as the focal point. However, when it comes to modern art as a vehicle to disseminate American liberalism, it faced, as we have seen, popular resistance from within. Undercover operations were a way to circumvent this problem. This violates the majority principle of democracy, but not necessarily its liberal perspective. As Gordon Wood, author of *The American Revolution: A History*, writes, "What really counts in maintaining democracy are the liberties protected by the Bill of Rights and the underlying conditions of the country – its culture, its social arrangements, its economic well-being, and the political experience of its citizens and their leaders" (Wood 2002: 21). Competition for incumbency seems to be of secondary importance.

If the financing were done openly, the liberal elite would see itself in conflict with the political sector which (a) relies on majorities and thus depends on popularity, and (b) whose members are, in general, not as well equipped to enjoy modern art as are the members of the elite. Moreover, it seems that some participants of the Berlin congress and affiliates to the CCF were unaware that they were, either directly or indirectly, financed by the CIA. Had they known, they would have left the projects it supported or publicly distanced themselves from their donors. In both cases, the effect would have probably been negative.

Some participants explicitly claimed that they did not know that they were financed by the CIA. They needed this umbrella to (a) keep up social respect,

(b) be acceptable to their cultural or political community, and (c) avoid political or social resistance and concomitant backlashes regarding their work. Secrecy was helpful and, to some extent, necessary for the conquest of the Western art community through sponsored exhibitions and gallery work. If the shows which finally installed Abstract Expressionism in Western Europe during the post-war period been openly financed by the US government, their impact would have been much reduced: the success of America's Cold War program depended on its ability to appear independent from government and representing the spontaneous convictions of freedom-loving individuals. This was, e.g., the credo of Allen Dulles. This is why secrecy was chosen.

To understand Abstract Expressionism's success, however, we must consider this element of secrecy. Georges Duby claims that "the most startling discoveries that remain to be made . . . will come from the attempt to find out what was left out of the discourse, whether voluntarily or involuntarily, to determine what was hidden, consciously or unconsciously" (quoted in Guilbaut 1983: 6). Naturally, a lot is left out when politics makes use of obfuscation[49] and secrecy. Schlesinger (2004: 447 and 448f.), special adviser to John F. Kennedy and Lyndon B. Johnson, claimed that "No one questions the state's right to keep certain things secret – weapons technology and development, intelligence methods and sources, diplomatic negotiations in progress, military contingency plans and the like." But the "real function of the secret system in practice is to protect the executive branch from accountability for its incompetence and its venality, its follies, errors and crimes"[50] – through "the disclosure of information to the Congress, press and people." Given the veil of secrecy, how should we understand politics?

Duby concludes:

> What we need are new scholarly tools, tools better adapted than those we now have to bringing out the negative in what we are shown, to laying bare the things that men deliberately cover up. At times these suddenly reveal themselves quite by accident, but most of the time they must be carefully deciphered between the lines of what is actually said.
>
> (Quoted in Guilbaut 1983: 6)

---

49 Obfuscation is the intentional reallocation of political issues into the private or bureaucratic sector to avoid the political debate and sanctioning by the voters. Magee and co-authors (1989) and Magee (1997) is the pioneering literature. I will not further discuss this model here, although it nicely demonstrates the power of secrecy in the political arena. See Holler (2012) for an application to standardization in the EU.

50 Sagar (2013), who motivated me to read Schlesinger (2004), discusses the possibility of a control of state secrecy by the legal sector, i.e., "lawmakers and judges." He concludes from his substantial analysis that this alternative "does not grant confidence that state secrecy will not be used to conceal wrongdoing. This is because the secrecy that these regulators must operate under makes it difficult to ascertain whether they have been able to resist interests who have every incentive to corrupt them" (Sagar 2013: 203).

Holler and Wickström (1999) present a highly stylized evolutionary model that analyzes effects of the obfuscation policy on the emergence and success of Abstract Expressionism. Andreozzi (2002b) uses this model to demonstrate that scandals are usually generated by young people. Are scandals a means of challenging obfuscation?

In 1966, a series of articles was published in the *New York Times* on the CIA's covert operations. Amidst reports on political assassinations and ruthless political intervention came details about the support which the CIA gave to the cultural sector. The upshot was that the moral authority which the intellectuals enjoyed during the height of the Cold War was "seriously undermined and frequently mocked" (Saunders 200: 6). Was this intended? Or, was it just the consequence of a change in art style: from Jackson Pollock's *drippings* to Andy Warhol's *Brillo Box* and his *Campbell's Soup Cans*? The latter works were definitively more appropriate to reflect the consumerism of capitalism than the former's worship of color and celebration of the lonely hero.

## 4.5 Machiavelli's conspiracy paradoxes

The collaboration of MoMA, the CIA, and the CCF in supporting Abstract Expressionism to make it the dominant Western esthetic and to export this art into every corner of the globe, especially of course, behind the Iron Curtain, contains elements of a conspiracy. In this section,[51] we want to study how to plan and execute a successful conspiracy, and how to fight success, from a more general perspective. We look at conspiracies and the inherent strategic relationship from the point of view of rational agents and demonstrate that in many cases an equilibrium does not exist from which recipes of rational behavior for the parties in question can be derived. The analysis is based on Machiavelli's very informative and highly competent writings on this subject.

### 4.5.1 Some paradoxes

In his *Discourses*, i.e., the *Discorsi* published posthumously with papal privilege in 1531, Machiavelli dedicated a full chapter to the discussion of conspiracy. This does not seem to come as a surprise if we share the common, but rather questionable (and unjustified) view that ranks Machiavelli as master of cruelties and betrayals.[52] However, the remarkable analytical and historical depth of his discussion might trigger second thoughts. I will mainly draw from the material of Chapter VI in Book III of the *Discorsi* entitled "Of Conspiracies," to further highlight the issue. This chapter summarizes most of what can be found on

---

51  This section is a revised version of Holler (2011), further elaborated in Holler and Klose-Ullmann (2016).
52  In a series of papers I tried to contribute to the qualification of this view (Holler 2007b, 2009b). Some of this material is also used in this text.

conspiracies in *The Prince* and the *History of Florence*, although Chapter XIX of the former and the Eighth Book of the latter contain additional treasures. Some of the material will be quoted below.

In his *Discorsi*, Machiavelli (1882a [1532]: 329) starts his lecture on conspiracy with a somewhat paradoxical observation: On the one hand, "history teaches us that many more princes have lost their lives and their states by conspiracies than by open war," and, on the other hand, conspiracies, "though so often attempted, yet they so rarely attain the desired object." The answer to this riddle is that conspiracies are ubiquitous but very often fail because preparation and execution were inadequate, the executors were incompetent or unlucky, and the situation was not what it was supposed to be. Economists would call these failures a "social waste." Moreover, the death of a prince does not always imply that a conspiracy is successful. Think of Brutus' fate and the result of his contribution to killing Caesar. In the end, Octavian followed in Caesar's footsteps and was honored as (God and) Imperator Augustus. The claim is that Brutus wanted to reinstall the Roman republic. His project failed.

Machiavelli promises that he will "treat the subject" of conspiracy

> at length, and endeavor not to omit any point that may be useful to the one or the other . . . so that princes may learn to guard against such dangers, and that subjects may less rashly engage in them, and learn rather to live contentedly under such a government as Fate may have assigned to them.
> (Machiavelli 1882a [1531]: 329)

Is Machiavelli's goal to reduce the social waste of unsuccessful conspiracies or to reduce the inclination of the people to revolt if they are unhappy with their prince? It seems that he is especially concerned about those high-ranking conspirators who "almost [themselves] king[s] . . . blinded by the ambition of dominion, they are equally blind in the conduct of the conspiracy, for if their villainy were directed by prudence, they could not possibly fail of success." Social waste again!

It seems quite paradoxical that Machiavelli's analysis sharpens the tools of both sides of the Conspiracy Game. Potential conspirators will learn when there is a chance of success and how to increase this chance. The princes are told how to reduce this chance. In the equilibrium we would see successful conspiracies only, triggered by circumstances that the princes could not avoid. The chance to face such situations can be minimized, and this might be Machiavelli's message, if the prince is "loved by the people," if he installs good laws and submits himself to these laws.

Given this interpretation, however, it seems rather paradoxical to assume that Machiavelli was interested in the social waste of unsuccessful conspiracy. On the contrary, he tried to teach "economic rationality" to the agents of both sides, which he did. He developed a rational theory of conspiracy that follows the pattern of a cost-benefit analysis – with the qualification that expected benefits are likely to be zero, if benefits are standardized such that zero is the minimum, and costs "converge to infinity" – in that case the conspiracy is expected to fail. Of course, the value of infinity is ill defined.

Montaigne points out another argument that is used not to join a conspiracy "even when the enterprise was just." When Brutus drew Statilius into the conspiracy against Caesar:

> he did not think mankind worthy of a wise man's concern; according to the doctrine of Hegesias, who said, that a wise man ought to do nothing but for himself, forasmuch as he only was worthy of it: and to the saying of Theodorus, that it was not reasonable a wise man should hazard himself for his country, and endanger wisdom for a company of fools.
>
> (Montaigne 1910 [1580]): 185)

This argument is of course eminent when expected costs to the conspirators are high and the corresponding private benefits are low. Then it needs saints, fools, or heroes to overthrow a tyrant.

There is still another puzzle involved: "conspiracies have generally been set on foot by the great, or the friends of the prince; and of these, as many have been prompted to it by an excess of benefits as by an excess of wrongs" (Machiavelli 1882a [1531]: 333). Plots are generally organized by "great men of the state, or those on terms of familiar intercourse with the prince" (Machiavelli 1882a [1531]: 332). Strong arguments exist for why only those agents can stage a successful conspiracy who are close to the prince, and why, as history shows, those who conspire enjoy generous benefits from this closeness:

> A prince, then, who wishes to guard against conspiracies should fear those on whom he has heaped benefits quite as much, and even more, than those whom he has wronged; for the latter lack the convenient opportunities which the former have in abundance.
>
> (Machiavelli 1882a [1531]: 333)

It appears that princely benefits to close friends do not prevent conspiracies, since this group of people can expect to achieve success. However, probabilities that capture expectations are not given by nature, but subject to the interaction of the agents involved. To some extent, the forming of expectations boils down to a game-theoretical problem but, as we will see, this does not guarantee that there is a satisfactory solution to it. Non-uniqueness of equilibria is ubiquitous and a source of uncertainty, even for rational agents.[53] Moreover, the set of agents, those who participate in the conspiracy and those who counteract it, is often subject to the course of the game itself.

Why did Machiavelli develop such a theory if not for demonstrating that the prince can avoid conspiracies if potential conspirators are rational enough to accept the benefits which a rational prince offers to them, given the risks

---

53 The Machiavelli Conspiracy Game, presented in Section 4.5.5 below, is characterized by one Nash equilibrium only, but both the equilibrium and the maximin solution are in mixed strategies and show substantial vagueness with respect to the strategies to choose and the expectations players form.

involved? Was this another step towards his demystification of power and politics, or did he want to demonstrate to the reader how skilled and capable he was in political reasoning? We will come back to this question. First, however, let us see how Machiavelli analyzes the strategies of the conspirators and how the prince counteracts.

In order to round off this list of puzzles it should be noted that unlike *Il Principe*, the *Discorsi* – the main arena of Machiavelli's discussion of conspiracy – is not dedicated to a prince but to two of Machiavelli's friends: Zanobi Buondelmonti and Cosimo Rucellai. Machiavelli is very explicit about this dedication and explains:

> I give some proof of gratitude, although I may seem to have departed from the ordinary usage of writers, who generally dedicate their works to some prince; and, blinded by ambition or avarice, praise him for all the virtuous qualities he has not, instead of censuring him for his real vices, whilst I, to avoid this fault, do not address myself to such as are princes, but to those who by their infinite good qualities are worthy to be such; not to those who could load me with honors, rank, and wealth, but rather to those who have the desire to do so, but have not the power. For to judge rightly, men should esteem rather those who are, and not those who can be generous; and those who would know how to govern states, rather than those who have the right to govern, but lack the knowledge.
>
> (Machiavelli 1882a [1531]: 91f.)

In 1522, Buondelmonti participated in the conspiracy against the Medici which, however, failed. He fled to France and served King François I until he could return, which was after the expulsion of the Medici in 1527.

### 4.5.2 The conspirator's strategies

Machiavelli identifies three phases of danger for the conspirators: the plotting, the execution of the plot, and the period after the plot has been carried out. If the plot is formed by a single person, then, of course, communication can be kept to a minimum and the "first of the dangers" is avoided. In addition, the project can be postponed or put to rest without major costs or risks. This could be a great advantage when its success does not look very promising, especially since the situation has changed. Many such plots never leave the state of planning and rejection: they are secret and remain secret, and we do not know of them. Machiavelli notes that

> it is not uncommon to find men who form such projects (the mere purpose involving neither danger nor punishment), but few carry them into effect; and of those who do, very few or none escape being killed in the execution of their designs, and therefore but few are willing to incur such certain death.
>
> (Machiavelli 1882a [1531]: 332)

Since the conspirator in a one-person plot is unlikely to be able to structure the minutes immediately following the execution in a constructive way, single assassins are likely to lose their lives even when they successfully kill a tyrant.

One-person plots are somewhat degenerated conspiracies. They lack the elements of communication, coordination, and trust that characterize non-degenerate conspiracies and often cause them to fail. However, as Machiavelli demonstrates, successful multi-person conspiracies are often designed such that they simulate one-person plots. The one-person plot is therefore a model case. But only plots that involve several persons presuppose a conspiracy proper, implying problems of coordination and perhaps communication as well. Machiavelli distinguishes between two arrangements of conspiracy proper: the two-person plot and the multi-person plot. The two-person plot has the disadvantage that possible actions are still constrained by numerical capacity. However, compared to a plot that involves more than two persons, it offers a series of advantages, as we will see. In fact, if there were more than two persons involved then, according to Machiavelli, most successful arrangements succeeded either reducing the situation to a two-person plot or, if possible, even to a one-person plot.

In cases of more than one agent, most conspiracies fail because of denunciation – not because of lack of means, or occasions. Machiavelli states:

> Denunciation is the consequence of treachery or of want of prudence on the part of those to whom you confide your designs; and treachery is so common that you cannot safely impart your project to any but such of your most trusted friends as are willing to risk their lives for your sake, or to such other malcontents as are equally desirous of the prince's ruin. [However,] men are very apt to deceive themselves as to the degree of attachment and devotion which others have for them, and there are no means of ascertaining this except by actual experience; but experience in such matters is of the utmost danger. And even if you should have tested the fidelity of your friends on other occasions of danger, yet you cannot conclude from that that they will be equally true to you on an occasion that presents infinitely greater dangers than any other.
>
> (Machiavelli 1882a [1531]: 334)

In other words, there is no adequate test for co-conspirators; the only test is the conspiracy itself. But is this a test? In general, it does not work like a test.

Alternatively, a potential conspirator could collect information on the willingness and competence of others who are candidates for conspiracy. In general, however, such information is scarce or even lacking, or likely to be biased. Indirect or flawed evidence can be deceptive and change the situation to the disadvantage of the conspirator. As Machiavelli observed:

> If you attempt to measure a man's good faith by the discontent which he manifests towards the prince, you will be easily deceived, for by the very fact of communicating to him your designs, you give him the means of putting an end to his discontent

by passing on this very valuable information to the prince. Machiavelli is more explicit about the problem of betrayal in his *Il Principe*:

> for he who conspires cannot act alone, nor can he take any associates except such as he believes to be malcontents; and so soon as you divulge your plans to a malcontent, you furnish him the means wherewith to procure satisfaction. For by denouncing it he may hope to derive great advantages for himself, seeing that such a course will insure him those advantages, whilst the other is full of doubts and dangers. He must indeed be a very rare friend of yours, or an inveterate enemy of the prince, to observe good faith and not to betray you.
>
> (Machiavelli 1882b [1532]: 61)

> It is thus that so many conspiracies have been revealed and crushed in their incipient stage; so that it may be regarded almost as a miracle when so important a secret is preserved by a number of conspirators for any length of time.
>
> (Machiavelli 1882a: 334)

Needless to say, a discovery from a lack of prudence increases with the number of conspirators involved and with the time of preparation that elapses. There can be imprudence that invites discovery by conjecture. Machiavelli reports the following incidence:

> The day before he was to have killed Nero, Scevinus, one of the conspirators, made his testament; he ordered his freedman Melichius to sharpen an old, rusty poniard, enfranchised all his slaves and distributed money amongst them, and had bandages made for tying up wounds. Melichius surmised from these various acts what was going on, and denounced it to Nero. Scevinus was arrested, and with him Natales, another conspirator, with whom he had been seen to converse secretly for a length of time. As their depositions respecting that conversation did not agree, they were forced to confess the truth, and thus the conspiracy was discovered to the ruin of all that were implicated.
>
> (Machiavelli 1882a [1531]: 335)

Of course, Scevinus' preparations were of utmost imprudence; however, if Natales, the second conspirator, had not been identified, Scevinus could still have made up a story and finding out the truth would have been impossible. In fact, it was in Scevinus' interest to make up a story which explained his preparations conclusively without any reference to a conspiracy. Competent conspirators should prepare an alternative story. These elements are reflected in the case of a conspiracy against Hieronymus, King of Syracuse:

> Theodorus, one of the conspirators, having been arrested, concealed with the utmost firmness the names of the other conspirators, and charged the matter upon the friends of the king; and, on the other hand, all the other conspirators had such confidence in the courage of Theodorus, that not one of them left Syracuse, or betrayed the least sign of fear.
>
> (Machiavelli 1882a [1531]: 335; with reference to Titus Livius)

A theory of rational decision making could reveal to us that, for Theodorus, it does not take much courage but rather requires the insight that if he confesses or names a conspirator who knows about the plot, the book will be thrown at him. (Those books can be very painful.) As long as none of the other conspirators was identified, the situation had the structure of a one-person plot in its planning stage. It is advisable to keep a multi-person conspiracy in this stage until its execution. Machiavelli illustrates the implementation of such a policy by the example of Nelematus, who

> unable to bear the tyranny of Aristotimus, tyrant of Epirus, assembled in his house a number of friends and relatives, and urged them to liberate their country from the yoke of the tyrant. Some of them asked for time to consider the matter, whereupon Nelematus made his slaves close the door of his house, and then said to those he had called together, 'You must either go now and carry this plot into execution, or I shall hand you all over as prisoners to Aristotimus.' Moved by these words, they took the oath demanded of them, and immediately went and carried the plot of Nelematus successfully into execution.
>
> (Machiavelli 1882a [1531]: 336)

Time, quickness, rapidity, speed, celerity often matter when it comes to the creation and use of secrecy. As Francis Bacon writes:

> generally it is good to commit the beginnings of all great actions to Argos with his hundred eyes, and the ends to Briareus with his hundred hands; first to watch, and then to speed. For the helmet of Pluto, which maketh the politique man go invisible, is secrecy in the counsel and celerity in the execution. For when things are once come to the execution, there is no secrecy comparable to celerity; like the motion of a bullet in the air, which flieth so swift as it outruns the eye.[54]
>
> (Bacon 2002 [1625]: 76f.)

However, the above example demonstrates that Nelematus not only relied on the speed of execution but also on the double-binding power of treachery. Those who can betray can also be betrayed. Often it is only a question who is the first-mover; Nelematus grabbed the first-mover advantage. However, if possible, a conspirator should confide his secret project to one person only, even when it involves a larger number of conspirators. One man

> whose fidelity he has thoroughly tested for a long time, and who is animated by the same desire as himself . . . is much more easily found than many . . . and then, even if he were to attempt to betray you, there is some

---

54 The hundred-eyed Argos was commanded to watch Io, who was a lover of Zeus. Briareus was a giant who helped Zeus to combat the Titans.

chance of your being able to defend yourself, which you cannot when
there are many conspirators . . . you may talk freely with one man about
everything, for unless you have committed yourself in writing the 'yes' of
one man is worth as much as the 'no' of another; and therefore one should
guard most carefully against writing, as against a dangerous rock, for nothing will convict you quicker than your own handwriting.

(Machiavelli 1882a [1531]: 337)

A handwritten message can transgress the bounds of a private communication
between two persons and make it public. What could have been merely one
man's word against another's becomes a potential threat when it is written
down.

In summary, Machiavelli identifies two risks

in communicating a plot to any one individual: the first, lest he should
denounce you voluntarily; the second, lest he should denounce you, being
himself arrested on suspicion, or from some indications, and being con-
victed and forced to it by the torture.

But he also suggests

means of escaping both these dangers: the first, by denial and by alleging
personal hatred to have prompted the accusation; and the other, by deny-
ing the charge, and alleging that your accuser was constrained by the force
of torture to tell lies. But the most prudent course is not to communicate
the plot to any one, and to act in accordance with the above-cited examples; and if you cannot avoid drawing someone into your confidence, then
to let it be not more than one, for in that case the danger is much less than
if you confide in many.

(Machiavelli 1882a [1531]: 338)

### 4.5.3 The counter-plot of the prince

There are numerous examples where the glory and the pomp of the prince
as well as his royal or divine position and reputation deters conspirators from
putting their daggers in his breast. Sometimes the prince's kindness or beauty
also prevents a successful execution. For instance, Giovan Battista, the designated murderer of Lorenzo de' Medici in what became the conspiracy of
the Pazzi, "was filled with admiration for Lorenzo, having found him to all
appearances quite a different man from what had been presented to him; and
he judged him to be gentle and wise" (Machiavelli 1882c [1532]: 372). And
the plot failed as Lorenzo survived – and took cruel revenge. However, history shows that this pattern, appealing to sheer properties of personality and
position, does not always work and the prince is well-advised to develop an
*ex ante* counter-strategy. In Machiavelli's writings, we find substantial material
that could help the prince discourage conspirators if he feels that glory, pomp,

reputation, and divinity may not be sufficient to protect his life and position. Of course, thinking about on-the-spot solutions, the corresponding strategies of the prince to counter a plot are generally defined by the action the conspirators take. Typically, conspiracy is a sequential game that sees the prince as a second-mover when it comes to the *execution*. But if secrecy works, the second-mover advantage shrinks. Often, however, conspiracies are triggered off by the prince himself and, in fact, he is the first-mover in this game. Of course, a poor policy could invite conspiracy, but often the princely invitation to plot is more specific.

In the extreme, a conspiracy can begin when the tyrant threatens to take away the fortune or the life of persons close to him. The deadly plot against Emperor Commodus, reported in the *Discorsi*, illustrates the second case: Commodus had

> amongst his nearest friends and intimates Letus and Electus, two captains of the Prætorian soldiers; he also had Marcia as his favorite concubine. As these three had on several occasions reproved him for the excesses with which he had stained his own dignity and that of the Empire, he resolved to have them killed, and wrote a list of the names of Marcia, Letus, and Electus,[55] and of some other persons, whom he wanted killed the following night. Having placed this list under his pillow, he went to the bath; a favorite child of his, who was playing in the chamber and on the bed, found this list, and on going out with it in his hand was met by Marcia, who took the list from the child. Having read it, she immediately sent for Letus and Electus, and when these three had thus become aware of the danger that threatened them, they resolved to forestall the Emperor, and without losing any time they killed Commodus the following night.
>
> (Machiavelli 1882a [1531]: 339)

Obviously, secrecy did not work for Commodus, but against him: "The body was secretly conveyed out of the palace, before the least suspicion was entertained in the city . . . of the emperor's death. Such was the fate of the son of Marcus, and so easy was it to destroy a hated tyrant" (Gibbon 1998 [volume I, 1776/77]: 87) – if secrecy works.

This case demonstrates that "the necessity which admits of no delay produces the same effect as the means employed by Nelematus" described above (Machiavelli 1882a [1531]: 339). It also reveals how a prince can provoke a conspiracy. This could be a profitable strategy, if the prince is aware of it, but it can be a deadly one otherwise. Of course, if a prince wants to avoid a conspiracy, then he should never design a situation in which the agent has only two alternatives: to perish or to fight. Yet, this can only be a necessary condition, but not a sufficient one should a conspiracy be avoided. The sequential structure

---

55  In Gibbon (1998 [volume I, 1776/77]: 87), the three names are Marcia, Eclectus, and Laetus.

of the execution of a conspiracy suggests that a high degree of unsteadiness in the prince's daily routine might be a good protection. Given the constraints of secret communications, conspirators have in general great difficulties to adapt to changing conditions or even to revise their plans. The standard example is the conspiracy of the Pazzi against Lorenzo and Giuliano de' Medici.[56] Plans were made that, in April 1478, the two should be killed at a dinner with Cardinal San Giorgio. While the two Medici men and the Cardinal attended Mass in the cathedral, the rumor spread that Giuliano would not come to the dinner. Plans had to be changed and it was decided to commit murder in the church. Not only did this alienate Giovan Battista, a competent conspirator who was assigned to kill Lorenzo, such that the roles had to be redistributed, but it led to a series of mistakes. Giuliano was killed by Francesco Pazzi as planned, but, because of the incompetence of Antonio da Volterra who was supposed to replace Giovan Battista, Lorenzo was able to defend himself and got away only slightly wounded. Not only did he become Lorenzo Magnifico and govern Florence with almost dictatorial power until his death in 1492, but he also had the means to go ruthlessly after those conspirators, who had not already been killed during the execution of the plot – like Francesco Salviati, the Archbishop of Pisa – and to erase the Pazzi family from the Florence scene.

In fact, when the conspirators tried to gain control over the government, the people of Florence, rather unexpectedly, rallied to the Medici. This proves that investing in the love of the people, as Machiavelli repeatedly pointed out, can be a very efficient means to counter conspiracy. He warned:

> of all the perils that follow the execution of a conspiracy, none is more certain and none more to be feared than the attachment of the people to the prince that has been killed. There is no remedy against this, for the conspirators can never secure themselves against a whole people.
>
> (Machiavelli 1882a [1531]: 345)

According to Shakespeare, Brutus and his affiliates were chased by the people of Rome after having been stirred up by Antonius reading Caesar's will to them.

Since the Pazzi conspiracy was supported by Pope Sixtus IV, a two-year war with the papacy followed placing a very heavy burden on the city of Florence. But Florence and the Medici survived and both had a brilliant future. Perhaps it should be noted that Lorenzo's son Giovanni ended up as Pope Leo X. Giulio, the natural son of Lorenzo's murdered brother Giuliano, followed him in the papacy as Pope Clement VII,[57] not to mention the fact

---

56  The Eighth Book of Machiavelli's *History of Florence* is dedicated to the description of this plot (see Machiavelli 1882c [1532]: 371ff.). The *Discorsi* (Machiavelli 1882a [1531]: 340f.) contains a summary.

57  In fact, Leo X was followed by a 'German Pope' with the name of Hadrian VI. However, the latter managed to survive this difficult situation for barely a year.

that Medici family members became Grand Dukes of Tuscany and mothers to French kings. However, we should emphasize that the support of the people of Florence on the day of the Pazzi conspiracy was decisive for the career of the Medici. Not only did Lorenzo survive, but his position was immensely strengthened by the unsuccessful conspiracy. Machiavelli concludes: "conspiracies rarely succeed, and often cause the ruin of those who set them on foot, whilst those against whom they were aimed are only the more aggrandized thereby" (Machiavelli 1882c [1532]: 368). The latter effect was definitively true in the case of Lorenzo and the Medici.

It seems that a prince who has the love of the people is relatively well protected if conspirators are rational and think about their lives and fate after execution:

> on the side of the conspirator there is nothing but fear, jealousy, and apprehension of punishment; whilst the prince has on his side the majesty of sovereignty, the laws, the support of his friends and of the government, which protect him. And if to all this be added the popular good will, it seems impossible that any one should be rash enough to attempt a conspiracy against him. For ordinarily a conspirator has cause for apprehension only before the execution of his evil purpose; but in this case, having the people for his enemies, he has also to fear the consequences after the commission of the crime, and can look nowhere for a refuge.
>
> (Machiavelli 1882b [1532]: 61)

To gain the love of the people can, however, be very costly and reduce the resources of the prince considerably, and there can be trade-offs which do not allow him to fully use this potential. This was the problem most of the Roman emperors faced:

> where in other principalities the prince had to contend only with the ambition of the nobles and the insolence of the people, the Roman Emperors had to meet a third difficulty, in having to bear with the cruelty and cupidity of the soldiers, which were so great that they caused the ruin of many, because of the difficulty of satisfying at the same time both the soldiers and the people; for the people love quiet, and for that reason they revere princes who are modest, whilst the soldiers love a prince of military spirit, and who is cruel, haughty, and rapacious. And these qualities the prince must practise upon the people, so as to enable him to increase the pay of the soldiers, and to satisfy their avarice and cruelty.
>
> (Machiavelli 1882b [1532]: 63)

Quite a few Roman emperors were installed, exploited and, in the end, even murdered by the soldiers that were meant to protect them. They did not, in contrast to the Medici, succeed in activating the people's love as a protection.

The Medici case also demonstrates the difficulties of conspiring against a multitude of people. As noticed by Machiavelli, to strike two blows of this kind at the same instant and in different places is impracticable, and to attempt to do so at different moments of time would certainly result in the one's preventing the other. So that, if it is imprudent, rash, and doubtful to conspire against a single prince, it amounts to folly to do so against two at the same time.

(Machiavelli 1882a [1531]: 342)

As a consequence, sharing power looks like a very promising device to decrease the potential of conspiracy. From here, it seems straightforward to argue in favor of a republic, or at least for the creation of a parliament. Here Machiavelli points to France as an example: "Amongst the well-organized and well-governed kingdoms of our time is that of France, which has a great many excellent institutions that secure the liberty and safety of the king. The most important of these is the Parliament, and its authority" (Machiavelli 1882b [1532]: 62). Machiavelli had met François I in Paris when he was sent as a special envoy (or "Secretary of State") by the Republic of Florence. However, Renaissance France was not known for its parliamentary system and its political system did not prevent the assassination of Henry III and Henry IV in later years.

Machiavelli observed that conspiracies

against the state are less dangerous for those engaged in them than plots against the life of the sovereign ... In the conduct of the plot the danger is very slight, for a citizen may aspire to supreme power without manifesting his intentions to any one; and if nothing interferes with his plans, he may carry them through successfully, or if they are thwarted by some law, he may await a more favorable moment, and attempt it by another way.

(Machiavelli 1882a [1531]: 345)

This applies to a republic that is already partially corrupted; "for in one not yet tainted by corruption such thoughts could never enter the mind of any citizen" (Machiavelli 1882a [1531]: 345). But, as the history of the Roman republic shows, which is the subject of his *Discorsi*, "such thoughts" were lingering in the background most of the time.

Back to principalities: if a successful conspiracy is obstructed by a multitude of targets to be conspired against, the multitude and anonymity of potential conspirators can also be a good protection for the prince, especially if the prince can avoid putting too much pressure on a single individual or a smaller group:

For if the great men of a state, who are in familiar intercourse with the prince, succumb under the many difficulties of which we have spoken, it is natural that these difficulties should be infinitely increased for the others. And therefore those who know themselves to be weak avoid them, for where men's lives and fortunes are at stake they are not all insane; and when they have cause for hating a prince, they content themselves with cursing and vilifying him, and wait until someone more powerful and of higher position than themselves shall avenge them.

(Machiavelli 1882a [1531]: 332f.)

Indeed "those who know themselves to be weak . . . are not all insane"; on the contrary, they might be called "rational." They view themselves as members of a "large group" as defined in Mancur Olson's seminal book *The Logic of Collective Action* (1965). Such a group does not contain a member whose potential and interest are strong enough to organize a conspiracy, irrespective of what the other members do, given the difficulties of execution and the draconic punishment in the case of failure. In principle, the prince can feel safe, even if there are many enemies, as long as there is no pioneer conspirator strong and interested enough to take the lead. Large groups are generally not self-organizing and membership remains dormant if the group does not offer selective incentives that cover membership costs and a premium for leadership. Membership costs can be extremely high in a conspiracy.

There is an additional element that may prevent actions against the prince, even when the group of potential conspirators is small, in the sense of Olson, and they know of each other. Each of them might hope that the other will do the dangerous job, to avoid risk of failure, on the one hand, and to qualify for a position of power after the successful conspiracy, on the other.[58] He who holds the dagger is hardly ever invited to become the murdered tyrant's successor.

As a consequence, the prince should choose a policy that does not polarize the opposition such that small groups can form. However, if he cannot avoid polarization, then it can be safer to have several opponents which compete with each other rather than a single rival who is strong and motivated enough to organize a conspiracy. If a prince cannot crush such a rival then he better create a second one. But as Machiavelli notes, "princes cannot always escape assassination when prompted by a resolute and determinate spirit; for any man who himself despises death can always inflict it upon others" (Machiavelli 1882b [1532]: 66). However, he also demonstrates that the prince has means to reduce the odds of conspirators and to get them interested in other more promising targets. Such targets are conquest, winning wars, becoming a hero.

### 4.5.4 What if a prince conspires?

Of course, the prince can also use conspiracy as a means to strengthen his position. This is the general experience we observe in the relationship of one prince to another; it found its ultimate incarnation in the idea and practice of secret diplomacy. In his *Secret Diplomatic History of the Eighteenth Century*, Karl Marx (1969 [1856/57]: 86) colorfully describes how England, from 1700, the date of the Anglo-Swedish Defensive Treaty, to 1719, was continually "assisting Russia and waging war against Sweden, either by secret intrigue or open force, although the treaty was never rescinded nor war ever declared." England betrayed her ally Sweden to serve the interests of Imperial Russia and her own hopes for large

---

58 The strategic problem can be represented as Volunteer's Dilemma; 'non-volunteering' is a likely outcome. See Section 3.5.4 above.

benefits out of a flourishing trade with Russia. Cases like this are abundant and many are well known. Perhaps less prominent are cases that show a prince who conspires against one of his ministers or generals, following Machiavelli's advice that "princes should devolve all matters of responsibility upon others, and take upon themselves only those of grace" (Machiavelli 1882b [1532]: 62).

The range of this strategy reaches from the obfuscation policy of democratic governments, which thereby hope to be re-elected,[59] to the prince sacrific-ing a confidant to gain the support of the people. "Having conquered the Romagna," Cesare Borgia, called "the Duke,"

> found it under the control of a number of impotent petty tyrants, who had devoted themselves more to plundering their subjects than to governing them properly, and encouraging discord and disorder amongst them rather than peace and union; so that this province was infested by brigands, torn by quarrels, and given over to every sort of violence. He saw at once that, to restore order amongst the inhabitants and obedience to the sovereign, it was necessary to establish a good and vigorous government there. And for this purpose he appointed as governor of that province Don Ramiro d'Orco, a man of cruelty, but at the same time of great energy, to whom he gave plenary power. In a very short time D'Orco reduced the province to peace and order, thereby gaining for him the highest reputation. After a while the Duke found such excessive exercise of authority no longer necessary or expedient, for he feared that it might render himself odious. He therefore established a civil tribunal in the heart of the province, under an excellent president, where every city should have its own advocate. And having observed that the past rigor of Ramiro had engendered some hatred, he wished to show to the people, for the purpose of removing that feeling from their minds, and to win their entire confidence, that, if any cruelties had been practised, they had not originated with him, but had resulted altogether from the harsh nature of his minister. He therefore took occasion to have Messer Ramiro put to death, and his body, cut into two parts, exposed in the marketplace of Cesena one morning, with a block of wood and a bloody cutlass left beside him. The horror of this spectacle caused the people to remain for a time stupefied and satisfied.
>
> (Machiavelli 1882b [1532]: 25)

This story not only tells us how a prince may establish the law and bring order, and to get rid of a possible rival and potential conspirator, but also how to satisfy the people who had to suffer in this process of transformation. Staging a conspiracy, however, is not always without risk even for the prince, especially if it should serve as a litmus test for the support of confidants:

---

59 This is the theme of a volume edited by Breton and co-authors (2007) on *The Economics of Transparency in Politics.* Section 4.4 (above) summarizes a contribution to this volume.

> Dion of Syracuse ... by way of testing the fidelity of someone whom
> he suspected ordered Callippus, in whom he had entire confidence, to
> pretend to be conspiring against him ... Callippus, being able to conspire
> with impunity against Dion, plotted so well that he deprived him of his
> state and his life.
>
> (Machiavelli 1882a [1531]: 349)

It seems safer for a prince just to pretend that there is a plot, assign the responsibility to some people whom he wants to get rid of, and then let justice prevail. It might be difficult to prove that the suspect is a conspirator, but more often, it is impossible to prove for a suspect that he is not. The veil of secrecy is asymmetric and in the end it is in favor with the powerful. There are numerous examples that testify this fact, and the powerful often make use of it. No wonder that if a prince discovers a plot, and "punishes the conspirators with death, it will always be believed that it was an invention of the prince to satisfy his cruelty and avarice with the blood and possessions of those whom he had put to death" (Machiavelli 1882a [1531]: 347). And often these beliefs are waiting to get corroborated.

Machiavelli offers

> an advice to princes or republics against whom conspiracies may have been
> formed. If they discover that a conspiracy exists against them, they must,
> before punishing its authors, endeavor carefully to know its nature and
> extent, – to weigh and measure well the means of the conspirators, and
> their own strength. And if they find it powerful and alarming, they must
> not expose it until they have provided themselves with sufficient force to
> crush it, as otherwise they will only hasten their own destruction.
>
> (Machiavelli 1882a [1531]: 347)

This quote is of interest in many ways: first, it mentions republics, and second, it is explicitly meant as advice. This brings us back to the question what motivated Machiavelli to present a "rational theory of conspiracy."

From Machiavelli's analysis follows that there are four closely neighboring categories: successful conspiracy, unsuccessful conspiracy, staged conspiracy, and pretended conspiracy. They are characterized by an *active* proposition of conspiracy. But there are also *passive* and counterfactual versions of conspiracy: the possible victim imagines that there is a conspiracy and even reacts on this imagination although there is none. For instance, in World War II, the British believed in the existence of a "fifth column," comprised of local civilians, mainly French or Belgian, who were eager to help the Germans make the English hurry to Dunkirk and leave the continent. This provoked a soldier of the London Regiment (Queen Victoria's Rifles) gun down a manifestly innocent old lady in Calais "in the belief that the Germans must be masters of disguise as well as of mobile warfare." A group of Belgian farm laborers were shot in a field: they "were accused of mowing grass 'in the formation of an arrow' to guide Stuka pilots to British troop formations" (Ferguson 2006: 28). While every British soldier knew of the fifth column, to the Germans it was unknown. (For further details, see Glyn Prysor's (2005) "The 'Fifth Column' and the British Experience of Retreat, 1940.")

### 4.5.5 The Machiavelli Conspiracy Game

Machiavelli did not elaborate on the passive version of conspiracy. If his analysis was meant to advise the conspirators and the prince, then this omission is plausible. There is hardly anything to learn from it for "people of action." At the outset of this chapter, we raised the question why did Machiavelli write so extensively on conspiracy? Is it for the purpose of teaching the prince and his rivals to behave efficiently? Does he want to make sure that those who are virtuous, whether conspirators or princes, are successful and thereby improve the "selection of the fittest" and thus contribute to the general welfare of mankind? Or is *Il Principe* simply a "handbook for those who would acquire or increase their political power" (Gauss 1952: 8) and the extensive treatment of conspiracy in *Discorsi* is a concomitant work that was merely intended to demonstrate the competence of its author?

In the appendix of Holler (2011), I tried to derive answers to some of these questions by means of game theory. There is a Conspirator $i$ with the two pure strategies: "Plot" and "Not plot." There is a Prince $j$ with the two pure strategies "Control" and "Not control." Variables $p$ and $q$ represent $i$'s probabilities for "Plot" and $j$'s probabilities for "Control," respectively.

The 2-by-2 payoff matrix in Figure 4.4 describes an *Inspection Game* (as analyzed in detail in Section 3.8.1), if payoffs are assumed to satisfy

(IG)  $a < b, a < c, d < b, d < c$ and $\alpha > \beta, \alpha > \gamma, \delta > \beta, \delta > \gamma$.

The payoffs are such that the equilibrium strategies $(p*, q*)$ and also the maximin strategies $(p°, q°)$ are mixed. Here $p*$ and $p°$ represent $i$'s probabilities for "Plot" while $q*$ and $q°$ represent $j$'s probabilities for "Control."

| Conspirator $i$ | Prince $j$ — Control $s_{21}$, q | Not control $s_{22}$, 1-q |
|---|---|---|
| Plot $s_{11}$, p | $(a, \alpha)$ | $(b, \beta)$ |
| Not plot $s_{12}$, 1-p | $(c, \gamma)$ | $(d, \delta)$ |

*Figure 4.4* The Machiavelli Conspiracy Game

The standard interpretation of mixed-strategy Nash equilibrium and the mixed-maximin solution implies that both players know the matrix, i.e., it is assumed that both players know their payoffs, but also the payoffs of the other party. This looks like a heroic assumption, but Machiavelli convincingly argues that conspirators are close to the prince: they know him. Moreover, when it comes to prominent issues, such as power and death, then at least the ordinal values should be common knowledge. However, the specification of probabilities $p*$ and $q*$ as well as $p°$ and $q°$ requires that the expected utility hypothesis applies, which allows for multiplying utilities and probabilities, and thus presupposes that utilities are cardinal. But we abstain from the assumption that utilities are interpersonally comparable: we cannot tell whether the prince is happier than the conspirator, or whether the reverse holds, although in some situations a conclusion seems to be straightforward.

The analysis of the Inspection Game (see Section 3.8 above) tells us that Conspirator $i$ chooses $p*$ such that the Prince $j$ is indifferent between "Control" and "Not control" and, of course, any $q$ that mixes the two. The corresponding property applies to $q*$. Thus, neither $i$ nor $j$ is motivated to deviate from $p*$ and $q*$, respectively. The trouble with this equilibrium is that, given $q*$, why should $i$ select $p*$, and why should $j$ select $q*$ if $i$ chooses $p*$, or if the Prince $j$ *assumes* that $i$ chooses $p*$? In other words, the Nash equilibrium $(p*,q*)$ is weak, i.e., if the conspirator deviates from $p*$, then, of course, his payoffs will not increase, given $q*$, as $(p*,q*)$ is an equilibrium, but neither will his payoffs decrease. The same applies if the Prince deviates from $q*$, given the Conspirator chooses $p*$. Why should a player choose a Nash equilibrium strategy if he expects that the other player chooses a Nash equilibrium strategy?

There are still other incentive problems with the Nash equilibrium $(p*,q*)$. For instance, if the benefits of a successful plot increases, the analysis of the Inspection Game in Section 3.8 tells us that this has no impact on the equilibrium behavior $p*$ of the Conspirator (although it seems plausible to expect that plotting becomes more likely). Although the Conspirator $i$ will not change his behavior, the $q*$ of the Prince $j$ will increase, notwithstanding the fact that there are no changes in the payoffs of $j$. Of course, $p*$ will not change despite of the changes in $i$'s payoffs, just because $q*$ changes to keep $i$ balanced choosing mixed strategy $p*$.

Because of these properties, we might think that the maximin solution $(p°,q°)$ is a more appropriate tool to describe decision making in a situation as described by the Inspection Game. Mixing in accordance to $p°$ guarantees a payoff $u_i(p°)$ which is identical to the payoff in accordance to the Nash equilibrium: $u_i(p°) = u_i(q*)$. The corresponding argument supports the maximin probability $q°$ for the Conspirator $j$. However, if $i$ is convinced that $j$ chooses in accordance with $q°$, then of course $i$ can do better, i.e., improve his or her expected payoff, by choosing a probability different from $p°$ for its mixed strategy. The pair $(p°,q°)$ is not a Nash equilibrium. In fact, both players could do better, *given the strategy of the other one*.

An alternative interpretation of the Inspection Game in Figure 4.4 says that it is the design of an individual agent, i.e., a player, given a particular strategic decision situation. The payoffs are his payoffs and the payoffs he or she assumes for the other player. If this applies to both the Prince and the Conspirator, then, in general, we will have two payoff matrices of the type in Figure 4.4. The assumed payoffs do not necessarily concur with the actual ones. Still, from the point of view of each of the two players, the interpretations and problems apply which we discussed for the game in Figure 4.4.

Whatever the interpretation of the game in Figure 4.4, game theory does not offer a clear-cut answer to a player on what to do – what strategy to choose. However, the game-theoretical analysis points out the complexity of the decision situation. The game looks rather trivial: two players, two pure strategies each, and still rational players do not know what to choose. Yes, game theory assumes that agents are rational. Players are assumed that they maximize expected utility. The analysis of the game in Figure 4.4 tries to find out about the probability of the various outcomes and the corresponding pay-off pairs. There is no uncertainty on the payoffs, but on the probabilities we can assign to their realization.

In his analysis of conspiracy, Machiavelli also assumes rational agents – however, not in the formally rigid way game theory does. But was he rational himself? He seemed to be intoxicated by the pleasures of thinking and writing, of delving into his own experience as high-ranking Secretary to the Second Chancery of the Republic of Florence and special envoy to the King of France, to Rome and even to Emperor Maximilian, on the one hand, and a victim of conspiracy, on the other. During his lifetime Machiavelli was repeatedly accused of conspiracy. When, in 1512, the conspiracy of Pietropaolo Boscoli and Agostino Capponi against the lives of Giuliano and Lorenzo de' Medici was discovered, Machiavelli was

> suspected of participation in this conspiracy, he was shut up in the prison of the Bargello, and had there to suffer the torture, the executioner having subjected him six times to the strappado. He was also kept for some days shackled, as we must presume from his writing that he had 'jesses' on his legs; it being well known that that word signifies the leather straps that hold one of the claws of the falcons.
>
> (Detmold 1882: xxviii)

Lorenzo de' Medici was a grandson of Lorenzo Magnifico and Machiavelli dedicated *Il Principe* to him.

> There is no mention of his torture in the public documents, nor in the resolutions of the Eight, where the condemnation of the other conspirators is recorded. But there can be no doubt about it, as he mentions it himself in a letter written to his friend Francesco Vettori on the 13th of March.
>
> (Detmold 1882: xxviii)

Vettori served Florence as diplomat and spent years as ambassador of his city in Rome. Over many years, he exchanged letters with Machiavelli. This material is a major source of the information we have about Machiavelli's life and work. They were friends, but not always on the same side of the political playing field. Detmold summarizes:

> Machiavelli was doubtless innocent of being a party to this conspiracy, which originated with Paolo Boscoli, a young man of one of the old and distinguished families of Florence, who had drawn Agostino Capponi into the plot. The latter committed the imprudence of letting fall a list of the conspirators, in going into the house of the Pucci; this list was picked up, and immediately communicated to the magistracy. Many of the most distinguished citizens were implicated, and Machiavelli amongst the rest.
>
> (Detmold 1882: xxviii)

This experience is strongly reflected in Machiavelli's theoretical discourse on conspiracy that we outlined above. Detmold continues:

> It is quite possible, however, that the list dropped by Capponi may have been merely a memorandum of those whom the originators of the conspiracy proposed amongst themselves to draw into the plot . . . Whilst this process was going on, Pope Julius II died, and the Cardinal Giovanni de' Medici was chosen as his successor, and assumed the title of Leo X. So soon as he heard of Machiavelli's imprisonment, he ordered his fetters to be struck off, and had him set free, as well as all the others who had been charged with being implicated in the Boscoli conspiracy.
>
> (Detmold 1882: xxviii f.)

The reaction of the newly elected Pope suggests that the conspiracy, at least to some extent, was staged by the Medici themselves: "Unhappily Boscoli and Capponi, having been found guilty, were executed before the Pope's pardon arrived" (Detmold 1882: xxix). It could well be that the list of conspirators that Capponi "let fall" was written by a Medici in order to get rid of some people that were a threat to the regained power of the family over Florence, or, at least, to push the claim to power with some vehemence.

It seems that Machiavelli was not involved in this conspiracy, if there was any at all. Detmold (1882: xxviii) concludes that

> the firm denial of Machiavelli under the pangs of torture ought certainly, with so honest and fearless a mind as his, to be taken for the truth, and should acquit him, not only of an unpatriotic act, but also of an act of folly in being one of a numerous body of conspirators, which folly no writer has ever exposed with greater clearness and more conclusive force of argument than himself.
>
> (Detmold 1882: xxviii)

But there is a certain spiritual conspiracy in Machiavelli's writing. The language is very plain, but people over the centuries have been seduced, again and again, to give highly controversial interpretations, many of which were not beneficial to Machiavelli's reputation. His most prominent critic was Frederick the Great, who published, with the help of Voltaire, an *Anti-Machiavel*, discussing chapter by chapter the immorality of *Il Principe* and its author, just a few weeks before Frederick succeeded his father as King of Prussia in 1740. (His political maneuvers, wars, and victories suggest that he benefitted a great deal from studying *Il Principe* in detail.) Shakespeare could not resist using the term "Machiavellian" for extremely mean behavior "of the Machiavellian type." Yet, a careful reader of Machiavelli's work reveals that he was a moral person. To him, a murder is a murder, even if the murderer is Romulus, the founding hero of Rome. He does not subscribe to an ethics which postulates "that the reason of state cannot be reduced to ordinary moral deliberation" – rulers may not be justified on moral grounds "when they lie, cheat, break promises, or even torture in order to further their state's welfare. And secrecy regarding such acts was often thought to be of the highest importance in furthering the designs of the state" (Bok 1982: 173). Machiavelli proposes all kinds of cruel policies for those who want to gain power and keep it, including conspiracy. He convincingly argues that in most cases these cruelties are necessary and cannot be avoided. Because they cannot be avoided, they might be justified by their success; however, in Machiavelli's view, this does not imply that they are inherently good.

Machiavelli did not discuss the moral dimension of conspiracy, or, more generally of secrets. Conspiracy is prominently a means, i.e., a strategy, in social interaction and secrets are related to it. Secrets can also be the result of "not knowing," because of the complexity of the social situation and of the world per se. In the next section, a moral dimension of secrets will be discussed. The section is about truth-telling, personal opinions, secrets, and the matter of personal integrity and its protection.

## 4.6 George Orwell's notebook: the moral dimension of secrets

What follows is not research about George Orwell as a writer and social activist, or a philosophical work on truth.[60] Rather, Orwell is taken as an important paradigmatic case in identifying the problems of telling the truth as a writer and cultural figure concerned with politics. Moreover, because Orwell was not only a paradigmatic case but also a public figure, an evaluation of his behavior could have an impact on our social behavior and our contemporary opinion about what is considered to be good and bad in politics and everyday life. The evaluation of public figures expresses social values and gives orientation

---

60  This section contains material published in Holler (2002b, 2005). Section 4.6.6 derives from Holler and Lindner (2004).

to society and, for this reason, many legal systems contain, on the one hand, rules designed to protect the reputation of such personalities, but, on the other, permit public dissemination of information about them and their private life.

In Orwell's case, the public evaluation of his character is of special importance, because truth and truthfulness were his major concerns throughout his writing. For many, he was an icon of truth and personal integrity. In his article "The Truth about Orwell," Spender (1972: 6) observes: "He is . . . a landmark in a political landscape which others may steer by." Yet, more than half a century after his death, there is an ongoing and often rather controversial discussion about Orwell's work and character. Was he a sincere, but perhaps ruthless, Cold War warrior, or was he corrupted by the "circumstances" of his day? Spender (1972; 6) observes that arguments "based on expediency, prudence, political sagacity attendant upon results had no appeal to him." As a consequence, there are not only contradictions in his work, but also in the interpretation of his work and political life. In his *Homage to Catalonia*, he declares: "I warn everyone against my bias, and I warn everyone against my mistakes. Still, I have done my best to be honest" (Orwell 1967[1938]): 170f.).

Orwell will serve us as a model of a left-wing Cold War intellectual. We shall reduce him to a silhouette portrait, but one that is alive enough to stir awareness of the truth problem in politics. Although one might well believe that truth is not an operational concept in politics its personification in terms of the reputation and personal integrity of public figures does in fact make it a relevant concept in the political arena. Thus, the legal rules governing the protection of privacy can have a strong impact on how this issue is tackled.

We will not deal with Orwell's struggle against his own Englishness or against the British hypocrisy regarding British colonial India, Burma, and the other colonies. Undoubtedly, Orwell "came to see the exploitation of the colonies as the dirty secret of the whole enlightened British establishment, both political and cultural" (Hitchens 2002a: 6). It is unavoidable, however, that we will have to consider both issues inasmuch as they are reflected in Orwell's work and the interpretation of its political message. As Timothy Garton Ash (1998: 10) says: "No one wrote better about the English character than Orwell, and he was himself a walking anthology of Englishness."

### 4.6.1 Prelude

In 1966, a series of articles was published in the *New York Times* on the CIA's covert operations. Amidst reports on political assassinations and ruthless political intervention, came details about the support which the CIA gave to the cultural sector (as discussed in Section 4.4 above). The consequence of this "confession" was that the moral authority which the intellectuals enjoyed during the height of the Cold War was "seriously undermined and frequently mocked" (Saunders 2000:6). Was this intended? What if the CIA had staged the discussion of its role in the Cold War cultural policy in order to tell the world how politically enlightened and sophisticated its leadership was, and perhaps still is, and how much it contributed to today's culture? And how corrupt intellectuals can be?

It is not always easy for a secret agency to bring to light the truth about its own merits. To some extent, it is paradoxical because of its self-reference. In Orwell's *Nineteen Eighty-Four*, we learn about truth from a book in the book, supposedly authored by the dissident hero Emmanuel Goldstein. Only towards the end of the book, when Winston Smith is tortured in the Ministry of Love, is he told by O'Brien, an officer of the Thought Police, that he, O'Brien, collaborated in writing the Goldstein book. Is this true? Or is it an "alternative fact"? We have no answer to this. In any case, that is where truth breaks down in Orwell's book and the attentive reader is left with the crumbs of a society which contradicts itself in values and action.

The logical structure of the book can be illustrated by the famous statement by Epimenides: "All Cretans are liars." Since Epimenides was a Cretan, the logical structure of this statement is self-referential and its truth value concurs with the sentence "I am lying," if we assume that Cretans lie all the time.[61] In his *Gödel, Escher, Bach*, Hofstadter (1980: 15ff.) used the term "strange loop" for such a self-referential system of statements.[62] "Strange loops" do not create secrets; they are not hiding information, but are subverting them. The creation of *alternative facts* is a way to achieve this. Combining state secrecy and democratic control "by the people" has a feature of the liar's paradox: "officials can use secrecy to conceal wrongdoing and to justify policies by claiming to have information that validates their decisions but which cannot be shared with the citizens" (Sagar 2013: 2). There are no means to find out whether state secrecy is in the interest of those who are governed or not. Yet, in Orwell's *Nineteen Eighty-Four*, there was another twist to the paradox.

Most likely, Orwell was not aware of the logical dilemma into which his book ran when he made the Goldstein book a possible product of the Thought Police. To some extent, he himself became a victim of the "strange loop" related to a posthumous interpretation of the story of the book. Orwell died in 1950. Before he died, he gave the specific instruction that *Nineteen Eighty-Four* should not be altered in any way. There was, however, a film of *Nineteen Eighty-Four* that was ready for distribution in 1956. Saunders (2000: 295ff.) reports that Sol Stein, executive director of the American Committee for Cultural Freedom, helped producer Peter Rathvon to provide a Cold War-era film version of *Nineteen Eighty-Four*. This needed a substantial reinterpretation of the book since Orwell's text is generally read as a protest against all lies,

---

61 For the relationship of secrets and lies, i.e., the "neighbourhood of truth," see McNutt (2009).
62 A "strange loop" relation is also the reason for "Russell's paradox," "this cousin of the liar's paradox," which made Frege "insert an appendix into the second volume of the *Grundgesetze* acknowledging the contradiction" (Leavitt 2006: 32). The story behind the paradox is: there is a (male) barber "who daily shaves every man in his town who does not shave himself and no one else. If the barber does not shave himself, he is one of the men who do not shave themselves, and thus must shave himself" (Leavitt 2006: 32).

especially against all tricks played by government, and as an expression of distrust against mass culture. The book ends with Winston Smith's spirit broken: he loved Big Brother. Needless to say, this ending was not acceptable. In fact, the film was given two different endings, one for the American audience and one for the British, and neither represented the ending of the book itself. In the British version, Winston Smith is shot down after crying "Down with Big Brother!" – and so is Julia. Unfortunately, so far I have no detailed information about the deviating US version.

The example demonstrates how detailed the interventions of a secret agency could be. However, perhaps we owe this very information to the agency itself, and the argument circles in an Orwellian loop. Karl Jaspers claims that "truth also needs propaganda," (quoted in Saunders 2000: 97), but there is the danger that truth becomes an impossibility.

History shows that the logical problem with *Nineteen Eighty-Four* was largely ignored by both parties: on the one side, we find those who wanted to learn from it the truth about the socio-politico system in which they lived, while the other side tried to suppress the book's distribution. *Nineteen Eighty-Four* itself became the equivalent to the Goldstein book in describing the reality of communist regimes. For instance, the Polish poet and essayist Czeslaw Milosz observed in his book, *The Captive Mind*, written in 1951–52 and published in the West in 1953:

> A few have become acquainted with Orwell's 1984; because it is both difficult to obtain and dangerous to possess, it is known only to certain members of the Inner Party. Orwell fascinates them through his insight into details they know well, and through his use of Swiftian satire. Such a form of writing is forbidden by the New Faith because allegory, by nature manifold in meaning, would trespass beyond the prescriptions of socialist realism and the demands of the censor. Even those who know Orwell by hearsay are amazed that a writer who never lived in Russia should have so keen a perception into its life.
>
> (Quoted in Hitchens 2002a: 55f.)

A Ukrainian edition of *Animal Farm* (Orwell 1945) also reached a certain number of readers. However, Hitchens (2002a: 92) reports that "most of the copies were seized and impounded by the American military authorities in Germany who turned them over to the Red Army for destruction." He concludes: "It was not only the British Ministry of Information which regarded Stalin's *amour-propre* as the chief object of propitiation in those days." Spender (1972: 6) reports that T.S. Eliot has turned down Orwell's manuscript of *Animal Farm* on behalf of the publisher Faber "on the grounds that it might harm Anglo-Soviet cultural relations."

Orwell himself and his writings are very useful objects to study the problems of truth, secrets, and politics. More than forty years after his death, he was accused of having handed a list of names to the Information Research Department (IRD) of the British Foreign Office in early 1949. The list included his assessment of whether the person was a potential Stalinist "fellow traveller."

This was but one of his contributions to the Cold War in which his authority was exploited by both the political Left and Right. In his younger years, Orwell was involved in other conflicts. Together with his first wife Eileen O'Shaughnessy, he participated in the Spanish Civil War, fighting for the Republicans and against Franco's regime,[63] where he was badly wounded. As a journalist and writer, he actively supported the withdrawal of the British from the Indian subcontinent where he had been born, and had served in the Indian Imperial Police in Burma. Orwell (1903–1950), a pseudonym for Eric Arthur Blair, was born in 1903 in Morihari in Bengal, India, the son of a minor customs official who was probably involved in the opium trade between British India and China. The family moved to England in 1907 and in 1917 he entered Eton. In 1921, he joined the Indian Imperial Police in Burma, from which he retired in 1927 (or 1928), determined to make his living by writing. His novel *Burmese Days*, first published in 1934, reflects his personal experience with British colonialism and this experience was extremely negative.

His rejection of colonialism was generalized in a critical attitude towards Englishness – a state of culture and mind from which he suffered so much. Of course, he could not accept Scottish nationalism either, but his main concern were totalitarian regimes, whether fascist or communist, socialist, or capitalist, and regimes which were on the way to becoming totalitarian and their inclination to "untruth." He blamed mass culture for preparing the soil for totalitarianism and moved to the Scottish island of Jura, a rather unpopulated part of the Hebrides. There "he found that keeping pigs could be a loathsome business" (Hitchens 2002a: 133). Notwithstanding, Orwell disliked the Scots and the cultish nature of Scottish nationalism and is one of the few writers of his period to anticipate the force of such nationalism (see Hitchens 2002a: 10). In *Burmese Days*, he let his British–Indian protagonist James Flory say to his native friend, Dr. Veraswami, that the British Empire is simply a device for giving trade monopolies to the English – or rather to gangs of Jews and Scotchmen (Orwell, n.d. [1934]: 40). However, one must be careful with Orwell not to identify his opinion with those of his protagonists. One should not confuse the medium with the message. For instance, it would be a misinterpretation to conclude from this quote that Orwell was an anti-Semite. His target were the British and their colonies. In a non-fictional essay of 1940, Orwell observes:

> It is much easier for the aristocrat to be ruthless if he imagines that the serf is different from himself in blood and bone. Hence, the tendency to exaggerate race-differences, the current rubbish about shapes of skulls, colour of eyes, blood-counts etc., etc. In Burma, I have listened to racial theories which were less brutal than Hitler's theories about the Jews, but certainly not less idiotic.
>
> (Quoted in Hitchens 2000a: 21)

This does not sound like the words of an anti-Semite.

---

63 See his *Homage to Catalonia* (Orwell 1967 [1938]).

### 4.6.2 Orwell's "List"

With the emergence of the Cold War, the Foreign Office, which had been erring on the side of Stalin for almost a decade, looked for advice on how to determine who was a possible fellow-traveller of Stalin and a "reliable" leftist. Its secret arm, the IRD, contacted Orwell for support. Phillip Deary, an Australian historian, wrote:

> Orwell's opposition to Soviet totalitarianism predated the Cold War. Its genesis lay in the Spanish Civil War. It was there that he witnessed at first hand how Stalinists and NKVD agents brutally trampled the tender shoots of libertarian socialism and how they deliberately falsified history.
>
> (Quoted in Lashmar and Oliver 1998: 98)

Orwell and his wife Eileen O'Shaughnessy were both enlisted in the militia of the heterodox Marxist POUM, the Workers' Party of Marxist Unification, which took an anti-Stalin position – rather than the Communist-run International Brigade. Hitchens conjectures that

> Orwell never knew it, but had he and his wife not managed to escape from Spain with the police at their heels they might well have been placed in the dock as exhibits for that very show trial. A memorandum from the archives of the KGB (then known as NKVD), dated 13 July 1937, describes him and Eileen O'Shaughnessy as 'pronounced Trotskyites' operating with clandestine credentials. It also asserts, with the usual tinge of surreal fantasy, that the couple maintained contact with opposition circles in Moscow.
>
> (Hitchens 2002a: 67)

None of this was true.

In Spain, Orwell had seen his leftist companions massacred by Stalin's agents. To Orwell, Stalinism was a negation of socialism, and it seems that he was more than willing to be of help to the IRD. He handed over a hand-written list of 35 names. Another story (see Lashmar and Oliver 1998: 95ff.) says that Orwell agreed that his notebook containing 130 names, listed and with comments, was sent to the IRD office. At that time, he was terminally ill at a sanatorium in Cranham. The notebook was copied and later returned to his home. According to Ash (1998: 12), Peter Davison, editor of a recent edition of *The Complete Works of George Orwell*, "gives us the true facts, in impeccable detail. In the late 1940s Orwell kept a small, pale blue notebook listing what he called 'crypto-communists and fellow-travellers.' Davison prints 135 names; another thirty-six have been withheld for fear of libel actions." According to Hitchens (2002b: 28), Davison was "the only scholar with comprehensive access to the archives," and he points out that Orwell's notebook is not the same as the "List." For example, the names of Charlie Chaplin and Stephen Spender are in the notebook, but not on the "List" as it was received by the IRD.[64] In the "List," the names are followed by comments such as "Political Climber. Zionist (appears sincere about this). Too dishonest to be outright F.T.," where F.T. is the abbreviation for "fellow traveler."

Ash (1998:12) concludes from the Davison edition that all Orwell did "was to pass on thirty-five *names* of people from his notebook. He did this not to get them spied upon by MI5, but to make sure that communists should not inadvertently be used as anticommunist propagandists." Somehow the puzzle about the number and the process of passing on remained.[65] But does it matter?

Saunders (2000: 300) is very critical about the "List," and so were others. Her arguments boil down to the observation "that by his actions, he demonstrated that he confused the role of the intellectual with that of the policeman." What was the role of an intellectual in the Cold War? Michael Foot, a former leader of the Labour Party and a friend of Orwell, found the "black-list" amazing; he was appalled. Tony Benn, another prominent Labour Party member, "was saddened to learn that Orwell 'gave in' to the pressure of the intelligence service" (Lashmar and Oliver 1998: 98). Although the arguments were weak, to see Orwell's "List" as an act of betrayal enjoyed quite extensive currency. For instance, Lashmar and Oliver remark:

> George Orwell's reputation as a left-wing icon took a body blow from which it may never recover when it was revealed in 1996 that he had cooperated closely with the IRD's Cold Warriors, even offering his own blacklist of eighty six Communist 'fellow-travellers.' As the Daily Telegraph noted, 'To some, it was as if Winston Smith had willingly cooperated with the Thought Police in 1984.'
>
> (Lashmar and Oliver 1998: 95)

In a recent comment on the discussion of Orwell's "List," Hitchens (2002a, 2002b) observes that Lashmar and Oliver are wholly mistaken, and not just in the number of names. First of all, it seems that Orwell said nothing in private that he did not say in public. The listed names were of public figures, like Congressman Claude Pepper and US Vice President Henry Agard Wallace, and only a few were known to him personally. The information contained in Orwell's "List" was public knowledge, no secrets, only its evaluation was private. To call it a "black-list" was utterly misleading. Moreover, it seems that this evaluation was given by a person who had enough practical experience

---

64 However, Ash (2003b) had a chance to see a copy of Orwell's "List" in the files of the IRD; he reports that it includes Charlie Chaplin's name.

65 Ash (2003b: 6) reports that the copy of the "List" contains 38 names, however, since "someone typed up this official copy of the original list that Orwell dispatched from his sickbed on May 2, 1949, to a close friend" the identity of the "List" can still be questioned.

and built up sufficient theoretical capacity to be qualified for this job. Peter Smolka, alias Smollett, was the only person on Orwell's "List," who was accused of being a Soviet agent. He was the very official in the British Ministry of Information who put pressure on the publisher to drop *Animal Farm*. Since then, it has been "conclusively established that Smolka was indeed an agent of the Society security" (Hitchens 2002b: 26).

Is somebody interested in cutting down the left-wing icon George Orwell and why? George Orwell was a man of the Cold War and he explicitly chose this role. Surprising as Orwell's behavior may seem, it is clear that, unlike many of his contemporaries, he was cynical towards the Soviet Union and, quite contrary to the belief of many right-wing Cold Warriors, he was never a Communist and never went through a phase of Russophilia or Stalin-worship or fellow-travelling. Consequently, he never had to be "cured" or "purged" by disillusionment. In 1947, Orwell wrote that in Spain he understood, "more clearly than ever, the negative influence of the Soviet myth upon the western Socialist movement" (Lashmar and Oliver 1998: 98). His concern was that Stalinism corrupted and discredited the socialist movement, and even made use of it to build up its totalitarian regime. However, some influential intellectuals from the Left did not accept this perspective, even before the existence of the "List" was made public. Hitchens (2002a: 46ff.) reports that Raymond Williams, a leading figure of the New Left in the 1950s, who once defended the Soviet Union's invasion of Finland in the period of the Hitler-Stalin pact in a Cambridge student pamphlet, pointed out a paradox which obviously misinterpreted Orwell, but still had a negative impact on the evaluation of Orwell's work and political message. In "his immensely influential book *Culture and Society* published in 1958," Williams claimed that the total effect of Orwell's work is paradoxical: "He was a humane man who committed an extreme of inhuman terror; a man committed to decency who actualized a distinctive squalor" (quoted in Hitchens 2002a: 48). Hitchens adds that this comes close to maintaining that Orwell invented the picture of totalitarian collectivism. Again, one must be careful not to identify Orwell's opinion as that of his protagonists.

One reason why the information about Orwell's "List" was received with alarm is that in the Cold War period, especially during Senator Joseph McCarthy's reign, many former Trotskyist or Communist intellectuals, e.g., James Burnham, excelled in drafting "one-sided reports for Red-hunting Senate investigation committees" (Tanenhaus 1999: 44). It seems that many of these reports were strategic, i.e., written to dissuade from the author's own leftist past. They delivered material for black-lists, banning people from work and public office, even "casting high officials such as Dean Acheson, George Kennan, and General George Marshall in treasonous roles" (Tanenhaus 1999: 47). Another possible form of strategic Red-hunting were public declarations, not very different from the confessions in Stalin's show trials. The consequences were, however, quite different.

### 4.6.3 *Truth and the destruction of icons*

The destruction of icons seems a very general experience of the post-Second World War period. Is this because truth-telling became a major issue in times of secret services and policies which referred to ideologies? Is it because of an even stronger position of the mass media in political life? In olden times, heroes lost their reputation when it turned out that they acted in a cowardly manner, but not because they lied or a secret was unearthed. (The brutal logic of heroism was to inflict harm on your enemies at all costs.)

In March 1983, Arthur Koestler, author of the anti-communist fiction *Darkness at Noon* and listed as a friend of Orwell,[66] who shared with him the experience of the Spanish Civil War, killed himself at the age of seventy-seven with an overdose of barbiturates and alcohol. Dying with him in his London flat was his third wife Cynthia Jefferies; she was twenty years younger than her husband. Julian Barnes, who calls himself a friend of Koestler, reports that in August 1998, Jill Craigie, film-maker wife of Michael Foot, told David Cesarani, author of the biography *Arthur Koestler: The Homeless Mind*,

> that in May 1952, after a pub-crawl in Hampstead (during which she drank only ginger beer), Koestler attacked and raped her at her flat. She did not tell anyone, not even her husband, for nearly 50 years; obviously, there were no witnesses, no police report, no corroborating evidence. She died in December 1999. Her account, though it stands by itself, sounds absolutely true.
>
> (Barnes 2000: 24)

The result of this disclosure was an outcry of disappointment from Koestler's community of friends and admirers, and a redefinition of his reputation in public life. Barnes (2000: 24) reports that Edinburgh University, "which received about a million pounds under the Koestlers' wills for a chair in parapsychology, reacted not by closing the department or returning the money but by removing Koestler's bust from display." Barnes adds that this was "an act of statuarial unpersonning worthy of the communism he spent much of his life exposing." Also, "unpersonning" is pivotal in Orwell's *Nineteen Eighty-Four*.

In his younger days, Koestler, who was born in Budapest in 1905, was an active communist. After an exciting youth in Vienna and Palestine, he spent the early 1930s as an influential communist journalist at Berlin. Why communism? His explanation was that he was filled with indignation about rich people who did not share the feelings of guilt he suffered from inequality. It

---

66 Orwell reviewed Koestler's *Darkness at Noon* in the *New Statesman* of January 4, 1941. (The review has been republished in the *New Statesman* of January 23, 2013.) It could well be that this book had a decisive impact on Orwell's later work.

was not envy that made him detest the rich, but their indifference to the poor and their spending of large sums of money with a clear conscience. Later, perhaps also out of his experience in the Spanish Civil War, Koestler changed his view on inequality and communism: he became rich through his writings and an outspoken anti-communist Cold War protagonist. On the occasion of the first meeting of the Congress of Cultural Freedom on June 26, 1950 in Berlin, Koestler proclaimed "indifference or neutrality in the face of such a challenge amounts to a betrayal and to the abdication of the free mind" (Lashmar and Oliver 1998: 125). The challenge was Stalin's communism. This was, as already mentioned, when, at the same meeting, the actor Robert Montgomery cried out that "there is no neutral corner in the Freedom's room!" (Saunders 2000: 79) – a possible reaction to the rather popular suggestion that Germany should be neutralized and then unified.

As already noted (in Section 4.4.2), the CIA made a large contribution to the financing of the Berlin congress and the Congress of Cultural Freedom (CCF) that emerged from the Berlin congress as a permanent institution. The CCF "secretly" financed Stephen Spender's magazine *Encounter*. In a recent biography of his parents,[67] Matthew Spender raises the question whether his knighted father was aware that *Encounter* was paid for by the CIA. (See the review of the biography by Tóibín 2016: 64).) (This shows that the secret CIA financing of *Encounter* is still an issue.) Stephen Spender founded *Encounter* in 1953, together with the journalist Irving Kristol, and served as its literary editor over several years. He finished in his engagement with *Encounter* in 1967 when the financing of the magazine by the CIA (and the British MI6) was uncovered by the *New York Times* and other daily newspapers.

Orwell wrote with Stephen Spender for Cyril Connolly's *Horizon* magazine in the 1940s. In the *New York Review of Books* of November 16, 1972, Spender contributed a review of books on George Orwell with the title "The Truth about Orwell." There had been a close relationship between the two. And Koestler?

It seems that Orwell shared the younger Koestler's view on inequality, but he was, as already said, never a Communist and he did not live long enough to enjoy the financial success of his books and the fame that accompanied them. However, in 1946, he proposed to Mrs. Celia Kirwan, a noted beauty and Arthur Koestler's sister-in-law. Kirwan rejected Orwell's offer. This was the very same Mrs. Kirwan who wrote to Orwell on April 30, 1949:

> Dear George, Thanks so much for helpful suggestion. My department were very interested in seeing them . . . they asked me to say they would be grateful if you would let us look at your list of fellow-travelling and crypto-journalists: We would treat it with the utmost discretion. Yours ever, Celia.
> (Quoted in Lashmar and Oliver 1998: 97)

---

67  The title of Matthew Spender's book is *A House in St John's Wood: In Search of My Parents*. It was published in the UK by William Collins in August 2015 and in the US by Farrar, Straus & Giroux in October 2015.

### 4.6.4 *Truth and propaganda*

On April 6, 1949, George Orwell wrote to Celia Kirwan:

> I could also, if it is of any value, give you a list of journalists and writers who in my opinion are crypto-Communists, fellow-travellers or inclined that way & should not be trusted as propagandists. But for that I shall have to send a notebook which I have at home, & if I do give you such a list it is strictly confidential, as I imagine it is libellous to describe somebody as a fellow-traveller.
>
> (Quoted in Lashmar and Oliver 1998: 97)

This confirms what has been said about Orwell's motivation and the status of the "List": if it were made public, it could damage the reputation of those described as "fellow-travellers." To publicly question the integrity of the listed persons, however, was not Orwell's aim, as we see from the quotation.

From his work at the BBC's Indian Service, Orwell was quite experienced in the evaluation of public and secret information and in circumventing censorship. Not everybody shared his view on the liberation of India. To Christopher Hitchens:

> there seems no doubt that Orwell made use of his BBC experience in the writing of *Nineteen Eighty-Four*. The room where the editorial meetings of Eastern Services were held was Room 101 in the Portland headquarters, itself one of the likely architectural models for the 'Ministry of Truth' (Minitrue). Moreover, the concept of doublethink and the description of vertiginous changes in political line clearly owe something to Orwell's everyday experience of propaganda.
>
> (Hitchens 2002a: 25)

There was, however, a new style of British propaganda. The ministry's general view was "that it was more effective to tell the truth, nothing but the truth, and as far as possible, the whole truth. What the propagandists learned was that propaganda was most effective if it was based on accurate factual information" (Lashmar and Oliver 1998: 19). This strategy, however, presupposed that accurate factual information was disseminated and that people believed in it. In this, the BBC played a major role: it informed and inspired trust. As George Orwell noted: "The BBC as far as its news goes has gained enormous prestige since about 1940 . . . 'I heard it on the radio' is now almost equivalent to 'I know it must be true'" (Lashmar and Oliver 1998: 19).

Truth is central to *Nineteen Eighty-four*, although we argued that the story is logically flawed. But the history of its interpretation demonstrates that there is a very fundamental truth in it: the cruelty of totalitarian systems. In *Burmese Days*, Orwell's protagonist James Flory betrayed his native friend Dr. Veraswami – and suffered for it. Truth was very important to Orwell in his writing, but also in his life. In his review, Ash observes with respect to Orwell:

In his best articles and letters, he gives us a gritty, personal example of how to engage as a writer in politics. He takes sides, but remains his own man. He will not put himself at the service of political parties exercising or pursuing power, since that means using half-truths, in a democracy, or whole lies in a dictatorship. He gets things wrong, but then corrects them.

(Ash 1998: 14)

This selected portrait concurs with Orwell's view on the relationship between truth and politics. In his 1935 essay "Politics and the English Language," he mused that "Political language and with variations this is true of all political parties, from Conservatives to Anarchists – is designed to make lies sound truthful and murder respectable, and to give an appearance of solidity to pure wind" (quoted in Hitchens 2002a: 71). Of a Russian agent in Barcelona charged with defaming the POUM fighters as Trotskyist Francoist traitors he writes, in *Homage to Catalonia*, "I watched him with some interest, for it was the first time that I had seen a person whose profession was telling lies – unless one counts journalists" (Orwell 1967 [1938]: 149f.).

The aside remark on the truth-telling journalists may express some contempt, but also some irony as Orwell worked, for many years, as a journalist himself. It implies a paradox. Perhaps Orwell wanted to demonstrate just how differentiated and complex truth-telling can be.

### 4.6.5 An afterword to truth-telling

Timothy Garton Ash, a British citizen, productive contributor to the *New York Review of Books* and reviewer of George Orwell (see Ash 1998), reproduced an interesting case of truth-telling. *The Times* of July 9, 2002 quoted "what someone told the *Times* journalist that Shirley Williams said that Tony Blair said that President Bush said to him. Blair's spokesman, Alistair Campbell, denied that Bush said anything of the sort." The denial was that President George W. Bush said: "The problem with the French is that they don't have a word for entrepreneur" (Ash 2003a: 32–34). It seems too much of an irony that George Orwell was born as Eric Arthur *Blair*.

Orwell made "the seldom observed distinction between the Cold War and the arms race or . . . between the Stalinization of Eastern Europe and the global ambitions of the United States" (Hitchens 2002a: 87). As early as 1947, Orwell wrote: "In the end, the European peoples may have to accept American domination as a way of avoiding domination by Russia, but they ought to realize, while there is yet time, that there are other possibilities." His favored alternative was obvious: "a socialist United States of Europe seems to me the only worthwhile political objective today" (quoted in Hitchens 2002a: 100).

It has been said that Orwell more or less copied his *Nineteen Eighty-Four* from Yevgeny Zamyatin's utopian fiction *We*. (The Russian title of the original text is *Мы*.) Zamyatin wrote this book in 1920. After its publication in the West, he had (and was allowed) to leave the Soviet Union; he died in Paris in 1937. There are strong similarities between *We* and *Nineteen Eighty-Four*. In *We*, the secret police are called "protectors" and the god-like Big Brother is called "benefactor." Freedom was bad in both scenarios: in *Nineteen Eighty-Four*, we learn that "Freedom is Slavery," while in the mathematically structured world of *We*, freedom is responsible for disorder, crime, and destruction. There is also an other-world in which the equivalent of Orwell's "proles" are called "MEPHIs"; the latter live on the other side of the "Green Wall," an area never seen by anyone of the established world. In the established world, regular inhabitants are known as numbers and organized accordingly. There is also a love story: in *We*, Julia and Winston Smith are foreshadowed by I-330 and D-503.

However, there are also substantial differences. He, D-503, was cured not through love and fear of torture by Thought-Police officer O'Brien, but through brain surgery. Unlike Julia, I-330 did not cooperate with the benefactor. She was physically tortured but did resist. Moreover, in *We*, there are revolutionary street fights between the MEPHIs and their supporters, on the one hand, and the established world represented by the benefactor, the protectors and the numbers, on the other, and the outcome is not decided before the novel ends. The established world is organized, on the basis of mathematical laws, as the "Only State," i.e., the world is not divided into three great super-states as in *Nineteen Eighty-Four*. However, do the super-power states really exist? In *Nineteen Eighty-Four*, we learn about the division of the world from Goldstein's book. We also learn that this book was possibly produced by the Ministry of Truth. This is where knowledge and information break down. The paradox of information and the impossibility of truth and thus of love are the prominent messages of *Nineteen Eighty-Four*. There seem to be more successful methods to dehumanize people than through brain surgery. This brings us back to the problem of truth. O'Brien would argue that untruth is necessary to avoid a world catastrophe. But in the end there is the Party's uninhibited greed for power in *Nineteen Eighty-Four*. As O'Brien claims: "Not wealth or luxury or long life or happiness; only power, pure power . . . The German Nazis and the Russian Communists came very close to us in their methods, but they never had the courage to recognize their own motives" (Orwell 1981 [1949]: 217).

In the case of Orwell's "List," "truth" was an issue of his opinions about other people. A first question could be: were these opinions justified? There are other questions: was it appropriate to pass these opinions on "in secret" for secret usage? Was this infringing the personal rights of the listed public figures, especially if they are not informed about this exchange of information and opinions? Does the public have the moral right to be informed when a public figure like Orwell comments on other public figures to a state agency? Obviously, these questions describe a trade-off. Legal rules and political culture provide constraints to possible answers. But then there is public opinion. After some turmoil, we can observe that Orwell fully regained his status of moral institution. The "List" seems to have been chucked into the wastepaper basket.

### *4.6.6 A formal model of doubts and truth-telling*

In this section, we shall discuss a simple game-theoretical model. The analysis is meant to demonstrate how the issues discussed above – and not just the Orwell case – could be submitted to a rigorous formal analysis. But it also shows limits of this approach. The game-theoretical analysis will demonstrate the complexity of the (modeled) decision situation, but it will not give us an answer to the question what rational agents are expected to choose.

Readers who are not all interested in formal analysis should be given a warning: the analysis offered here requires the knowledge of the four basic arithmetical operations, only, and some very general thinking. It could be read as an exercise in intermediate game theory. However, primarily, the analysis is meant to illustrate the effect of raising doubts about Orwell's willingness to be sincere about his anti-Stalinist, left-wing liberal position and to defend it. John Bayley's (2001) review of a Jeffrey Mayers' book *Orwell: Wintry Conscience of a Generation*, was headlined "The Last Puritan." To some extent, this label summarizes the conclusion that the public draws from the discussion that followed the outcry about the "List." Bayley (2001: 50) writes, Orwell's "death at the age of forty-seven was a sad loss to letters, as it was to writers and public men of conscience and integrity." Orwell was "neutral in religious matters," but his friend Anthony Powell could not avoid saying that Orwell "was in his way a sort of saint." Hitchens (2002a: 124) reports this quote.

Not everybody saw Orwell as a saint and some have interpreted his cooperation with the Information Research Department, as we have seen, as strategic behavior – as a submission to the pressure of the intelligence service. Was Orwell of the sincere Cold Warrior type $(t_s)$ or was he a "weak" strategic opportunist of dubious moral standards $(t_w)$ – as it is often said of Arthur Koestler?

Now, who is the judge? The press, or, more generally, the public opinion makers, including the various reviewers quoted above? Of course, to some extent, opinion makers reflect the values of their readers and listeners, but sometimes the role and impact of newspaper owners, politicians, and of those who pay for advertisements is essential. However, it is said that in the long run, information can only be successful if it is accurate. Unfortunately, there is no proof for this conjecture, but it seems more or less evident that, *ceteris paribus*, telling the truth could be cheaper. From *Nineteen Eighty-Four*, we can see how costly it is to revise history, including the risk that the revision is not completely successful. But again and again, the powerful try to get their history into the books, and often they are successful.

For the sake of the argument, let us assume that the public opinion makers (POMs) draw some benefits from attacking a strategic figure of type $t_w$ (e.g., a Koestler type), while they run into problems if their attack was directed to a person who turns out to be a sincere figure of type ts (e.g., an Orwell type). However, as we have seen, even in Orwell's case, there were doubts about his integrity after the public was informed about his "List." Those POMs who argued that Orwell's "reputation as a left-wing icon took a body blow from which it may never recover" (see Lashmar and Oliver's (1998: 95) quote above), however, lost face. Notwithstanding, there was a relatively high a priori expectation that Orwell would turn out to be a weak type $t_w$ and, thus, their attack would be successful.

Let us denote by $p°$ the probability of $t_w$ that summarizes this expectation. In the case of Orwell, we may assume that each member of the POMs community had a different value for $p°$ and those with a high value were more inclined to attack than those with a low value. Let us further suppose that both groups – those who attacked Orwell, and those who did not and perhaps even defended his reputation – were informed in a reliable way that he had given the "List" to the IRD in 1949. The only difference is that each group drew a different conclusion from this action. The latter group interpreted it as a sign (or signal) that he was sincere (of type ts) about his anti-Stalinism, while the other group saw it as sign of opportunistic behavior (corruption), or that he had to give in to the pressure of the intelligence service (see Tony Benn above), which identified him as weak type $t_w$.

Mary McCarthy, a former admirer of Orwell, commented "on what she saw as Orwell's move to the right" that "it was a blessing he died so early" (see Saunders 2000: 301). Obviously, there were people who no longer believed he was sincere. Was it a reasonable strategy of Orwell to give the "List," if he was sincere, or was this a signal that he had merely chosen an easy way to please the authorities during the Cold War era? (The latter has been said of Koestler.) What can the POMs conclude from his sharing the "List"? From the exchange of notes with Celia Kirwan, we learn that Orwell took an active part in the "List" project. In his life and writings, he gave ample evidence that he can put himself into other people's shoes and thereby understand their needs and plans. It seems appropriate to assume that he had a similar approach when he developed the idea of passing the "List" to the IRD. In other words, a game-theoretical approach seems to be adequate for analyzing Orwell's behavior and evaluating the conclusions which the POMs drew from it.

While I brooded over such an analysis, it dawned on me that the strategic situation of the players – Orwell and the POMs – is equivalent to the signaling game analyzed in Cho and Kreps (1987).[68] Orwell is identical with player A who can be of type $t_w$, i.e. weak, or type $t_s$, i.e. strong. Player A has two possible strategies: "to give the 'List'" (List) and "not to give the 'List'" (No List). Of course, the latter strategy makes sense only if there is the temptation to give the "List" and there is the chance that rejecting this temptation becomes known to a wider audience *some days in the future*. Player B, a member of the POMs, does not know what type player A is. B can attack A by aggressively reporting on A, i.e., choosing "Attack," or abstain from an attack, i.e., choosing strategy "No Attack." The common form of attack is "scandalization," i.e.,

---

68 See Holler and Lindner (2004) for an application analyzing the effects of mediation. The presentation of the model follows this article closely.

creating a scandal by assuming a more or less hypothetical interest of a third party (e.g., the general public or a third-party victim as in the Koestler case).[69] Looking for a sensation is perhaps a less aggressive form of attack.

This model assumes that player A knows his type, i.e., Orwell knows whether he is of type $t_w$ or $t_s$, and that this information is "private." This implies that B does not know A's type.[70] Consequently, B does not know whether he is playing the game on the left or on the right in Figure 4.5. B can, however, observe whether A has chosen to give the "List" or not, before B decides whether to attack. This assumes that not giving the "List" will be revealed, e.g., when Orwell's life will be studied in posterity, and Orwell cares about his post-mortem reputation.

Of course, the payoffs given in Figure 4.5 for the various outcomes are highly questionable. It is assumed that it is good for B (a POM) to attack, if A (Orwell) is weak, and it is bad for him if A is strong. A positive outcome to B earns a value of 1, a negative a value of 0. This reduces the strategic problem of B to forming expectations on the type of A – whether A is strong or weak. The intuition is the following. A journalist (or writer) profits from a scandalous story if it is seen by the readership as adequate (and the attacked person does not respond). It seems that this applies, at least for the time being, to the case of Koestler. However, if the attacked person is strong and the scandalous story is convincingly rejected – either by the person him-/herself or by "defenders" as in the case of Orwell – the attacking party may lose their reputation and regret his/her choice of strategy.[71]

| | | B | | | | B | |
| | | Attack | No Attack | | | Attack | No Attack |
|---|---|---|---|---|---|---|---|
| | List | (-3,1) | (-1,0) | | List | (-2,0) | (0,1) |
| A | | | | A | | | |
| | No List | (-2,1) | (0,0) | | No List | (-3,0) | (-1,1) |
| | | Weak A($t_w$) | | | | Strong A($t_s$) | |

*Figure 4.5* The Orwell signaling game

69  See Holler (1999, 2002a) and Marciano and Moureau (2013) for the analysis of the scandal phenomenon.
70  By introducing alternative *types* for a player we apply Harsanyi's (1967/68) approach to the modeling of incomplete information. Complete information assumes that players know their payoffs and the payoffs, i.e., the types, of the other players.
71  In his comments to an earlier version of this model, Alain Marciano, i.e., one of the two editors of Holler (2005), pointed out that the attitude of the other journalists should be important to the payoffs of B: "One journalist may find an interest in revealing the existence of the list but his attitude will provide him with great benefits if his or her colleagues follow him and use the disclosed information. On the contrary, if he is not followed, he may suffer from professional sanctions (for instance, for having tried to destroy an icon)." This supports, by and large, the structure of the payoffs assumed for player B.

The payoffs of A (Orwell) are more differentiated. The best he can earn is 0. This is his value if either (i) he is strong and produces the "List" and there is no attack, or (ii) he is weak, there is no attack and he does not produce the "List." Obviously, an attack gives values of -2 or even -3 to A. At least for some period of time, Orwell's image suffered from the press coverage about the "List," as the reactions of Michael Foot and Tony Benn and the comments of Paul Lashmar and James Oliver and of Frances Stoner Saunders (see above) demonstrate. Of course, this was posthumous. If the "List" was inconsistent with his political view, if Orwell was weak, then there would be even more damage as the -3 in the left-hand matrix compared to the -2 in the right-hand matrix indicates. Giving the "List" is a dominant strategy to the strong A, while it is a dominated strategy to the weak one. In case of complete information, we should expect that the players choose their dominant strategies and the decision problem is easily solved. However, as B does not know whether A is weak or strong, there are the possibilities that (a) the weak A imitates the strong one and (b) the strong A chooses a strategy undercutting this possibility. However, even a strong A prefers not to give the "List" and not be attacked to giving the "List" and being attacked. Even a "strong" Orwell was not looking for a scandal which questions his sincerity.

We can only guess that Orwell preferred to remain silent about the fact that he gave the "List" to the IRD. Had he known that the "List" would be discussed in the press, he might have been more careful in his *wording*, but – as it seems today – hardly about its *content*. It would be highly misguided to assume that Orwell was not concerned about his reputation as a writer and left-wing activist. We noted above that before he died, he gave the instruction that *Nineteen Eighty-Four* should *not* be altered in any way – albeit somewhat in vain. He also gave the order that some of his weaker texts should not be reprinted – he did not succeed here either, but for other reasons. Therefore, it is not unfounded to assume that Orwell thought about how future generations would evaluate his work and activities. The fact that he was dead for more than forty years before the media exploited the issue of the "List" is not of major relevance: The world has not changed so much that the issues of secrecy and truth-telling in politics have become irrelevant. The Cold War may be over, but wars themselves are not, and ideologies (and religions) still matter. There is no "end of history."[72]

Moreover, the press is interested in the truth issue even more than ever, if only to increase sales by pointing out (or creating) scandals. You need only put yourself into the shoes of a journalist, forget your moral qualms and your good education, and ask yourself whether you would attack the icon Orwell after you heard about the "List." Of course, you do not know how the "public" will react, but in the short run, it is very likely that news about the "List" could have

---

72 Contrary of what was proposed by Francis Fukuyama in his best-selling book *The End of History and the Last Man* (New York: Free Press, 1992).

a positive effect on the sales of the newspaper you work for. In the medium run, however, it could turn out that the icon is re-established and your reputation as a journalist and the reputation of your newspaper will suffer from "scandalizing" the "List." Perhaps you will even lose money or your job. Would you attack Orwell after hearing about the "List" – and after receiving some names included in the "List" together with some comments? What do you conclude from the fact that Orwell had given the "List" in the first place? Are there any good arguments which support his decision even today, or was it the foolish action of a terminally ill man? In other words, can you conclude that he was strong or weak in the way as defined by Figure 4.5 and the underlying story?

In order to give an answer to the latter question, we apply a rigorous game-theoretical analysis. In what follows, we restrict ourselves to the abstract description and leave it to the reader to think of A as Orwell and of B as a journalist or writer who is looking for a sensation or a chance to create a scandal. Following Cho and Kreps (1987), we assume that B expects A to be of type $t_w$ or $t_s$ with probabilities $p° = 0.1$ and $1 - p° = 0.9$, respectively. The qualitative results remain the same with every probability assumption in which A is more likely to be strong than weak.

Given these priors, B should *not* attack if there is no further information. But there is further information: B can observe whether or not A has given the "List." Today it is common knowledge that A did give the "List." This raises the question as to whether this is rational within the bounds of our model. If, from a strategic point of view, A wants to evaluate whether or not he should give the "List," then he has to form expectations about whether B will ultimately attack. The answer to this question is by backward induction. The first step is to find out about the reasoning of B which is at the end of the decision chain. If B has to decide whether or not to attack, then he has to form expectations about whether A is "strong" or "weak." A game-theoretical interpretation of A's giving the "List" could be helpful in this respect on the grounds that it can be interpreted as a signal in the sense of Spence (1974) – of being strong (or weak). However, as we shall see, there are problems with this.

If we consider that the game in Figure 4.5 is played sequentially, A moves first and B can see the choice of B before choosing his strategy, then we can identify two Nash equilibria,[73] if A is more likely to be strong than weak.

Equilibrium I is a pooling equilibrium which is characterized by the fact that A gives the "List," irrespective of his type; and B does not attack because the utility[74] to B of "no attack" is larger than B's utility gained from "attack," i.e.,

---

73 These are "sequential equilibria" because the game is sequential and one player has incomplete information so that the equilibria are subject to beliefs. See Kreps and Wilson (1982a, 1982b) for the pioneer papers.

74 In game-theoretical terms, payoffs are also known as "von Neumann and Morgenstern utilities" which satisfy the expected utility hypothesis. Consequently, we do not have to distinguish between expected utilities, utilities, and payoffs.

$u_B(\text{no attack}) = 0.9 \cdot 1 + 0.1 \cdot 0 > u_B(\text{attack}) = 0.9 \cdot 0 + 0.1 \cdot 1.$

To prevent A being identified as weak, if he is weak, we assume that A assumes that B attacks with a probability $q \geq 0.5$ if A does not give the "List." Given this assumption, A will give the "List" even if A is weak. In fact, not giving the "List" is taken as a signal that A is weak. Consequently, B updates his priors. If B's posterior beliefs are such that he expects A to be weak with probability $p > 0.5$, then B prefers to attack. Obviously,

$$u_B(\text{no attack}) = (1 - p) \cdot 1 + p \cdot 0 < u_B(\text{attack}) = (1 - p) \cdot 0 + p \cdot 1, \text{ if } p > 0.5.$$

If $p = 0.5$, then B is indifferent between attacking and not attacking.

Equilibrium I (List, No Attack) implies that B cannot identify A as being weak or strong; this is the essence of a pooling equilibrium. Thus, the signal of giving the "List" and the underlying reasoning is not particularly helpful for B to identify A being strong or weak, but it prescribes No Attack as optimal strategy. That is, the behavior of B will not depend on whether A is of type $t_w$ or $t_s$, but B's payoffs are larger if A is strong. If A is weak and B does not attack, as implied by equilibrium I, then B misses a chance to achieve a larger payoff.

It is "unfortunate" to B that Equilibrium II (No List, No Attack) is a pooling equilibrium, too. Here is a situation in which A does not give the "List" irrespective of his type. To keep a strong A from preferring not giving the "List," it suffices that A assumes that B will attack with probability $q \geq 0.5$ if B learns that A gave the "List." But how can we rationalize this assumption? We simply assume that B believes A to be weak with probability $p° > 0.5$, if A gives the "List." This assumption is possible (i.e., consistent) because giving the "List" is out of Equilibrium II, and yet it does not look very convincing.

In his non-fiction work *The Log from the Sea of Cortez*, John Steinbeck (1976 [1941]: 147) wrote: "Even erroneous beliefs are real things, and have to be considered proportional to their spread or intensity. 'All-truth' must embrace all extant apropos errors also, and know them as such by relation to the whole, and allow for their effects." Is $p° > 0.5$, if A gives the "List," such an "apropos error"?

Equilibrium II (No List, No Attack) demonstrates that it could be to the advantage of a weak A not to give the "List." But are B's beliefs, underlying Equilibrium II, reasonable? Cho and Kreps (1987) provide an argument that they are not. A weak A will get a payoff of 0 in equilibrium. By giving the "List," the best he could get is a payoff of $-1$. To give the "List" makes no sense if A is weak, although it will if A is strong: $t_s$ receives a payoff of $-1$ in the equilibrium by not giving the "List" but can *conceivably* get 0 from offering the "List." If B follows his *intuition* and puts no probability weight on a weak A if B observes the fact that the "List" was given, then an A who gave the "List" would be expected to be strong and B would not opt for an attack. More generally, the *intuitive criterion* of Cho and Kreps implies that type ti would not reasonably be expected by B to send out-of-equilibrium message m if the best ti could get from m is less than ti could get from the equilibrium outcome. If a strong A realizes this argument he will always give the "List" – which "breaks" Equilibrium II and suggests Equilibrium I, i.e., giving the "List" and "No Attack."

We might think of an equilibrium in mixed strategies as discussed in the Inspection Game (see Section 3.8 above). Because of the sequential structure of the game, there must be a "means" such that a weak A could convey that he will play a mixed strategy after B made his choice of attacking or not. I cannot see any setting by which a "weak" Orwell can bind himself to *randomize* on giving the "List" after B has chosen to attack (or not to attack). In fact, if Orwell does not give a "List," then the precondition of an attack is missing – an attack is not feasible. This problem also discredits Equilibrium II. However, above we argued that not giving the "List" might be revealed in the future, and Orwell cares about his post-mortem reputation.

The selection of Equilibrium I is also confirmed by the results for very low $p°$. In the absence of a weak A, i.e., $p° = 0$, there is no asymmetric information and, of course, the strong A will give the "List." We would not expect this scenario to significantly differ from the one for very low $p°$. This enforces the selection of Equilibrium I.

It is notable that for $p° < 0.5$, $p°$ being the prior of A being weak, both equilibria suggest that B will not attack. For the given priors, this result coincides with the rational decision of B, if B cannot gain information about A's willingness to give the "List." Thus, it seems that, in the given case, giving the "List" or not does not have any influence on the decision of B. Yet, if we accept Cho and Kreps's (1987) *intuitive criterion*, then Equilibrium I will be selected and we would expect A to give the "List," irrespective of his type, and B will not attack. Consequently, B will identify A as weak, if A does not give the "List," and thus attack. (But on what issue?) Hence, Equilibrium I does not provide B with any information as regards A's type, but it forces A to give the "List" and rationalizes B's renunciation of an attack as a best reply to A giving the "List."

The *intuitive criterion* has been criticized because of the logical difficulties which arise when interpreting disequilibrium messages as signals (see Mailath et al., 1993). However, Equilibrium II can also be excluded by applying the concept of *strategically stable equilibria* by Kohlberg and Mertens (1986). An application of this concept selects a subset of the equilibria which fulfills the *intuitive criterion* proposing that off-equilibrium beliefs have to be reasonable "in some sense." Therefore, if there are no strong (exogenous) indicators for A being weak, Equilibrium I seems adequate describing the outcome of the game if the two players act rationally.

Now, what does it say in terms of Orwell and the "List"? If Orwell was convinced that his giving the "List" was an appropriate tool in the political battle against Stalinism (and fascism), as we can conclude from his letter to Celia Kirwan, then this was a rational behavior. This behavior, however, could be imitated by a weak type of Orwell who gave the "List" for strategic reasons hoping that this would not be observed and cause an attack. Of course, even a strong Orwell would not be happy to read in the *Daily Telegraph* the comment on his "List": "To some, it was as if Winston Smith had willingly cooperated with the Thought Police in *1984*." However, this attack was not supported by the equilibrium analysis if the a priori expectation $1 - p°$ for Orwell being strong (or sincere) was larger than 0.5. Either the *Daily Telegraph* was misled in the a priori value $p°$, or was biased in a way such that the payoffs were very different from those shown in Figure 4.5, or did not care about its reputation which, by and large, indeed suffered from the attack on Orwell. An alternative interpretation is that those who were responsible for the comment in the *Daily Telegraph* did not understand the game situation – or had serious problems with the *intuitive criterion*.

Of course, we should not assume that any of the agents of the above strategic decision problem followed the pattern of game-theoretical reasoning presented here. The analysis is meant to demonstrate how convoluted the most simple modeling of decision making can grow if there is a secret.

# 5  Justice in the end?

In the final scene of *The Good, the Bad, and the Ugly*, Tuco is shoveling open the grave of the "Unknown" with Blondie's gun pointing at him. When the $200,000 treasure is unearthed, with a stroke of his shovel, Tuco cuts open one sack and the gold dollars pour out. Blondie directs Tuco to stand on the rotten wooden cross of the tomb with a hangman's noose around his neck and his hands tied behind his back. While Tuco balances on the tip of his shoes so as not to fall from the unsteady cross and break his neck, Blondie shifts half of the bounty onto his horse, leaving the other half in full view of the trembling, shaking, sweating Tuco. When doling out the shares of treasure, Blondie mumbles something like "Seems like in the old days. Four for you, and four for me." And following this, just like in the old days, he will cut the rope suspending Tuco from a distance with a perfect shot of his perfect rifle. Tuco will drop face-first onto the bags of gold dollars left to him. After having done this job, Blondie will ride away – on the only horse available – accompanied by the unearthly sound of Ennio Morricone's magnificent music – the best film music ever.

In this scene, the loaded gun in Blondie's hand implies a second-mover advantage, which he, somewhat surprisingly, does not exploit with respect to sharing the treasure. This adds a surreal touch to the movie – or should we say: another one. Was it, as claimed by Bondanella (2001: 261) "male cameraderie, a bond central to the traditional Western formula," that "has crept back into Sergio Leone's interpretation of the American West?" If so, then this sequence had the features of a parody.

Blondie has the air of an angel vanishing into the distance. But why did, first of all, Tuco accede to step onto the shaking cross in order to have a hangman's noose fixed around his neck? Blondie wouldn't shoot him, would he? Tuco's having a noose around his neck and hands tied behind his back, standing on an unsteady, weather-beaten cross, seems to be the much more dangerous alternative.

The hanging ritual at the end of the movie could be interpreted as a reference to the earlier business relationship between Tuco and Blondie – which now comes to an end. On the other hand, it looks like an act of purification, i.e., a degradation of resentments. It seems that Blondie feels that there are still unpaid bills to settle. Earlier in the movie, there was a scene when Tuco put a rope around Blondie's neck. It was only because a shell exploded next to the house and destroyed its ceiling, that *this* rope did not put an end to Blondie's life. And then there was the march through the desert. Without the half-dead Bill Carson making his appearance, Tuco's departure would have left Blondie roasted by the desert's sun and lack of water until his final collapse.

The shaking cross under Tuco's boots is a strong symbol. Does it refer to crucifixion and the suffering for sins? Perhaps only after this purification and the balancing of Blondie's sentiments was a sharing-out of the treasure possible. Of course, sharing in equal parts came as a surprise after the overpowering greed for money that dominated this movie. What was a long story dripping with blood, ended as a fairy tale, which even attained some degree of fairness. The equal-share outcome concurs with the meet-them-halfway solution that Berz (2015) identifies as "just or fair" for dividing a "cake" in the business world.[1] Blondie and Tuco were business partners, and Blondie's remark "Seems like in the old days" evokes this partnership and the need for a fair solution related to it. But in the case of Tuco and Blondie, this was only a partial solution. All the others who showed up in the movie, mostly dead, were not involved. It would be difficult to identify the fairness of equal-share outcome with justice in this case. "Justice as fairness"[2] will not work. Moreover, it seems that Tuco was not convinced of the fairness of the outcome. He cursed Blondie, shouting, "Hey Blondie! You know what you are? Just a dirty son of a bitch!", still with his hands tied behind his back and the severed noose around his neck.

Perhaps Tuco was worried about not having a horse and being abandoned in this desert environment. In bargaining theory, this situation could be illustrated by a non-convex payoff space. Perhaps Tuco saw himself defeated and the equal share, given the circumstances of the share-out, was just a final blow to demonstrate Blondie's victory. It seems that money is just a symbol of power in this movie. Is the greed for money just a substitute for the hunger for power? The heroes do not spend money. When Tuco goes shopping for a gun, he gets a gun plus the shopkeeper's money. Is this fair?

On December 24, 2013, Queen Elizabeth II signed a pardon for Alan Turing's conviction for gross indecency. The posthumous pardon was justified by Turing's outstanding contributions to the war effort. Previously, on September 10, 2009, Prime Minister Gordon Brown had apologized, describing the treatment of Turing as "appalling." He acknowledged:

---

1 It also concurs with the outcome which derives from the Nash bargaining solution (Nash 1950a) if the (cooperative) bargaining game is symmetric, i.e., if the conflict payoffs are equal and the payoff space is symmetric with respect to the 45-degree line. However, there is no way to sign enforceable contracts. Van Damme (1987: 127) discusses how this result can be achieved in a non-cooperative setting in which the outcome is determined by a Nash equilibrium. Yet, technically speaking, watching the movies final scene, we see a dictator game enfolding.

2 This is the headline of the first chapter of John Rawls's *A Theory of Justice* (1971).

While Turing was dealt with under the law of the time, and we can't put the clock back, his treatment was of course utterly unfair, and I am pleased to have the chance to say how deeply sorry I and we all are for what happened to him.

(Brown 2009)

Justice can be unfair.

History gives us second-mover advantages to re-evaluate its course. In his apology speech, Brown confirmed the suicide hypothesis and emphasized Turing's homosexuality and how it burdened the last years of his life. He talked about the "theatre of mankind's darkest hour" and Turing's commitment to fighting fascism. He did not mention Turing's outstanding theoretical work in mathematics and computer science, his pioneering contribution to artificial intelligence, and his interest in mathematical biology (which might explain why there was cyanide in his home). Was this fair?

Justice in the end, or is it all about power? "You may run the risk, my friend, but I do the cutting." The discussion will be continued.

# References

Ahlert, M. (2014), "A Conceptual Model of Desire-Based Choice," Halle/Saale: Martin-Luther-University Halle-Wittenberg, Volkswirtschaftliche Diskussionsbeiträge 75.

Airaksinen, T. (2011), "Secrets of Science in Bacon's New Atlantis," in: T. Airaksinen and M.J. Holler (eds.), *Secrets of Secrets II* (*Homo Oeconomicus* 28), Munich: Accedo-Verlag: 415–435.

Airaksinen, T. (2012), "Desire and Happiness," *Homo Oeconomicus* 29: 393–412.

Airaksinen, T. (2013), "Sade, or the Scandal of Desire," *Homo Oeconomicus* 30: 369–384.

Airaksinen, T. (2014a), "An Introduction to Desire," *Homo Oeconomicus* 31: 447–461.

Airaksinen, T. (2014b), "There are Countless Ways to be Happy," Presentation at the Frankfurt School of Finance, October 9, 2014. Quotes have been confirmed by T. Airaksinen.

Akerlof, G. (1970), "The Market for Lemons: Quality Uncertainty and the Market Mechanism," *Quarterly Journal of Economics* 89: 488–500.

Allais, M. (1953), "Le comportement de l'homme rational devant le risque: critique des postulats et axiomes de l'école américaine," *Econometrica* 21: 503–546.

Alvaredo, F., Atkinson, A.B., Piketty, T., and E. Saez (2013), "The Top 1 Percent in International and Historical Perspective," *Journal of Economic Perspectives* 27, 3: 3–20.

Amir, L.A. (2014), *Humor and the Good Life in Modern Philosophy*, Albany: State University of New York Press (SUNY).

Anderson, K. (2014), "Rampant Remakery: Yojimbo vs. a Fistful of Dollars," April 7. http://nerdist.com/rampant-remakery-yojimbo-vs-a-fistful-of-dollars/. Accessed April 25, 2018.

Andreozzi, L. (2002a), "Oscillations in the Enforcement of Law: An Evolutionary Analysis," *Homo Oeconomicus* 18: 403–428.

Andreozzi, L. (2002b), "Society Saved by Children: The Role of Youngsters in the Generation of Scandals," in: M.J. Holler (ed.), *Scandal and Its Theory II* (*Homo Oeconomicus* 19), Munich: Accedo-Verlag: 199–205.

Andreozzi, L. (2004), "Rewarding Policeman Increases Crime: Another Surprising Result from the Inspection Game," *Public Choice* 121: 69–82.

Arrow, K.J. (1963 [1951]), *Social Choice and Individual Value* (2nd edition), New York: John Wiley and Sons.

Arruñada, B. (2017), "Property as Sequential Exchange: The Forgotten Limits of Private Contract." Available at: https://papers.ssrn.com/sol3/papers.cfm?abstract_id=2879827. Accessed January 3, 2018.

Arundel, A. (2001), "The Relative Effectiveness of Patents and Secrecy for Appropriation," *Research Policy* 30: 611–Q24.

Ash, T.G. (1998), "Orwell in 1998," *New York Review of Books* 45 (October 22):10–14.

Ash, T.G. (2003a), "Anti-Europeanism in America," *New York Review of Books* 50 (February 13): 32–34.

Ash, T.G. (2003b), "Orwell's List," *New York Review of Books* 50 (September 25): 6–12.

Ash, T.G. (2015), "Defying the Assassin's Veto," *New York Review of Books* 62 (February 19): 4–6.

Atkinson-Griffith, N. (2002), "Artist's Statement," in: *Nicola Atkinson-Griffith's "Secrets of the World,"* Symposium, introduced and edited by M.J. Holler (*Homo Oeconomicus* 18), Munich: Accedo-Verlag: 538.

Aumann, R.J. (1985), "On the Non-transferable Utility Value: A Comment on the Roth-Shafer Examples," *Econometrica* 53: 667–677.

Aumann, R.J. and M. Maschler (1972), "Some Thoughts on the Minimax Principle," *Management Science* 18: 54–63.

Avenhaus, R. (1997), "Entscheidungstheoretische Analyse der Fahrgastkontrolle," *Der Nahverkehr* 9: 27–30.

Avenhaus, R., Canty, M., Kilgour, M., von Stengel, B., and S. Zamir (1996), "Inspection Games in Arms Control and Disarmament, Invited Review," *European Journal of Operational Research* 90: 383–394.

Bacon, F. (2002 [1625]), *Essays or Counsels, Civil and Moral*, London: Folio Society.

Bain, J.S. (1956), *Barriers to New Competition*, Cambridge, MA: Harvard University Press.

Barnes, J. (2000), "The Afterlife of Arthur Koestler," *New York Review of Books* 47 (February 10): 23–25.

Bauer, C.P. (2013), *Secret History: The Story of Cryptology*, Boca Raton, London, and New York: CRC Press/Taylor & Francis Group.

Baumol, W.J. (1977), "On the Proper Cost Tests for Natural Monopoly in a Multiproduct Industry," *American Economic Review* 67: 809–822.

Baumol, W.J., (1982), "Contestable Markets: An Uprising in the Theory of Industry Structure," *American Economic Review* 72: 1–15.

Baumol, W. J., Bailey, E. E., and R.D. Willig (1977), "Weak Invisible Hand Theorems on the Sustainability of Multiproduct Natural Monopoly," *American Economic Review* 67: 350–365.

Baumol, W.J., Panzar, J. C., and R.D. Willig (1982), *Contestable Markets and the Theory of Industry Structure*, San Diego: Harcourt Brace Jovanovich.

Bayley, J. (2001), "The Last Puritan," *New York Review of Books* 48 (March 29): 47–50.

Beaulier, S. and B. Caplan (2007), "Behavioral Economics and Perverse Effects of the Welfare State," *Kyklos* 60: 485–507.

Berggren, N., Elinder, M., and H. Jordahl (2008), "Trust and Growth: A Shaky Relationship," *Empirical Economics* 35: 251–274.

Bernheim, B.D. (1984), "Rationalizable Strategic Behavior," *Econometrica* 52: 1007–1028.

Bertrand, J.L.F. (1883), "Compte-rendu de Théorie de la richesse social par Léon Walras de Recherches sur les principes mathématiques de la théorie des richesses par Augustin Couront," *Journal des Savants* 67 (September): 499–508.

Berz, G. and M.J. Holler (2014), "The Good Fairy and the Bad Raisin Pickers: The Dilemma of Renewable Energy," *ISE/CCR Working Paper*, No. 1, October. Available at: www.ifamd.de/aktuelles.html. Accessed April 25, 2018.

Berz, G. (2015), *Game Theory Bargaining and Auction Strategies: Practical Examples from Internet Auction to Investment Banking* (2nd edition), Basingstoke: Palgrave Macmillan.

Binder, C. (2014), "Preference and Similarity between Alternatives," Erasmus University, Rotterdam (manuscript).

Binmore, K. (1992), *Fun and Games: a Text on Game Theory*, Lexington, MA and Toronto: D.C. Heath and Co.

Binmore, K., and A. Shaked (2010), "Experimental Economics: Where Next?" *Journal of Economic Behavior & Organization* 73: 87–100.

Black, D. (1948), "On the Rationale of Group Decision Making," *Journal of Political Economy* 56: 23–34.

Black, D. (1958), *The Theory of Committees and Elections*, London and New York: Cambridge University Press.

Blaseio, H. (2016), "The Road to Novelty," SSRN.

Blind, S. (2002), "Shall I Sell You My Secret? On Blackmailers, Traitors, Good Secrets, and Secret Goods," in: *Nicola Atkinson-Griffith's "Secrets of the World," Symposium*, introduced and edited by M.J. Holler (*Homo Oeconomicus* 18), Munich: Accedo-Verlag: 565–569.

Bloom, P. (2008), "First Person Plural," *The Atlantic* 302, no. 4 (November): 90–98. Available at: www.theatlantic.com/magazine/archive/2008/11/first-person-plural/307055/,3/18-18/18. Accessed April 26, 2018.

Bok, S. (1982), *Secrets: On the Ethics of Concealment and Revelation*, New York: Pantheon Press.

Bolle, F. (1998), "Rewarding Trust – An Experimental Study," *Theory and Decisions* 45: 85–100.

Bondanella, P. (2001), *Italian Cinema: From Neorealism to the Present* (3rd edition), New York: Continuum International Publishing.

Brams, S.J. (1975), *Game Theory and Politics*, New York: Free Press.

Brams, S.J. (1983), *Superior Beings: If They Exist, How Do We Know?* New York et al.: Springer.

Brams, S.J., and A.D. Taylor (1996), *Fair Division: From Cake-Cutting to Dispute Resolution*, Cambridge: Cambridge University Press.

Breton, A., Galeotti, G., Salmon, P. and R. Wintrobe (eds.) (2007), *The Economics of Transparency in Politics (Villa Colombella Papers)*, Aldershot: Ashgate Publishing.

Brown, G. (2009), "Gordon Brown: I'm Proud to Say Sorry to a Real War Hero," *Telegraph* (September 10). Available at: www.telegraph.co.uk/news/politics/gordon-brown/6170112/. Accessed April 26, 2018.

Bulow, J.I., Geanakoplos, J.D., and P.D. Klemperer (1985), "Multimarket Oligopoly: Strategic Substitutes and Strategic Complements," *Journal of Political Economy* 93: 488–511.

Cabanne, P. (1967), *Entretiens avec Marcel Duchamp*, Paris: edition Pierre Belfond (*Dialogues with Marcel Duchamp*, translated by R. Padgett, New York: Viking Press).

Caryle, C. (2015), "Saving Alan Turing from His Friends," *New York Review of Books* 62 (February 5): 19–21.

Cendrowski, S. (2012), "How Long does a Razor Really Last? Gillette Comes Clean," *Fortune* (June 7).

Cheng, L.K. and M. Zhu (1995), "Mixed Strategy Nash Equilibrium Based Upon Expected Utility and Quadratic Utility," *Games and Economic Behavior* 9: 139–150.

Chiasson, D. (2015), "Where's Brando?" *New York Review of Books* 62 (January 8): 18–19.

Cho, I.K. and D. Kreps (1987), "Signalling Games and Stable Equilibria," *Quarterly Journal of Economics* 102: 179–221.

Coase, R.H. (1960), "The Problem of Social Cost," *Journal of Law and Economics* 3: 1–44.

Cockroft, E. (1974), "Abstract Expressionism. Weapon of the Cold War," *Artforum* 12 (June): 39–41.

Cohen, W.M., Nelson, R., and J.P. Walsh (2000), "Protecting Their Intellectual Assets: Appropriability Conditions and Why U.S. Manufacturing Firms Patent (or Not)," NBER Working Paper no. 7552.

Cole, D. (2014), "The Three Leakers and What to Do About Them," *New York Review of Books* 51 (February 6): 7–11.

Cole, D. (2016), "The Trouble at Yale," *New York Review of Books* 63 (January 14): 4–8.

*Collier's Encyclopedia* (1969), Volume 23 of 24 Volumes, New York: Crowell-Collier Educational Corporation.

Condorcet (1785), *Essai sur l'application de l'analyse à la probabilité des décisions rendues à la pluralité des voix*, Paris: L'Imprimerie Royale.

Condorcet (1989), *The Political Theory of Condorcet*, translated and edited by Fiona Sommerlad and Ian McLean, Social Studies Faculty Centre Working Paper 1/89. Oxford: Faculty of Social Sciences, Oxford University.

Copeland, B.J. (2004), *The Essential Turing*, Oxford et al.: Oxford University Press.

Copeland, B.J. (2012), *Turing: Pioneer of the Information Age*, Oxford et al.: Oxford University Press.

Cox, A. (1983), *Art-as-Politics: The Abstract Expressionist Avant-Garde and Society*, Ann Arbor: University of Michigan Research Press.

Danto, A.C. (1992), *Beyond the Brillo Box: The Visual Arts in Post-Historical Perspective*, New York: Farrar Straus Giroux.

Danto, A.C. (1999), *Philosophizing Art: Selected Essays*, Berkeley, Los Angeles and London: University of California Press.

Davis, M. (2000), *Engines of Logic: Mathematicians and the Origin of the Computer*, New York and London: W.W. Norton & Company.

Debreu, G. (1979 [1959]), *Theory of Value: An Axiomatic Analysis of Economic Equilibrium*, New Haven and London: Yale University Press.

Debreu, G. (1991), "The Mathematization of Economic Theory," *American Economic Review* 81: 1–7.

de Hart Mathews, J. (1976), "Art and Politics in Cold War America," *American Historical Review* 81: 762–787.

Deley, A.T. (2013), "Bob Dylan and Plagiarism: To Catch a Master Thief," *Dissident Voice: A Radical Newsletter for Peace and Social Justice* (December 12).

DeParle, J. (2007), "The American Prison Nightmare," *New York Review of Books* 56 (April 12): 33–36.

Detmold, C.E. (1882), "The Life of Machiavelli," in: *The Historical, Political, and Diplomatic Writings of Niccolò Machiavelli*, translated from the Italian by Christian E. Detmold, in four volumes, Boston: James R. Osgood; Vol. 1: XV–XLI.

Dewey, J. (1979 [1938]), *Experience and Education*, New York: Collier Books, and London: Collier Macmillan Publishers.

Diekmann, A. (1985), "Volunteer's Dilemma," *Journal of Conflict Resolution* 29: 605–610.

Diekmann, A. (1986), "Volunteer's Dilemma. A Social Trap without a Dominant Strategy and Some Empirical Results" in: A. Diekmann and P. Mitter (eds.), *Paradoxical Effects of Social Behavior. Essays in Honor of Anatol Rapoport*, Heidelberg and Vienna: Physica-Verlag: 187–197.

Diekmann, A. (1993), "Cooperation in an Asymmetric Volunteer's Dilemma Game: Theory and Empirical Evidence," *International Journal of Game Theory* 22: 75–85.

Downs, A. (1957), *An Economic Theory of Democracy*, New York: Harper.

Dresher, M. (1962)"A Sampling Inspection Problem in Arms Control Agreements: A Game Theoretic Analysis," Memorandum RM-2972-ARPA, The RAND Corporation, Santa Monica, California.

Duchamp. M. and V. Halberstadt (1932), *L'Opposition et Cases Conjugees, Opposition und Schwesterfelder, Opposition and Sister Squares*, Paris and Brussels: L'Echiquier.

Dudley, L. (2002), "The Secrets of Small Worlds," in: *Nicola Atkinson-Griffith's "Secrets of the World,"* Symposium, introduced and edited by M.J. Holler (*Homo Oeconomicus* 18), Munich: Accedo-Verlag: 548–550.

Dufwenberg, M., Gneezy, U., Güth, W. and E van Damme (2001), "Direct Versus Indirect Reciprocity: An Experiment," in: J. Frohn, W. Güth, H. Kliemt, and R. Selten (eds.), *Making Choices I (Homo Oeconomicus* 18), Munich: Accedo-Verlag: 19–30.

Dylan, B. (2005), *Chronicles: Volume One*, New York: Simon & Schuster.

Dyson, G. (2012), *Turing's Cathedral: The Origins of the Digital Universe*, London: Allen Lane.

Eco, U. (1986), *Art and Beauty in the Middle Ages*, New Haven, CT and London: Yale University Press.

Faulhaber, G. (1975), "Cross-subsidization: Pricing in Public Enterprises," *American Economic Review* 65: 966–977.

Fehr, E. and K. Schmidt (1999), "A Theory of Fairness, Competition, and Cooperation," *Quarterly Journal of Economics* 114: 817–868.

Ferejohn, J.A., and M. P. Fiorina (1975), "Closeness Counts Only in Horseshoes and Dancing," *American Political Science Review* 69: 920–925.

Ferguson, N. (2006), "A 'Miracle of Deliverance'?" *New York Review of Books* 53 (November 30): 26–29.

Feynman, R.P. (1985), "*Surely You are Joking, Mr. Feynman!*" *Adventures of a Curious Character*, New York and London: Norton.

Foucault, M. (2004), *Death and the Labyrinth*, New York and London: Continuum.

Frey, B.S. (1997), *Not Just For the Money: An Economic Theory of Personal Motivation*, Cheltenham: Edward Elgar.

Frey, B.S. and A. Stutzer (2002), "What Can Economists Learn from Happiness Research?" *Journal of Economic Literature* 40: 402–435.

Frey, B.S. and M.J. Holler, (1997), "Moral and Immoral Views on Paying Taxes," in: S. Hellsten, M. Kopperi and O. Loukola (eds.), *Taking the Liberal Change Seriously*, Aldershot et al.: Ashgate.

Frey, B.S. and M.J. Holler (1998), "Tax Compliance Policy Reconsidered," *Homo Oeconomicus* 15: 27–44.

Friedman, W.F. and C.J. Mendelsohn (1994 [1938]), *The Zimmermann Telegram of January 16, 1917, and its Cryptographic Background* (War Department, Office of the Chief Signal Officer, Washington, GPO, 1938), Aegean Park Press.

Fudenberg, D. and J. Tirole (1985), "Preemption and Rent Equalization in the Adoption of New Technology," *Review of Economic Studies* 52: 383–401.

Fustel de Coulange, N.D. (2006 [1864]), *The Ancient City: A Study of the Religion, Laws, and Institutions of Greece and Rome*, Mineola, NY: Dover Publications.

Gallini, N.T. (2002), "The Economics of Patents: Lessons from Recent U.S. Patent Reform," *Journal of Economic Perspectives* 16: 131–154

Gauss, C. (1952), Introduction to Niccolò Machiavelli's *The Prince* (Mentor edition), New York: Mentor Books.

Gibbon, E. (1998 [volume I, 1776/77]), *The History of the Decline and Fall of the Roman Empire* (28 Selected Chapters), Ware: Wordsworth.

Gibson, A. E. (1997), *Abstract Expressionism. Other Politics*, New Haven and London: Yale University Press.

Girard, R. (1972), *La violence et le sacré*, Paris: Editions Bernard Grasset.

Glaeser, E.L. (2006), "Paternalism and Psychology," *University of Chicago Law Review* 73: 133–156.

Golding, J. (2003), "Divide and Conquer," *New York Review of Books* 50 (January 16): 32–35.

Goldman, A.H. (2009), *Reasons from Within*, Oxford: Oxford University Press.

Gottlieb, A. (2016), "Who Was David Hume?" *New York Review of Books* 63 (May 26): 68–70.

Guilbaut, S. (1983), *How New York Stole the Idea of Modern Art*, Chicago, IL: Chicago University Press.

Güth, W., Königstein, M., Marchand, N. and K. Nehring (2001), "Trust and Reciprocity in the Investment Game with Indirect Reward," in: J. Frohn, W. Güth, H. Kliemt, and R. Selten (eds.), *Making Choices II (Homo Oeconomicus* 18), Munich: Accedo-Verlag: 241–262.

Gylling, H.A. (2009), "Conservatism and Secrecy," in: T. Airaksinen and M.J. Holler (eds.), *The Secrets of Secrets (Homo Oeconomicus* 26), Munich: Accedo-Verlag: 143–159.

Haladyn, J.J. (2010), *Marcel Duchamp. Ètant donnés*, London: Afterall Books.

Halpern, S. (2014), "The Creepy New Wave of the Internet," *New York Review of Books* 61 (November 20): 22–24.

Halpern, S. (2016a), "Going Dark," *New York Review of Books* 63 (May 26): 20–22.

Halpern, S. (2016b), "Our Driverless Future," *New York Review of Books* 63 (November 24): 18–20.

Harsanyi, J.C. (1967/68), "Games With Incomplete Information Played by 'Bayesian' Players," *Management Science* 14: 159–182, 320–334, 486–502.

Harsanyi, J.C. (1977). *Rational Behavior and Bargaining in Games and Social Situations*, Cambridge: Cambridge University Press.

Hastings, M. (2016), "What's New About the War?" *New York Review of Books* 63 (March 10): 28–30.

Hauptman, W. (1973), "The Suppression of Art in the McCarthy Decade," *Artforum* 12 (October): 48–52.

Hendricks, K. (1992), "Reputation in the Adoption of a New Technology," *International Journal of Industrial Organization* 10: 663–677.

Herzberg, F. (1966), *Work and the Nature of Man*, Cleveland, OH: World Publishing.

Herzberg, F., Mausner, B., and B.B. Snyderman (1959). *The Motivation to Work* (2nd edition), New York: John Wiley.

Hill, R. and T. Myatt (2010), *The Economics Anti-Textbook: A Critical Thinker's Guide to Microeconomics*, Halifax and Winnipeg: Fernwood Publishing, and London and New York: Zed Books.

Hillinger, C. and V. Lapham (1971), "The Impossibility of a Paretian Liberal: Comment by Two Who Are Unreconstructed," *Journal of Political Economy* 79: 1403–1405.

Hillman, A. (2010), "Expressive Behavior in Economics and Politics," *European Journal of Political Economy* 26: 403–418.

Hitchens, C. (2002a), *Why Orwell Matters*, New York: Basic Books.

Hitchens, C. (2002b), "Orwell's List," *New York Review of Books* 49 (September 26), 26–28.

Hochschild, A. (2017), "When Dissent Became Treason," *New York Review of Books* 64 (September 28): 82–85.

Hodgson, G.M. (2010), "A Response," in: M.J. Holler (ed.), *Symposium: Letter to the Queen* (*Homo Oeconomicus* 27), Munich: Accedo-Verlag: 329–389.

Hoffmann, J. (2002), "Notes from the Pit," in: *Nicola Atkinson-Griffith's "Secrets of the World,"* Symposium, introduced and edited by M.J. Holler (*Homo Oeconomicus* 18), Munich: Accedo-Verlag: 551–553.

Hofstadter, D.R. (1980), *Gödel, Escher, Bach: An Eternal Golden Braid*, New York: Vintage Books.

Holler, M.J. (1982), "The Relevance of the Voting Paradox: A Restatement," *Quality and Quantity* 16: 43–53.

Holler, M.J. (1984), "Collective Choice Approach to Individual Decision Making," in: M.J. Holler (ed.), *Coalitions and Collective Action*, Würzburg und Wien: Physica-Verlag: 338–344.

Holler, M.J. (1985), "The Theory of Contestable Markets: Comment," *Bulletin of Economic Research* 37: 65–67

Holler, M.J. (1986a), "Moral Sentiments and Self-Interest Reconsidered," in: A. Diekmann and P. Mitter (eds.), *Paradoxical Effects of Social Behavior. Essays in Honor of Anatol Rapoport*, Heidelberg and Vienna: Physica-Verlag: 223–233.

Holler, M.J. (1986b), "The Mixed Strategy Equilibrium Trap," in: M.J. Beckmann et al. (eds.), *Methods of Operations Research* 54, Meisenheim: Verlag Anton Hain, 249–258.

Holler, M.J. (1990), "Unprofitability of Mixed Strategy Equilibria in Two-Person Games: A Second Folk-Theorem," *Economics Letters* 32: 319–332.

Holler, M.J. (1993), "Fighting Pollution when Decisions are Strategic," *Public Choice* 76: 347–356.

Holler, M.J. (1994), "Regulatory Policymaking in a Parliamentary Setting: Comment," *Jahrbuch für Neue Politische Ökonomie*, Volume. 13, P. Herder-Dorneich, K.-H. Schenk and D. Schmidtchen (eds.), Tübingen: Mohr-Siebeck.

Holler, M.J., (ed.) (1999), *Scandal and Its Theory I* (*Homo Oeconomicus* 16), Munich: Accedo Verlag.

Holler, M.J., (ed.) (2002a), *Scandal and Its Theory II* (*Homo Oeconomicus* 19), Munich: Accedo Verlag

Holler, M.J. (2002b), "Artists, Secrets, and CIA's Cultural Policy," in: B. Priddat and H. Hegmann (eds.), *Finanzpolitik in der Informationsgesellschaft. Festschrift für Gunther Engelhardt*, Marburg: Metropolis-Verlag: 13–33.

Holler, M.J. (2002c), "Shall I Give You My Secret? An ARTS&Games Reconsideration," in: *Nicola Atkinson-Griffith's "Secrets of the World,"* Symposium, introduced and edited by M.J. Holler (Homo Oeconomicus 18), Munich: Accedo-Verlag: 539–543.

Holler, M.J. (2005), "George Orwell and his Cold Wars: Truth and Politics," in: J.-M. Josselin and A. Marciano (eds.), *Law and the State: A Political Economy Approach*, Cheltenham: Edward Elgar: 121–141.

Holler, M.J. (2006), "Adam Smith's Model of Man and Some of its Consequences," *Homo Oeconomicus* 23: 467–488.

Holler, M.J. (2007a), "Adam Smith's Model of Man and why the Market Program Failed," in: J. Lemetti and E. Piirimäe (eds.), *Human Nature as the Basis of Morality and Society in Early Modern Philosophy*, Helsinki: Acta Philosophica Fennica: 169–185.

Holler, M.J. (2007b), "The Machiavelli Program and the Dirty Hands Problem," in: P. Baake and R. Borck (eds.), *Public Economics and Public Choice: Contributions in Honor of Charles B. Blankart*, Berlin et al.: Springer, 39–62.

Holler, M.J. (2007c), "The Artist as a Secret Agent: Liberalism Against Populism," in: Breton, A., Galeotti, G., Salmon, P., and R. Wintrobe (eds.), *The Economics of Transparency in Politics (Villa Colombella Papers)*, Aldershot: Ashgate Publishing: 73–96.

Holler, M.J. (2008), "Re-defining Arts, Readymades, and Secrets," *Homo Oeconomicus* 25: 437–450.

Holler, M.J. (2009a), "The Zimmermann Telegram: How to Make Use of Secrets?" in: T. Airaksinen and M.J. Holler (eds.), *The Secrets of Secrets (Homo Oeconomicus* 26), Munich: Accedo-Verlag: 23–39.

Holler, M.J. (2009b), "Niccolò Machiavelli on Power," in: M. Baurmann and B. Lahno (eds.), *Perspectives in Moral Science. Contributions from Philosophy, Economics, and Politics in Honour of Hartmut Kliemt*, Frankfurt: Frankfurt School Verlag, 335–354; republished in L. Donskis (ed.) (2011), *Niccolò Machavelli: History, Power, and Virtue*, Amsterdam and New York: Rodopi.

Holler, M.J. (2009c), "John von Neumann und Oskar Morgenstern," in: H. Kurz (ed.), *Klassiker des ökonomischen Denkens*, München: Verlag C.H. Beck, 250–267.

Holler, M.J. (2010), "The Two-Dimensional Model of Jury Decision Making," *Journal of Public Finance and Public Choice (Economia delle Scelte Pubbliche)* 28: 29–42 (published in 2012).

Holler, M.J. (2011), "On Machiavelli's Conspiracy Paradoxes," *Homo Oeconomicus* 28: 549–569; republished in: F. Cabrillo and M. Puchades Navarro (eds.) (2013), *New Thinking in Political Economy (Constitutional Economics and Public Institutions). Essays in Honour of José Casas-Pardo*. Cheltenham: Edward Elgar: 125–145.

Holler, M.J. (2012), "Efficiency or Obfuscation," in: P. Behrens, T. Eger, and H.-B. Schäfer (eds.), *Ökonomische Analyse des Europarechts*, Tübingen: Mohr Siebeck: 367–375.

Holler, M.J. (2013a), "Mehrdimensionale Konsumentscheidungen und Manipulation der Nachfrage," in: M. Held, G. Kubon-Gilke and R. Sturn (eds.), *Jahrbuch Normative und institutionelle Grundfragen der Ökonomik, volume 7*, Marburg: Metropolis: 99–118.

Holler, M.J. (2014), "There Are No Desires in Economics," in: T. Airaksinen (ed.), *Desire and Desires (Homo Oeconomicus* 31), Munich: Accedo-Verlag: 597–616; repr. in (2015), *Acta Aerarii Publici* (Universitas Matthiae Belii) 12: 4–21.

Holler, M.J. (2015), "Welfare, Preferences and the Reconstruction of Desires," *International Journal of Social Economics* 42: 447–458.

Holler, M.J. (2016), "What John von Neumann Did to Economics," in: G. Faccarello and H.D. Kurz (eds.), *Handbook on the History of Economic Analysis, Volume I: Great Economists since Petty and Boisguilbert*, Cheltenham and Northampton, MA: Edward Elgar: 581–586.

Holler, M.J. and V. Høst (1990), "Maximin vs. Nash Equilibrium: Theoretical Results and Empirical Evidence," in: R.E. Quandt and D. Triska (eds.), *Optimal Decisions in Markets and Planned Economies*, Boulder, CO, San Francisco, CA and London: Westview Press: 245–255.

Holler, M.J., Høst, V. and K. Kristensen (1992), "Decisions on Strategic Markets – An Experimental Study," *Scandinavian Journal of Management* 8: 133–146.

Holler, M.J. and B. Klose-Ullmann (2008), "Wallenstein's Power Problem and Its Consequences," *AUCO Czech Economic Review* 2: 195–216.

Holler, M.J. and B. Klose-Ullmann (2010), "Art Goes America," *Journal of Economic Issues* 46: 89–112.

Holler, M.J. and B. Klose-Ullmann (2013), "*One Flew Over the Cuckoo's Nest*: Violence, Uncertainty, and Safety," in: H.-H. Kortüm and J. Heinze (eds.), *Aggression in Humans and Other Primates: Biology, Psychology, Sociology*, Berlin and Boston, MA: De Gruyter: 163–180.

Holler, M.J. and B. Klose-Ullmann (2016), "Machiavelli's Conspiracy Games," in: L. Donskis and O. Loukola (eds.), *Secrets and Conspiracies*, Amsterdam and New York: Rodopi, forthcoming.

Holler, M.J. and B. Klose-Ullmann (2018), *Game Theory for Those Who Manage*, forthcoming.

Holler, M.J. and M. Leroch (2008), "Impartial Spectator, Moral Community and Legal Consequences" *Journal of the History of Economic Thought* 30: 297–316.

Holler, M.J. and M. Leroch (2010), "Efficiency and Justice Revisited," *European Journal of Political Economy* 26: 311–319.

Holler, M.J. and I. Lindner (2004), "Mediation as Signal," *European Journal of Law and Economics* 17: 165–173.

Holler, M.J. and S. Napel (2007), "Democratic Decision Procedures, Stability of Outcome, and Agent Power, with Special Reference to the European Union," in: J.C. Pardo and P. Schwartz (eds.), *Public Choice and the Challenges of Democracy*, Cheltenham: Edward Elgar: 220–234.

Holler, M.J., and B.-A. Wickström (1999), "The Use of Scandals in the Progress of Society," in: M.J. Holler (ed.), *Scandal and Its Theory (Homo Oeconomicus* 16), Munich: Accedo-Verlag: 97–110.

Holt, J. (2012), "How the Computers Exploded," *New York Review of Books* 59 (June 7): 32–34.

Hoppe, H. (2000), "Second-Mover Advantages in the Strategic Adoption of New Technology Under Uncertainty," *International Journal of Industrial Organization* 18: 315–338.

Høst, V. and M.J. Holler (1990), "Maximin vs. Nash equilibrium: Theoretical Results and Empirical Evidence," in: R.E. Quandt and D. Triska (eds.), *Optimal Decisions in Markets and Planned Economies*, Boulder, CO, San Francisco, CA and London: Westview Press: 245–255.

Hotelling, H. (1929), "Stability in Competition," *Economic Journal* 39: 41–57.

Inglehart, R., Basañez, M., Diez-Medrano, J., Halman, L., and R. Luijkx (eds.) (2004), *Human Beliefs and Values: A Cross-Cultural Sourcebook Based on the 1999–2002 Values Surveys*, Mexico City: Siglo XXI Editores.

Jensen, R. (1982), "Adoption and Diffusion of an Innovation of Uncertain Probability," *Journal of Economic Theory* 27: 182–193.

Jensen, R. (1992), "Innovation Adoption and Welfare Under Uncertainty," *Journal of Industrial Economics* 40: 173–180.

Jevons, W.S. (1888 [1871]), *The Theory of Political Economy* (3rd edition), London: Macmillan.

Johnson, S. (2005 [1765]), *Mr. Johnson's Preface to his Edition of Shakespeare's Plays* (Online reprint). Ian Lancashire (ed.) (online edition published by RPO Editors, Department of English, and University of Toronto Press as *Samuel Johnson (1709–1784)*: Preface to his Edition of Shakespeare's Plays (1765). ed.). London: J. and R. Tonson and others.

Kahn, C.M. and D. Mookherjee (1992), "The Good, the Bad, and the Ugly: Coalition Proof Equilibrium in Infinite Games," *Games and Economic Behavior* 4:101–121.

Kahneman, D. (2003), "Maps of Bounded Rationality: Psychology for Behavioral Economists," *American Economic Review* 93: 1449–1475.

Kahneman, D. (2013), *Thinking, Fast and Slow*, New York: Farrar, Straus and Giroux.

Kahneman, D. and A. Tversky (1979), "Prospect Theory: An Analysis of Decision under Risk," *Econometrica* 47: 263–291.

Kaplan, S.N. and J. Rauh (2013), "It's the Market: The Broad-Based Rise in the Return of Top Talent," *Journal of Economic Perspectives* 27 (Summer): 35–56.

Keegan, J. (1990), *The Price of Admirality: The Evolution of Naval Warfare*, Harmondworth: Penguin Books.

Keynes J.M. (1936), *The General Theory of Employment, Interest and Money*, New York: Harcourt, Brace and Co.

Kilgour, D.M. (1972), "The Simultaneous True," *International Journal of Game Theory* 1: 229–242.

Kilgour, D.M. (1974), "The Shapley Value for Cooperative Games with Quarelling," in: A. Rapaport (ed.), *Game Theory as a Theory of Conflict Resolution*, Boston, MA: Reidel.

Kilgour, D.M. (1975), "The Sequential Truel," *International Journal of Game Theory* 4: 151–174.

Kilgour, D.M. (1978), "Equilibrium Points of Infinite Sequential Truels," *International Journal of Game Theory* 6: 167–180.

Kilgour, D.M. and S.J. Brams (1997), "The Truel," *Mathematics Magazine* 70: 315–326.

Klemisch-Ahlert, M. (1993), "Freedom of Choice: A Comparison of Different Rankings of Opportunity Sets," *Social Choice and Welfare* 10: 189–207.

Kliemt, H. (1986), "The Veil of Insignificance," *European Journal of Political Economy* 2: 333–344.

Klose-Ullmann, B. (2015), "Desire on Stage," *Homo Oeconomicus* 32: 489–508.

Knack, S. and P. Keefer (1997), "Does Social Capital have an Economic Pay-Off? A Cross-Country Investigation," *Quarterly Journal of Economics* 112: 1251–1288.

Koch, K. (2002), "Inside and Outside: *Nicola's Game*," in: *Nicola Atkinson-Griffith's "Secrets of the World,"* Symposium, introduced and edited by M.J. Holler (*Homo Oeconomicus* 18), Munich: Accedo-Verlag: 554–560.

Kohlberg, E. and J.-F. Mertens (1986), "On the Strategic Stability of Equilibria," *Econometrica* 54: 1003–1037.

Kosuth, J. (1974), "Art After Philosophy," in: G. de Vries (ed.), *On Art: Artists' Writings on the Changed Notion of Art after 1965* (German-English edition), Köln: Verlag M. DuMont Schauberg.

Kramer, G.H. (1973), "On a Class of Equilibrium Conditions for Majority Rule," *Econometrica* 41: 285–397.

Kreps, D.M. and R. Wilson (1982a), "Sequential Equilibrium," *Econometrica* 50: 863–894.

Kreps, D.M. and R. Wilson (1982b), "Reputation and Imperfect Information," *Journal of Economic Theory* 27: 253–279.

Kultti, K., Takalo, T. and J. Toikka (2006a). "Simultaneous Model of Innovation, Secrecy, and Patent Policy," *American Economic Review (AEA Papers and Proceedings)* 96: 82–86.

Kultti, K., Takalo, T. and J. Toikka (2006b), "Cross-Licensing and Collusive Behavior," *Homo Oeconomicus* 23: 181–194.

Kultti, K., Takalo, T. and J. Toikka (2007). "Secrecy Versus Patenting," *RAND Journal of Economics* 38: 22–42.

Kurz, H.D. (2012), "Schumpeter's New Combinations: Revisiting his *Theorie der wirtschaftlichen Entwicklung* on the Occasion of its Centenary," *Journal of Evolutionary Economics* 22: 871–899.

Kurz, H.D. (2016a), "Adam Smith on Markets, Competition and Violations of Natural Liberty," *Cambridge Journal of Economics* 40: 615–638.

Kurz, H.D. (2016b), *Economic Thought: A Brief History*, New York: Columbia University Press.

Lashmar, P. and J. Oliver (1998), *Britain's Secret Propaganda War*, Stroud: Sutton.

Leavitt, D. (2006), *The Man Who Knew Too Much: Alan Turing and the Invention of the Computer*, New York and London: Atlas Books (W.W. Norton & Co.)

Lehtinen, A. (2011), "The Revealed-Preference Interpretation of Payoffs in Game Theory," *Homo Oeconomicus* 28: 265–296.

Leonard, R. (2010), *Von Neumann, Morgenstern, and the Creation of Game Theory: From Chess to Social Science, 1900–1960*, New York: Cambridge University Press.

Lewis, A. (2009), "Justice Holmes and the 'Splendid Prisoner'," *New York Review of Books* 56 (July 2): 44–47.

Lewis, D. (1988), "Desire as belief," *Mind* 97: 323–332.

Lewis, D. (1996), "Desire as belief II," *Mind* 105: 303–313.

Lichtenstein, S. and Slovic, P. (1971), "Reversals of Preference Between Bids and Choices in Gambling Decisions," *Journal of Experimental Psychology* 89: 46–55.

Machiavelli, N. (1882a [1531]), *Discourses on the First Ten Books of Titus Livius*, in: *The Historical, Political, and Diplomatic Writings of Niccolò Machiavelli*, translated from the Italian by Christian E. Detmold, in Four Volumes, Boston, MA: James R. Osgood and Co.; Vol. 2: 93–431.

Machiavelli, N. (1882b [1532]), *The Prince*, in: *The Historical, Political, and Diplomatic Writings of Niccolò Machiavelli*, translated from the Italian by Christian E. Detmold, in Four Volumes, Boston, MA: James R. Osgood and Co.; Vol. 2: 1–88.

Machiavelli, N. (1882c [1532]), History of Florence, in: *The Historical, Political, and Diplomatic Writings of Niccolò Machiavelli*, translated from the Italian by Christian E. Detmold, in Four Volumes, Boston, MA: James R. Osgood and Co.; Vol. 1: 3–420.

Madrick, J. (2014), "Innovation: The Government was Crucial After All," *New York Review of Books* 61 (April 24): 50–53.

Magee, S.P. (1997), "Endogenous Protection: The Empirical Evidence," in: D.C. Mueller (ed.), *Perspectives on Public Choice: A Handbook*, Cambridge: Cambridge University Press.

Magee, S.P., Brock, W.A., and L. Young (1989), *Black Hole Tariffs and Endogenous Policy Theory*, Cambridge: Cambridge University Press.

Mailath, G.J., Okuno-Fujiwara, M. and A. Postlewaite (1993), "Belief-Based Refinements in Signalling Games," *Journal of Economic Theory* 60: 241–276.

Mani, A., Mullainathan, S., Shafir, E. and J. Zhao (2013), "Poverty Impedes Cognitive Function," *Sience* 341 (August 30): 976–980.

Manin, B. (1997), *The Principles of Representative Government*, Cambridge: Cambridge University Press.

Marciano, A. and N. Moureau (eds.) (2013), *The Bright Side of Scandals (Homo Oeconomicus 30)*, Munich: Accedo-Verlag.

Markoff, J. (2014), "Fearing Bombs That Can Pick Whom to Kill," *New York Times* (November 11). Available at: https://www.nytimes.com/2014/11/12/science/

weapons-directed-by-robots-not-humans-raise-ethical-questions.html. Accessed April 8, 2018.

Marx, K. (1969 [1856/57]), *Secret Diplomatic History of the Eighteenth Century and The Story of the Life of Lord Palmerston*, London: Lawrence & Wishart.

Maschler, M. (1966), "A Price Leadership Method for Solving the Inspector's Non-Constant Sum Game" *Naval Research Logistics Quarterly* 13: 11–33.

Maslow, A.H. (1943), "A Theory of Human Motivation," *Psychological Review* 50: 370–96.

Maslow, A. H. (1954), *Motivation and Personality*, New York: Harper.

May, K.O. (1954), "Intransitivity, Utility, and the Aggregation of Preference Patterns," *Econometrica* 22: 1–13.

Mazzucato, M. (2014), *The Entrepreneurial State*, London and New York: Authem Press.

McKelvey, R.D. (1976), "Intransitivities in Multidimensional Voting Models and Some Implications for Agenda Control," *Journal of Economic Theory* 12: 472–482.

McKelvey, R.D. (1979), "General Conditions for Global Intransitivities in Formal Voting Models," *Econometrica* 47: 1085–1111.

McNutt, P.A. (2009), "Secrets and Lies: The Neighbourhood of No-Truth," in: T. Airaksinen and M.J. Holler (eds.), *The Secrets of Secrets (Homo Oeconomicus 26)* Munich: Accedo-Verlag: 161–171.

Merrill III, S. and B. Grofman (1999), *A Unified Theory of Voting: Directional and Proximity Spatial Models*, Cambridge: Cambridge University Press.

Metcalfe, J.S. (1998), *Evolutionary Economics and Creative Destruction (The Graz Schumpeter Lectures)*, London: Routledge.

Milgrom, P. and J. Roberts (1982), "Limit Pricing and Entry Under Incomplete Information: An Equilibrium Analysis," *Econometrica* 50: 443–460.

Miller, N.R. (1982), "Power in Game Forms," in: M.J. Holler (ed.), *Power, Voting and Voting Power*, Würzburg and Wien: Physica-Verlag.

Millis, W. (1935), *Road to War: America 1914–1917*, Boston, MA and New York: Houghton Mifflin.

Mishra, R.K. (2014), "Miller's *All My Sons* in the Light of Aristotle's *Poetics*," *International Journal on Studies in English Language and Literature* 2: 25–28.

Modigliani, F. (1958), "New Developments on the Oligopoly Front," *Journal of Political Economy* 66: 215–232.

Modigliani, F. (1959), "Reply," *Journal of Political Economy* 66: 418–419.

Moldovanu, B. and M. Tietzel (1998), "Goethe's Second Price Auction," *Journal of Political Economy* 106: 854–859.

Montaigne (1910 [1580]), *Essays of Montaigne*, translated by C. Cotton, revised by W.C. Hazlett, New York: Edwin C. Hill.

Morgenstern, O. (1976), "The Collaboration Between Oskar Morgenstern and John von Neumann on the Theory of Games," *Journal of Economic Literature* 14: 805–816.

Moulin, H. and B. Peleg (1982), "Cores of Effectivity Functions and Implementation Theory," *Journal of Mathematical Economics* 10: 115–145.

Mullainathan, S. and E. Shafir (2013), *Scarcity: Why Having Too Little Means So Much*, New York: Times Books.

Nash, J.F. (1950a), "The Bargaining Problem," *Econometrica* 18: 155–162.

Nash, J.F. (1950b), "Equilibrium Points in n-Person Games," *Proceedings of the National Academy of Sciences of the United States of America* 36: 48–49.

Nash, J.F. (1951), "Non-Cooperative Games," *Annals of Mathematics* 54: 286–295.

Nentjes, A. (2012), "On the Right to Repeat Oneself," *Homo Oeconomicus* 29: 413–431.

Northrop, E. (2000), "Normative Foundations of Introductory Economics," *American Economist* 44: 53–61.

Nurmi, H. (1982), "Power in an Ideological Space," in: M.J. Holler (ed.), *Power, Voting and Voting Power*, Würzburg and Vienna: Physica-Verlag: 256–269.

Nurmi, H. (1988), "Assumptions of Individual Preferences in the Theory of Voting Procedures," in: J. Kacprzyk and M. Roubens (eds.), *Non-Conventional Preference Relations in Decision Making*. Berlin et al.: Springer: 142–155.

Nurmi, H. (2002), *Voting Procedures under Uncertainty*, Berlin et al.: Springer.

Nurmi, H. (2006), *Models of Political Economy*, London and New York: Routledge.

Nurmi, H. (2010), "Thin Rationality and Representation of Preferences with Implications to Spatial Voting Models," in: S. Greco, R.A. Marques Pereira, M. Squillante, R. Yager, and J. Kacprzyk (eds.), *Preferences and Decisions*, Berlin, Heidelberg and New York: Springer: 321–337.

Nurmi, H. and T. Meskanen (2000), "Voting Paradoxes and MCDM," *Group Decision and Negotiation* 9: 297–313.

Olson, M. Jr. (1965), *The Logic of Collective Action*, Cambridge, MA: Harvard University Press.

Ortmann, A., Fitzgerald, J. and C. Boing (2000), "Trust, Reciprocity, and Social History," *Experimental Economics* 3: 81–100.

Orwell, G. (no date given [1934]), *Burmese Days*, San Diego, CA, New York and London: Harvest.

Orwell, G. (1967 [1938]), *Homage to Catalonia*, London: Secker & Warburg.

Orwell, G. (1980 [1945]), *Animal Farm*, Harmondsworth: Penguin Books.

Orwell, G. (1981 [1949]), *Nineteen Eighty-Four*, Harmondsworth: Penguin Books.

Owen, G. (1995), *Game Theory* (3rd edition), San Diego, CA et al.: Academic Press.

Pattanaik, P. K. and Y. Xu (1990), "On Ranking Opportunity Sets in Terms of Freedom of Choice," *Recherches Economique de Louvain* 56: 383–390.

Paz, O. (1978), *Marcel Duchamp: Appearance Stripped Bare*, New York: Arcade Publishing.

Pearce, D.G. (1984), "Rationalizable Strategic Behavior and the Problem of Perfection," *Econometrica* 52: 1029–1050.

Phelps, E. (2016), "What is Wrong with the West's Economics?" *Homo Oeconomicus* 33: 3–10, Reprinted from *New York Review of Books* (August 13, 2015): 54–56.

Picker, R. C. (2010), "The Razors-and-Blades Myth(s)," John M. Olin Law & Economics Working Paper No. 532, University of Chicago Law School.

Piketty, T. and E. Saez (2006), "The Evolution of Top Incomes: A Historical and International Perspective," *American Economic Review (Papers and Proceedings)* 96: 200–205.

Plott, C.R. (1967), "A Notion of Equilibrium and its Possibility under Majority Rule," *American Economic Review* 57: 787–806.

Pollock, J. (2006), *Thinking About Acting: Logical Foundations for Rational Decision Making*, New York: Oxford University Press.

Prysor, G. (2005), "The 'Fifth Column' and the British Experience of Retreat, 1940," *War in History* 12: 418–447.

Raub, W. and T. Voss (2017), "Micro-Macro Models in Sociology: Antecedents of Coleman's Diagram," in: B. Jann and W. Przepiorka (eds.), *Social Dilemmas, Institutions and the Evolution of Cooperation. Festschrift for Andreas Diekmann*, Berlin: De Gruyter.

Reinganum, J. (1981), "On the Diffusion of New Technology: A Game Theoretic Approach," *Review of Economic Studies* 48: 395–405.

Riker, W. (1982), *Liberalism Against Populism*, San Francisco, CA: Freeman.

Rosen, S. (1981), "The Economics of Superstars," *American Economic Review* 71: 845–858.

Rubinstein, A. (1988), "Similarity and Decision-Making Under Risk (Is There a Utility Theory Resolution to the Allais Paradox?)," *Journal of Economic Theory* 46: 145–153.

Russell, J.M. (1984), "Desires Don't Cause Actions," *Journal of Mind and Behavior* 84: 1–10.

Saari, D. (1995), *Basic Geometry of Voting*, New York et al.: Springer.

Saari, D. (2011), "'Ranking Wheels' and Decision Cycles," *Homo Oeconomicus* 28: 233–263.

Sagar, R. (2013), *Secrets and Leaks: The Dilemma of State Secrecy*, Princeton, NJ and Oxford: Princeton University Press.

Samuelson, P.A. (1938), "A Note on the Pure Theory of Consumers' Behaviour," *Economica* 5: 61–71.

Sandler, I. (1970), *The Triumph of American Painting: A History of Abstract Expressionism*, New York and Washington, DC: Praeger Publishers.

Sanouillet, M. and E. Peterson (eds.) (1989 [1973]), *The Writings of Marcel Duchamp*, Boston, MA: Da Capo Press.

Saunders, F.S. (2000), *The Cultural Cold War: The CIA and the World of Arts and Letters*, New York: Free Press. (Revised version of *Who Paid the Piper: The CIA and the Cultural Cold War*, London: Granta Publications, 1999, by the same author.)

Scanlon, T. (1998), *What We Owe to Each Other*. Cambridge, MA: Harvard University Press.

Schelling, T. (1982), "Ethics, Law, and the Exercise of Self-Command," The Tanner Lectures on Human Values, University of Michigan: 1–35.

Schinzel, H. (2012), "Who is Afraid of Red, Yellow and Blue III: Vandalism and Freedom," *Homo Oeconomicus* 29: 237–245.

Schlesinger, A.M., Jr. (2004), *The Imperial Presidency*, New York: Mariner Books.

Schofield, N. (1983), "Generic Instability of the Majority Rule," *Review of Economic Studies* 50: 695–705.

Schofield, N. (2008), *The Spatial Model of Politics*, London: Routledge.

Schofield, N. (2009), *The Political Economy of Democracy and Tyranny*, Munich: Oldenbourg Verlag.

Schumpeter, J.A. (1928), "The Instability of Capitalism," *Economic Journal* 38: 361–386.

Schumpeter, J.A. (1983 [1934], *Theory of Economic Development* [1911/1912 first published as *Theorie der wirtschaftlichen Entwicklung*. Duncker & Humblot, Berlin), New Brunswick, NJ, and London: Transaction Publishers.

Schumpeter, J.A. (2010 [1942]), *Capitalism, Socialism and Democracy* (with a new introduction by Joseph E. Stiglitz), New York and London: Routledge.

Sedgwick, J. (2002), "Giving Up Secrets by Moving in the 'Right Direction': *Nicola's Game* Revisited," Symposium, introduced and edited by M.J. Holler (*Homo Oeconomicus* 18), Munich: Accedo-Verlag: 544–547.

Selten, R. (1971), "Anwendungen der Spieltheorie auf die Politische Wissenschaft," in: H. Maier, K. Ritter and U. Matz (eds.), *Politik und Wissenschaft*, Munich: C.H. Beck, 287–320.

Selten, R. (1973). "A Simple Model of Imperfect Competition where 4 are Few and 6 are Many," *International Journal of Game Theory* 2: 141–201.

Sen, A.K. (1970), "The Impossibility of a Paretian Liberal," *Journal of Political Economy* 78: 152–157.

Sen, A.K. (1971), "The Impossibility of a Paretian Liberal: Reply," *Journal of Political Economy* 79: 1406–1407.

Sen, A.K. (1976), "Liberty, Unanimity and Rights," *Economica* 43: 217–245.

Sen, A.K. (1982), "Liberty as Control: An Appraisal," *Mid-West Studies in Philosophy* 7: 207–221.

Sen, A.K. (1985). *Commodities and Capabilities.* Amsterdam and New York: North-Holland.

Sen, A.K. (1989), "Development as Capability Expansion," *Journal of Development Planning* 19: 41–58.

Senior, N.W. (1854), *Political Economy*, London and Glasgow: Richard Griffin and Co.

Shaw, B. (1964 [1919]), *Heartbreak House*, Harmondsworth: Penguin Books.

Sherman, R. and T.D. Willett (1967), "Potential Entrants Discourage Entry," *Journal of Political Economy* 75: 400–403.

Schroeder, T. (2004), *Three Faces of Desire*. New York: Oxford University Press.

Smiley, X. (2014), "Kim Philby: Still an Enigma," *New York Review of Books* 61 (December 4): 45–46.

Smith, A. (1982 [1759]). *The Theory of Moral Sentiments*, D.D. Raphael and A.L. Macfie (eds.), Indianapolis, IN: Liberty Press.

Smith, A. (1981 [1776/77]), *An Inquiry into the Nature and Causes of the Wealth of Nations*, R.H. Campbell and A.S. Skinner (eds.), Indianapolis, IN: Liberty Press.

Smith, V.L. and J.M. Walker (1993), "Monetary Rewards and Decision Cost in Experimental Economics," *Economic Inquiry* 31: 245–261.

Spence, A.M. (1974), *Market Signaling*, Cambridge, MA: Harvard University Press.

Spencer, B. (2002), "Trust in Secrets," in: *Nicola Atkinson-Griffith's "Secrets of the World,"* Symposium, introduced and edited by M.J. Holler (*Homo Oeconomicus* 18), Munich: Accedo-Verlag: 563–564.

Spender, S. (1972), "The Truth about Orwell," *New York Review of Books* 19 (November 16): 3–6.

Starr, P. (2014), "A Different Road to a Fair Society," *New York Review of Books* 61 (May 22): 33–36.

Steinbeck, J. (1976 [1941]), *The Log from the Sea of Cortez*, Harmondsworth: Penguin Books.

Steunenberg, B. (1994), "Regulatory Policymaking in a Parliamentary Setting." in: P. Herder-Dorneich, K.-H. Schenk und D. Schmidtchen (eds.), *Jahrbuch für Neue Politische Ökonomie*, Vol. 13, Tübingen: Mohr-Siebeck, 66–71.

Stigler, G.J. (1966): *The Theory of Price* (3rd edition), New York and London: Macmillan.

Stigler, S.M. (1980), "Stigler's Law of Eponymy," in: T.F. Gieryn (ed.), *Science and Social Structure: A Festschrift for Robert K. Merton* (Transactions of The New York Academy of Sciences Series II, Volume 39).

Strouhal, E. (2012), *M. Duchamp/V. Halberstadt: Spiel im Spiel, A Game in a Game, Jeu dans le Jeu*, Nürnberg: Verlag für Moderne Kunst – Kunsthalle Marcel Duchamp – N°5.

Sturn, R. (2010), "On Making Full Sense of Adam Smith," *Homo Oeconomicus* 27: 263–287.

Sudgen, R. (1985), "Liberty, Preferences, and Choice," *Economics and Philosophy* 1: 213–229.

Sunstein, C.R. (2013), "It Captures Your Mind," *New York Review of Books* 60 (September 26): 47–49.

Sylos Labini, P. (1962), *Oligopoly and Technical Progress*. Transl. by E. Henderson, Cambridge, MA: Harvard University Press.

Tanenhaus, S. (1999), "The Red Scare," *New York Review of Books* 48 (January 14): 44–48.

Tellis, G.J., and P.N. Golder (1996), "First to Market, First to Fail? Real Causes of Enduring Market Leadership," *Sloan Management Review* 37: 65–75.

Tirole, J. (1988), *The Theory of Industrial Organizations*, Cambridge, MA, and London: MIT Press.

de Tocqueville, A. (1956 [1835 and 1840], *Democracy in America*, New York: Mentor Books.

Tóibín, C. (2016), "The Talented, Trapped Spenders," *New York Review of Books*, 63 (April 7): 63–65.

Tsebelis, G. (1990), "Penalty has no Impact on Crime: A Game Theoretic Analysis," *Rationality and Society* 2: 255–286.

Tuchman, B. (1971), *The Zimmermann Telegram*, New York: Bantam Books.

Turing, A.M. (2004), *The Essential Turing: Seminal Writings in Computing, Logic, Philosophy, Artificial Intelligence, and Artificial Life Plus the Secrets of Enigma*, B.J. Copeland (ed.), Oxford: Clarendon Press.

van Damme, E. (1987), *Stability and Perfection of Nash Equilibrium*, Heidelberg et al.: Springer.

van Damme, E., Binmore, K.G., Roth, A.E., Samuelson, L., Winter, E., Bolton, G.E. Ockenfels, A., Dufwenberg, M., Kirchsteiger, G., Gneezy, U., Kocher, M.G., Sutter, M., Sanfey, A.G., Kliemt, H., Selten, R., Nagel, R., and O.H. Azar (2014), "How Werner Güth's Ultimatum Game Shaped Our Understanding of Social Behavior," *Journal of Economic Behavior & Organization* 108: 292–318.

Vannucci, S. (1986), "Effectivity Functions, Indices of Power, and Implementation," *Economic Notes* 25, 92–105.

Vannucci, S. (2002), "Effectivity Functions, Opportunity Rankings, and Generalized Desirability Relations," *Homo Oeconomicus* 19: 451–467.

Veblen, T. (1979 [1899]), *The Theory of the Leisure Class*, New York: Penguin Books.

von Neumann, J. (1959 [1928]), "On the Theory of Games of Strategy," in: A.W. Tucker and R.D. Luce (eds.), *Contributions to the Theory of Games, Volume 4. Translation of "Zur Theorie der Gesellschaftsspiele," Mathematische Annalen* 100: 295–320.

von Neumann, J. and O. Morgenstern (1944), *Theory of Games and Economic Behavior*, Princeton, NJ: Princeton University Press.

von Stackelberg, H. (1934), *Marktform und Gleichgewicht*, Vienna and Berlin: Verlag von Julius Springer.

Walker, M. and J. Wooders (2001), "Minimax Play at Wimbledon," *American Economic Review* 9: 1521–1538.

Walras, L. (1954 [1874]), *Elements of Pure Economics, or the Theory of Social Wealth (Éléments d'économie pure ou théorie de la richesse sociale)*, translated by William Jaffe, London: Allen and Unwin.

Weber, M. (1948 [1924]), "Class, Status and Party," in: H.H. Gerth and C.W. Mills (eds.), *Essays from Max Weber*, London: Routledge and Kegan Paul.

Weber, M. (2005 [1922]), *Wirtschaft und Gesellschaft. Grundriß der verstehenden Soziologie*, Zweitausendeins: Frankfurt am Main.

Weesie, J. (1993), "Asymmetry and Timing in the Volunteer's Dilemma," *Journal of Conflict Resolution* 37: 569–590.

Wilde, O. (1997), *Collected Works of Oscar Wilde*, Ware: Wordsworth Edition.

Wiles, J. (2006), *Mixed Strategy Equilibrium in Tennis Service*, Thesis, Trinity College, Duke University, Durham, NC.

Williams, T. (1947), *A Streetcar Named Desire*, New York: A New Directions Book, James Laughlin.

Williamson, O.E. (1975), *Markets and Hierarchies: Analysis and Antitrust Implications*, New York: Free Press.

Wittman, D. A. (1973), "Parties as Utility Maximizers," *American Political Science Review* 67: 490–498.

Wittman, D. (1985), "Counter-Intuitive Results in Game Theory," *European Journal of Political Economy* 1: 77–89.

Wittman, D.A. (1993), "Nash Equilibrium vs. Maximin: A Comparative Statics Analysis," *European Journal of Political Economy* 9: 559–565.

Wood, G.S. (2002), "Rambunctious American Democracy," *New York Review of Books* 49 (May 9): 20–23.

Wood, M. (2013), "Discovering Orson Welles," *New York Review of Books* 60 (December 19): 75–78.

Zak, P.J. and Knack, S. (2001), "Trust and Growth," *Economic Journal* 111: 295–321.

Zola, E. (1867), "Une nouvelle manière en peinture: Eduard Manet," *Revue du XIXe siècle* (January 1).

# Index

For Product Safety Concerns and Information please contact our EU representative GPSR@taylorandfrancis.com Taylor & Francis Verlag GmbH, Kaufingerstraße 24, 80331 München, Germany

Printed and bound by CPI Group (UK) Ltd, Croydon, CR0 4YY

01/05/2025

01858446-0001